Religion in 50 Words

Religion in 50 Words: A Critical Vocabulary is the first of a two-volume work that seeks to transform the study of religion by offering a radically critical perspective. It does so by providing a succinct and critical examination of the key words used in the modern study of religion. Arranged alphabetically, the book explores the historic roots, varied uses, and current significance and utility of the technical terms used within the current field of religious studies. These are the terms that both students and scholars routinely deploy to think about, describe, and analyze data—sometimes without realizing that they are themselves technical tools in need of attention.

Among the topics covered:

- Belief
- Critical
- Culture
- Definition
- Environment
- Gender
- Ideology
- Lived religion
- Material religion
- Orthodoxy
- Politics
- Race
- Sacred/profane
- Secular
- Theory

This book submits all of its terms to a critical interrogation and subsequent re-description, thereby allowing a collective reframing of the field. This volume is an indispensable resource for students and academics working in religious studies.

Aaron W. Hughes is the Philip S. Bernstein Professor in the Department of Religion and Classics at the University of Rochester, USA.

Russell T. McCutcheon is University Research Professor and Chair of the Department of Religious Studies at the University of Alabama, USA.

"Covering an essential set of concepts, *Religion in 50 Words* offers vital grounding for the study of religion—helping readers to understand what we often overlook: how we secure and what we mean by the words we use when studying religion. They name and tackle the fundamental question: what do words have to do with the study of religion? I highly recommend this book."
Anthony B. Pinn, Rice University, USA

"This substantive and singular guide describes and analyzes the embedded and extended meanings of the categories and terms used in the contemporary study of religion. Written in an informative rather than normative tone, it will help students of religion clarify our thinking and say what we mean."
Wm Scott Green, University of Miami, USA

"A scholar is only as good as her tools, and with this volume Hughes and McCutcheon have provided scholars of religion with a metaphorical whetstone on which they can sharpen their most important tools: their concepts. In each of these fifty chapters, Hughes and McCutcheon outline the contours of the fault lines in the field, show how different scholarly approaches utilize broadly shared concepts but often for competing purposes, and evaluate the relative merits of rival approaches. This volume will be of interest to both seasoned scholars and students new to the field looking for a survey of our field's contested vocabulary."
Craig Martin, St. Thomas Aquinas College, USA

"*Religion in 50 Words* is not just another collection of useful (or useless) words for studying religion. It is a masterful introduction to the *critical* use of terms in the academic study of religion. Written by two of the most qualified scholars to undertake such an endeavour, this volume opens up the interdisciplinary 'field' that is the study of religion."
Kocku von Stuckrad, University of Groningen, The Netherlands

Religion in 50 Words
A Critical Vocabulary

**Aaron W. Hughes and
Russell T. McCutcheon**

LONDON AND NEW YORK

First published 2022
by Routledge
2 Park Square, Milton Park, Abingdon, Oxon OX14 4RN

and by Routledge
605 Third Avenue, New York, NY 10158

Routledge is an imprint of the Taylor & Francis Group, an informa business

© 2022 Aaron W. Hughes and Russell T. McCutcheon

The right of Aaron W. Hughes and Russell T. McCutcheon to be identified as authors of this work has been asserted by them in accordance with sections 77 and 78 of the Copyright, Designs and Patents Act 1988.

All rights reserved. No part of this book may be reprinted or reproduced or utilised in any form or by any electronic, mechanical, or other means, now known or hereafter invented, including photocopying and recording, or in any information storage or retrieval system, without permission in writing from the publishers.

Trademark notice: Product or corporate names may be trademarks or registered trademarks, and are used only for identification and explanation without intent to infringe.

British Library Cataloguing-in-Publication Data
A catalogue record for this book is available from the British Library

Library of Congress Cataloging-in-Publication Data
A catalog record for this book has been requested

ISBN: 978-0-367-69045-8 (hbk)
ISBN: 978-0-367-69047-2 (pbk)
ISBN: 978-1-003-14018-4 (ebk)

DOI: 10.4324/9781003140184

Typeset in Times New Roman
by Apex CoVantage, LLC

Contents

List of consultants   viii
Acknowledgments   x

Introduction: a user's guide   1

1 Affect   11

2 Authenticity   18

3 Authority   23

4 Belief   26

5 Canon   32

6 Classification   35

7 Cognition   41

8 Comparison   47

9 Critical   52

10 Culture   58

11 Definition   64

12 Description   70

13	Diaspora	76
14	Environment	79
15	Essence	84
16	Experience	88
17	Explanation	95
18	Faith	101
19	Function	104
20	Gender	111
21	History	116
22	Identity	123
23	Ideology	130
24	Indigeneity	136
25	Interpretation	142
26	Law	150
27	Lived religion	153
28	Material religion	159
29	Method	167
30	Methodological agnosticism	173
31	Origin	181
32	Orthodoxy	187

33	Phenomenology	193
34	Pluralism	199
35	Politics	206
36	Power	212
37	Practice	220
38	Primitive	225
39	Race	232
40	Redescription	240
41	Religion	247
42	Religious literacy	255
43	Sacred/profane	263
44	Secular	270
45	Society	278
46	Status	284
47	Text	287
48	Theory	295
49	World religions	302
50	Worldview	310

Appendix: a word on etymologies   313
Index   315

Consultants

Michael Altman, Department of Religious Studies, University of Alabama, USA.
Christopher Cotter, Department of Theology and Religious Studies, University of Chester, UK.
Daniel Dubuisson, Centre National de la Recherche Scientifique, Lille, France.
Steffen Führding, Institute for the Study of Religion, Gottfried Wilhelm Leibniz Universität, Hannover, Germany.
Naomi Goldenberg, Department of Classics and Religious Studies, University of Ottawa, Canada.
Margarita Guillory, Department of Religion, Boston University, USA.
Mitsutoshi Horii, Faculty of English and IT Management, Shumei University, Japan.
Sylvester Johnson, College of Liberal Art and Humanities, Virginia Tech, USA.
Adil Hussain Khan, Department of Religious Studies, Loyola University, New Orleans, USA.
Barbara Krawcowicz, Department of Jewish Studies, Jagiellonian University, Poland.
Craig Martin, School of Arts & Sciences, St. Thomas Aquinas College, USA.
Richard Newton, Department of Religious Studies, University of Alabama, USA.
Brent Nongbri, History of Religions, Norwegian School of Theology, Religion and Society, Norway.
Suzanne Owen, Leeds Trinity University, UK.
Steven Ramey, Department of Religious Studies, University of Alabama, USA.
Adele Reinhartz, Department of Classics and Religious Studies, University of Ottawa, Canada.

Peggy Schmeiser, Johnson Shoyama Graduate School of Public Policy, University of Saskatchewan, Canada.
K. Merinda Simmons, Department of Religious Studies, University of Alabama, USA.
Leslie Dorrough Smith, Women's and Gender Studies Department & Department of Religious Studies, Avila University, USA.
Teemu Taira, Department of Study of Religions, University of Helsinki, Finland.
Vaia Touna, Department of Religious Studies, University of Alabama, USA.
Robyn Faith Walsh, Department of Religious Studies, University of Miami, USA.

Acknowledgments

Writing such a volume had been in the back of our minds for quite some time. We recall our friend, Willi Braun, reporting how Jonathan Z. Smith had once told him that he wished that he had written a book akin to Raymond Williams *Keywords: A Vocabulary of Culture and Society* (1976), the very book that has inspired us here. It was more formally conceived and then proposed to Routledge's Rebecca Shillabeer in the early summer of 2020—to whom we are grateful for contracting the volume. We also wish to express our appreciation for the input of the four anonymous reviewers whose comments helped to make this a stronger volume by, for example, suggesting a variety of key terms that we have added to our list. Then, throughout the Fall of 2020, the book that you now hold became the ideal sort of COVID-19 writing project for both of us—Aaron in New York state on the southern shores of Lake Ontario and Russell in Tuscaloosa, Alabama—given that we were each mostly working away from our offices, largely teaching remotely due to the in-person risks of the virus. With university libraries either closed to patrons or offering limited services and hours, we were therefore reliant to a large degree either on periodically carting a box of books home or, more likely than not, the many online resources to which each of our university's libraries luckily subscribe (e.g., electronic journals and a variety of other research databases). And so, while many of us who joined book clubs long ago probably still own that old blue, photoreduced two-volume *Oxford English Dictionary* (complete with the rectangular magnifying glass stored in a little drawer at the top) there is nothing now quite like the full entries and embedded links for over 600,000 words (including plenty of examples of various historic and contemporary usages) that are now available at the online OED. We should also acknowledge how useful Google's various digital resources have become, between scholarly articles that are searchable via Google Scholar, the partial or, in many cases, complete scans of recent and historic books and manuscripts that are part of Google Books, not to mention its ngram viewer initiative, which searches and then graphs the frequency of word and phrase usage from 1500 to 2019, along with links to examples of such usage as found in its archive of already scanned materials. These were all among the now handy resources on which we relied while working away from our offices—tools that we do not take for granted given that we are each old enough to easily imagine them as not existing at all. We certainly recall the days of heading to the reference room to flip through the pages of the American Theological Library Association's (ATLA) thick, semi-annual volume, *Religion Index One: Periodicals*, in search of the details on articles and authors. Thus, tackling a project like this at a time such as this is certainly something that would have been unthinkable to a previous generation of scholars. Our indebtedness to those working in the digital humanities therefore needs to be noted—an indebtedness that hopefully makes apparent just how closely integrated so-called traditional humanistic scholarship now is with the digital realm; after all, an awful lot of behind-the-scenes work with computer code, not to mention all those people who have scanned all of those books' pages (sometimes leaving more than just hints of their trace via the scans of gloved hands that pop up every now and then), was necessary for us to learn more about how precursors to this or that word somehow made its way into English sometime in the twelfth or thirteenth century.

Along with acknowledging the importance of these resources, we would also like to mention colleagues who, though no less immersed in a rather unusual COVID-19 semester of their own, each agreed to join the project as consultants (with their names listed at the opening of the volume). Not only did some read early drafts of many of the entries that follow, offering feedback that helped us to revise much of what is to come, but they were all invited to read and comment on the completed manuscript, prior to its submission to the publisher. We recognize that, even though we are co-authors, each bringing different expertise to bear, we hardly exhaust that growing subfield that some now call critical religion. Recruiting colleagues who also identify with the attitude of this approach, to provide input of their own, therefore helps to make the volume all the stronger, we think, by being more representative and therefore, we hope, more useful to readers (whether they are students or colleagues). We are therefore grateful for the time and energy that our consultants each put into this project.

Introduction
A user's guide[1]

> [A]cademic subjects are not eternal categories...
> Raymond Williams, *Keywords: A Vocabulary of Culture and Society*

Scholarly analyses are only as good as the words in our possession and scholars' agreement on how they are used and what they do. Words function as the basic tools that we use to name things, to bring features of the world that catch our attention or our curiosity into sharper focus, and to construct a set of narratives about them and their relationships to other things, all of which are often passed on from generation to generation. But words may also do more than just name things that are already out there; they may very well constitute or, as some scholars say, individuate items from their hectic background, making it possible for us to distinguish and thereby talk about something that, lacking the word (and, yes, all that goes with it) we might not have even noticed. Yet we rarely reflect carefully on our choice of words or consider them to be not just tools but also historical artifacts with a past, with implications, and even with limits; instead, scholars often prefer to assume that their words are as natural as that which they use them to name. We ignore all this, however, at our own peril—especially when that "we" names a group of scholars who see themselves as occupying a common field, with a common focus and a shared pursuit. It is especially challenging in the field that we, the authors, share; since the European-inspired academic study of religion is, at most, about 150 years old, and because it was preceded by many generations of theological speculation, there is—despite the appeals of many to the contrary—much room for confusion and slippage. The book that follows is meant to confront that slippage, head-on, by focusing on our words. Not just any words, of course, but some of those that have created and continue to define the academic study of religion.

DOI: 10.4324/9781003140184-1

2 *Introduction: a users guide*

Although we are both critical of some of the work now carried out by those who count themselves as members of this field (notably named a discipline in some parts of the world—the terms come with implications), we hope that each of our previous works have also made evident that we are both mindful of the importance of understanding the history of the field—after all, where it came from, as the old saying goes, helps us to understand where it might be going. It is for that reason that the rationale for this book, intended as a primer for a vocabulary necessary for what some are now calling a critical study of religion (more on that below), is explicitly rooted in another little book, first published 50 years ago by Eric J. Sharpe (1933–2000), the noted historian of our field. His 1975 book, *Comparative Religion: A History* once counted among a small number of required readings for students of religion in our own academic generation. But the book that we have in mind here is probably lesser known these days: his *Fifty Key Words: Comparative Religion* (1971), a small volume appearing in a series that was also devoted to such other titles as theology, philosophy, the Church, sociology, and the Bible. The books that appeared in the series along with Sharpe's certainly tell us something about an earlier moment in the field's history (there is, for example, no volume on the Qur'an, let alone one devoted to the Synagogue or the Temple). Moreover, the words that he decided to cover in his volume signal an obvious deference to Christianity—and, more than likely, a particular type of Protestantism—which may not have been obvious at the time, but certainly cannot go unnoticed today. Such "keywords" for the entire field of comparative religion therefore included the likes of: creation, divination, eschatology, evil, heaven and earth, incarnation, judgment, mana, priest, prophet, revelation, salvation, sanctuary, scripture, shaman, and worship. Moreover, these words often are used as having matter-of-fact definitions and little about them (let alone the wider assumptions that drive their use) is scrutinized or questioned. This means that the messiness of such words—their investments in ideology or class structure, for example, pointing to heated debates over how they have been used and what they do or do not name and accomplish—is overlooked, thereby naturalizing how they happen to be used now (along with the interests of their users). Neat and simple definitions are given, reinforcing popular usage, with which most readers might just nod their head and keep reading. All the words (and the assumptions on which they are premised) are left standing at the end of the book in much the same manner that they had before.

Take Sharpe's entry on God as but one quick example. The opening sentence reads as follows: "It is a truism to say that the question of belief in God or the gods is determinative for most historical religions. . ." But is it really a truism? Not anymore, we would suggest, if ever it actually was. The long-standing assumption that religion is best or properly defined as having something to do with a god, despite still being widely shared to this day (such as almost any dictionary definition of religion, let alone scholars who continue to assume as much), is hardly the only way of defining religion. This should be obvious to anyone acquainted with the variety of definitions that are out there in the literature. In fact, once common debates on whether Buddhism is or is not a religion (dating to at least the nineteenth century) hinged on taking this definition as self-evident—a debate that quickly evaporates if one opts to define religion in some other way, as the opium of the people, following Karl Marx, for instance. The classification of religions into certain subcategories, such as that once common designation "historical religions"—namely those that can be traced back several centuries or millennia to what are claimed to be historical figures and events—was largely driven by Christian scholars prioritizing their own familiar themes and then looking for them elsewhere, in the unfamiliar. To this we could also add the still prominent idea of "world religions," including various subtypes (like so-called Eastern and Western religions) or even Sharpe's own use of the once popular term "the great religions." All of these categories are now seen by many scholars as highly problematic for a wide variety of reasons and thus in need of careful rethinking (which might result in their removal from our common vocabulary). Case in point: as recently as the mid-1970s scholars still routinely classified all religious traditions simply into "Christian" and "non-Christian," much as Sharpe did in his volume, leaving us in no doubt concerning the self-invested manner in which scholarship on religion often proceeds. And as for the emphasis on this thing called belief in the aforementioned quotation—a word often assumed to correspond to some internal set of assumptions or propositions that can be enumerated or stated by means of what many would call a creed or simply a statement of belief, whose recitation is often thought to signal one's membership in a group—well, it is no longer so obvious. As the terms that follow reveal in some detail, the complexity of our terminology—and thus the things they name—are often presented to us as being far simpler and easier than they might actually be.

With this problem of simplicity and ease in mind, we should also note that, in our reading, the goal of many scholars of religion is either to chronicle (and thereby merely describe) how people already talk about themselves and their worlds or to arrive at some sort of mutual understanding amidst the different religions. The latter is on particular display in the discourses associated with interreligious or interfaith dialogue, something that has become one of the hallmarks of contemporary religious studies (at least in some of its guises). Although we distance ourselves from such versions of the field, we find the ongoing tendency to take the people whom we study for granted instructive. For we maintain that one of the central problems of the field is that scholars of religion (many of whom are still from, and were therefore trained in, North America and Europe, often arriving at the field via prior theological interests or investments of their own) have long taken a certain sort of common sense or even folk vocabulary for granted. This is precisely what Sharpe did with those discourses on god, belief, etc.—simply adopting such terms and using them *as if* they also constituted a scholarly vocabulary or cross-cultural utility. Addressing this problem is at the heart of the entries that follow.

Consider again Sharpe's entries, among which, of course, was also such classic comparative religion topics as: ancestor-worship, animism, comparative method, initiation, myth, phenomenology of religion, ritual, tabu, totem, and so on. Taken as a whole, the entries largely present topics of relevance to but one religion—to wit, Christianity—that just happen to be familiar enough to many in the field (at least 50 years ago). His readers would of course see no difficulty in raising them to the status of cross-cultural, comparative categories, reasoning that, for example, if "we" had priests and prophets, well, "they" probably do too. For instance, in the country where we are both employed as professors, the federal authorities routinely discuss the tax implications for those non-profits designated as churches, thereby using a term of obvious, local significance to Christians as if it can easily carry the weight of cross-cultural difference, thereby standing in also for mosques, temples, synagogues, gurdwaras, and so on. While we do not wish to be so crass as to liken a previous generation's work as being akin to someone from, say, England, arriving ashore in India, a few hundred years ago, and asking someone there "What's the name of your Bible?" we nonetheless see this as being not so far off from where the field once was and, lamentably, where it still might be, at least in some of its versions. In many ways this is understandable, to be sure, since research has long established that each of us confronts the unknown by means of models that we then generalize and extend from the already known.

But—or so we have both long argued, and as we hope to demonstrate in our own volume devoted to keywords here—scholarship requires us to do something other than merely adopting, even if later stretching, one local discourse and then using it *as if* it was a scholarly discourse capable of providing a systematic model for understanding the world around us.

This point strikes us as still eluding many in the field. This might not be that surprising, after all, since, generally speaking, it is often *their* shared local vocabulary that is being stretched and thus *their* common sense that is being extended to other cultures and societies. Perhaps these problems would have been painfully obvious to readers of Sharpe's volume if he had instead adopted a viewpoint dominant in some *other* part of the world, one that was alien to his readers' local understanding. What would have happened, for example, if he had written in the voice of someone unfamiliar with North America or Britain and who was, say, local to somewhere like Saudi Arabia and therefore brought up taking "things Muslim" for granted, or, let's say again, the voice of an author from South Korea or someone from . . . (you get our point, we hope). Such a writer, hoping to reach readers in the English-speaking market, many of whom undoubtedly take "things Christian" for granted, could certainly not just start generalizing from *their* local context as a way to talk about what they thought was *our* universal. They would use, for example, such terms as "hadith" or "hajj" (terms no less technical, let alone local, than "god" and "belief") as if they were natural and then use them to name concepts assumed to be similar in other religions. In fact, in writing that very sentence we were tempted, as is customary in scholarly writing, to italicize those two Arabic terms since they are, after all, foreign words. Yet, most scholars never consider italicizing the word church, used above, despite the fact that the term is both technical and foreign as well, inasmuch as it is used by a specific subgroup of people we happen to study and derived from a much earlier proto-Germanic word. So that instinct to mark the difference or historicity *of just some words*, or the temptation to take certain locals for granted, betrays the very point that we are trying to make here. A major argument that weaves throughout all that follows is that the field of religious studies can do so much better than simply reproducing and using mostly Christian terms as if they were naturally extendable and evidenced all around us. To stay with the above example, jihad is frequently described as a subset of "Just War Theory" and hadith as a species of "Commentary," "Text," or "Canon"—all terms well established in Christian discourses. Perhaps readers, upon finishing this book, will come to understand why we see such approaches as anything but scholarly.

The question, then, is *what is scholarly*, and how, in deriving a vocabulary capable of doing scholarly work, we might accept but also build on the assumption that all of us are rooted in some local context. We do not write here, as Sharpe and many of our other predecessors did, assuming that we are each somehow objectively floating outside reality as we carefully describe its inner workings. (In fact, we are aware of very few who do assume that today, making the object of those continued critiques of the presumed neutrality of the study of religion a red herring.) Nothing might make the problem with that once dominant position more obvious than co-writing with someone else, as we have done before and as we are pleased to be doing once again here, for we each come to the blank page and the various rewrites of draft entries with our own history, assumptions, aims, style, etc. So how can we *retool*, and not just stretch, our inevitably local words along with the local interests of which they are representative and which they help to achieve, doing so in a way that is capable of giving voice to both of our curiosities? Might we even just invent some new words of our own, or devise brand new uses for old words, to do the new sorts of work that we both hope to accomplish? After all, words, like academic subjects, did not simply fall to us from the heavens, already made; instead, they are the tools that our predecessors devised and defined, with the aim of doing specific work that they wanted done, and which were then passed along to us inasmuch as we shared in those labors. But these words—and the scholarly narratives that they produce—also limit us, potentially preventing us from seeing or imagining outside of the terms of reference they have created. What if we wanted to do something new, and something different? What if we were not content with Sharpe's introduction defining our field as "the (as far as possible) objective study of religious beliefs and practices, ancient and modern, along historical and analytical lines"? Surely we would need new tools. Is it possible, in other words, to develop a new way of talking about the world, in the pursuit of different ends—a way that can be adopted by those who, *regardless of their own local setting*, might also wish to talk about the world in a way that not only looks for similarities and differences across local settings and times but also tries to offer an account of sameness and difference?

This is the place, then, to be a little more specific about what we mean by a *critical* study of religion, and how it can be informed by the vocabulary that follows. By that term we do not mean, of course, to criticize religion or the people who identify as religious (whatever they may mean by that)—we are not here to inform people how to perform their own rituals properly or the correct way to tell the stories that they tell. Indeed, our work has never been critical of religion or the religious, if by that one means intervening in debates and practices that scholars usually examine when they say they study religion; rather, we have often been critical of the scholarly moves and frames used by scholars to study them in an academic context—studies that sometimes, in our view, improperly intervene in disputes taking place among the people being studied, thereby taking sides or normalizing just some of the claims or practices while exoticizing yet others. In fact, it would be quite unfortunate if being "critical of religion" was the take-away from this volume—we might caution that those in disagreement with the version of the field we recommend may be tempted to characterize our work in just that way, making it all the easier to dismiss. Now, we do indeed recognize that there are those who use the designation in this manner, aiming to find what they represent as *better* ways of being religious, as judged from this or that set of values or interests; this, however, is not our approach. Instead, our aim is to steer entirely clear of such judgments, aiming, instead, to place ourselves in a tradition that develops and uses technical tools capable of studying religion—which includes even calling something religion to begin with!—as something thoroughly human. We therefore study, if we frame it a little differently, what people designate *as* religious and whatever its opposite might be (after all, being designated as something presupposes those other things that are not). As will become evident soon, many of the terms we use to carry out this work operate in complex relationships with their opposites—much as up presupposes down and cold is meaningless without an idea of what it means to be hot—as ways of charting territory and identity. Things get interesting, of course, when this way of mapping our world bumps up against things that are rather more complicated and ambiguous than such paired concepts can manage—like the often-cited person standing on the threshold of the room, neither in nor out, thereby confounding the rules for behavior either inside or outside of the room. In our reading, religious acts—as well as designating just some acts *as* religious—are nothing more or less than part of the spectrum of ordinary human behaviors and human creations, and thus something that can be scrutinized as can be any other human claim, action, or institution. In a word, a critical approach places this thing called religion—however one defines the term—firmly within the changeable and contestable landscape of history and culture (words that, like many we have been using here, are themselves also tools that will occupy our attention in the pages that follow). Should one consider religion to be something more or other than that, then there are plenty of other books and intellectual pursuits to follow in achieving those other ends. But those are not ours.

But with this final point in mind—i.e., seeing the study of religion, and claims that something is religious, as an historical and cultural effect—we come to the second, rather more influential, book that we also have in mind in tackling this shared project, one first published the year after Sharpe's own volume. That other book is *Keywords: A Vocabulary of Culture and Society* (1976), by Raymond Williams (1921–1988), a Welsh literary theorist known for his work linking literary works to practical issues of ownership and power. In doing this, he went against how others had traditionally studied literature, literariness, and the supposedly ethereal meaning thought by many to lurk within a story or a poem. His *Keywords* (which, unlike Sharpe's book, is still in print and in use) has been helpful to scholars well beyond literary or culture studies—indeed, scholars such as us. In tracking down the derivation and various modern uses of terms that we commonly use in studying groups of people, Williams's entries steer clear of making normative claims (that is, this is how we must use this or that word) and instead make plain the sometimes happenstance twists and turns taken by our words along with their sometimes unintended effects. In so doing, he draws attention to our way not just of talking *about* the world but, more than this, our way of *constituting* a world that we see to be worth talking about in either this or that way—doing so by being cognizant of how words work in relation to yet other words, constituting a vocabulary, which is so much more than a mere list. From aesthetic to consumer, ethnic, family, hegemony, modern, private, tradition, and work, Williams helps readers to do just what we hope to do in a rather less ambitious volume that is aimed primarily, but certainly not exclusively, at our own scholarly field, namely, to investigate clusters of words while *retooling* or, in a word, *redescribing* (yet another word that will deserve some attention) those familiar terms that many students and scholars often use without giving them much thought. In so doing, we show the assumptions and interests that they entail and the linguistic, methodological, and theoretical relations they imply, all in hopes of furthering a scholarly and critical discourse devoted to studying claims about a thing in the world that many of us, for good or ill, call "religion." (For more on a discursive approach to the study of religion see Jay Johnston and Kocku von Stuckrad's co-edited volume, *Discourse Research and Religion: Disciplinary Use and Interdisciplinary Dialogues* [2020].)

Each entry in our book therefore follows Williams's lead by first identifying where our terminology comes from (what we might call historicizing our discourse). In addition, we then move on to demonstrating the various ways in which scholars have used or still employ these terms, making evident the larger conversations—and, sometimes, disagreements—enabled by saying one wishes to understand religion as opposed to explain it. We will not shy away from making recommendations of our own for future use for some of these terms but, to get there, we also aim to be fair in making readers aware of who has been using these terms in order to do what sort of work. Even if readers do not wish to follow our lead we hope nonetheless to nudge their work along by acquainting them with their tools' sources and, just as importantly if not more so, their implications. That there are far more terms than just the 50 that we have selected—some with the help of the anonymous reviewers who gave us feedback on the idea earlier on— should be obvious. (Williams's own book, for example, had 50 just by the time he made it to F in his alphabetical table of contents.) But we have to start somewhere and, ideally, we would like to keep it all succinct enough to offer a book that is affordable, that can be readily used, and that can prompt the sort of debate that keeps a scholarly field healthy and dynamic. Our choices were certainly not arbitrary, and we hope that many of the terms will, as in Williams's own book, be recognized as operating within clusters—though, of course, we have also included some that are simply representative of noteworthy trends or developments in the current field and thus something deserving of a reader's attention. To highlight these clusters, at the end of each entry we provide a list of those other terms in the book that are directly relevant to the term under discussion. For the sake of convenience, we also list those relevant terms in the second volume, *Religion in 50 More Words*. Hopefully, those who see unfortunate gaps in our table of contents will fill them in with some etymological digging of their own, finding forgotten uses for terms and suggesting ways of their own to revise them or, in some cases, maybe recommending that we just retire them altogether.

The present study therefore seeks to provide a succinct historical, social, political, and institutional examination of many of the interconnected key technical terms that together comprise the architecture of the modern study of religion, all of which is aimed at both students and colleagues in the field. Our goal, then, is to get at the historic beginnings, common uses through time, and current significance and utility of many of the basic technical terms used within the current field of religious studies. These are the terms that both students and scholars routinely deploy to create a domain in which to think about, describe, and analyze their data. In submitting these terms to a critical interrogation and subsequent redescription, we hope to facilitate further a collective reframing of the field. Though, as we just noted, our ideal audience is students and scholars in religion, we also trust that this volume will be of interest to readers in other academic fields who routinely choose to study religion in their own work but who may lack the technical training offered by the academic study of religion.

One final word, before we begin: as will be evident from a quick look at the table of contents, this is not a book like Ron Geaves's pocket-sized *Keywords in Religious Studies* (2006)—with succinct entries often used when describing and comparing religions (such as his asceticism, flagellant, Gaia, initiation, neo-pagan, penance, and schism—many of which, by the way, also lean heavily on Christian sources). It is also not a book in the style of the many edited handbooks that are now available (with Mark C. Taylor's *Critical Terms for Religious Studies* [1998] being the first of these modern resources to be published), each with multiple authors providing an often uneven overview of the literature on this or that topic. Nor does it merely present a collection of religious terminology, as in a phenomenological lexicon of first order terms, what one would find in a dictionary of world religions. For, as important as such comparative terms as canon, myth, ritual, and tradition may be for carrying out some of our work, we decided to pull the camera back considerably further in this volume and instead focus on the far more general and, we hope, shared theoretical vocabulary that all students and scholars in our field may wish to hone and employ, whether they study people or texts, actions and objects, or institutions. Regardless of the group, historic period, or region that we each study, we would hope that all scholars are engaged in definition and description, distinguishing religious from non-religious things, and studying how these items or actions intersect with other aspects of the human—and that such scholars are up to the task of fine-tuning their vocabulary and their tools as a way of improving their work.

We are therefore inviting readers of this book to examine the fact that many of us all somehow just apparently seem to know that a scholar of religion ought to be able to use such terms as karma, mitzvah, Tao, sin, and gurdwara, thereby qualifying each *as* distinctly religious and therefore seeing them as somehow inherently related to each other. And to do this we may need a whole new critical vocabulary—or at least a new way of using some of our old words.

Note

1 Like the Appendix, this Introduction appears in both this volume and, with slight revision, in *Religion in 50 More Words*.

1 Affect

In recent years, the term "affect"—as opposed to saying that something has an effect, i.e., consequence or practical implications—has received considerable attention in the Humanities in general, and the study of religion in particular. This is on account of the late-twentieth century rise of "affect theory"—an approach in culture studies and social theory that is seen by some as indebted to the French philosophers Gilles Deleuze (1925–1995) and Pierre-Félix Guattari (1930–1992) and their collaborative reading of the work of the earlier Dutch philosopher Baruch Spinoza (1632–1677). The latter understood "affect" to name a body's capacity for action and as a site on which action is exerted. This approach (one that critiques the once widely held position that saw mind and body as unrelated domains, with mind taking the more prominent role, or the so-called mind-body problem) draws attention to and thereby understands a broad range of what at least some might describe as the possibly subconscious feelings that people—and perhaps even entire social groups—experience. These can include such dispositions as emotions and moods, which, in turn, are presumed to impel us toward action, thought, and ever-changing forms of social relation with others. The propensity for theoretical overdetermination, and the problem of researchers sometimes relying uncritically on texts and participant self-reports to mediate between such overdetermination on the one hand and the presumably active, inner lives of social actors (whether living or long dead), on the other, however, may raise as many questions for the critical scholar as a focus on affect attempts to solve. That scholars in other fields approach these issues differently, must be noted of course. We think here of the cultural theorist Lauren Berlant, and her work on how sentimentality in American popular culture (i.e., identifying with the feelings of others) functions socially and politically (e.g., *The Female Complaint* [2008, 100]), as well as the contemporary literary scholar Frances McDonald, and her work on representations of laughter in American literature. But, at least for some in the study of religion, affect theory has taken a perhaps predictable path toward studying the inner world of the social actor.

The English noun that stands in for this approach, "affect" (obviously related to such other words as "affectation" and "affection," along with its opposition, "disaffection") derives from the classical Latin *affectus*. The latter term is used to denote a mental or emotional state or, significantly, a perceived inner reaction (notably one that is passing, better captured today by the word "effect" [Latin *effectus*], as in a result or a consequence of a previous prompt). The term can also name a physical state (sometimes used to designate one that is thought to be a result of a disease). Among its synonyms are: influence or impression, disposition, eagerness, zeal, purpose or even devotion. We see this in the modern usage of Pope Francis's so-called apostolic letter, dating from September 2020, entitled *Scripturae sacrae affectus* (English: Devotion to Sacred Scripture), a document that marked the 1,600th anniversary of the death of Jerome, a fifth-century Roman Catholic theologian. In post-classical Latin, the term was sometimes given a valence, thus signifying not just desire but *evil* desire, as used in, for example, the Vulgate (the later fourth-century Latin translation of the Christian bible, whose New Testament was originally in the Greek that was commonly used during the Hellenistic era—called Koine Greek). Consider, for example, 1 Thessalonians 2:2, "sed ante passi et contumeliis affecti. . ." (rendered in the so-called Douay English translation of 1582 as: "But having suffered many things before, and been shamefully treated. . ."). Early on, the English term was used to refer to the manner in which one is inclined or disposed toward something. Thus we arrive at Geoffrey Chaucer's *Troilus & Criseyde* (1385): "And therto dronken hadde as hoot and stronge, As Crassus dide for his affectis wronge" (Book III, line 1391). Consider also the pamphlet, *The Supper of the Lord* (1533)—originally attributed to the fictitious Nicholas Twonson of Nuremberg but, by 1573, credited to the English Protestant Reformer, William Tyndale (1494–1536)—"God is searcher of heart and reins, thoughts and affects" (266, quoting the 1850 edition), or, as late as Francis Bacon's 1626 work, *Sylua Syluarum Or A Natural History in Ten Centuries*: "The affects and Paffions of the Heart and Spirits, are notably difclofed by the Pulfe" (25, section 97, quoting the 1670 edition).

By the end of the nineteenth century, however, the term began to take on a more technical and specialized meaning. This was especially the case in what were then the nascent social and biological sciences, and to such an extent that all of these more general uses of the term had, for the most part, by then become obsolete—especially evident in what were then the new academic fields of Psychology and Psychiatry. We see this change, for instance, in the American philosophy and evolutionary psychologist

Affect 13

James Mark Baldwin's *Handbook of Psychology: Feeling and Will* (1891): "Affects therefore are the feeling antecedents of involuntary movements; as motives, including affects, are the inner antecedents of acts of will" (vol. 2, 314, quoting the 1891 edition). Baldwin (1861–1934)—after whom the "Baldwin effect" is named—argued that an organism's ability to learn new behaviors can affect its reproductive success and, thus, influence the genetic makeup of its species through the Darwinian process of natural selection. The still noted philosopher and psychologist from roughly the same time, William James (1842–1910), who was himself a key figure in the early formation of the study of religion, also employed the term in his *Collected Essays & Review* (1894): "We may also feel a general seizure of excitement, which . . . German writers call an *Affect*, and which is what I have all along meant by an emotion" (358, quoting the 1920 edition). This is how the term continues to be employed to this day, where an affect is used, primarily, though by no means exclusively, in psychology and among some affect theorists to refer not simply to emotions but also to the observable expressions, gestures, postures, that are said to accompany (and thereby publicly signal) the presumed presence of inner states and dispositions. Affectations, in other words, allow the observer to infer the existence of such inner states. Sometimes, of course, such affectations can be read pejoratively, as gestures or flourishes that are judged as unnecessary, ostentatious, or, simply put, showy. In Henry Fielding's novel, *Joseph Andrews* (1742), we read in the Preface: "Now Affection proceeds from one of two Causes, Vanity or Hypocrisy. . ." (6, citing the 1967 edition).

On account of its presumed ability to signify events or states present only in the internal life of individuals, the private domain associated with experience, it was probably only a matter of time before the term became associated with religion, itself understood during the modern period as naming a unique inner disposition expressed outwardly. Here, we see it relate to the already well-established efforts to protect religious claims from Enlightenment-era critique by asserting it to be a non-rational sentiment—a point shared with Donovan Schaefer's well-received book, *Religious Affects: Animality, Evolution, and Power* (2015), inasmuch as it is aimed at addressing what he understands as scholars' over-emphasis on studies of belief. We therefore see the term employed in close relation to religion as early as the American theologian, Jonathan Edwards (1703–1758), such as in his *A Treatise Concerning Religious Affections* (1746), a work that played a key role in what is often referred to as the "First Great Awakening" of the early- to mid-eighteenth century, and which sought to renew individual piety and religious devotion in England and in the colonies that would soon become the United States. For example, Edwards argues in the book's first section, "On the Nature of Affections, and Their Importance in

Religion," that Christians do not pray in order to "declare our wants and desires, in order to inform God," but, rather "to affect our own hearts, and so to prepare ourselves for the reception of the blessing we ask" (34), adding: "If the things of religion are rightly understood, they *will* affect the heart"— while those unaffected are characterized as "spiritually blind" (40). We also think here of the once influential work of the German pietist theologian, Friedrich Schleiermacher (1768–1834):

> true religion resides very much in the affections . . . God has given to mankind affections for the same purpose as he has given all the faculties and principles of the human soul, that they might be subservient to the great business for which man was created—the business of religion.
> (41, quoting the "somewhat abridged" 1824 edition)

Within the academy, the term initially was mostly confined to the realm of psychology, but in the 1990s we witness a crossover to the fields commonly grouped together as the Humanities, with the rise of what later comes to be known as "affect theory" (often dated to the early 1960s). This approach groups feelings, emotions, and moods—i.e., a set of subjectively experienced and self-reported dispositions—into discrete categories of analysis, to then determine the ways in which they are exhibited within or projected onto social, cultural, and political contexts. Or, as phrased by Schaefer in the Introduction to his above-mentioned book: "Affect shapes this interaction between knowledge, religion, and power." Affect theorists thus seek to approach the study of culture, history, and politics in such a manner that attention is placed on what they understand as the expression and motive force of a set of prior, non- or pre-linguistic, and thus interior, forces or dispositions. They do this, moreover, as a way to account for how collections of individuals come to agree on, say, the cultural conventions of their lives—though, to be fair, there are no doubt those who would agree that language and culture *shape* or *condition* affective states and responses (as does Schaefer in his more recent *The Evolution of Affect Theory: The Humanities, the Sciences, and the Study of Power* [2019]). It is not immediately clear, however, whether many would hold the further position that situation and setting (i.e., discourse and structure) *produce* what members of groups subsequently internalize *as* pre-social sentiments. The latter position has been suggested by the cultural anthropologist at the University of Tübingen, Monique Scheer, in a 2012 article entitled "Are Emotions a Kind of Practice (and is that What Makes Them Have a History)? A Bourdieuian Approach to Understanding Emotion." She argues there that because habitus (a term derived from Pierre Bourdieu's [1930–2002] sociological work, naming the internalization of our cultural setting and its standards) "is the precondition for subjectification . . . [i]t can and does produce the behaviors and thought patterns of intentionality or a 'free will,' if that is what a specific community demands of its subjects" (*History & Theory* 51/2: 206). She continues: "The 'interior' as the locus of 'true feelings' and the self is also a product of a habitus that daily engages in denigrating the 'exterior' and 'emancipating' the subject from it." However, should one *not* follow Scheer's more thoroughgoing social theory—something akin to Bruce Lincoln's own early interest in the discursive context of what he termed sentiments of affinity and estrangement (see the second edition of his *Discourse and the Construction of Society* [2014], 8–9, 74, 94, 103)—then although they may be *influenced* by setting, intuitive, pre-ideological affects are instead assumed to make us (and by us we no longer just mean human beings as distinct from the animal kingdom) what and who we are. Now they are neither under our rational control nor even necessarily within our conscious awareness and, as such, they can only sometimes be captured or adequately expressed in language. In fact, an over-reliance on not just conscious belief but also on the role of language is among affect theory's targets. It is somewhat ironic, however, that such studies in the field today are often represented as part of a larger materialist move found in such subfields as embodied religion (e.g., Elaine A. Peña's work, *Performing Piety: Making Space Sacred with the Virgin of Guadalupe* [2011]), or what is sometimes also termed religion on the ground (in that they both aim to move away from traditional studies of texts and elite practitioners' self-reports)—thus affect theory's focus on what is assumed to be a pre-expressive inner sentiment or experience that is only secondarily materialized or embodied, as it were.

One might therefore see how this approach can signal a set of problems that have plagued the study of religion since its inception. We refer, namely, to the basic question: what is the nature of, and how do we study, such seemingly inner states as religious experience? As will be the case with so many of the keywords that follow, there exists an overwhelming tendency in the academic study of religion to conceptualize, and then study, religion (and by extension that which is often designated as the sacred) as existing either before or beyond language and history. The study of affects, it would seem, is no different. How, after all, can one understand that which is considered to exist beyond or prior to our categories of analysis? Affect theory, whether intentionally or not is not really the issue, thus provides a new way to talk about old issues in the field—issues that we maintain have little or no place in the study of religion—such as common presumptions about religion being based in non-rationale experience. While the latter term, experience, may play a role in managing the social sphere—i.e., as a discourse to legitimate certain political or social choices as opposed to others—there is no way, despite the claims of colleagues in the Cognitive Science of Religion

(CSR), to study the internal thought, experiences, and motivations of social actors, especially those of people living hundreds or thousands of years ago. It is for this reason that we propose to discuss *claims of* experience rather than experiences themselves. For instance, in an article titled "Affect and the Study of Religion" (published in *Religion Compass* 9/10 [2015]: 335–345), Jenna Supp-Montgomerie maintains that affect theory, in turning attention from the individual as the bearer of emotion to the social lives that emerge between bodies and things, offers new insights into theorizing about religion. Regardless how this approach is adopted in other fields, the move from texts, beliefs, and practices to such things as corporeality and materiality may not so much represent a new way to theorize religion as stand in for an updating or even rebranding of the status quo in the field, which emphasizes experience and emotion over history, politics, economics, and other material condition.

It is also interesting that the generally recognized founder of at least one strand of affect theory, the psychologist (and not scholar of religion) Silvan Tomkins (1911–1991)—whose writings influenced the literary critic and early queer theorist Eve Kosofsky Sedgwick's (1950–2009) own work in the mid-1990s—argued, in his multi-volume *Affect Imagery Consciousness* (1962–1991): "In Christianity the covenant is less exclusive and more loving and thereby provided a purer and more universal love as a model and as an ideal for all" (vol. 3, part 2, 774, citing the complete edition from 2008). Though the son of Russian Jewish immigrants in America, Tomkins here taps into a much earlier and well-known set of normative Christocentric tropes. Not unlike an earlier generation of scholars of religion, who unthinkingly used Christianity (let alone certain of its denominations) as their lodestar to compare and contrast other religions, Tomkins echoes a certain structural bias in a field where his theories are now applied and elaborated. We also witness this in some of the applications to which affect theory has been used in the study of religion. For example, Peter C. Hill and Ralph W. Hood, Jr.'s "Affect, Religion, and Unconscious Processes" (*Journal of Personality* 67/6 [1999]: 1015–1046), tries to use a Cognitive-Experiential Self-Theory (CEST) model to explain religious experience by showing how the latter represents the need to manage pleasure and pain, the need for a coherent conceptual system, the need for self-esteem, and the need for relatedness. Or, again, consider the collection of essays edited by John Corrigan, *Feeling Religion* (2018), in which contributors demonstrate how an understanding of emotion sheds light on equally problematic—though they would, of course, likely never use the term "problematic"—categories such as religion, spirituality, and the secular. In many ways, however, this is tantamount to using an unknown to explain yet another unknown. And if these examples are all concerned with modern issues, then we see how

Affect 17

affect theory can be used to make sense of the past in, for example, the American historian Barbara H. Rosenwein's *Emotional Communities in the Early Middle Ages* (2007), which argues, in a rather circular fashion, that religious beliefs affected emotional styles even as those same styles helped to shape religious expression.

Problematic in all of this, at least for the critical scholar, is the widely shared assumption that we can somehow use either written texts or people's self-reports as a gateway to understand the pre-expressive, emotional world of living or long dead people. If this is difficult to do with a living author, just imagine how much more difficult (if not impossible) it is to do so with someone who lived close to 800 years ago. Texts, let alone participant responses to an ethnographer's queries, we maintain, should *not* be regarded as directly mediating some authentic and non-textual experience or emotional state, as some affect theories claim. Instead, both should be approached as specific and always situated discursive moments, with each using a host of rhetorical devices, grounded in particular social, political, historical, let alone class, racial, and gendered contexts. We would therefore do well not to look too quickly beyond each of these to some pre-social and presumably universal sentiment.

Affects, and the modern approach used to understand them, may very well be little more than a repackaged way to talk about the ever problematic category in the field known as experience. Like the latter, affects are difficult to ascertain, largely unrepresentable and unpresentable, and therefore given to theoretical incoherence despite claims concerning their priority or originality—all features that, unfortunately, are still all too common in the field. That we, as researchers, no doubt presume ourselves to have them (whether affects or experiences) strikes us as a flimsy basis to then infer their existence elsewhere and in other people, especially if we have failed to take seriously the larger structured settings in which we live and work and which may very well have—recalling Scheer's argument—produced this impression in us in the first place.

In this volume see: authenticity, belief, culture, experience, gender, history, material religion, politics, race, religion, sacred/profane, secular

In *Religion in 50 More Words* see: immanence/transcendence, meditation, mysticism, piety, soul, spirituality

2 Authenticity

There exists a widespread assumption, among both scholars and the general public alike, that certain ways of being religious are more pure and thus faithful to some posited original than others—an assumption that can also be seen in how religion itself is distinguished from, and often valued over, other aspects of social life. It is little wonder, then, that we often find associations between the words "religion" and "authenticity." The latter term implies an authoritative genuineness or purity that is perceived to be something closely akin to an object's or a person's true nature as opposed to some derivative, watered-down, or accidental quality. In the study of religion, authenticity is a value judgment that implies that someone or something (such as interpreting a text or performing a social identity) is represented as the only, the essential, or the natural and thus inevitable option. Claims that something or someone is authentic necessarily implies that someone or something is inauthentic and thus secondary, polluted, or flawed. Such a judgment is therefore always political, inasmuch as it is explicitly involved in not just arranging but also ranking and valorizing the world, and it therefore deserves our critical attention, especially when we see how self-serving such judgments can be—inasmuch as they generally reproduce sets of normative assumptions about what religion ought to be (a point apparent in Susan Sanderson, Brian Vandenberg, and Paul Paese's study of how health professionals distinguish mental health crises from so-called authentic religious experiences; see their "Authentic Religious Experience or Insanity?" in the *Journal of Clinical Psychology* 55 [1999]: 607–616).

This now common English word "authentic" is derived from the Hellenistic Greek, *aúthentikós*: *auto* ("self") + *hentes* ("doer" or "being"), which connotes a sense of doing or accomplishing something for oneself, thereby implying a sense of originality and autonomy—thus signifying early on something akin to an original as opposed to a copy. The modern term, which has a number of historic senses, entered English by way of French and, earlier, from the ancient Latin *authenticus*, which from late antiquity to the

DOI: 10.4324/9781003140184-3

medieval period designated, among other things, a type of music associated with Christian worship. The thirteenth-century Old French *autentique* eventually resulted as a term used to denote authoritative documents (e.g., legal texts—such as Thomas Wilson's later *The arte of rhetorique for the vse of all soche as are studious of eloquence* [1553], which described covenants and deeds as "autentique"). Soon thereafter the term was extended to a characteristic possessed by a certain group of people, notably those who were seen to be especially credible, legitimate, licensed, and thus qualified to speak or act in specific settings (making plain the implicit and long-standing association between authenticity and authority). Consider the fifteenth-century Scottish poet Robert Henryson and his translation and adaptation of 13 of Æsop's fables in his own book, *The Morall Fabillis*. In one of its poems, "The Trial of Fox," the wolf—who is portrayed as educated and with expertise in the law—is characterized as follows: "He is autentik, and ane man of age" (see line 1013). Eventually the word comes to designate items or people that are particularly unvarnished and therefore presumed to be natural and genuine, while simultaneously lacking affectation or gimmicks, thereby making them particularly trustworthy and therefore legitimate. In Chaucer's late-fourteenth-century poem, "The Book of the Duchess," we witness the following description of a knight's deceased love: "Though her stories be autentike. . ." (line 1086). We also read in Richard Watson's 1796 *An apology for the Bible, in a series of letters, addressed to Thomas Paine*:

> A genuine book, is that which was written by the person whose name it bears, as the author of it. An authentic book, is that which relates matters of fact, as they really happened. A book may be genuine without being authentic. And a book may be authentic without being genuine.
> (See letter II)

Something is authoritative by virtue of its being self-contained or self-created—returning us to the much earlier Greek sense of accomplishing something by oneself, with no help from another. We see this in the Cambridge University Divinity Professor, William Whitaker's polemical, anti-Catholic work, *A disputation on Holy Scripture against the papists, especially Bellarmine and Stapleton* (1849):

> The papists themselves confess that the church does not make the scripture authentic, but only declares it. But if the scriptures be first authentic of itself, then certainly it necessarily follows that it must be authentic also to us. That is called authentic, which is sufficient to itself, which commends, sustains, proves itself, and hath credit and authority from itself.
> (chpt. 11, 332)

Despite how the term is most often used by speakers—as if it selects out and names a quality in an object that makes it either authentic or inauthentic—*claiming* that something is authentic, or possesses some quality known as authenticity (an early eighteenth-century variant), is ultimately a performance of judgment on the part of a speaker. As in Whitaker's above criticism of Roman Catholicism, this judgment functions to isolate and then prioritize one option among others. We also see this in claims about something being an authentic work of art, authentic Mexican food, authentic olive oil, or that only sparkling wines originating from a specific region in France can legitimately be called champagne. In his chapter "Weavers and Dealers: The Authenticity of an Oriental Carpet" (in *The Social Life of Things* [1988]), the anthropologist Brian Spooner (1935) therefore concludes that claims of authenticity are *not* about the items so described but, instead, all about the speakers who use the claim to sanction a ranking of those items for their own purposes. He notes, for example, that judging a so-called Oriental carpet's authenticity developed only once the mass-production of such rugs had happened—a situation in which industrialized supply suddenly outpaced demand—thus making such claims part of their branding and marketing rather than a description of some supposed feature of the weaving, its pattern, or material. Unless we try to argue that religion is mysteriously set apart from all other aspects of human history and culture (as some do, to be sure), then this applies to claims about authentic religion or authentic forms (e.g., Islam, Hinduism) as well.

It is therefore important to hear claims of authenticity as just that, *claims* made by social actors in hectic social settings, all of whom are trying to manage an economy of competing contenders (i.e., a market suddenly flooded with carpets). There is an unfortunate tendency, however, to look for the authentic (i.e., original, universal, true, essential, etc.) dimension of a religion (often linked to some sort of inner and thus private sentiment, such as a unique aspect of what is usually called experience) or to identify some historical or regional variation of a particular religion as more or less authentic (i.e., orthodox, normative, credible, correct, preferred, etc.). Such judgment, to invoke one of the term's meanings, provides sufficient evidence to question how seemingly disinterested descriptions of authentic religion might be, prompting us instead to hear such assertions as far more prescriptive, invested, and socially formative than they initially appear. This judgment coincides with the tendency to privilege and thereby protect those claims, actions, and organizations designated *as* religious from rigorous scrutiny by asserting that they are uniquely self-created or, as scholars have often said, *sui generis*. The latter term, so common in the phenomenology of religion, is Latin for "self-caused" or "one of a kind"—a position that is meant to prevent others from reducing religion to what might be considered even more basic and non-religious aspects. We thus see how easily a long history of usage for the term "authentic" can be linked to modern efforts to cordon off a select aspect of the human as somehow pure and authoritative. We can easily see this happen when members of the groups themselves make such claims, with the aim of promoting their own groups and interests. Consider the late Ray C. Stedman's once bestselling book, *Authentic Christianity: Trading Religion & Rules for True Faith* (1996)—described as "revealing the real purpose, simplicity, and joy of true Christianity." Despite the claim to universality, the work ends up being a particular type of evangelical Protestantism supposedly free of non-essential rituals and based on a, as its members would say, personal relationship with Jesus Christ, itself a common anti-Papal polemic that dates from the Protestant Reformation in the early- to mid-sixteenth century. Then there is R. Albert Mohler Jr.'s July 15, 2002, letter to the editors of *The New York Times*, written in his capacity as the then President of the Southern Baptist Theological Seminary (in Louisville, KY): "an Islam that settles for religious pluralism is not authentic Islam, and Christianity without zeal for conversion is not true Christianity." In fact, commentaries on something called authentic Islam seem to be a favorite for recent media and even political and scholarly efforts in parts of the world, aiming to sanction certain forms as being more authoritative than others. Such references to authenticity as if it simply named an obvious characteristic of religion appears just as easily in the work of scholars, both past and present. Consider a 2020 peer reviewed article in *Archive for the Psychology of Religion* entitled "An Authentic Feeling? Religious Experience Through Q&A Websites" (published in 42/2: 211–231) which, in part, is aimed at "improving social research about the Authenticity of the religious feeling." Or, more classically, consider C. Jouco Bleeker (1898–1983), once noted scholar at the University of Amsterdam and longtime contributor to the International Association for the History of Religions (IAHR, the field's only international organization), who, like others in the once influential field of phenomenology of religion, understood scholars' roles to be "to distinguish what is genuinely religious from what is spurious" (as he wrote in the opening to his collected essays, *The Sacred Bridge* [1963]). Here he assumes religion to embody that which is, as the historian of the field, Jacques Waardenburg (1930–2015) once characterized such work, "tuned into the holy or the divine" (writing in "Religion between Reality and Idea" in *Numen* 19 [1972]: 187 n. 147). Such terms are ill-defined and correspond to the usually preferred designation of "the sacred," a term that has been favored by generations of scholars intent on identifying and naming what they held to be the unique and therefore essential element as somehow authentic or real, what a much earlier generation might well have even named as natural or even primitive and earliest religion.

Contrary to how the term "authentic" is customarily used, it is best that critical scholars recall Spooner's conclusion and avoid employing the term as if it innocently describes an actual or obvious quality inherent to either objects or people. One cannot, for example, look more closely or carefully at a carpet or a devotee to discern either's authenticity, for doing so merely sanctions an implicit set of assumptions and the asserted and therefore undefended value/ranking system that (unknowingly perhaps) guides its use—with as many contesting systems being present as there are people contesting who and what counts as the real or the natural. Instead, claims that either this or that is the authentic form of some religion should prompt us to scrutinize the interests of the one who makes such a claim about the world and to investigate the effects of employing it, should its use be heard as persuasive and uncontested.

In this volume see: experience, identity, interpretation, orthodoxy, phenomenology, religion, text

In *Religion in 50 More Words* see: emic/etic, evil, idol, nones, piety, renunciation, spirituality

3 Authority

Many in both the general public and in the study of religion alike persist in understanding things designated *as* religion to be concerned with what the German Protestant theologian Paul Tillich (1886–1965) famously termed "faith in an ultimate concern" (as he argued in *The Dynamics of Faith* [1957]). It perhaps makes sense, then, that items commonly associated with religion, and thus carrying the adjective "religious," are often represented as being of heightened relevance and legitimacy—at least when compared to those that are seen as mundane, everyday, or, in a word, profane. So it should come as no surprise that the noun "authority," along with its adjective "authoritative," is a familiar word in scholarship on religion. We frequently encounter the phrase "an authoritative text," for example, or a certain tradition is described as carrying weight or authority (a phrase found as early as William Shakespeare's *Henry VIII* [Act 3, Sc. 2]). Yet studying authority often risks erasing the prior and ongoing historical and human situations in which status, deference, and privilege are claimed and established, let alone reproduced and, sooner or later, contested, undermined, and replaced. Instead, as we see in Paul Hedges and Christina Welch's chapter on sources of authority in religion, scholars often end up merely paraphrasing how practitioners' accounts, such as concluding that "for members of the LDS church (commonly known as Mormons), authority lies in a text" (in Hedge's edited book, *Controversies in Contemporary Religion* [2014], 68). However, appealing to the less represented verb we might instead ask why has this, or any, collection of diverse texts, and certain readings of them, been *authorized*—by whom and to what effect? Such a question, we would hope, makes evident the distance between a critical study of something called authority and one that is merely descriptive and thus less interested in theorizing something that is often taken for granted as simply inhabiting and thus animating items or people.

The word "authority" dates from the Anglo-Norman terms *auctoreté* and *auctoritie*, used as early as the twelfth century. Interestingly, it is not used in

DOI: 10.4324/9781003140184-4

the now common sense of a natural quality, but instead refers to a relational status and thus something that enables one to make claims on others. The latter includes giving orders or someone able to make legitimate claims about the world, akin to a modern notion of being a witness or spokesperson. Authority, in this much earlier sense, was therefore a social product of people in ranked situations. Ultimately traced to the much earlier Latin *auctoritas* (signifying everything from the right to own things to prestige and esteem—and itself linked to the Latin *auctor*, from which the modern word "author" eventually develops, as someone seen as a legitimate source), it is therefore difficult to see the earlier term as anything but a designator concerned with social relationships and their consequences.

To be fair, Hedges and Welch do note that the King James Bible "*is considered* authoritative" (emphasis added), going on to outline the exclusive male leadership within the church's formal hierarchy. They also note that "the authority of the church [is] firmly in the hands of men," that "men are authority figures with the family," as well as showing an interest in Latter Day Saints women's responses to male authority. But all of this seems to portray authority as a thing or quality that is possessed or exercised—no doubt a characterization that people within the groups we study may offer when we ask them questions about their groups—rather than seeing authority as the product of a variety of prior social acts and conditions. Instead, it might be more profitable to ask *why* one subgroup exercises certain powers in this specific example, not to mention *what* practical circumstances and techniques reproduce a structure of authority in which over half of the populations is systematically and consistently excluded from accessing the levers of influence.

This alternative set of questions gains inspiration from University of Chicago historian of religions, Bruce Lincoln, notably his book, *Authority: Construction and Corrosion* (1994) as well as his essay, "How to Read a Religious Text" (*History of Religions* 46/2 [2006]: 127–139). The latter deviates from the usual preoccupation of identifying the original version of a text in order to ascertain what it might have once "really meant." Instead, Lincoln consistently presses the view that texts are artifacts of prior human situations (let alone artifacts used in contemporary situations)—situations in which actors make choices that have effect. Thus, "who speaks here" becomes a scholar's concern, rather than reading texts as speaking for themselves, such as someone claiming that "the *Bhagavad Gita* says. . . ." Quoting Lincoln: "Who is trying to persuade whom of what in this text? In what context is the attempt situated, and what are the consequences should it succeed?" (127). Such "destabilizing and irreverent questions" (as he characterized them in the related comments from Thesis 4 of his "Theses on Method" (*Method & Theory in the Study of Religion* 8/3 [1996]:

225–227) cut to the heart of the mechanism by which authority systems are perpetuated: they are dehistoricized and represented as something other than specific social actors' situated claims in a hectic economy of competing claims. Any approach that fails to pose Lincoln's questions therefore risks participating within what he might term a regime of authority, thereby reifying rather than studying the divisions of social agency and rank within the groups under study.

Not unlike how beliefs and experiences can be redescribed as evidence of prior social situations, so too authority becomes not something that "lies within" items. Authority, much like the thing we call an identity, is thus the result of claims and contests among a group's many members, with followers always implicated in how they are governed. For, as Lincoln makes evident throughout his above-mentioned book, *Authority*, social legitimacy derives from those over whom so-called leaders exercise their status—whether via the members' active agreement or apathy and inaction. Leadership and legitimacy are thus best studied as always *given to* actors by others, as opposed to something supposedly grabbed or possessed. And, as bestowed, they can always be revoked.

In this volume see: authenticity, belief, experience, faith, identity, power, redescription, sacred/profane, status

In *Religion in 50 More Words* see: church, commentary, cult, dialogue, founder, hagiography, idol, liberation, paganism, priest/prophet, reformation, tradition, value

4 Belief

Many have long relied on "belief system" as a handy synonym for what others might just simply call a religion or a world religion (sites where people are said to "make their beliefs tangible" [quoting Elaine Peña's *Performing Piety* [2011]). Yet, this common word "belief" is much more complex than it might at first appear, entailing assumptions about religion and even what it means to be human, and so for this reason it deserves closer scrutiny. For the term often turns on the presupposition that internal dynamics—often of a mysterious and highly personal nature—manifest themselves in publicly observable actions, and it is the former as opposed to the latter that are of concern to both the so-called believer as well as those who study them. This focus on the internal, though common throughout the field, requires some scrutiny.

Predecessors to the modern English term "belief" first appeared in Old English—dating from roughly the fifth to eleventh centuries—as *be* (prefix) + *yleve*, which most likely is a variant or alteration modeled on an even earlier Latin term. The word shows considerable semantic overlap with the later French loan word "*foi*" to which it is related. Early on both terms found a home within Christian discourses and, theologically, there was an early distinction between the two words with "belief" referring either to the intellectual or reasoned assent to certain stated propositions (or what Christians often called dogmas and creeds). For example, the three parts of the so-called Apostles Creed, which is widely adopted in Christianity, begin with: "I believe in God, the Father almighty, creator of heaven and earth . . . I believe in Jesus Christ, his only Son, our Lord . . . I believe in the Holy Spirit . . . ." Reciting such creeds therefore functions much as an oath might—as an authoritative, public demonstration of group membership. "Faith," on the contrary, was often used to name (such as for those who designated themselves as "the faithful") a personal and likely non-rational trust, commitment, or state of assuredness that seemingly defied evidence or which did not rely upon reason and argumentation. To believe, then, often involved a

Christian's stated acceptance of the existence of God and, more technically, the exact nature of God and God's intervention in human history in the form of Jesus Christ (e.g., Christology, the systematic statement and study of the nature and mission of Jesus Christ). This now important semantic distinction, between English's belief and faith, is significantly absent from the cognate Germanic languages, for example, the German term *Glaube* includes both senses (such as the title of Friedrich Schleiermacher's famous work in systematic theology, *Der christliche Glaube* [revised ed., 1830–1831], usually translated as *The Christian Faith*—a famous title that noticeably avoids the term religion, a word found in German as well as in English).

The term "belief" has a lengthy history in English, something that now includes popular usage (we think of Neil Diamond's pop hit song from 1966, "I'm a Believer," which, notably, is premised on the role empirical evidence plays in arriving at a conclusion for, as the lyric goes, "Then I saw her face, now I'm a believer. Not a trace, of doubt in my mind. . ."). In scholarship, however, the earliest attestations of the term are all theological in scope. As early as the twelfth century, for example, it is used to refer explicitly to a mental action, habit of trusting, or having confidence in a person or thing. It thus came to denote the trust that a so-called Christian believer places in their idea of God. The *Oxford English Dictionary* attributes its first recorded use in *Ælfric*'s *Homily on Nativity of Christ* (ca. 1125) in the context of the Christian ritual known as the eucharist (from the Greek, to give thanks), also known for some as communion: "Ðesne laf we æteð þonne we mid bileafan gað to halige husle ure hælendes lichame" ("This loaf we eat when we with belief got to the holy Eucharist of Our Lord's body"). Here the notion of belief is coupled with having the correct understanding of a particular Christian ritual (for example, its meaning and its relation to Christian doctrine, not necessarily its proper performance). This notion of belief, as an inward state of agreement, is certainly in keeping with the late antique Christian—and, as of the sixteenth century and after, the Protestant Christian—emphasis on belief over acts. This distinction became from the earliest period a convenient way to differentiate Christian belief from Jewish ritual, and, later, was relied upon to minimize what Protestants portrayed as Roman Catholicism's excessive focus on what was characterized as disingenuous and thus empty and insincere outward performance. Recall the Apostle Paul's famous dictum: "A person is not a Jew who is one only outwardly, nor is circumcision merely outward and physical. No, a person is a Jew who is one inwardly; and circumcision is circumcision of the heart, by the spirit, not by the written code. Such a person's praise is not from other people, but from God" (Romans 2: 28–29)—a strategic de-emphasis of action that can be found all throughout the ancient world, e.g., Philo of Alexandria's (b. 20 BCE) *Questions and Answers on Exodus* 2.2:

"the proselyte is the one who circumcises not the foreskin but the pleasures and desires and other passions of the soul." In fact, we would argue that this handy distinction between inner and outer, between claims concerning non-empirical states of awareness or feelings, on the one hand, and, on the other, public behaviors and modes of social organization—coupled with the ranked prioritization and valuing of the former over the latter—has become a key element of modernity. This is related to the now common assumption that a shared, interior human nature unites the species despite plenty of observable differences. If so, then the discourse on belief (akin to the discourse on faith) may be understood to have become part of the way in which the modern self and the idea of the individual, and thus also the human, are today understood, represented, and organized.

Belief—or, more correctly, the claim of having such an inner state as a belief—therefore became the primary means to adjudicate who was and who was not in the "proper" community, indicating that a term of supposed individual awareness can instead be understood as an effective social designator. Tracking beliefs, or more accurately public professions and thus performance of belief, functioned as a quasi-checklist that determined membership within a larger social group, providing a convenient way to organize and separate people (even to persecute them). Beliefs, then, as well as those said to hold them, could be seen as either proper (orthodox) or improper (heterodox). It should be clear that implicit in the notion of claims involving belief is a certain normativity, i.e., tracking is not simply about *making* a list but also of *ranking* the elements of that list as better or worse. Since socially formative decisions were being made as to who was a true believer and who was not (making these others freethinkers, unbelievers, or even heretics or infidels), authoritative collections of beliefs, sometimes also referred to as creeds or dogmas, had to be made and policed. These checklists, as it were, could then be assented to (or not)—with the implications of disagreement taking a number of forms, including banishment or even death (sometimes in what many would today see as simply horrendous ways). It is probably for this reason that another early use of the term is to be "out of belief," as in to have "fallen out of the Word," as some Christians might today classify a type of preaching that, at least to their way of thinking, deviates from their group's orthodoxy. Though this use of the term is now largely obsolete, it was once used to refer to those who were outside what would have then been referred to as the Christian faith—whether as non-Christians or, as was more often the case, the wrong kind of Christians (with Christian vs. non-Christian once being a dominant way of classifying people, a binary system even adopted by early and, in some cases, surprisingly recent scholars of religion). In the sermons of the Scholastic theologian John Wyclif (1330–1384), for example, to be "out of bileve" is equivalent to have "misturned fro Goddis wille" (i.e., to have ignored God's will).

A less theological valence to the term began to appear in the sixteenth century. Used in an expanded sense, belief now came to designate a basic or ultimate principle or presupposition of knowledge in general, where it was now used primarily in the plural. Such beliefs, now understood in a more philosophical sense, were those things that could be innately and thus legitimately held (for, often, one not just has or possesses but also holds a belief). In 1590, for example, the author and courtier Sir Philip Sidney (1554–1586) wrote: "My only defence shall be beleefe of nothing." This use of the term would seem to denote the acceptance of what is believed to be a fact—akin to the pop song mentioned earlier—as we would today phrase it (leading to a modern usage such as "I don't believe you" said as a way of contesting someone else's claims or even pronouncing something to be "unbelievable," that is, defying credulity). This quotation is also interesting in the sense that it refers to a belief in nothing, which implies a certain agnosticism (a term coined by the English scholar, Thomas Huxley, in 1869, to denote a position against unverifiable speculation and thus one that admits to the limits of human of knowledge, such as determining whether or not a god exists) or even atheism (itself an older term, borrowed by from late-sixteenth-century French, to name the lack of belief in the existence of god, with the negative prefix a- added to the Greek-derived term theism, for a belief in a god).

It is clear from this brief history that the term "belief" is firmly embedded within a specifically European discourse on knowledge and legitimacy, one that seeks to differentiate between good or proper beliefs and bad or improper ones, with an eye toward social formation on the one hand and social differentiation on the other. It is a key element in a group of associated terms that, while subjective in the sense that it is presumed by those using it to name something internal and thus private and personal to the so-called believer, it also plays a crucial dimension in definition and maintenance of a community (in distinction from the nonbelievers let alone those who believe what is then labeled unorthodox or heretical and extremist things). There is, however, often a conflation between these two uses with those concerning an internal dimension—often associated with claims about having had an experience—privileged over the external social one. Moreover, this communal sense of the term is often used in a manner that allows one to speak, often in reified and essential terms, of concepts like "Christian belief." Though the use of such a term rarely qualifies *what kind* or, better put, precisely *whose* Christian belief—suggesting that such a generalization is not intellectually sloppy so much as a strategic effort to emphasize but one form, as if universal, to the exclusion of its potential competitors.

The term "belief"—as in the popular and already-mentioned synonym for religion, "belief system"—is also problematic when used to describe groups outside of the Christian context. We often find this, for example, in world religions textbooks, religious literacy guides, or even in official government documents in what are often termed pluralistic, liberal democracies. While Christianity—at least as dominantly represented by many who claim membership in this obviously wide-ranging group—is said to be predicated on belief (and this is why historically it has been so important for theologians to identify and then separate proper from improper beliefs) most other groups studied by scholars of religion emphasize aspects or features other than internal assent to a set of dogmas. Traditional forms of Judaism, for example, emphasize action and thus those actions understood as rituals over belief. While the concept of a Messiah figure is important throughout much of Judaism, for instance, public declarations of belief in such a figure, let alone specifications on the details, is not necessary to be part of the community (i.e., it is not used as litmus test of group membership—yet other things are, of course, such as lineage or participation in certain ritual occasions). Significantly, it was only when what we today commonly designate as Judaism became an accepted part of the modern (largely Christian) European nation-state that a set of things known as "Jewish beliefs" had to be articulated (e.g., identifying it with ethical monotheism, the belief in a single god that is the source of all morality). While in Islam, belief is important (known in Arabic as *iman*, or what came to be known as Muslim articles of faith, including the belief in the existence of Allah), it in no way functions in the same manner as it does within Christianity. To talk about the belief systems of other religions therefore often signifies an attempt at Christian-inspired interreligious dialogue, in which others are understood, and thereby remade, in the image of the discourse's dominant members.

To correct many of these problems (such as the presumption of a nonempirical essence that animates public behavior), scholars have therefore begun to emphasize action in place of studying a group's beliefs. They regard the latter not merely as the secondary site where prior belief is externalized, expressed, or symbolized—a once prominent theory of ritual—but, instead, as providing the practical, organizational conditions in which self-perception inevitably takes shape (i.e., the setting in which people come to assume they have such things as beliefs). Thus, according to such an alternative approach, belief is the residue of prior conditions that enable social actors to perceive and then represent themselves *as if* they have dynamic, pre-social inner states that only later motivate their actions. In this model, actors who, for instance, recite a pledge of allegiance for the first time, or who make the sign of the crucifix on their chests, are not doing it *because* they believe themselves to be the member of a group, but, instead, they are following prior (and in some cases, long forgotten) instructions of authorized elders and thus matching the observable behaviors of their peers, in a specific social setting. Doing so repeatedly and in unison a sufficient number of times allows them to eventually take for granted that they can

Belief   31

understand the *effect* of collective action (i.e., a feeling of membership) as if it were the *cause* of collective action. In other words, if queried they would more than likely report that they recite the pledge *because* they are a patriot or that they make the sign of the cross *because* they are a devout member of the Roman Catholic Church. Undoubtedly, those scanning this very text perceive themselves to be English readers but, adopting this critical stance, such an identity can instead be understood as the *result* of the long-standing and continually reinforced, routinized practice of reading certain texts in specific ways—practices, we must admit, which were forced upon all of us (i.e., taught) at a very young age, without our consent.

What should be evident is that belief is a rather more complicated topic than is usually evident in the field's common emphasis on the self-reports of people routinely represented as believers. That scholars should so quickly and uncritically adopt such local discourses and then proceed to use them as if they are correct or consequential for cross-cultural scholarly work—assuming, for instance, that beliefs cause people to behave in certain ways—is, of course, the question that can be posed by an exploration not just of "belief" but, more importantly perhaps, of the discourse on belief. In fact, posing such questions may allow us to move our work considerably away from the commonsense model of belief to one that theorizes such claims as claims that always occur in contestable social settings, where the discourse on belief is used by social actors in response to the challenge of the unfamiliar and the different, to draw a line between self from other in a competitive social economy. If so, then this makes claims of belief claims "an agonistic affirmation," as nicely phrased by Donald S. Lopez, the scholar of Tibetan Buddhism, who has persuasively argued that "the statement, 'I believe in. . .,' is sensible only when there are others who 'do not'. . . . [It is] a means of establishing a community against 'the world'. . ." ("Belief" in Mark C. Taylor's *Critical Terms for Religious Studies* [1998], 33). If so, then hearing someone say, "Well, I believe in . . ." or finding something in the archives called "a statement of faith," should signal to the critical scholar a social situation of contest rather than an innocent expression of some sort of inner disposition. After all, at least in our experience people do not go around spontaneously reporting on their beliefs to empty rooms.

In this volume see: experience, faith, orthodoxy, religion, religious literacy, world religions

In *Religion in 50 More Words* see: afterlife, animism, atheism/theism, emic/etic, idol, immanence/transcendence, meditation, mysticism, piety, reformation, spirituality, theology

5 Canon

Frequently we hear that a religious text is "canonical" or forms part of a particular religion's "canon." This term, like so many in the field, is a term of relevance to the members of the groups we study that has been simply reinscribed in the academic study of religion, where it is now used generically and often interchangeably with cognate terms like "scripture" or "holy books." Rarely is there any focus on *how* the term authorizes certain texts and discourses—and, of course, those who interpret them—over other possible candidates. For to make a text canonical is ultimately a political act, one grounded in choice and often contention. Accordingly, time and energy ought to be expended ascertaining how, when, where, and, importantly, by whom the quality of canonicity is determined, ascribed, and, significantly, policed and thereby maintained. While the term was initially used to refer to the so-called Christian canon, meaning the laws and decrees of the Church, something that could also be easily expanded to refer to a collection or list of authoritative biblical books accepted by the Christian Church as genuine and inspired, it has now been expanded to refer to the "canons" of other religions. Within this context, most traditions are now assumed to be in possession of their own distinct canonical—and thus essential and orthodox—texts. Judaism, for instance, possesses the Hebrew Bible, the Mishnah, the Babylonian Talmud, in addition to a host of other commentaries and legal codes that certain forms of Judaism deem as authoritative (that other forms do not regard them as such is also telling). We thus witness a triangulation between canon, authority, and normativity.

The Greek word *kanōn* was most likely derived from *kānna* (a bulrush reed or rod; also related to the English term "cane"), a Semitic loan word from the Greek. Its original meaning seems to be a stick used to measure something. In Greek, it could also be used to designate a specific and technical meaning associated with a standard of excellence (e.g., a carpenter's or bricklayer's measuring stick or square). In some early attestations, a canon was a person, referring to a cleric who lived with others in a house meant for

DOI: 10.4324/9781003140184-6

clergy or, later, in one of the houses within the precincts of a major church or cathedral. A person designated as "a canon" was expected to conduct their life according to the customary discipline or rules of the church. In Old English the term came to refer to those rules, laws, or decrees of the Church, particularly those laid down by an ecclesiastical Council—hence the term "canon law." As early as (the Venerable) Bede's late ninth-century work, *Ecclesiastic History*, for example, we see references to "canones boca" (that is, books of the Canon) to refer to the books of the Bible. Then, again, in Shakespeare's comedic *All's Well that Ends Well*, Parolles informs Helen that: "Besides, virginity is peevish, proud, idle, made of self-love—which is the most inhibited sin in the canon" (Act 1, Sc. 1). Canon here refers to the rules associated not so much with the Church, but with the rules of propriety for an aging woman.

Despite its origins in ancient Greek, the term canon is intimately connected to the history of Christianity where it refers primarily to the collection of what are believed to be authentic biblical books—a collection characterized as closed, as in excluding further additions or revisions. Here we should perhaps remember all those other texts that were deemed inauthentic and thus excluded from the biblical canon—such as the so-called non-canonical texts, e.g., The Gospel of Thomas or the Gospel of Mary—that emphasized certain aspects of Jesus's person and role (known as the doctrine of Christology) that the early Church's leadership had rejected as heterodox. Again, we witness the political skirmishes involved in the act of deeming something canonical or not. This use of the term canon, to refer to biblical books, may be found as early as the prologue to the fourteenth-century *Wycliffe Bible* where, for example, we read: "In the bigynnyng of canon, that is, of the bok of Genesis." It is only in the nineteenth century that we witness this meaning transferred to any set of books described as sacred to those outside Christianity. This new, wider usage, not coincidentally, is connected to the rise of the comparative study of religion. In his *Introduction to the Science of Religion* (1873), for example, Friedrich Max Müller (1823–1900) writes: "We have in the history of Buddhism an excellent opportunity for watching the process by which a canon of sacred books is called into existence" (29). Increasingly it became customary—as it still is today—to speak of a "Hindu canon," a "Zoroastian canon," an "Islamic canon," etc. Of course the term can also be secularized and not just universalized, to refer, for example, to the "Shakespearean canon" or, more generally, a "literary canon" (whose contents literary critics have fought in recent decades). Thus, we now hear calls to "expand the canon" or "decolonize the canon" so as to include works of writers traditionally excluded from onetime authoritative collections (e.g., women, racialized minorities).

A traditional or, at least, descriptive approach to the study of religion is often interested in describing the contents of canonical texts, and then interpreting their contents. For example, in the introduction to their *Reinventing the Tripitaka* (2017), Jiang Wu and Greg Wilkinson write that the "history of East Asian Buddhism is concomitant with the translation, compilation, and circulation of Chinese Buddhist texts. The most important form of such textual creations is the Chinese Buddhist Canon" (xiv). Rarely, however, is energy focused on the slippage that occurs when we apply a term with heavy Christian overtones and uses to other texts from different religious traditions. What does it mean, to stay with the aforementioned example, to call the *Tripitaka* a canon, let alone part of the "Chinese Buddhist canon"? More importantly, however, when we use the term canon simply as a synonym for a collections of privileged texts or as to denote what are imagined to be a set of eternal ideas immune from history, we risk overlooking all of those very human, and thus political, contestable, and idiosyncratic aspects behind such formation. This, as Jonathan Z. Smith (1938–2017) reminds us, in his essay "Sacred Persistence: Toward a Redescription of Canon" (in his 1982 book, *Imagining Religion*), is ultimately a situated issue of choice, and we, as critical scholars, should be attentive to such situations and such choices—not only in our own work, but in how that very work itself functions in what are often called "classic canonical formations."

In this volume see: authority, classification, comparison, ideology, politics, power, text, world religions

In *Religion in 50 More Words* see: church, commentary, founder, fundamentalism, hagiography, priest/prophet, reformation, theology, tradition, understanding

6 Classification

It is still commonplace to find scholars of religion who maintain that any imposition from outside risks nullifying the authentic meanings and disclosures of those understood to be religious insiders. Those who attend a little more carefully to the material conditions of scholarship, or indeed of human cognition more generally, would maintain a rather different position and instead argue that the world does not spontaneously self-organize or speak for itself to senses that only passively receive the information. Knowledge production, after all, results from curious observers organizing their worlds in novel ways, often by placing unanticipated things beside one other to draw attention to what might have been unforeseen similarities and unanticipated differences—all in the service of arriving at new knowledge. Classification is thus every bit as important as definition, in this process of intellection, if by the former we mean not just naming but also devising a system that makes it possible to decide that the items of the world have relationships with each other. An interest in studying such systems means that scholars will focus on how the people under study organize their own world, to be sure, but it is also important to be aware that scholarship comes with its own set of interests and own systems of organization and rank—after all, scholars are people too.

Classification has a long history—as long, one could argue, as there has been human beings intent on making claims about their world and the items within it. Put most simply, to claim that this is not that, that I am not you, and that we are here or now and not there or then all presuppose an organizational system that makes such comparisons possible. Conclusions about like and unlike are reached—and, if we're not mindful, easily taken for granted as natural or inevitable—by us, the people who devised the prior system of relationships in the first place, the one that enabled us to decide that she was older than him. Our habit of overlooking these organizational systems prevents us from ever entertaining that our taxonomies—or classificatory systems—are hardly innocent, universal, or representative only of mere intellectual curiosities. In fact, there is a tendency to valorize the results of our classification systems, either implicitly or explicitly, such that a similarity is understood as a positive trait while a difference might be seen as an unfortunate shortcoming. Once common divisions of the world into what were then termed Western and non-Western peoples, or Christian and non-Christian, for example, or even earlier divisions between national and universal religions (a forerunner to the modern world religions discourse) or the still prominent distinction between monotheism and polytheism, produce conclusions about the world inspired by a particular way of organizing it (i.e., there's "us," on the one hand, and, on the other, everyone else)— one that may strike many today as rather dated or even suspect. Case in point: one must be persuaded by a certain sort of theological argument to conclude that Christianity, complete with what some might consider three gods (called the father, the son, and the holy spirit), as well as a devil and a host of demons and angels, is a monotheistic religion. Despite decades of criticism of such systems, identifying their self-serving nature, they have proven remarkably resilient, however. We think here of the literary critic, Edward W. Said (1935–2003) and his still provocative criticism of a system of knowledge he termed Orientalism, including the European strategy of caricaturing "the other" (in the case of Said's work, the Muslim world) as a means of defining the limits of self, i.e., who "we" are, in distinction from who we see "them" to be. Classification is thus closely linked to basic, socially formative acts, making it hardly the innocent activity that it is sometimes taken to be.

The word "classify" entered English as a derivation from the earlier fourteenth-century French term *classe*, itself derived from the much earlier Latin *classis*, which once named a military unit. The Latin term was eventually linked to the manner in which the legendary sixth King of Rome, Servius Tullius (r. 578–535 bce) is said to have divided the population for the purposes of military service and taxation, with each of the six classes of the population further subdivided into what were called centuries (of 100 each). By the sixteenth century the term was regularly used to name a collection of things that are said to share some required trait, such as in the entry for December in the almanac appended to John Evelyn's *Sylva or, A Discourse of Forest-Trees and the Propagation of Timber* (1664): "And thefe [i.e., plants] we have diftributed likewife, into the *three* following *claffes* . . ." (122 of the 1671 edition). Eventually, the term takes on a rather technical designation in the modern taxonomy of the natural world (traced to the eighteenth-century Swedish botanist, Carl Linnaeus), with classes coming below phylum and above order in an elaborate classification system, such as the class Mammalia, of which there are a variety of orders, one of which is Primates, which, eventually, in the so-called tree of life, includes human beings. More commonly, the term has come to name a group of students, even the place in which they meet for instruction (i.e., the classroom—originally hyphenated—along with classmate, both of which are attested in the early eighteenth century). The term can also be used for naming one's level of expertise or competence and training (such as the different classes of a driver's license), though since at least the seventeenth century it has often been used to name a grouping of people organized in terms of their wealth and thus their economic rank and social standing, e.g., the working class. We read, for example, in James Nelson's *An Essay on the Government of Children* (1753): "I will felect five Claffes: *viz*. the Nobility, the Gentry, the genteel Trades, all thofe particularly which require large Capitals, the common Trades, and the Peafantry" (273 of the 1761 edition). From this focus on associating or differentiating people based on their level of affluence (or, as a Marxist scholar might phrase it, their relationship to the modes of production, i.e., whether they earn their living by selling their own labor or by investing the capital produced by other people's labors), we eventually derive the modern notion of "being classy," a usage dating at least to the final third of the nineteenth century. It is worth noting that "classic" also derives from the Latin via the later French *classique*, which references the members of the supervisor grouping, pre-dating but related to the modern economic sense of the term.

From the late eighteenth century on we find the verb "classify" naming the act of placing an item into a class and, by extension, creating a system of related classes for the purpose of ordering items, people, or information. We see this, for example, in Rev. Charles Henry Hartshorne's 1840 book, *An Endeavour to Classify the Sepulchral Remains in Northamptonshire; or, A Discourse on Funeral Monuments in that County, Delivered before the Members of the Religious and Useful Knowledge Society, at Northampton*: "I will briefly classify them, so that you may see their respective ages and relative value in point of activity" (17). The noun "classification" (from the Latin *classificatio*) developed along with it, such as the English scientist and Anglican priest, William Whewell, and his *An Essay on Mineralogical Classification and Nomenclature with Tables of the Order and Species of Minerals* (1828). These examples are certainly related to the simultaneous interest in reassessing how the natural world was understood throughout the nineteenth century. We see this in scientific advances of the era (e.g., Charles Darwin's mid-century theory of natural selection) as well as information then returning from the colonies, via letters, diaries, reports, etc., to centers of learning and governance across Europe, forcing scholars to begin to reconsider, among other examples, long-standing assumptions of Christian uniqueness. It should thus come as little surprise that these terms begin to appear more often in print during this period.

In the study of religion, the interest to group what one considered like with like, in distinction from that which was assumed to be different, dates to the earliest period in the field's history. This further reinforces the notion that gains in knowledge do indeed come about by means of comparison—more often than not, driven by the search for universal or essential sameness. While the central role of a variety of self-interested Christian theologians cannot be overlooked in driving much of the early work in the field (and thus their common though self-beneficial designation of the world into Christians vs. non-Christians or, even earlier, Christians vs. either pagans or heathens), efforts to move away from such obviously theological systems resulted in the mid- to late-nineteenth-century development of the world religions classification system—though pretty much all of the earliest scholars of religion continued to rank religions in a hierarchy that mostly resulted in Christianity being at the top. Dutch and German Protestant theologians, as the beneficiaries of a tremendous amount of colonial-era information on "the heathens," came to understand that unanticipated similarities between "them" and "us" required a more nuanced classificatory approach to the religions of the world. Distinguishing between what in English we would call world religions, on the one hand, and what they designated as Ethnic or National Religions, on the other, their early attempt at a more systematic scheme divided religions based upon the degree to which they were seen to have spread beyond what was presumably their original kin group. Settling first on only Christianity and Buddhism as truly world religions—as scholars used the term at the time—all other religions, such Judaism and what was then known by Europeans as "Hindoosim" and "Mohammadanism," were agreed to have remained limited to their original lands and people, thus making them so-called national religions.

As flawed as we may now see such an effort to have been, however, the discourse on world religions has remained, though changing significantly over time, and today still comprises the dominant manner in which religions are arranged and studied. It remains so dominant that pretty much all knowledge in the field currently revolves around it, from curricula (the world religions course is, for most students, their entry-level class, with upper-level classes focused on merely one of the members of this family, or one of their aspects) and scholarly conferences (with program units largely devoted to this or that world religion or one of their features, such as myths, rituals, texts, etc.) to the way that departments hire faculty (often looking for a specialist in each of the world religions) and the way that publishers accept manuscripts and put authors into print, not to mention the way booksellers arrange their products on shelves or online. That there today exists a potent critique of this still widespread classificatory system (called by some the world religions paradigm) should not be overlooked, of course.

But adequate or not, such classificatory systems at least make plain that the effort to know the world is intimately linked to the effort to name and divide it up—making the study of a group's manner of classifying their world a primary means for studying groups (a point evident from the early French sociologists Émile Durkheim and Marcel Mauss's once influence book, *Primitive Classification* [1903], to such later works as the anthropologist Rodney Needham's *Symbolic Classification* [1979]). This involves ascertaining and then highlighting what members of a particular grouping are thought to have in common (or not). It is also clear that the classifier, not unlike the comparativist, plays a significant (though often overlooked) role in the production of such knowledge, inasmuch as they must decide the criteria that drive their system of organization—ensuring that we never forget that knowledge is as much a product of history as is what gets to count as a religion. No doubt the field's early name (at least in much of the English-speaking world), Comparative Religion, made some of this clear, despite earlier confidence in the objectivity of the scholar. The way to know something about one religion was, for the early comparativists, to know something about many other members of the same class, as one of the founders, F. Max. Müller (1823–1900) once phrased it, citing an earlier claim by the Frankfurt-born writer, Johann Wolfgang von Goethe (1749–1832), with regard to language ("he who knows one knows none"). It is the importance of comparison, carried out by means of a classificatory system of our own devising, one that is representative of our own interests and goals as scholars, that continues to be of relevance in the field today. This is in spite of the fact that some scholars claim to be able to transcend their own setting and, as phenomenologists used to put it, describe the world as it presents itself to us. Instead, siding with Claude Lévi-Strauss (1908–2009), the founder of the method known as structuralism—as described by Jonathan Z. Smith (1938–2017) in the opening to his essay "Classification" in the *Guide to the Study of Religion* (2000)—we would argue that classification systems are the inevitable and necessary basis for all knowledge. We see this when Lévi-Strauss concluded, early on in his life, that the only way to "see" something in the field *as* a dandelion was to be able to see the sum total of the differences and similarities between this one item and all that surrounds it, making claims about the dandelion the result of this oscillation of similarities and differences. "The dandelion cannot be 'intelligible' by itself," Smith concludes, "but only as 'much more,' as constituted by the totality of those relations of similarities and differences that allow one to 'isolate' it" (35). Contrary to those who try to divest themselves of both theory and method, in order to let the objects or people under study supposedly to speak for themselves, Smith then concludes that "objects are 'given' as 'bundles of relations' as part of the process of intellection itself." Classification, as flawed as any one system can be, is all we have if we wish to make sense of our world—with the job of scholars not only to be articulate in their use, but to be forthcoming in admitting to their existence and open to their criticism and revision. This begins with scrutinizing the criteria in terms of which any system of relations is established and the possible reasons for their selection and use as opposed to the many other possible options.

In this volume see: authenticity, comparison, definition, phenomenology, world religions

In *Religion in 50 More Words* see: animism, atheism/theism, civil religion, cult, east/west, emic/etic, evil, idol, magic, monotheism/polytheism, myth, nones, paganism, piety, priest/prophet, reformation, ritual, sect, spirituality, syncretism

7 Cognition

Cognition, an English term of increased use since the 1950s, has, like so many others, a general and often agreed-upon meaning in other disciplines and fields of study but then also one that seems to be confined to those who study religion. The latter field has a tendency to take words with fairly complex and technical meanings only to domesticate them by, among other things, adapting or even removing their precision so that they become rather generic and thus deprived of their former analytic rigor. Cognition is just such a word. If the more customary sense of the word refers to epistemology and the action or faculty of knowing (including sensation, perception, conception), then some scholars who study religion tend to use it in quite the opposite sense, to refer not to the procedures of perception and thinking per se, but, instead, to denote feelings, sentiments, and volitions. As is the case with other terms, once we append the adjective "religious" to it—in this case resulting in "religious cognition" (a term with a dramatic rise in use in the last few decades)—the term can be used, once again, to refer to almost any sort of affect or experience construed *as* religious, be it by a practitioner or a scholar (or the third option that supposedly bridges these two, now named by some as the scholar-practitioner). Apart from the far more precise use of the term in the subfield known as the Cognitive Science of Religion (CSR)—an active, international research area that dates to the late twentieth century—it is a term that a critical scholar might reconsider using in their own work.

The modern English word derives from *cognit-*, the participial stem of the Latin verb *cognōscĕre* (i.e., to know or to have knowledge of). It is found in English as early as the fifteenth century, as in the poet and Augustinian friar, Osbern Bokenham's (ca. 1393–ca. 1464) *Lyvys Seyntys* (English: *Lives of Saints* [1447]): "Illumynyd she is wyth clere cognycyoun In hyr soule" (134, lines 335–336 quoting from the life of Marye Mawdelyn [i.e., Mary Magdalene] in Carl Horstmann's 1883 German edition of Bokenham's *Legenden*). Though we see here how the term would seem to refer

DOI: 10.4324/9781003140184-8

to some vague notion of clarity in the soul (not unlike contemporary usage in certain quarters of the study of religion), other early uses of the term could be more technical, referring not just to the *fact* of thinking but the *act* or the *processes* by which we are able to have knowledge about objects in the world. Thus we read in George Henry Lewes's (1817–1978) *History of Philosophy from Thales to Comte* (1867): "A faculty of cognition a priori" (betraying the influence of Immanuel Kant's [1724–1804] philosophy at the time), which, in distinction from the sort of "sensuous knowledge" that is derived from "the world of experience," leads to the "higher world of cognition," synonymous for Lewes with knowledge (vol. 1, cxiii and 308, citing the fourth edition of 1871). Or, from the following year, consider an article in *The New York Teacher and the American Educational Monthly* ("A Journal of Popular Instruction and Literature" [1868]): "Thought, then, is a cognition, not immediate and irelative, as is a perception, an intuition, an imagination, but mediate and relative" (vol. 5, 42). Thus the more technical use of the term in the modern era generally names higher-order mental processes as well as their result. This is conveyed in the gerund "thinking," also suggested in the common translation of René Descartes's original French *"pense"* (*"Je pense, donc je suis"*) to the Latin *cogito*, (*"Cogito, ergo sum"*) and eventually to the well-known English version of his famous formula: "I think, therefore I am" (see the opening to Part IV in his *Discourse on the Method* [1637]).

As far as the study of religion is concerned, there is a tendency to try to use the term "religious cognition" in the more technical sense, despite the fact that, appeals to scientific understanding notwithstanding, it is rarely able to escape the more generic sense. Attempts to find a specifically religious type of knowledge or reasoning process, no matter how rigorous or naturalistic such attempts may now seem, risk reproducing assumptions about that which is designated *as* religious as being somehow unique and set apart from other intellectual processes. It is also worth pointing out that current efforts to study why, for example, human beings tend to report believing in spiritual beings, as a previous generation of scholars might have phrased it, are obviously rather different than much earlier studies of what might have then been called a religious *mentalité*. We see the latter, for example, in "[t]he religious mentality . . . was given its most complete and brilliant expression by the keen minds of Athens" (in a letter to the editor of the weekly *The Living Church* newsletter, October 25, 1919, 926). Or, again, in the Orientalist title of the 1929 book by Lütfi Levonian (1881–1961)—onetime preacher at the Martyrs' Church, an Armenian Evangelical Church then located in Turkey prior to Armenians being forced to leave that country—*Moslem Mentality: A Discussion of the Presentation of Christianity to Moslems*. Despite such differences, they nonetheless share the presumption that something different is happening when it comes to how minds process, or function, with regard to so-called religious claims—some sort of mental difference that requires a specific approach or training to understand.

The deployment of the term "cognition" in the study of religion therefore runs the gamut from the generic to the ostensibly scientific. We see the former, for example, when John Hick (1922–2012), the English theologian and once influential philosopher of religion, seeks to define some vague sense of religious cognition by connecting it to two equally murky terms, experience and faith. "I am seeking to understand," he claims, "that which occurs when the religious man, and more specifically the Christian believer, speaks of 'knowing God' and goes on to explain that this is a knowing of God by faith" (in his "Religious Faith As Experiencing-As," *Royal Institute of Philosophy Lectures*, vol. 2: *Talk of God* [1969], 20–35). The term, especially in the field perhaps inappropriately known as History of Religions, can then be used as a cross-cultural category. We witness this in Herbert V. Guenther's essay, "Some Aspects of Tibetan Religious Thought" (*History of Religions* 6/1 [1966]: 70–87), where he writes that "Knowledge belongs to the being of man, and just as his being may reveal itself as decisive existence or as a nondescript state, so also knowledge has a double nature. The one is cognition (*rig-pa*) . . ." (83). Guenther subsequently goes on to describe this "cognition" as having "the intangible flavor of what we may call 'value' . . . a cognition whose mood is one of unchanging bliss . . . it is also an aesthetic apprehension of reality" (83). Not unlike a lot of scholarship from the 1960s and 1970s, the term here would seem to be related to some sort of experiential understanding of the so-called sacred. It is perhaps in this rather generic, even theological, sense that the John Templeton Foundation (named after the Wall Street financier and philanthropist who founded it), funds a wide number of theological and scientific research programs (having spent over $1.5 billion to date). It has a keen interest in this very area, as detailed on its Religious Cognition site. "This strategic priority," the Foundation reports, "concerns basic scientific research into the nature of cognitive and affective processes." Why? To understand, among other things, the acquisition and transmission of religious beliefs—a no doubt legitimate and fascinating research topic, but one that becomes all the more significant given the Foundation's overall goal: to answer "the deepest and most perplexing questions facing humankind." As the site goes on: "Our vision is one of infinite scientific and spiritual progress." Once again, we see cognition used in a sense that, ultimately, supports what could be understood as a form of spiritual improvement.

More recently—especially since the early 1990s and with the publication of E. Thomas Lawson and Robert N. McCauley's co-written book, *Rethinking Religion: Connecting Cognition and Culture* (1990)—the term "cognition" in the study of religion is used rather more technically. Primarily it is associated with what is known as the Cognitive Science of Religion (CSR), a highly collaborative research specialty which studies religious thought and behavior (e.g., ritual) from the perspective of the cross-disciplinary cognitive sciences. It is a field that draws on work carried out from within evolutionary science, such as cognitive psychology, developmental psychology, linguistics, neuroscience, etc. CSR's aim is to demonstrate (i.e., explain) just how human minds acquire, generate, and transmit so-called religious thoughts, practices, and schemas by means of humankind's ordinary cognitive capacities. CSR's aim is a large vision, to be sure, with dedicated research centers around the world, e.g., centered around the work of the anthropologist, Harvey Whitehouse, at Oxford University in the UK; the productive Religion, Cognition, and Culture research program at Aarhus University in Denmark; and the Laboratory for Experimental Research on Religion (LEVYNA), an active center at Masaryk University, Czech Republic. CSR, however, remains marginal to the rest of the field, whether on account of the generally humanistic approach that still dominates elsewhere (and which resists all explanatory attempts in the field) or on account of criticisms by those in the field who are more influenced by social constructionist approaches and thus unpersuaded by CSR's desire to offer a naturalistic explanation of religion. Such criticisms notwithstanding, recent years have witnessed an explosion in the emergence of journals or scholarly associations devoted to the issues of religious cognition, with names such as the *Journal of Cognition and Culture* (Brill), *Journal for the Cognitive Science of Religion* (Equinox), *Religion, Brain, and Behavior* (Taylor & Francis), and the *Journal of Cognitive Historiography* (Equinox). To such journals we could also add the International Association for the Cognitive Science of Religion (IACSR), an affiliate of both the American Academy of Religion (AAR) and the International Association for the History of Religions (IAHR). All of these periodicals and organizations seek to, in the words of the first journal listed above, explore "the mental foundations of culture and the cultural foundations of mental life." For after all, whatever else religion is, it is at least a series of associated ideas (about the world, about how to act, about which groups are worth joining and at what cost to the members, and about the many powerful beings who are claimed to populate the universe, etc.) that have very successfully been passed down through the generations. Human cognition thus functions as a relevant approach for scholars interested in the acquisition and transmission of such ideas.

While we can certainly appreciate CSR's desire to naturalize the study of religion, doing so by connecting it to routine patterns of intellection, as opposed, say, to imprecise and even inchoate notions like experience or the sacred, several key issues still deserve more attention. First off, we can witness some of the problems that CSR gets into in its members' sometimes close affiliation with funding derived from organizations like the aforementioned Templeton Foundation. Referring once again to its website, its goals are described as follows: "This strategic priority concerns basic scientific research into the nature of cognitive and affective processes and content involved in beliefs, experience, knowledge, attitudes and behaviors related to God and other supernatural agents." The smooth transition between, or association of "science" and "God"—something that animates an entire tradition of liberal theological scholarship, concerned with the consilience of religion and science—is something that some have certainly flagged. To this, we could also highlight the strategic lack of important qualifiers, such as "culturally-postulated," when the Foundation references claims about such things as God and other supernatural agents. All of this is potentially problematic, given the fact that the existence of such agents would seem to be taken for granted here, as opposed to being queried or just assumed to be the result of the natural features of human cognition. We see the latter, for example, in our tendency to project the existence of intentional agents virtually everywhere, in our effort to account for the behavior of the natural world—something that Justin Barrett termed the Hyperactive Agency Detection Device (HADD). According to Barrett: "Part of the reason people believe in gods, ghosts and goblins also comes from the way in which our minds, particularly our agency detection device (ADD) functions" (see his 2004 book, *Why Would Anyone Believe in God?* [31]). The human tendency to detect agency everywhere is a concept central to the early work of the anthropologist, Stuart Guthrie, such as his book on anthropomorphism, *Faces in the Clouds: A New Theory of Religion* (1993). This book is indebted to the even earlier work of the Scottish philosopher, David Hume, e.g., his *The Natural History of Religion* (1757): "We find human faces in the moon, armies in the clouds; and by a natural propensity, if not corrected by experience and reflection, ascribe malice or good-will to every thing, that hurts or pleases us" (sec. 3: 29, citing Howard E. Root's 1956 edition). In this category we could also cite the work of the Professor of Sociocultural Anthropology and Psychology, Pascal Boyer, among others. Indeed, many of the priorities that the Templeton Foundation is interested in funding will likely make a critical scholar of religion pause. One such initiative is "religious and spiritual development," defined as if this were a necessarily good thing or "experiences of the divine." (For a critique of this curious relationship between private monies and CSR research, see the chapter "'Show Me the Money': Big-Money Donors and the Cognitive Science of Religion" in the edited volume, *Theory in a Time of Excess* [2017], 115–120).

The second issue worth considering is that some in CSR do not appear to be interested in developing a technical definition of religion, preferring to use the term in scholarship pretty much as it is popularly used among the population at large. This succeeds in keeping their key analytic term as ambiguous (and thus problematic) as anyone else in the study of religion. We think here of Lawson and McCauley's early and admittedly groundbreaking application of findings from linguistics to the study of ritual, but in which specifically religious rituals are those that involve culturally postulated superhuman agents—an approach curiously reminiscent of E. B. Tylor's advocacy for "belief in spiritual beings" as the essential aspect of all religion, from well over a century and a half ago. Third, not unlike those functionalists from early in the field's development, CSR risks reducing "religion" to cognition, thereby ignoring a host of social, political, ideological, and historical contexts. It should be said, of course, that there are debates within CSR on this very point, with initiatives such as those at Aarhus University, where the link to culture is just as important an emphasis. Fourth, CSR, with its focus on presumably universal cognitive processes, and despite the appearance in recent years of resources such as the online Database of Religious History, seems to be largely uninterested in history or the historical record. Even if those engaged in CSR are interested, they may lack the tools (i.e., philological, historical) to make any meaningful contribution to the work of historians who actually study these periods. Religious texts and rituals, stripped of their discrete specificity, are assumed to be representative of a universal theory of basic human cognition—a reduction that sometimes inspires a backlash from others who are equally committed to naturalistic studies of religion.

In this volume see: affect, belief, critical, definition, experience, function, history, sacred/profane

In *Religion in 50 More Words* see: emic/etic, God, mysticism, myth, piety, ritual, soul

8 Comparison

The now common English term "compare" derives from the Latin verb, *comparare*, signaling two things grouped together or matched and paired, because they are seen to be equal or the same. The term eventually entered English through Old French (*comperer*), sometime in the early fifteenth century, and can be evidenced in the later (1611) usage that is found in the King James Bible: "She [Wisdom] is more precious than Rubies: and all the things thou canst desire, are not to be compared vnto her" (Proverbs 3:15). Nothing, it is clear from this, should be seen as being akin to Wisdom, inasmuch as its status is lessened if it is likened to anything else. Or consider the opening lines of William Shakespeare's still well-known 1609 Sonnet 18: "Shall I compare thee to a summer's day? Thou art more lovely and more temperate. . . ." Or, again, in Moliere's protagonist Alceste who, in the play *The Misanthrope* (1666), says: *"rien n'est comparable à mon amour extrême"* (Act 4, Sc. III; nothing compares to my exceeding love). This same usage, which presumes comparison to concern sameness and thus identity, is dominant even to this day, when we think of such diverse examples as the common instructions still given in classrooms to "compare and contrast" or even Prince's 1985 pop song, famously covered by Sinéad O'Connor in 1990, "Nothing Compares 2 U," i.e., nothing is equivalent to you, ensuring that you are a privileged case. That this sense of incomparability appears in early-seventeenth-century love sonnets and modern pop songs about love makes sense—both striving to set the object of affection apart from all others. More technically, however, we now realize that to compare two items always presupposes both similarity *and* difference, recognizing that no two things can, by definition, ever be identical. Even so-called identical or monozygotic twins have differences, if nothing else because one is there and the other is here (though in 2008 it was also demonstrated that their genomes can actually differ as well, despite long-standing assumptions to the contrary). This means that two very similar things are still distinguishable—for, if utterly indistinguishable, we would have to conclude that only one thing was present. For scholars, the act of comparing two or more things forms the basis for all new knowledge, inasmuch as intellectual gains result from extending the known and the familiar to the unknown and the unfamiliar, with the familiar, on occasion, being stretched to such an extent that it fails, prompting us to reconsider how to understand some novel item. Comparison is therefore a complicated activity despite, like so many of the terms discussed in this volume, it often being assumed to be natural and effortless. For precisely this reason little energy is sometimes expended to ascertain its motivations and its possible ends or implications.

Consider the September 17, 2020, media reports in the United States, which covered then Attorney General, William Barr's comments from the previous evening at a Constitution Day event at Hillsdale College, a private school in the state of Michigan. The College, as described on its website, positions itself as "an independent institution of higher learning founded in 1844 by men and women 'grateful to God for the inestimable blessings' resulting from civil and religious liberty." Barr's words below are of interest to us because they center around a comparison that caught the attention of many, as evidenced by the loud applause of those in attendance at the event. But his comments also attracted the interest of commentators who instead described them as, at least in one case, "incendiary hyperbole designed to feed a sense of paranoia and fear" (according to political commentator John Meacham, featured on CNN that same evening). At what was the applause, on the one hand, and, on the other, the rather critical response aimed? Well, according to the Attorney General: "You know, putting a national lockdown, stay at home orders [in response to COVID-19], is like house arrest. Other than slavery, which was a different kind of restraint, this is the greatest intrusion on civil liberties in American history." According to Barr, the COVID-prompted lockdown in the United States is "like" house arrest and, apparently, the institution of slavery as well, inasmuch as they are both represented as subtypes of a common, larger category (i.e., state-sanctioned restraint that limits personal freedoms). That this apparent likeness inspired applause from some and criticism from others, cannot be overlooked, indicating that despite being a commonplace activity in which we all engage daily, the effort to find similarities and differences is certainly more complicated—and in this case, much more political or ideological—than we might at first think.

This complexity involves recognizing not just that comparison is about difference as much as similarity (as some, but not all, now do) but also that it turns out to be more about the one doing the comparison than it is about some supposedly enduring or essential feature in the two items being compared. Finding certain similarities or differences is, after all, a way to advance a position or a viewpoint—i.e., because these two things are alike or are different we should therefore act in this or that manner. This begins to become more apparent once we leave behind comparisons that might strike us as rather mundane or self-evident (e.g., claiming that this is heavier than that) and, instead, consider what is entailed in likening staying in your home during a pandemic (so as to avoid contracting or conveying a potentially deadly illness) to the history of forced bondage and legally sanctioned servitude. Yes, one might claim that getting a tattoo today is like having one's head cut off by a guillotine during the French Revolution, inasmuch as both involve the skin being pierced. Yet other differences between these two items are certainly worth emphasizing and that make this one particular similarity seem highly problematic, since only one constitutes a form of execution, and thus a difference of what we might conclude to be of tremendous consequence. We can therefore understand the reaction by political commentators when the US Attorney General saw a likeness worth highlighting between so-called COVID-19 lockdowns and slavery—a similarity, should one advance such a position, that helps one to undermine the credibility of lockdowns inasmuch as they are apparently similar to an historical institution widely recognized today as abhorrent. Within this latter context, even that seemingly benign comparison mentioned above, concerning one thing simply being heavier than the other, might not be as innocently or neutrally descriptive as it first appears, inasmuch as it could be a conclusion that sorts and evaluates people in consequential ways (such as discrimination based on body type). While this might seem to some to be of rather less impact than the Attorney General's comparison, both are socially formative, helping to craft a specific type of world, comprised of certain sorts of social actors in certain sorts of social settings.

Comparison, then, is not just a way of producing knowledge but also an invested process that produces knowledge with different investments and effects. The way in which two items are put beside one other (and which two items, we should ask?) is not dictated by the items themselves, as if their similarities or differences are either indisputable or intrinsic. Instead, the items are related by the one who is doing the choosing—i.e., change the comparativist and the comparison alters as well. In the study of religion, it was the late Jonathan Z. Smith who persuasively argued precisely this point, on a variety of occasions, against the backdrop of a field whose history is populated with frequent assertions of how one religion (i.e., Christianity) is superior to others or how all religions share a certain trait. More generally, we also see this act of comparison to show how religion is incomparable to all other aspects of the human. The latter coincides with recurring efforts to identify fundamental similarities among religions (in the plural and particular), across time and region, all in an effort to make claims about religion (in the singular and universal), seeing the latter as an essential, unique, and timeless aspect of human nature. Contrary to this long-established tradition in the field, Smith not only argued that similarity *and* difference are both entailed in all comparisons, but that items in the world do not self-arrange or self-classify. On the contrary, the things in the world about which we claim to know something are placed into their various relationships of similarity and difference (e.g., these are religions and those are political systems) by curious and invested observers proactively arranging their worlds. These observers include everyone from an Attorney General interested in criticizing various US governors' stay at home orders to someone judging people's height to determine who gets to go on the Ferris wheel. We also see this in our own field, when scholars use comparative categories like myth, ritual, pilgrimage, prayer, text, etc., to name and organize different things and actions, from different contexts and historical periods, *as if* they are members of the same class, all for purposes of making claims about the world.

That this more critical perspective on comparison—one that sees it as a tool that situated people use to organize their world in specific ways, for specific purposes (among which undoubtedly are scholarly purposes)—is especially relevant in the study of religion. "To know one [religion]," in the oft-quoted locution of F. Max Müller (1823–1900), "is to know none." Scholarly judgments from that era about the familiar and the strange were taking place in a setting in which what were then read as perplexing reports of so-called practices of "the savages" and "the heathens" in the colonies were arriving back in metropoles such as London, Amsterdam, and Paris. Such practices were perplexing precisely because of how familiar they seemed to be despite what struck those early comparativists as their obvious exoticness (and perhaps even danger). Comparison arose here on account of the inevitable failure of local understandings (e.g., claims concerning the uniqueness and thus incomparability of Christianity) when confronted with new and unanticipated information (e.g., reports of the surprisingly familiar-looking beliefs and practices of people from other parts of the world).

The challenge is twofold. First, how to articulate one's comparative work—making as plain as possible the larger concern or interest by means of which one has placed two items, two behaviors, two groups of people beside each other in our mind's eye. It is ultimately such a placement that allows us to conclude that they are either similar or different (or, more properly, their degree or extent of similarity or difference). This risks the authority of scholarly claims, of course, or at least as some have rather confidently made them, for now the conclusion is not that "all religious people believe in a god" but, rather, "given that I have defined religion as 'belief in a god,' it allows me to talk about these discrete groups and then to come to conclusions about them in this specific way." As for the second challenge: how to argue that the knowledge gained by juxtaposing this to that, *in this particular manner*, is consequential and therefore significant enough to discuss. Thinking again of Smith, the question "So what?" was ever-present in his work. What persuasive reasons can one provide to readers or to students to help them to understand that this difference between two things that they had previously assumed to be like is worth their time, has effect, and therefore tells us something that we did not already know about the world? For if any two items are indeed comparable—i.e., can be placed, by the comparativist, into a variety of possible relationships to make evident both similarities and differences—then the question is why should we regard this similarity at the expense of that difference? Making that case is left up to the critical scholar of religion who understands that, despite the claims of the people whom we might study, the world does not come pre-sorted and that their own questions and curiosities are therefore instrumental in making the world knowable.

In this volume see: classification, description, essence, identity, religion

In *Religion in 50 More Words* see: animism, atheism/theism, commentary, conversion, cult, dialogue, east/west, emic/etic, founder, idol, initiative, magic, monotheism/polytheism, nones, sect, syncretism, understanding

9 Critical

Critical, like the words "critic" and "criticism," has a general sense of finding fault, belittling, or being censorious. Such a charge is frequently leveled, especially in religious studies, at those who are imagined as being too skeptical of the claims of so-called believers (i.e., the people under study) or of the work or methods of their colleagues. Note the work that the qualifier "too" is doing here—drawing attention to a usually unmarked point beyond which continued pressing of one's scholarly peers may be represented by them as being ill-mannered or even uncollegial. However, and this is where ambiguity and confusion sets in—Michel Foucault (1926–1984) himself noted how the notion of critique was multivalent and always defined by that to which the term was related (see his influential essay "What is Critique?" in the edited collection, *The Politics of Truth* [2007])—the term can also connote learned appreciation and refined judgment (especially in the sense of art and literature, as in being an art critic or engaging in literary criticism). Neither of these latter two senses, however, are assumed to be aimed at undermining the cultural productions that they discuss—if anything, they imply a notion of respectful commentary on art and literature, both seen as notable instances of enduring human creativity. (Though, yes, the artist or the writer may sometimes be dismayed at how their work is read and interpreted.) Like many other terms included in this volume, it is precisely this ambiguity that is sometimes exploited to weaken a term that could be useful to the scholar when studying religion, let alone naming something as religion, as a human production.

"Critical" first entered the English language from the Latin *criticus* and also the earlier Greek *kritokós* as a noun, with the latter often referred to a "judge," namely, one who has knowledge of the law and can therefore credibly adjudicate a case or an issue. The term's earliest use in English dates to the early seventeenth century where, as an adjective, it referred primarily to the act of judging, especially in the sense of doing so unfavorably or in a manner that finds fault with one party. Thus we read, for

DOI: 10.4324/9781003140184-10

Critical 53

example, in William Shakespeare's *Midsummer Night's Dream* (1605): "That is some Satire keene and criticall" (Act 5, Sc. 1, 54). Or when, in *Othello* (1604), Iago informs Desdemona that he has nothing good to say about her: "I am nothing, if not Criticall" (Act 2, Sc. 1, 122). Running alongside this meaning of fault-finding, however, is the act of exercising what is considered to be a critical, i.e., careful, judgment. This sense of the term, now largely obsolete, is related to the softer sense of appreciation, which has replaced it (e.g., an art or music appreciation course at a contemporary university, akin to a wine tasting which is about understanding and appreciating similarities and differences among brands and vintages). Historically, we witness this, for example, in the English playwright, Colley Cibber's (1671–1757) play *Love Makes Man* (1701): "Well, Madam, you see I'm punctual . . . I'm always critical—to a Minute" (v. 53). In this latter sense, the "critical" person is someone who takes extra care by being precise and punctual. Yet a third modern use of the term "critical" sees it connected to the noun "theory," as in "critical theory," which can either generally designate a certain style of scholarship (akin to the approach of this very volume) or, more specifically, can name the original German *kritische Theorie*. This latter, more precise sense is usually associated with the emergence of what is today known as the Frankfurt School, wherein a group of influential Marxist philosophers and political theorists (e.g., Theodore Adorno [1903–1969], Walter Benjamin [1892–1940], Max Horkheimer [1895–1973], and Herbert Marcuse [1898–1979]), who were dissatisfied with early-twentieth-century socio-economic systems (e.g., capitalism, communism, and fascism), sought to use open-ended and self-critical investigations to examine the workings of society, including its institutions and class relations. For some today, references to critical theory and critical theorists may very well designate work carried out in their scholarly tradition, aimed at identifying how power and authority function within a group in order to liberate people from their effects—something quite challenging to do given the many forms power can take. This is evident in Horkheimer and Adorno's ironic, mid-1940s observation that "the emancipation of women has culminated in their being trained as a branch of the armed forces" (see their co-written *The Dialectic of Enlightenment*, 185 [citing Edmund Jephcott's 2002 translation]). Although such a normative interest in emancipation, based as it is on a confidence in how social life ought to be arranged, does not animate the use of the term in this volume, the current effort to historicize (i.e., to reframe items taken to be self-evident, timeless, or universal, within their sometimes overlooked, contestable settings, all in order to see them as situated human products that are indicative of certain sorts of human relations) owes much to this tradition of scholarship.

What should by now be clear is that although in its most general or even popular sense the term "critical" implies censure and fault-finding (e.g., to criticize someone), its more specialized usage gravitates toward a refinement of taste, cultivation, and discrimination. In the latter sense it has become associated with the domain of certain classes (often upper or elite) and even professions—a status quo, if you will—that are presented as being responsible for the standardization or even policing of taste and sensibilities. While recent years have sometimes seen the attempt, on account of the first sense of the term's meaning (e.g., fault-finding), to replace it with cognates such as "objective," "value-free," or "disinterested," the second notion of judgment and its pretense to the authority of a class, guild, or profession remains.

These very different senses of the term—(1) "critical" as censorious; (2) "critical" as refined judgment and appreciation; and (3) "critical" as in a type of theory—create real confusion whenever the term is used. In the academic study of religion, the term certainly possesses this wide semantic range, but the default meaning tends to be the second, such as those scholars who produce what are called "critical editions" of noteworthy texts, complete with extensive notes and commentary, all designed to enhance the readers understanding of the text (e.g., Gavin Flood and Charles Martin's new translation of *The Bhagavad Gita* [2014], part of Norton's Critical Editions series—a wide-ranging series which includes the King James Bible as well as *Macbeth*, Jane Austen's *Persuasion*, and Solomon Northup's *Twelve Years a Slave*). We point out here that the tendency among some scholars of religion is first to approach their topic of study aiming to judge which example of, say, Hindu or Muslim behavior is proper, accepted, and thus orthodox; and, second, to develop their own appreciation of these authorized beliefs and practices. The result is, lamentably, often a version of the field more akin to a liberal theological attempt to generate interreligious dialogue and mutual understandings among the "correct" religious people and groups—something often seen implicitly driving the world religions paradigm that still dominates the field.

This confusion, as we would certainly characterize it, over the role of the scholar of religion means that "critical" (like its associated terms critic and criticism) is often employed ambiguously (and, we would add, perhaps on purpose) to give the guise that one's work is more "critical" (i.e., disinterested, scholarly, rigorous, etc.) than it may in fact be. For one thing, the term can often mean that when one says one is being "critical" (e.g., "I am a critical scholar of religion"), one is in fact doing little more than using the term in the second sense above (as indicative of a refined taste or attitude of appreciation). We see this in how the field is littered with books—from introductory textbooks to specialized studies meant for other experts—that, while purporting to be "critical," do little more than engage in simple description of the topics under study (perhaps offering what anthropologists once called thick description). Like connoisseurs (from the French verb, to know), many see their role to be the development of increasingly finer nuance in their detailed description of, for instance, a work of art or the taste of a wine. We see this in the study of religion in books with titles such as Ross Aden's *Religion Today: A Critical Thinking Approach to Religious Studies* (2013) or in a study with the title *Investigating the Resurrection of Jesus Christ: A New Transdisciplinary Approach* (2020) by Andrew Loke, which appears in the book series entitled *New Critical Thinking in Religion, Theology and Biblical Studies*. One has to wonder in these two examples just what work the adjective "critical" is doing. It is clear from such titles, including the contents of such works, that in these books and series the term "critical" is invoked in the sense of exercising what they imagine to be careful judgment or nuanced observation, a usage far from being as productive or provocative of thought as some might like. This is especially evident when we realize that the first routinely reproduces a commonsense view of the field (e.g., the manner in which, say, the well-known but nonetheless problematic east/west dichotomy is simply used throughout the work to distinguish people and religions instead of being historicized and interrogated). The second, moreover, is concerned with "using historical arguments that the best explanation for the origination of the belief that Jesus resurrected is that it happened" while also arguing "that the best explanation for the occurrence of this event is that God raised Jesus from the dead" (Loke, 38). The implication, of course, is that such work appears to be more theoretically sophisticated than some will surely read it to be—though we would agree that they are likely more nuanced when compared to outrightly theological studies of religion. Once again, we see the second use of the term subsume all others.

The other use of the term "critical" in the modern academic study of religion is that of scrutinizing a certain posture towards data that are construed *as* religious, not unrelated to Judith Butler's characterization of Foucault's project as aiming "to establish critique as the very practice that exposes the limits of that epistemological horizon itself" (see her "What is Critique? An Essay on Foucault's Virtue" in *The Political: Readings in Continental Philosophy* [2002], 212–222). As already noted, one frequently hears the charge that so-and-so is "too critical" or "overly critical"—a usage that seems more concerned with disciplinary boundary management, thereby conserving a certain way of naming and knowing about religion, than with assessing what possible advances in knowledge may result from such approaches. Such judgments are generally deployed to refer to those who reduce the claims or behaviors of participants "to mere data" and who generally use skeptical methods and theories (e.g., so-called naturalistic or explanatory approaches) that go beyond the acceptance or mere paraphrases of how the people under study represent or understand themselves. It is interesting that while those who engage in charging colleagues with being too "critical" nonetheless frequently assert that they themselves are engaging in "critical" work (defined in a different sense, of course)—making clear that there is a certain normativity, let alone ambiguity, to the term's use.

It is important to note here that the sort of implicit gatekeeping that the seemingly related term "rigorous" can sometimes accomplish in the field—i.e., criticizing other's work for its "lack of rigor," an ill-defined term that has as much elasticity and thus as many nefarious uses as does the problematic term "collegial"—is, in our estimation, different from what we here propose for this important term "critical." Instead of relying on an unarticulated definition, which thereby opens the door to a usage that may seem commonsensical to those (whether due to their sheer numbers or rank and privilege) in a position to operationalize the interests that drive such negative judgments, we propose explicitly delineating such terms, in detail, so as to minimize their ideological utility. Scholars should therefore, we recommend, be prepared to elaborate and persuasively defend precisely what so-called critical, let alone rigorous, scholarship entails or involves, always holding such understandings open to the scrutiny of their peers. Shared governance concerning the limits and style of the profession are, at the end of the day, the only legitimate mechanism that scholars have to regulate their common work.

Moving forward it would therefore seem that these three distinct uses of the term should be separated clearly from one another, and kept separate, given that each sense of the word results in a rather different (sometimes diametrically opposed) approach to the study of human culture, let alone those specific cultural productions designated *as* religious. This would assist scholars to make better sense of the significant differences between the normative approach of, for example, the peer-reviewed journal *Critical Research on Religion*—self-described as "examin[ing] religious phenomena according to both their positive and negative impacts"—and the international school of thought now known by some as Critical Religion. The latter, at least as phrased by the UK-based Critical Religion Association, begins from a very different starting point: "'religion' as a category has little meaning on its own because the boundaries around what is and what is not 'religion' are so blurred when related to other categories (such as politics, economics etc.)." For while the first and third uses of the term, as identified above, are somewhat compatible with one another, the second is where the problems reside on account of its investiture in cultured judgment and tasteful appreciation (akin to judging which impacts of religion are positive and which are negative)—traits of a caretaking study of religion that, we would argue, are anything but critical.

In this volume see: culture, description, explanation, orthodoxy, theory, world religions

In *Religion in 50 More Words* see: cult, emic/etic, idol, magic

10 Culture

Culture, as Raymond Williams noted, "is one of the two or three most complicated words in the English language" (*Keywords* [1976], 25). This is on account of the fact that the term, while part of common discourse, is also central to many intellectual disciplines and subdisciplines, where, as he goes on to argue, it is frequently used "in several distinct and incompatible systems of thought." Its ambiguous deployment in the study of religion, often as naming that which is imagined to be something that is distinct from religion, is no less problematic, as is the vague way in which it is sometimes used as if synonymous with the entire domain of human practice and organization. The ambiguity and thus imprecision that results from its wide semantic range places it alongside a variety of other terms in our field that are themselves of questionable value to the critical scholar.

The now widely used English term "culture" derives from the Latin noun *cultura*, which comes from verb *colere* ("to cultivate"). As already noted, it would come to possess a rather wide range of meanings that includes: the twelfth-century sense of farming the land; to improve or refine oneself and one's status through training or education, i.e., self-discipline; to rear or raise, a sense prominent up until the mid-nineteenth century (in the sense of plants, animals, or, since at least the late nineteenth century, even bacteria); to inhabit; to honor with worship, and, only late in its history (i.e., later nineteenth century), the by now popular sense of a distinctive set of traits or a so-called way of life and worldview that defines a particular people (or a subgroup within, those who are judged to be cultured), a nation, or a society. Though many of the word's various meanings gradually separated from one another, they still on occasion overlap, further complicating the term's usage. Moreover, from the past participle of *colere* (*cult-*), we derive the sense of a system of rituals or worship. Cult, from the Latin *cultus*, is attested in English as early as the late fifteenth century; for example, from William Caxton we read: "Whan they departe fro the culture and honour of theyr god" (1483). In this latter

DOI: 10.4324/9781003140184-11

sense, honor supplements culture here as virtue whereby the pious perform what we would today consider their religious duties.

Despite this use of culture as what many would today commonly understand as religious worship, the primary etymology of the term comes from Old French, *couture*, whose meaning refers to animal husbandry and working (i.e., cultivation of) the land. In the course of the sixteenth century, the idea of culture as "tending to something" expanded to include the process of human development itself. Thus Thomas Hobbes (1651): "The education of Children [is called] a Culture of their minds" (*Leviathan* Part II, chpt. xxxi, 189) and Samuel Johnson in "The Mischief of Falsehoods: The Character of Terpicula" (January 7, 1752): "She therefore neglected the culture of an understanding which might have supplied the defects of her form and applied all her care to the decoration of her person" (see F. P. Walesby's *The Works of Samuel Johnson* [1825], vol. II, 382). From this use in reference to minds and education we gradually witness the term employed in the sense of something that resembles its current meaning, but not until the eighteenth century and not really common before the middle of the nineteenth. Only then does "culture" begin to take on the notion of all those distinctive ideas, customs, social behaviors, or ways of life believed to be common to, or distinctive of, a particular people, nation, or society. Thus the Polish-born writer, Adam Gurowski's *Slavery in History* (1860): "This Egyptian or Chamitic civilization, too, preceded by many centuries the Shemitic or Aryan cultures" (6–7). Notice in this last sense the term is used in the plural. Nations, and groups within nations, now become defined and identified by their respective "cultures."

This sense of the term, now by and large the primary one, remained relatively rare until the early twentieth century. With the rise of European Romanticism, the term (whether culture in English, *Kultur* in German, or *couture* in French) now becomes even further dislodged from its earlier meanings and comes to designate the *raison d'être* of a group, i.e., that set of essential characteristics that are said to define one group from all others. We see this clearly in the writings of the philosopher and poet, Johann Gottfried von Herder (1744–1803), who argued that there was no universal human culture, but, rather, distinct cultures, traditions, and languages that exist on different levels of development throughout the globe. It is this sense of the word—though, we would hope, lacking the paternal, developmental, and often even outrightly racist tone of earlier work—that is often picked up by the modern academy. Thus, the English historian and politician, Edward Augustus Freeman (1823–1892), writing in volume I of his six-volume *The History of the Norman Conquest of England, Its Causes and Its Results* (1867–1879): "A language and culture which was wholly alien to them . . ." (1867, chpt. IV, 167)—though compare this with this author's use of the same word, but in a different sense, in volume IV of the same work: "The foreign Prelate might be, as a rule, a man of higher culture than his English predecessor . . ." (1875, chpt. XIX, 301). Or, more recently, consider also Edward Sapir (1884–1939), writing in his *Language: An Introduction to the Study of Speech* (1921, quoting the 1949 edition): "Historians and anthropologists find that races, languages, and cultures are not distributed in parallel fashion" (208) and "the history of language and the history of culture move along parallel lines" (219). It is also in this sense that, with the addition of a modifying noun, it becomes possible to speak of a social movement and those who subscribe or belong to it (e.g., popular culture, mountain climbing culture, or fostering a culture of openness).

It is worth pausing for a moment to observe that, as argued by Williams in another of his books, *Culture & Society: 1780–1950* (1958), this modern sense of the term (e.g., to be cultured, possessing cultured tastes, being a member of a culture, etc.) rose to prominence in English literature and writing beginning with the late-eighteenth-century's so-called Industrial Revolution in England. Specifically, he found the word to be commonly used as part of socially and politically conservative reactions to the rising urbanization that resulted during this period, as well as the presence of increasingly democratic forms of government throughout the nineteenth century. Such linkages between what was then called culture and the so-called values assumed to inform and be conveyed by it (a so-called heritage that, or so it was claimed at the time, should be preserved or protected), makes evident that the term has a history that involves the maintenance of contestable identity and status, in response to perceived challenges or threats.

In sum, the word today seems to be used in three distinct, if overlapping, ways: (1) as an abstract noun that describes intellectual and aesthetic development as part of a ranked status system; (2) an independent noun that describes the cumulative way of life of a particular period, people, or group; and (3) an independent and abstract noun that indicates intellectual and artistic production (again, as part of a ranked status system). We see the use of (2) perhaps most clearly in the writings of those Victorian scholars who are often associated with the foundational texts of the academic study of religion (along with other modern scholarly disciplines, e.g., sociology or anthropology). For example, in Émile Durkheim's still read sociological study, *Les formes élémentaires de la vie religieuse* (1912), where we find such usages as "human culture" (e.g., Book III, chpt. I, sec. iii) and the once popular idea of cultures being more or less advanced (see Book II, chpt. V, sec. I; the anthropologist, Mary Douglas [1921–2007], part of the later Durkheimian tradition, went on to complicate this considerably, with her so-called grid/group theory—see James Spickard's "A Guide to Mary Douglas's Three Versions of Grid/Group Theory" in *Sociological Analysis*

50/2 [1989]: 151–170). We also see this in the main title of the once influential book by the early English anthropologist, Edward Burnett Tylor. His two-volume *Primitive Culture: Researches into the Development in Mythology, Philosophy, Religion, Language, Art and Custom* (1871) seeks to define the attributes—specifically religious—of modern "primitives" as a way to explain the natural origins of religion at what he considered to be the dawn of humanity, ultimately concluding that "belief in spiritual beings," Tylor's preferred definition (and one not far off how some scholars define religion today), was actually a mistake due to the limitations of early human cognition and problem-solving. The complex sense of the three usages noted above indicate intellectual tensions—so common in the Humanities in general and the study of religion in particular—between a general sense of ranked human development on the one hand and the local ethos of the particular groups and subgroups that comprise humanity on the other.

In terms of the word's deployment in the modern study of religion, we witness equal ambiguity and confusion. Frequently it is used interchangeably—especially in the second and third senses of the term above—with the no less problematic term "religion." Witness, for example, the title of the academic journal *Culture & Religion*, which is described on its webpage as "lying at the interface between the study of religion and other academic studies of culture." Such usage paradoxically imagines religion to be a part of culture, but, picking up on a long-standing tradition in the field, also implies that they are somehow distinguishable, and that the former, if studied properly, needs to be approached differently than other aspects of the more mundane latter. Relatedly, we frequently witness the deployment of terms like Islamic, Jewish, Buddhist, and other such "religious" cultures (e.g., Muslim culture, somewhat akin to the once prominent term "Islamic civilization"), but very little energy is expended trying to define what makes a particular culture Islamic or Jewish or Buddhist. In all of these examples, culture, understood as historical, situated, contingent, etc., seems to be imagined to be but one aspect or manifestation of some prior, essential thing called religion—something that can supposedly help to account for certain aspects or features of religion, but without religion ever being reduced to it. In some cases, especially in the subfield of Jewish studies, it has become fashionable in recent years to study something referred to as Jewish culture (often more specifically defined as American Jewish culture) instead of Judaism (which is instead conceived as a religion). As with the now popular move toward plural nouns—as in studying Judaisms rather than Judaism—this, however, creates just as many problems as it is supposed to solve. For example, eating traditional "Jewish" food—without attendant Jewish texts or ritual practices (which are often relegated to the religious dimension)—is now thought to provide a way of being Jewish and of maintaining Jewish continuity but without being religious (e.g., the identifier "cultural Jew" or someone being "a cultural Catholic"). Yet scholarly works that seek to examine—or, perhaps better, celebrate—some amorphous expression like Jewishness often end up further reifying it. For while Jews are imagined to fit into larger cultural contexts, this is accompanied by a simultaneous desire to demonstrate how they are nonetheless uniformly unique in their expression of a shared identity, within those larger, changeable, and plural contexts. This sometimes means examining how Jewish people have absorbed or adopted non-Jewish forms (e.g., humor, film, food) and then somehow "judaized" them. This is analogous to those trends in the parent field of religious studies (parent, that is, if Judaism is approached as a religion) that seek to "analyze" amorphous but situated concepts such as the sacred or experience.

Yet other times the term "culture" is used to name and thereby differentiate all too neatly and conveniently some historical thing, act, or even affect from that which is imagined to be some more pure, ahistorical, and sacred notion of religion. For example, the practice of female circumcision (or what is also termed by yet others, female genital mutilation—one's choice of term tells us much about one's position on it, of course) in places like Africa and the Middle East is often imagined by scholars to be a "cultural" practice as opposed to a religious one because religion is widely presumed to be, by definition, a force for good in the world, implying that so-called religious elements have been improperly appropriated or applied to legitimize the practice. Often, culture or politics or the secular, or whatever else is imagined in such an approach as corrupting religion—which includes so-called religious extremism—is therefore problematically opposed to what is represented as an apolitical and original form of orthodox and thus proper spirituality. In like manner, we see this dichotomy when, for instance, scholars of Islam inform readers "that 69.4 % of men who committed honor killings in Jordan *did not perform their daily prayers*, and that 55 per cent *did not fast*" (emphasis added). As John Esposito and Dalia Mogahed go on: "That these men fail to observe the most obligatory rituals of Islam suggests that their act of murder is not motivated by religious zeal or devotion" (as quoted in their widely discussed 2007 book, *Who Speaks For Islam? What a Billion Muslims Really Think* [123]). Or, as phrased in a variety of online posts, from 2008, about the book: "Sexism [is] committed by men, not religion." By this account it would seem that, for so many scholars of Islam, and indeed scholars of religion more generally, religion can be co-opted and corrupted by the culture in which it is inevitably situated, expressed, and practiced. We see here the classically idealist notion of religion as an internal, apolitical, and private disposition that is only secondarily exercised in public, a stance nicely evident early on in the field's history when the American psychologist, William James (1842–1910), argued in his *The Varieties of Religious Experience: A Study of Human Nature* (1902), that "the originally innocent thing" of a charismatic founder's religious experience was prone to be "contaminate[d]" by "the spirit of politics and lust of dogmatic rule" associated with later disciples and followers (1905, 335).

This particular sense of the term "culture," naming changeable context and thereby working in concert with "religion" to protect the domain named by the latter by assigning unsavory elements to the former (e.g., the designation of "religion and culture") is particularly in vogue among many current scholars of religion. We witness this especially with those who imagine and then study religion as a source for good in the world and as therefore helping to improve what they see as problematic cultural forms, such as injustices based on race and gender. For this reason, many who are both within and outside of the academy, argue that religion, seen as distinct from culture, can be used to make it better—an approach that further requires such proponents to identify some criterion to distinguish good and proper religion from what are then represented as derivative and flawed cultural forms whose followers have "hijacked the tradition."

All of these problematic and ambiguous uses of the term "culture" emerge out of its complex etymological history. Equal parts Romantic and analytical, with a class- or identity-based effect often added, the term has been deployed for many reasons, often at cross purposes with one another. Most importantly, however, is that we realize that the term is, at least traditionally, heavily invested in Romantic notions of peoplehood (whether serving so-called conservative or progressive causes). As critical anthropologists have long known, for whom it functions as their primary taxonomic tool, culture, not unlike "religion" in our field, often signals something special, something that makes one group fundamentally distinct (and often privileged) from all others. Both terms, then, were and continue to be deeply involved in contestable acts of identification, whether for humanity as a whole (in that religion is assumed to be a universal acquisition of the species) or the various groups within it, each assumed to possess their own discrete and unique ethos—something nicely exemplified in the work of the anthropologist, Kamala Visweswaran, e.g., her *Un/common Cultures: Racism and the Rearticulation of Cultural Difference* (2010).

In this volume see: experience, explanation, gender, identity, politics, race, religion, sacred/profane, secular

In *Religion in 50 More Words* see: cult, east/west, emic/etic, immanence/transcendence, paganism, ritual, sect, tradition, value

11 Definition

From the Old French *definer*, itself from the much earlier Latin *dēfīnīre*, the English verb, "to define" and the noun, "definition" (Latin: *dēfīniō*), entered the English language in the early fifteenth century. Both noun and verb signify the act of marking a limit or a boundary, thus also to bring something to a conclusion—hence the word also developing into a term for making a declaration of limit. One might think also of the related adjective "definitive," denoting a precise limit, but also suggesting that what is described is done so in a final or authoritative sense. "Who wrote Shakespeare's plays?" asks an August 7, 2020, article in *The Atlantic*, before continuing with the pronouncement: "A definitive statement of authorship may be hard to come by...." By the mid-seventeenth century the modern understanding of the term appears in the sense that the word comes to name the act of identifying the limits of a specific item or word. Definition now is about collecting together the central or key characteristic or characteristics for the sake of appearing in a dictionary (from the Latin, *dictiō* + *ārius*, i.e., pertaining to words, or wordbook). We see this exemplified in John Milton's *Tetrachordon: Expositions upon the foure chiefe places in Scripture which treat of Mariage, or nullities in Mariage* (1645), a tract directed at the English parliament and arguing in favor of legalizing divorce: "Definition is that which refines the pure effence of things from the circumftance" (18).

This link between essentialism and definition makes sense if by definition we mean the act of limiting something, implying that all members of the class must necessarily share in some specified trait, without which they would cease to be members of that class (their *sine qua non*, or, literally, without which not). We often find this mutual understanding in our field, such as Max Weber's early-twentieth-century classic, the posthumously published *The Sociology of Religion* (1920), whose opening chapter, "The Rise of Religions," begins (in its English translation) as follows: "It is not possible to define religion, to say what it *is* at the start of a presentation such as this. Definition can be attempted, if at all, only at the conclusion of the study." Why? Because, as Weber immediately goes on to state: "[t]he essence of religion is not even our concern. . . . ." Thus, for Weber, to define meant to arrive at the necessary and fundamental characteristic shared by all members of a given class of items. Its essence or what others call its substance (hence we might refer to it as a substantive definition) is not possible to name, he informs his readers, until all members of the group have been examined and determined to possess it or not. In this way, Weber is exemplary of the long-standing trend to connect definition to description—case in point, Jay Wexler's recent book on US law and new religious movements, *Our Non-Christian Nation* (2019), where, to exemplify the difficulty of defining religion, he writes: "Seriously, try to define the term and see if you can come up with an acceptable formulation, one that captures all those belief systems you think are religious and excludes all those that aren't" (13). Apparently, one tries to define religion already knowing which things are religious, thus *defining* them by *describing* them. But given the lack of an *explicit* definition or set of criteria that might exercise some degree of limit to the possible items requiring his attention (i.e., his search for this elusive essence), it is not clear how either Weber or Wexler know what to describe when they set out to study religion. This is a problem that should strike us as being in need of further consideration. Surely it was not just by chance that Weber's book, for example, was divided into chapters on such topics routinely associated by many with religion (at least with Christianity): prophets, the problem of evil, mysticism, salvation, and ethics. Instead, and whether he realized it or not, and protestations to the contrary, Weber had no choice but to rely upon an *implicit* and therefore unarticulated definition that enabled him to know or intuit that, for example, Christian, Hindu, and Buddhist groups were relevant to his work. The trouble with such implicit or unarticulated definitions, however, is that they often mimic and thereby uncritically reinforce whatever happens to be the common understanding among a group, which subsequently functions as the scholar's analytic framework despite the fact that such usages were never intended as the basis for cross-cultural comparative work.

Alongside such a traditional, not to mention problematic, understanding of definition (i.e., as an effort to identify an inherent characteristic) there also exist far more nuanced uses of the term. Ludwig Wittgenstein's (1889–1951) influential proposal for a so-called family resemblance approach to defining objects, on the one hand, and, on the other, stipulative definitions (a word thought to be from the Latin *stipulari*, to make a bargain, contract, or promise).

Regarding the first, Wittgenstein, an Austrian-born philosopher, is often cited as finding essentialist approaches to definition as misguided, inasmuch as he argued (in his *Philosophical Investigations* [1953]) that people tend to address the unknown by means of the known. Having already a prototypical understanding of something in mind (probably part of the folk classification system that they were taught as children), people then extend them to a new or alien scenario, using it as a model, exemplar, or prototype against which they assess the unfamiliar. Should a German Shepherd, for whatever reason, constitute someone's prototypical dog then its familiar, observable traits, for them, become the standard against which other animals are compared, all to determine whether they are members of the so-called family of dogs (i.e., whether they more or less match the prototype). Such a family resemblance approach shifts the burden to the definer, especially when it comes to making judgments on boundary cases, i.e., those cases where something shares very few characteristics with one's prototype. (How few are too few, and at what point will we draw the line, assert a boundary, and say that it is not a dog?) This also holds for scholars, inasmuch as they must recognize that they simply happen to have become accustomed to German Shepherds as exemplars of dogs or, returning to the history of our field, Christianity as a religion; that is, the prototype must be understood as not being definitive but, instead, merely handy or useful. Such an approach therefore argues that our models must continually be open to revision.

With regard to the second development, and not unrelated to the way that a family resemblance approach shifts attention to the definer from, at least in Weber's approach, the item being defined (the latter is sometimes known by the Latin term, *definiendum*, with the words used to define something referred to as the *definiens*), stipulative definitions also draw our attention to the scholar. To give an example: one might establish that, for the purposes of some study, religion will be defined as "the acknowledgment and recognition of all our duties as if they were divine commandments" (quoting the once famous definition from Immanuel Kant's *Religion Within the Boundary of Pure Reason* [1793]). Or, instead, maybe as "belief in spiritual beings" (from the influential, though minimal, definition of the early anthropologist Edward Burnett Tylor [1832–1917]). We must fully recognize that neither definition has a necessary nor determinative relation to what religion *really is* or *ought to be*. Instead, the definition is selected and proposed by the individual for their specific purposes and the requirements of their context, making clear that the object of study is itself a discursive object that exists within parameters that they themselves have established. This was quite evident to Humpty Dumpty in Chapter 6 of Lewis Carroll's *Through the Looking Glass and What Alice Found There* (1871), when he defines "glory" to mean "a nice knock-down argument." Alice predictably contests this curious definition, to which he replies, "When *I* use a word . . . it means just what I choose it to mean—neither more nor less." Ideally, of course, a discursive object is shared across enough researchers so as to constitute an academic field as opposed to an idiosyncratic item of interest to but one person (as was the case in Humpty Dumpty's definition). That such shared or adopted understandings can indeed be linked to the authority of the speaker cannot go unnoticed, to be sure, such as the famous 1893 US Supreme Court case of *Nix v. Hedden*, in which no less than an Associate Justice stipulated that, for purposes of trade and tariff, tomatoes would be considered in US law as vegetables and not, botanically speaking, as fruit, as tomato importers had argued in court. Not only does this approach to definition require us always to consider who is setting the terms but also to keep in mind that issues of definition often arise where and when something is at stake. This is the case with religion, inasmuch as the constitutions of many modern liberal democracies allow religions and religious people certain privileges, or exemptions, when it comes either to taxation or expression. Debates over what is and what is not religion therefore arise regularly—case in point, so-called Pastafarianism (dated to 2005 in the US state of Kansas) and its adherents desire to have their official ID photos taken with pasta strainers on their heads.

But despite greater precision over what it means to define, there are still many scholars who are openly critical of what others see as the necessity of an explicit definition of religion. Rather than presupposing precise definitions (inasmuch as they assist scholars to focus attention and thereby manage, by minimizing, what constitutes a legitimate object of study worth our attention), there are those who maintain that a lack of definition is advantageous, since it prevents the scholarly observer from interfering (that is, limiting or restricting) with the phenomenon under study. Many scholars of religion (let alone those who study myth, ritual, tradition, etc.) therefore go about their work without ever actually defining their object of study—studies that make plain that each of their presumed objects of study are not necessarily coterminous with religion as the term is used in yet another scholar's work, prompting us to wonder if they are actually examining the same thing. Case in point, consider two current research initiatives, the first social scientific and the other more humanistic: the Database of Religious History (religiondatabase.org) and the American Religious Sound Project (https://religioussounds.osu.edu). The former recruits an international team of historical and ethnographic specialists to write entries on religions from around the world (creating what it refers to as "the world's first comprehensive online quantitative and qualitative encyclopedia of religious cultural history"). The latter relies on a large team of coordinators and affiliates to create and post audio files that offer "resources for studying and interpreting the diversity of American religious life by attending to its varied sonic cultures." However, in both cases the object of study, religion, is left undefined. While the latter project "seek[s] to represent religion as fully entangled with and embedded within other aspects of social life, rather than as discrete or separate" (as described on its FAQ page), it also notes there that the recordings "reflect subjective choices made by our teams of faculty, staff, and student researchers, done as much as possible in consultation with the communities being recorded." This ensures that there is no guarantee that the same criteria have, or criterion has, been used across the site's various items, despite its attempt to draw conclusions from them all concerning something called religion in general, let alone to understand its diversity in the United States. Simply put, lacking a definition, then of what are the site's instances all an example? As for the former, in an article on the initiative that was published in the *Journal of the American Academy of Religion* (85/2 [2017]), Edward Slingerland and Brenton Sullivan note that "it is important to keep in mind that we are not so much interested in defining 'religion' in the abstract [at the Database of Religious History] as we are in locating the components of a particular religious group" (323). Once again, without a clear—and, importantly, shared—definition of what religion is how do we know what it is that apparently has components, let alone how do we know that each contributor is talking about the same thing across the database's wide-ranging articles? In fact, just because the same word, religion, is used in both, why should we even assume that these two resources are even studying the same thing? After all, as made evident in this very volume, the same word is often used very differently, to do rather different work.

Although both initiatives lack an overall definition of their object of study (something that, curiously, they each see as a benefit), they certainly have no problem with making subsequent claims about religion in general as well as about its various subtypes or components. This may strike readers as puzzling—unless, of course, a commonsense or authoritative folk definition, implicit to and thus shared by members of the groups from which their contributors come, is simply being asserted and used *as if* it provides an adequate scholarly definition. The trouble is, of course, that this term religion is used so broadly by members of various groups—and, we cannot overlook, *used not at all by members of yet other groups, present and past, which scholars of religion might nonetheless still wish to study*—that elevating but one local usage *as if* it is adequate to the task of scholarship seems shortsighted at best and, at worst, intellectually sloppy and possibly even irresponsible. This term religion is so widely used throughout the world today (a world which, due in part to the colonial-fueled spread of European languages, now extends to virtually the entire globe), that it is now taken by many to be an obvious element of all human life. This results in many scholars somehow just knowing what it is (the old "I know it when I see it" position, a phrasing linked to a 1964 US court case, *Jacobellis* v. *Ohio*, concerning obscenity laws). All too frequently one witnesses scholars claim that to offer a definition actually gets in the way of their work by inserting their own views between them and their research subjects—sometimes claiming that any such scholarly reframing does an injustice to the people being studied (a view that often animates criticisms of scholars of religion who use the word "data" to name the claims, actions, etc., they study). We would argue quite the opposite, in fact, for the scholar's views and assumptions are always there (something that yet others would argue that the word "data" always makes evident, so as preventing anyone from concluding that the scholar somehow had access to what some would refer to as the whole or authentic people being studied). Thus, an explicit definition acts as a control on scholarship by introducing public precision, thereby impeding the ability to advance, as if authorized, a form of local common sense (and promoting along with it its interests and effects in the world), one that may happen to be familiar to the individual scholar's own social group. Critical scholarship, then, should instead aim to moderate and, where possible, eliminate such problems by moving from reproducing certain implicit folk conceptions to the development of technical, clearly stated, and defensible stipulative definitions—even going so far as to entertain carrying out an ethnography of definitions (i.e., making definitions themselves one's data), with little concern for arriving at the correct way to define something like religion. For just as chemists employ a technical, theoretical language to study something only they designate as H_2O rather than what we all commonly call water, so too scholars of religion should, at minimum, redescribe their main term, religion, making plain the assumptions and interests that are driving their use of the term by recognizing that scholarly definitions are actually theories in miniature.

In this volume see: classification, comparison, description, essence, phenomenology, redescription

In *Religion in 50 More Words* see: atheism/theism, civil religion, cult, dialogue, emic/etic, evil, fundamentalism, idol, magic, monotheism/polytheism, nones, paganism, piety, syncretism, understanding

12 Description

Description, one of the most overused and simultaneously undertheorized methods employed in the academic study of religion, derives simultaneously from the French *descripcioun* and the Latin *dēscriptiōn-*. The primary meaning of both involve listing those observable, characteristic features and details deemed significant to understand a place, item, or person as distinguishable from its surroundings. Often, a description, then, is—not unlike definition—an attempt to portray a thing's or a person's key trait(s). Late-fourteenth-century usage includes Chaucer: "Auarice, after the descripcion of seint Augustyn, is likerousnesse in herte to haue erthely thynges" (1391), where the vice of avarice (or greed) is implied to be just as "described" by Augustine (i.e., as the source of suffering by focusing on a so-called transitory good in place of God, e.g., recounting himself as previously being "greedy of enjoying things present, which passed away and wasted my soul" [*Confessions* [401], Book VI, 11.18, in Edward B. Pusey's translation]). This is typical of description, where one invokes it rhetorically, not just to make but also to secure a particular point—here being that greed is the desire "to have earthly things," a claim that can go unchallenged on account of it being associated with the famous early Christian theologian and saint. Therefore, despite the appearance that description is obvious to all and sundry, it is more often than not a socially formative act, based on social interests that prompt an actor to choose to focus on (i.e., describe) something but, necessarily, to the exclusion of all else, all for the purpose of shaping the reader's or listener's perception of the world or an issue. Typically, the element of choice entailed in all description often gets lost, in that the interests animating the selection of focus may be so widely shared that the item being described strikes many as so obviously interesting or important and central as to be a brute fact whose assumed status prompts it to stand out from its environment and thereby compelling its naming and careful observation. This is in evidence when we witness people claim such things as "Well, it goes without saying . . ." or "As everyone knows . . ."

DOI: 10.4324/9781003140184-13

However, such claims themselves betray a setting in which this is obviously not the case (otherwise one would not make such pronouncements); working to recover the contestable situations behind seemingly simple descriptions is among the tasks of the critical scholar.

A description is thus a possibly idiosyncratic and always partial list of qualities or features that the describer *decides* to use or otherwise highlight and thereby mark-out as characteristic of something. Thus, William Shakespeare in the very late sixteenth century: "Pay him six thousand . . . before a friend of this discription shall lose a haire" (*Merchant of Venice*, Act 3, Sc. 2, 299). As just argued, though, left muted or unstated, most often, is *who* gets to decide just what those characteristics might be and, of course, *why* they are emphasized at the expense of other possible candidates. In describing the height of two items one leaves unstated anything about their mass, their placement, the substance from which they were made, their manufacturing date, their use, and so on. In this sense, description is necessarily connected to interpretation. Though the latter is often assumed to read into something (by determining its meaning) while the former is usually assumed to be the result of neutral and therefore disinterested observation. Historically, the idea of describing the essential traits of an individual could also be stretched to include the common features of a group. We witness this in cognate meanings, now obsolete, wherein description is an enumeration of individuals in a census (Old French ca. mid-thirteenth century), where it can also refer to the act of registering the names of individuals or citizens for some purpose. This might be connected to the fact that such individuals were often regarded as little more than chattel for the landed aristocracy. Thus, the Christmas day sermon of the fourteenth-century English theologian, John Wyclif: "Syryne . . . bigan to make þis discripcion" (see Sermon 90 in the *Select English Works of John Wyclif*, vol. 1, *Sermons on the Gospels for Sundays and Festivals* [1869]). There would therefore seem to be an inherent tension in the first and primary sense of description—in which all of those items that are considered to be main features are used to give a person or object definition—with the second sense being much more superficial, in that it only lists the names of individuals in some sort of register without mentioning so-called essential characteristics (unless, of course, they are the essential characteristics of the landowner).

By the late sixteenth and early seventeenth century, description begins to take on the connotation of a representation in art. Thus, John Gregory in *Posthuma* (1649): "This Description is . . . of the Earth and Water both together, and it is don by Circles." This new use of the term brings out a little more clearly the fact that that which is described is not the *actual* object or person, but, rather, a visual or literary representation, or perhaps even a representation of a representation. For instance, we read in the English novelist, William Makepeace Thackeray (1811–1863): "Let any man look at that second plate of the murder on the Thames, and he must acknowledge how much more brilliant the artist's description is than the writer's" (*An Essay on the Genius of George Cruikshank* [1884], 54). The implication here seems to be that artists and writers seem to be engaged in some sort of duel to ascertain who can offer the best description of a person, a place, or an event.

Also relevant, especially to the academic study of religion, is the idea that something is beyond or defies description, in the sense that it cannot be represented or otherwise mediated in or through language—hearing someone say "I can't quite put it into words" would be a commonly heard example (consider also the French, frequently used in English, "*Je ne sais quoi*" [literally, "I do not know what"]—ironically used as if it names a quality of objects). We see this as early as the early seventeenth century; thus, Joseph Morgan in his 1725 translation of Muhammad Rabadan's *Mahometism Explained* (vol. II, chpt. xxiii, 76): "I could plainly see the Hosts of Cœlestial Potentates, with Legions of immortal Nymphs, lovely beyond all Description." This usage extends into the present with, for example, the entry on the bazaars in Damascus in Macmillan's *Guide to Palestine and Egypt*: "The fascination of this bazaar is beyond all description" (1901, 135). This notion of "beyond description" for that which is unspeakable or cannot be expressed in language—itself an authorizing technique that erases choice and portrays items as self-evidently significant—plays a noticeable role in our field, especially as it relates to the omnipresent, if extremely imprecise and problematic, term "the sacred." We read, for example, in Mircea Eliade's (1907–1986) well-known *The Sacred and the Profane: The Nature of Religion* (1959) that "the sacred is pre-eminently the real, at once power, efficacy, the source of life, and fecundity" (28). If the sacred is the real, then, according to Eliade's reasoning, the real is, well, sacred, and then the two, together, are the source for a host of other amorphous and imprecise concepts (life, power, and the like). This is a classic move of the now often-critiqued school of thought known as phenomenology, at least as the term came to be employed in the study of religion, which uses descriptions of a wide range of often distinct phenomena (i.e., that which presents itself to the senses, as a phenomenologist might phrase it) to point back toward that from which they are inferred to manifest themselves. More often than not this essence is the aforementioned sacred, that which is posited as existing beyond, because it came before, language, thus placing it beyond all forms of categorization, definition, and thus beyond all description. But, of course, that which cannot be described and classified cannot be known. Taking this position seriously requires us to inquire how the scholar (let alone the practitioner, who might equally employ this rhetoric of unknowability—such as

David Bryant's January 8, 2013, article in *The Guardian* newspaper in the UK, whose headline read: "God is Unknowable: Stop Looking for Him, and You Will Find Faith") can even know what they claim to be speaking about. That a special sort of insight is then claimed (in the above case, it is known as faith) makes evident the difference between the claims made by critical scholars of religion and the sorts of claims that might be made by the people whom such scholars study.

As already suggested above, in terms of method, description (and the results of descriptive work) is everywhere in the field of religious studies. In classic phenomenology, as just witnessed, description plays a large role in classification since the scholar of religion is ultimately the one who is responsible for organizing the items under consideration into what are often taken to be their distinct categories. It is not uncommon, for example, to see groupings, such as sacrifices, sacraments, sacred space, sacred time, scriptures, canons, festivals, rituals, and myths—all derived through the act of description. But from the above examples, it seems fair to conclude that description is, unfortunately, used in a number of contradictory ways in the field, itself perhaps not surprising given the different meanings involved in the historic use of the term. For one thing, when scholars engage in description—i.e., describing the contents of a particular text, ritual, or the like—many seem to think that this is tantamount to engaging in theory. Describing what a text "says," however, is being neither theoretical nor critical. For instance, consider that, in his essay "Myths as Religious Explanations" (*Journal of the American Academic of Religion* 48/3 [1980]: 175–190), the philosopher Jack Carloye (1927–2019) argues that "descriptions of which myths are constituted are grounded in mythopoeic experiences" (175). This would seem to mean that, for him, the description of a myth (which includes how the subject under study might account for the narrative's existence or origin) somehow allows the scholar uninhibited access into the experience of another. In this sense, too much scholarship in the study of religion is about simple description, often reproducing sets of participant assumptions (at least for those practitioners seen by the scholar as acceptably or not constituting a threat) and masquerading as theoretically grounded insights. In cases where the people under study are not seen in such a benign or favorable manner, the scholar would likely never consider their task completed until they moved well beyond mere description of the people's claims or texts and, instead, pressed on to account for *why* anyone could see things in the manner as they do. We think here of the many studies of marginal or non-dominant groups, as carried out by scholars of religion (so-called cults or New Religious Movements [NRMs]), in which failing to offer an explanatory account for the group's very existence or for its member's self-understandings and actions would be seen as rather problematic inasmuch as it might risk lending the impression that their claims and practices were acceptable or normal. The degree to which work that presents itself as solely descriptive is seen in the field as sufficient is therefore a political issue often linked to the degree to which the scholar or reader identifies with the people or items under study and thereby authorizes their claims and actions by repeating them or merely paraphrasing them via a scholar's descriptive work.

What should be evident by now is that description, despite frequent appeals to the contrary, is neither objective nor value neutral. Describing, say, the contents of a text or the nuances of a ritual means that the scholar has no option but to make choices about what items in the world to focus upon and which of its many aspects to emphasize, marginalize, or otherwise just ignore. This choice, we hope, would be guided by an explicit and defensible theory, providing a rationale to one's colleagues and readers as to why one wishes something to occupy their attention. Here, we might quote from Jonathan Z. Smith's (1938–2017) Introduction to *Imagining Religion* (1982, xi): "The student of religion must be able to articulate clearly why 'this' rather than 'that' was chosen as an exemplum." In this oft-quoted passage, Smith articulates the importance of self-conscious choice. To this, we could also add the tale told by the philosopher of science, Karl Popper (1902–1994), in his book *Conjectures and Refutations: The Growth of Scientific Knowledge* (1963), concerning his onetime request to his students: "Take pencil and paper; carefully observe, and write down what you have observed!" (61, quoting the 2002 edition). This request, the starting point of the traditional scientific method, ends up puzzling the students, until told *what* to observe, *how* long, and *why*. Popper concludes not only that observation requires prior choice but also that "its description presupposes a descriptive language . . . it [also] presupposes similarity and classification, which . . . presuppose interests, points of view, and problems." In a word, it requires the sort of theory that can lead to articulate and defensible choices.

For example, in choosing to argue that Maimonides's *Guide of the Perplexed* (the twelfth-century classic of medieval Jewish thought) is a work of philosophy as opposed to theology (or even vice versa), and then providing a description of the work as one or the other, will certainly focus on specific aspects (to wit, philosophical ones) as opposed to others (e.g., its theological parts). In this respect, description is intimately connected to some of the issues and problems witnessed above and raised under definition. We can also witness some of the political uses to which description can be put in works devoted to the topic of early Islam, a period that is notoriously difficult to describe on account of the paucity of sources contemporary with the events they narrate. In more sympathetic or outrightly apologetic readings, however, scholars often have no problem telling their readers that

Description 75

they "consult the widest range of sources about Muhammad" (e.g., Omid Safi's *Memories of Muhammad* [2009], 17), that they read *later* sources with "careful, judicious scrutiny" (e.g., Asma Afsaruddin's *The First Muslims* [2008], xx), or that their descriptions present that which "is strictly faithful to classical biographies (as far as facts and chronology are concerned)" (e.g., Tariq Ramadan's *In the Footsteps of Muhammad* [2007], xi). The assumption here, of course, is that description is tantamount to the simple summary of contents that are themselves stable, objective, and of obvious importance as scholars take their own reading of the tradition, as they understand it, and offer it as something universal and natural. Here, again, it is clear how description and interpretation mutually reinforce one another.

Instead, going back to Smith, description—understood now as being animated by a prior theory of human action and institutions—ought to be but the first level or order of scholarship, the first thing one does when one encounters a new social fact (e.g., something designated by the scholar as a text, a ritual, etc.). Frequently, at this stage of the encounter, insider language is used or paraphrased to summarize the content. As part of this initial encounter with an unfamiliar source, the scholar necessarily puts that which has just been described into academic categories (e.g., text, ritual, etc.) that not only make sense to scholars of religion (given that they have been created by the scholar for their analytic purposes) but that also allows them to place the unfamiliar into relationships of similarity and difference with other items already categorized in that same manner, data from other historical or geographic locales. This comparative act is foundational to the academic enterprise, inasmuch as it makes generic items of a people's day-to-day life into objects of scholarly study (i.e., data) and thus things that can be analyzed using a critical vocabulary and methods (as opposed to being protected or merely appreciated as "special" and thus self-evidently important and interesting). Smith was especially interested in redescription—the final act of reconsidering the initial description, in light of the subsequent comparative work, by which something new about the item may now become apparent to the scholar. Such an act, Smith argues, leads to a better understanding of the utility of our analytic terms and categories, and, just as importantly, sharpens our understanding of the various spheres of human creativity.

In this volume see: classification, definition, essence, interpretation, method, phenomenology, redescription

In *Religion in 50 More Words* see: commentary, dialogue, emic/etic, idol, nones, paganism, understanding

13 Diaspora

The noun "diaspora" dates to the late seventeenth century where it is believed to derive from Hellenistic Greek (and then Latin), from *dia* (meaning, among other things, through or by mans of) + *sporá* (as in to sow or spread seeds, from which we also derive the English "spore" and even "sporadic"). Our modern term is thus linked to a Greek word that we would today translate as "disperse," as in to spread items out among other things. John Owen (1616–1683), the English theologian, is cited, in a posthumous publication, as describing "the Jewish Diafpora" (in his *A Plea For Scripture Ordination or, Ten Arguments From Scripture and Antiquity Proving Ordination by Presbyters Without Bifhops to be Valid* [1694], 13)—a usage that, in the study of religion at least, provides one of the most common examples of the term's use. The so-called scattering of the 12 tribes of ancient Israel is known as the Exile (Hebrew: *galut*)—an occurrence said to have taken place first in the eighth century BCE with the dispersal of the northern ten tribes and then again, 200 years later, by the so-called Babylonian exile of the members of the remaining southern tribe of Judah. Thus Psalm 137:4: "How could we sing the songs of the Lord while in a foreign land?"—a poem or song whose equally famous opening line reads: "By the rivers of Babylon we sat and wept, when we remembered Zion" (New International translation). The long-standing representation of Jewish people as comprising what we would today call an ethnicity or a nationality—well prior to the now common designation of Judaism as a world religion—but with no homeland (something some believe to have been corrected with the founding of the modern state of Israel in 1947, but which continues to provoke controversy concerning those who claimed their own right to a land which was previously known as Palestine) is traced by many to these mythic events narrated in the Hebrew Bible.

Over the past several decades this still common designation has, with increasing frequency, been applied far wider, to name the process by which migration (whether forced or chosen) spreads the members of any group far from what its members consider to be their native land. People being "diasporic" or "in the diaspora" comes to name those not just away from home but those working to recreate identities alien to their current setting but familiar to memories of a distant or lost homeland. Such social actors have recently caught the attention of scholars interested in efforts to recreate displaced identities. In the study of religion alone, we witness this in works such as: Joseph M. Murphy's *Working the Spirit: Ceremonies of the African Diaspora* (1995), Steven Vertovec's *The Hindu Diaspora: Comparative Patterns* (2001), R. Marie Griffith and Barbara Dianne Savage's *Women and Religion in the African Diaspora: Knowledge, Power, and Performance* (2006), Paul C. Johnsons's *Diaspora Conversions Black Carib Religion and the Recovery of Africa* (2007), Ted Trost's edited collection, *The African Diaspora and the Study of Religion* (2008), Michael Hawley's edited book, *Sikh Diaspora: Theory, Agency, and Experience* (2013), the *Routledge Handbook of the Indian Diaspora* (2017), Ana Cristina O. Lopes's *Tibetan Buddhism in Diaspora: Cultural Re-signification in Practice and Institutions* (2018), and Duke University Press's book series, Religious Cultures of African and African Diaspora People, described as "investigat[ing] the epistemic boundaries of continental and diasporic religious practices and thought and explores the diverse and distinct ways African-derived religions inform culture and politics."

Diaspora studies present a useful example of how nostalgia can be understood as a product of the stressed present, pitched outward and backward in time, though bearing all the marks of the contemporary (despite being couched in the symbols of elsewhere). For once one leaves, the idea of a home quickly becomes just that—an idea, based on a (perhaps shared) memory that freezes invariably a moment, a setting, a series of social relations, etc., in time. In much earlier times, home continued to move and change, as naturally happens, yet to the one at a distance it remained a static idea, one that became condensed into a relatively small set of symbolically potent (and thus strategically useful) images, sounds, styles, tastes, and smells. Yet the idea of home that becomes so useful to those living overseas risks becoming a caricature to those who remain in the so-called homeland. Think of the 2002 film, *My Big Fat Greek Wedding* (written by its star, Nia Vardalos) and its endearing but comic portrait of longtime Greek immigrants to the United States. It soon becomes clear in conversation with people living in Greece today that the film was as well accepted there as in North America, though in Greece it was seen as a parody not of Greeks in general, as North American viewers may have assumed it was, but, more specifically, of their older relatives who, having emigrated to North America a generation or more ago, hold dear an image of home well out of pace with Greece today. Thus the idea of home, not unlike positing an originary point, meets the needs of the displaced community, failing to be in one-to-one sync with an actual place—an insight that makes sense of the American author Thomas Wolfe's well-known posthumous novel, *You Can't Go Home Again* (1940).

The literature of diaspora studies, then, is in how representations of near and far, here and there, present and past, can be seen to be mutually informing rather than a simple binary pair in which each is the straightforward opposite of the other. Also evident in a critical appraisal of this literature is how identity is an ongoing collaborative exercise (and thus a verb, i.e., identification, more than the static and substantive noun that it is often taken to be), which works with what is at hand, which includes a memory divorced from the inevitably dynamic present of a faraway place.

In this volume see: authenticity, belief, culture, identity, indigeneity, origin, race, society

In *Religion in 50 More Words* see: conversion, east/west, initiation, paganism, pilgrimage, syncretism, tradition

14 Environment

Environment is a noun of multiple origins—partly a borrowing from French and partly formed, by derivation, within English from *environ*, an Anglo-Norman transitive verb denoting the act of enclosing (i.e., inhabiting, guarding) and *-mentum*, the Latin suffix commonly used to form nouns from verbs, thereby denoting the result or product of the action of the verb. Environment is thus the area surrounding a place or thing; the environs, surroundings, or physical context and thus setting. Thus, the British writer, Thomas Carlyle (1795–1881): "Baireuth, 'with its kind picturesque environment' . . ." (writing in *The Foreign Review and Continental Miscellany*, vol. 5 [1830], 34). The noun can also be used to refer to the physical surroundings or conditions in which a person or other organism lives and develops, and that otherwise effect its life, existence, or traits. In this vein, the philosopher Henry Sidgwick (1838–1900) writes: "every sentient organism tends to adapt itself to its environment" (*The Methods of Ethics*, Book II, chpt. VI [1874], 194, quoting the seventh edition). This, in turn, leads not only to the more modern sense of the environment being akin to the natural world (an association far more prominent in the mid- to late twentieth century) but also to the social world, such as the political or religious circumstances in which a person lives, with the assumption, especially in the study of religion, that one's religious environment determines, to whatever extent, how one will act. Though, we should also note from the outset, that for some today, these two terms do rather different work, with "environment" signifying the larger or pre-signified setting in which symbolic or cultural "worlds" are established. Critical scholars likely will not find this distinction all that helpful, however, given how it promotes many scholars' fantasy of somehow accessing a pre-linguistic and thus pre-social reality. Within this latter context, physical and natural environments are now reimagined as a metaphysical or transcendent one, namely, that which provides the immaterial conditions that are said to give definition to a particular country or social group. Think of Max Weber's (1864–1920)

DOI: 10.4324/9781003140184-15

classic *Sociology of Religion* (1920), which works on the assumption that religion functions as one of the core forces in society, that which motivates people to think and act in certain ways as opposed to others. Weber was particularly interested in ascertaining the religious reasons and motivations behind different societies, cultures, and economics, something that he imagined as crucial to understanding the differences between, for example, the so-called East and the West. According to Weber, such religious motivations led to the genesis of rational bourgeois capitalism, and its attendant accumulation and concentration of wealth (i.e., capital), from within certain religious contexts and not others. We witness this in his classic, *The Protestant Ethic and the Spirit of Capitalism* (1905), which argued that the so-called spirit of capitalism is somehow inherent to what he characterized as Protestant religious values, especially that of one of its denominations: Calvinism. This latter tradition, he argued, was responsible for the "disenchantment of the world," something that was also responsible for leading to more rational forms, including that of scientific thought. In addition to this rather essentialist notion of religious environment, consider the more recent and popular book by Stephen Prothero, tellingly titled *God is Not One: The Eight Rival Religions That Run the World, and Why Their Differences Matter* (2010). This work also attempts to argue that religious environments subsequently structure society, economics, and politics—as in defining how a particular people or group think.

Of course, environment has other meanings in the study of religion. It can, often in theological fashion (at least for so-called monotheistic religions), denote the natural world that God is said to have created for humans, something that, for instance, is described in the Genesis origins narrative. Thus we read in Ayo Fatubarin and Olusegu Alokan's article, titled "Religion, Man and His Environment": "the creation of the environment demonstrates the thoughtfulness of God, in first creating all things man needs on the planet earth, before creating man" (*British Journal of Education* 1/2 [2013]: 49). It is common, though perhaps not as overt in the previous example, for some to envisage religion as not just providing, or narrating the establishment of, a generic environment but, instead, as establishing a certain sort of setting, one that provides the conditions necessary for human's protection and flourishing. This idea of a "religious environment" or even a "spiritual environment," is one wherein individuals are presumed to be nourished and where they learn and live out religious and moral truths, something that is increasingly and conveniently put in counterpoint with the so-called secular. Dutch anthropologist and scholar of religion, Birgit Meyer, for example, uses the term "religious environment" as referring to "crosscutting formats for doing religion" (see her "Afterword," *Social Analysis* 64/1 [2020]: 134). Though it is difficult to see how this differs from "religious community," it is perhaps worth noting that a religious environment—like any other noun with the adjective "religious" appended to it—is assumed by many scholars to name something set apart from the rest of culture. More often than not, this is presumed to be a space (or a region, or community or the like) that is somehow infused with if not the sacred (as it was for Eliade) then at least some set of supposedly unique or deep values that are imagined to define a community.

The most recent and by far most prominent use of environment in the study of religion is to connect the field to discourses associated with environmentalism (itself a term of greater use in the last third of the twentieth century). We therefore witness the subfield of "religion and ecology" along with such terms as "dark green religion" and "dark green spirituality" (credited to Bron Taylor) naming diverse traditions in which nature is itself assumed to be sacred (e.g., his book *Dark Green Religion: Nature Spirituality and the Planetary Future* [2010]). Perhaps most notable in this regard is the work of Mary Tucker and John Grim, the couple that founded the "Forum on Religion and Ecology" at Yale University—which dates to the "Religions of the World and Ecology Conference Series," held at Harvard between 1996 and 1998. The Yale forum is described on its website as:

> an international multireligious project contributing to a new academic field and an engaged moral force of religious environmentalism . . . it explores religious worldviews, texts, and ethics in order to contribute to environmental solutions along with science, policy, law, economics, and appropriate technology.

We see in this description the theme, so common for many throughout the history of the field, that religion is a force for good in the world that, *when understood properly*, can lead to positive change (as assessed by the writer, of course). Left out of this discussion, of course, is the idea that, should we just adopt the colloquial definition of the term, groups often named as religious can easily be argued to have played a leading force in environmental degradation throughout the world, especially with the sometimes prominent emphasis on the natural world existing for human consumption and pleasure. Carrying out its work from within the world religions paradigm, evidenced in part by its "religion and . . ." format, the Forum produced a series of volumes (e.g., *Judaism and Ecology*, ed. Hava Tirosh-Samuelson; *Daoism and Ecology*, eds. N. J. Giradot, James Miller, and Liu Xiagon; *Indigenous Traditions and Ecology*, ed. John Grim), all of which are listed on their website simply as "[specific religion] Volume." Indeed, many conferences and workshops continue to be devoted to topics of religion and ecology, such as the recent workshop at Michigan

State University's Muslim Studies Program on "Islam, Environmental Science, and Conservation," where papers were presented on topics as diverse as "The Quran and the Environment" (by Abdalmajid Katranji, Michigan State University), or "Is there an Islamic Tree Species?" (by Atus Syahbudin, Universitas Gadjah Mada).

Many of these events, forums, and books reproduce the generic theme that is still prominent throughout much of the field: religion can make the world a better place on account of the fact that *all* religions are imagined as not just essentially the same but also as promoting justice (environmental, racial, gender, and so on and so forth). Such an interpretation or understanding of religion, of course, makes the environment—to return us to the phenomenology of those like Eliade—into the source of the sacred, with humans now imagined as its stewards. For instance, in her 2014 American Academy of Religion Presidential Address, "Interrupting Your Life: An Ethics for the Coming Storm" (later published in *JAAR* 84/1 [2016]: 3–24), Laurie Zoloth articulated what she called a "theology of interruption." The latter, in her own words, is described as "a moment of justice, or beauty, or compassion, or grace, in such an unjust world." Religion, as is sometimes typical for scholars, is thus represented as the unproblematic solution, and never portrayed as a term or category to be queried or questioned.

What should be clarified, though, is that the set of claims, practices, and institutions grouped together by a researcher *as* religion may indeed provide an operating environment in which justice, beauty, or compassion are realized or promoted. We do not contest this. But, as that old saying goes, the devil is in the details. It might, then, be more interesting to inquire into related questions, such as *which* conception of justice, *what* model of beauty, let alone compassion *for whom*? After all, anyone aiming for historical or cultural specificity in their work will quickly realize that these matters are not nearly so straightforward as to enable people simply to make general or universal claims about, for example, justice. If anything, overlooking the situationally specific nature of such claims and failing to grapple with the multiple, and sometimes conflicting sense of justice, let alone beauties and degrees of compassion, may only function to authorize one among many by representing it as the lone or self-evident option. To name but one example: so long as laws are written in a fashion that protects, by justifying, a wide assortment of actions of police officers, actions that strike members of the community as egregious and unwarranted acts of violence will continue to go unpunished. This is because the legal environment, as long-established by both the political and judicial system, is such that those acts cannot, by definition, be considered unjust or illegal (regardless of how wrong some may argue this to be). This could change, of course, given that these legal contexts are historical and thus contingent and thus always open to renegotiation, though the considerable weight of tradition often prevents this from happening, or at least happening easily or to any great degree. The common scholarly association between religion and goodness, evident in the frequent association for some scholars between that which they designate as religion and that which they understand to be beneficial to the natural environment, fails to inquire into the interests that support and produce varying senses of the good, or the justice, let alone the natural. (On the latter, see Elizabeth Bird's essay, "The Social Construction of Nature: Theoretical Approaches to the History of Environmental Problems" in *Environmental Review* 11/4 [1987]: 255–264.) Instead, as we recall a 2016 scholarly essay in the field doing (that is, Nadeem Mahomed and Farid Esack's essay, "The Normal and Abnormal: On the Politics of Being Muslim and Relating to Same-Sex Sexuality," *JAAR* 85/1 [2017]: 224–243), scholars often acknowledge that such a thing as justice is a fraught idea yet their work then proceeds *as if* the difficulties were somehow magically settled without ever being explored and debated. This is a common activity where authors regularly engage in scholarly practice of mulling over the difficulties of defining religion in the opening pages to a study, only to proceed without having ever settled on a definition, as if we all just know what religion is. As a result, a rather specific conception is advanced but without ever being articulated explicitly or defended persuasively—an authorizing move that effectively establishes a very particular sort of environment in which our work takes place while ensuring that it is beyond critique since its structure is simply assumed. Instead, we propose that a critical approach should be eager to focus on the often unseen and therefore unexamined conditions and operations that make each setting possible and persuasive, aiming not just to inhabit or reproduce it but also to scrutinize its mode of production and its manufacturing history.

In this volume see: culture, definition, description, interpretation, origin, phenomenology, sacred/profane, secular, worldview

In *Religion in 50 More Words* see: creation/endtimes, dialogue, spirituality, theology, tradition

15 Essence

Although once prominently used in scholarship on religion, playing a central role in how the scholars' object of study was defined and understood, today the idea of an essence (and its often-paired concept, manifestation) no longer appears as frequently in the literature. However, many of the assumptions driving its former use may be as present as ever, indicating why it should continue to occupy the attention of critical scholars.

From the Latin *essentia*, itself is linked to the prior Greek noun *ousía* (derived from the Greek verb for "to be"), the word seems to have entered English sometime in the late sixteenth or early seventeenth century. Writers eventually adopted the French spelling and it functioned to name a fundamental and thus enduring character, quality, or trait of an item—sometimes also called its substance (Latin verb *substare*, to stand under)—which thereby establishes or defines the item's very identity. For instance, in the first dialogue of the 1601 treatise, *Dialogicall Difcourfe of Spirits and Divels* (co-written by the preachers John Deacon and John Walker and published in London), the character Orthodoxus discusses whether angels were created or are eternal, describing "their effence, or nature it felf." This defining aspect, nature, or essence, is generally assumed to be non-empirical and internal, i.e., not associated simply with observable or outer aspects of the item under study. The modern term's ancient precursors appeared in texts we would today designate as philosophical, e.g., Aristotle's fourth century BCE texts *Metaphysics*, *Categories*, and *Topics*, where we learn that the substance of a thing is to be distinguished from its mere accidents, i.e., those properties that something may or may not have while still remaining the same thing. These discussions then find their way into early Christian theology, e.g., the writings of Tertullian (the late-second-century Roman author), which played an influential role in shaping modern understandings of the doctrine of the Trinity. We read, for example, how the Christian god is conceived as having three persons, with the so-called son and holy spirit being seen as, in English translation, "partners in the Father's substance"

Essence 85

(*Adversus Praxean* [*Against Praxis*], 3 [1920 ed.]). Or, again, in the even more influential work of Augustine (354–430), where the technical term "essence" is instead preferred (e.g., *De Trinitate* [*On the Trinity*], Book VII). Apart from also naming what remains once something has been concentrated or distilled, a usage not far from identifying the required, elemental, or necessary components of something (as in the essential works of some author), this vocabulary becomes a standard item of what we would today refer to as a philosophically idealist approach. We often see this in the history of European writing that prioritizes that which is presumed to be an inner or even spiritual and thus defining characteristic over outer traits that are claimed to be secondary, derivative, and merely happenstance and therefore contingent (what are sometimes called accidents), characteristics that are assumed to be prone to deterioration and pollution. This stance is in opposition to a philosophically materialist stance, classically associated with a writer like Karl Marx (1818–1883), whose work instead prioritizes such things as ownership and the production and circulation of goods as providing the practical conditions in which value systems are created and maintained.

In the study of religion, the word "essence" has often been associated with a style of essentialist definition, which aims to define by identifying the *sine qua non* or indispensable element of something, e.g., that feature without which something would not be religious. It is also connected to the term "manifestation," a word generally meaning to take a tangible form that exhibits or demonstrates something to the senses, i.e., to make something manifest. For example, take John Whitehead's *A Manifestation of Truth* (1662), a treatise written to defend Quakerism. Understandably, perhaps, it was also a term used by so-called spiritualists in the nineteenth century to name the form taken by a spirit whom they had conjured. Most famously for the student of religion, perhaps, the two terms occur in the translated title of an early classic of the field by the Dutch Egyptologist Gerardus van der Leeuw (1890–1950): *Religion in Essence and Manifestation: A Study in Phenomenology* (German: *Phänomenologie der Religion*), which was published in 1933 and first appeared in English in 1938. A student at the University of Leiden of the Norwegian scholar, W. Brede Kristensen (1867–1953)—who himself studied also Leiden under the Dutch scholar Cornelis Petrus Tiele (1830–1902), credited, along with F. Max Müller (1823–1900), as founding the field of Comparative Religion—van der Leeuw was one of the major early translators of a prior school of thought, philosophical phenomenology, applying it to the study of religion. Should someone be aware of outline of the philosophical tradition in this subfield, and the works of its major thinkers (e.g., Edmund Husserl [1859–1938], Martin Heidegger [1889–1976], and Maurice Merleau-Ponty [1908–1961]),

86 *Essence*

then the emphasis of the phenomenology of religion on identifying the universal essence of religion by using the comparative method for cross-cultural and historical studies of its varied forms (i.e., the plural religions, understood as manifestations of religion, in the singular) will be puzzling. For the earlier philosophical tradition, despite admitted differences in how it was practiced by different scholars throughout its history, was mainly concerned with studying human consciousness, from the subjective point of view, so as to better understand the medium in which experiences of the world can be said to take place (indicating why phenomenology has sometimes been called transcendental idealism, as in Husserl's work, or even a metaphysics of experience by others). Thus, philosophical phenomenology was not so concerned with things in themselves (i.e., the ontology, or being-ness, of things in the world—such as ascertaining the essence of religion, itself one among many items in the world) as with how things *appear to us* in our experience (opting to refer to things as phenomena, to mark the mediated role played by consciousness itself) and thus with determining the prior conditions that allow us to experience the world to begin with. Thus, such work sometimes was concerned with pure or transcendental consciousness—work that was criticized by some as focusing on a disembodied thinker, alienated from an actual world (thus, in response, the development of what was called existential phenomenology, notably under Heidegger's influence). What sets the phenomenology *of religion* apart, then, is its presumption that one can infer something about the objects of experience (i.e., religion or, as some phenomenologist prefer, the experience of the sacred) from a sufficient comparative study of varied phenomena—hence the prominence of comparative studies of myths, rituals, symbols, texts, and institutions in such phenomenological work. We think here of the well-known example of Mircea Eliade (1907–1986) and his interest in studying what he referred to as the sacred as a structure of consciousness. In fact, the modern world religions textbook and its survey course could be considered to be an inheritor of this tradition, inasmuch as each chapter or unit studies the historical and regional details of one so-called faith tradition all in order to gain some insight into the overall or overarching phenomenon that is religion in the singular. Depending on the rationale informing a particular department, an entire degree in the field could be driven by a phenomenological approach, inasmuch as the essence of religion can only be inferred after aspects of each of the religions have been surveyed and studied.

As discredited as this approach may now seem to be (despite the world religions course not only populating most departments' curricula but also constituting one of their most important courses), and as out of place as a term like essence may at first appear to be in the modern field, the critical scholar may find that this way of defining and then studying religion remains

Essence 87

surprisingly relevant for many in the field today. For example, consider those scholars who, contrary to the phenomenological tradition in the field, now seem to emphasize carefully empirical specificity in their work (e.g., subfields known now as lived religion, embodied religion, material religion, or religion on the ground). Despite the focus on tangible bodies and observable practices—rather than just studying texts and their interpretation—those working in what is called embodied religion still seem to presuppose that some *thing* has been embodied. This is perhaps not dissimilar to eighteenth- and nineteenth-century writers discussing "embodied spirits" or, as noted in an issue of the 1848 magazine, *The Christian Pioneer*, Jesus Christ was "virtue embodied" (116, in a section entitled Anecdotes, Selections, and Gems). That such contemporary scholars think far more broadly than did their Christian theological predecessors must be acknowledged, of course. Yet the prominence of claiming that it is the sacred which is being embodied or, more broadly, this thing commonly designated as meaning, suggests that earlier thoughts on how comparative study of discrete empirical manifestations might shed light on a disembodied prior and causal essence may continue to exert more influence in the modern field than we might realize. This is important for the critical scholar to bear in mind, for advances in the field away from either explicitly theological or pseudo-theological positions may not be as great as some claim.

In this volume see: comparison, definition, experience, lived religion, material religion, method, sacred/profane, world religions

In *Religion in 50 More Words* see: emic/etic, evil, immanence/transcendence, liberation, meditation, piety, soul, spirituality, symbol, theology

16 Experience

"Experience," particularly as it is qualified by the adjective religious, i.e., religious experience, is probably among the most important terms in the history of the academic study of religion. Such importance, though, tends to be based less on analytic utility than upon its ambiguity and imprecision, with more vague concepts *seeming* to be more useful, given the almost unlimited breadth of their application. The term "experience" is certainly no different, based as it is on assumptions concerning private feelings or sentiments—recall the influential German Protestant theologian Rudolf Otto (1869–1937) and how he located religion in an experience of what he called the "numinous" or the "wholly other" (from his book *Das Heilige*, usually translated as *The Idea of the Holy* [1917]). By its very nature, then, the essential core to religion was claimed to be non-rational, making religion not just about something other than so-called beliefs, but also resulting in its resistance to clear and precise definition. Instead, Otto argued that researchers must be open to the reality of the experience itself and be ready to experience it for themselves, an approach that calls into question the usual basis for what was once called the "science of religion." Although the word "experience" may seem to have a self-evident place in almost any academic field, since it is, after all, etymologically related to the word "experiment" (namely, the act of putting something to public test for the sake of clarification and verification), when it comes to the study of religion it is often used to undermine the empirical and the public by means of the subjective and the private. That the claims being made about the priority or sanctity of these supposedly internal dispositions are themselves public, and are therefore part of negotiations and disagreements between situated social actors who each have interests, deserves more scholarly attention, however.

The modern English word "experience" derives from the earlier French *expérience*, which in turn is based on the present participle of the Latin *experīrī*, *experient-em*, meaning to try, or to put something to the test. The earlier meaning of the term, now largely obsolete, is thus the act of

DOI: 10.4324/9781003140184-17

determination and, when used in the sense of a court trial, in determining guilt or innocence based on factual evidence. This is where the relation with the other modern noun, "experiment," comes in, derived from the same root. Thus, the English poet John Gower, writing in 1393: "At Avynon the xperience Therof haþ ȝoue an euidence" (*Confessio Amantis*, vol. I, 14). The term, in other words, was associated with practical demonstration, as we see, for example, in Geoffrey Chaucer's *Treatise on the Astrolabe* (1391): "I . . . found the point of my rewle . . . a lite[l] with-in the degree & than haddy of this conclusioun the ful experience" (15). This usage was characterized by the literary critic, Raymond Williams, as "experience past," naming the accumulated evidence from past lessons, as in the modern sense of having "work experience" (see his entry on experience in *Keywords: A Vocabulary of Culture and Society* [1983]).

Undermining this early meaning, experience would later come to signify a state of mind or feeling that was (and still is) claimed to form, among other subjective states, part of one's ongoing inner religious life (a sense of the word instead termed by Williams "experience present"). Thus the theologian, John Owen (1616–1683), in his *Two discourses concerning the Holy Spirit, and His work: the one, Of the Spirit as a comforter, the other, As He is the author of spiritual gifts* (1674): "Testified unto by the Experience of them that truely believe" (49). Or, as we read in Jonathan Edwards's *A treatise concerning religious Affections* (1746): "Those Experiences which are agreable to the Word of God, are right" (vol. II, 45). It is in this sense that John Wesley (1703–1791), one of the founders of the modern Protestant denomination known as Methodism, is famously said to have experienced what he later described in his journal as a strange warming of his heart during a meeting on the evening of May 24, 1738. This was his so-called Aldersgate experience, named after the street where the meeting took place, and from which he concluded: "I felt I did trust in Christ, Christ alone for salvation; and an assurance was given me that He had taken away my sins, even mine, and saved me from the law of sin and death" (*The Journal of the Rev. John Wesley*, vol. 1 [1827], 97; Methodist churches to this day annually celebrate Aldersgate Day on whichever Sunday falls closest to May 24). That this sense of experience is not only linked to moments characterized as religious (such as the often-described Buddhist goal of experiencing the disillusion of self, described by the metaphor of emptiness) should be clear, for we find it used in any setting where the speaker aims to convey a sense of legitimacy. Of note is that both senses of the modern word can be invoked simultaneously, as in the common phrase "the British experience," implying both an accumulation of historical examples but which are all said to exemplify a universal and still present disposition, e.g., "the unconquerable British spirit."

In the study of religion, "experience" is frequently associated with this latter sense of some vague feeling or inner and self-authenticating state. It is assumed that the meaning of such observable items as symbols, scriptures, practices, etc., derive from a private experience in the minds (or hearts?) of religious founders, their disciplines, and subsequent practitioners. Such experiences are therefore assumed to constitute the essence of religion, something expressed (literally, pushed outward) differently into various contexts, to be sure, but something which, after careful comparative analysis, can be demonstrated by such scholars to be uniform across settings. In fact, this could be said to be the driving force behind the world religions paradigm, including the efforts to encourage interreligious dialogue. This, in turn, gives rise to the notion that attaining or having such experiences is the goal of religious life, where it is somehow connected to equally murky concepts such as "truth" and "authenticity," despite the fact that many languages neither possess a word for "experience" nor its sometimes linked concept, "spirituality." This approach has influenced the field of religious studies to such an extent that many have maintained that if scholarship does not give sufficient (and, some would add, respectful) attention to the participant's experience (or, we might more critically add, their reports or claims of experience), or what is sometimes simply called the experiential dimension of religious practice, such studies are said to be reductionistic. The latter leads to the charge that such scholars "do not take religion seriously." Given the close association between this understanding of experience, on the one hand, and common assumptions about human nature, on the other, such scholarly approaches are further characterized as disrespectful to and thus dismissive of the people under study.

Shifting attention from these supposed experiential states and, instead, looking at the claims that such states exist and persist, the scholar of Buddhism, Robert Sharf, has argued that appeals to experience became a convenient way for Christian theologians in the nineteenth century to bypass criticism that sought to undermine their own religious truth claims. The rhetoric of experience, as we might now call it, was therefore used in settings of social contest and thus in situations of disagreement, for what better way to rebuff one's critics than to argue that their object of derision belonged to the inner and thus unassailable spiritual world of the individual (see Sharf's essay "Experience" in *Critical Terms in Religious Studies* [1998], 94–116). Wayne Proudfoot, in his widely acclaimed book, *Religious Experience* (1985), traces this turn to inner sentiment, away from empirical reality, to the influential German theologian Friedrich Schleiermacher (1768–1834), who argued against the Kantian position of his day, which denied metaphysics and simultaneously maintained that religion was reducible to a system of beliefs or morality (a reading of Schleiermacher contested by Theodor

Vial in his book, *Modern Religion, Modern Race* [2016], 67). Veritable religion, Schleiermacher maintained against precisely such a critique, is instead predicated on a feeling of the infinite, making it, as Otto later reinforced, a non-rational disposition or awareness, and thus not something to be critiqued by so-called Enlightenment rationality. It was, instead, something to be *felt*—a feeling of absolute dependence, as Schleiermacher put it in his famous work of systematic theology, *Der christliche Glaube* (English: *The Christian Faith*).

Predictably, such a position proved amenable to many in Europe because if at first it protected their understanding of Christianity, it could subsequently be expanded at will to include religion writ large (as this category was then expanding in its application). The increasing use of the rhetoric of experience (represented as worldwide traditions of spiritual, mystical, contemplative, visionary experience) therefore demonstrates the continued universalization of Christianity by demonstrating religion's own universality. Moreover, in privileging religious experience, some scholars could later argue that all religious traditions emerged from, and were therefore all attempts to give expression to, a common apprehension of the sacred. Observable differences in belief and practice could now be reduced to factors thought to pre-date, or even to lie outside of, historical or cultural contexts. This sense of experience therefore intersects with the East/West understanding of the world, wherein the "East" is imagined to represent the meditative and thus experiential traditions whereas the supposedly more rational traditions are of the "West"—think, for example, of stereotypes of the Indian yogi engaged in silent meditation. D. T. Suzuki (1870–1966), the popular Japanese interpreter of Zen Buddhism for European and North American audiences, argued, for example, that Zen is pure experience, with the experience of satori claimed to pass beyond all rational understandings, thereby enabling one to experience "the absolute oneness of things" (see "Practical Methods of Zen Instruction," in his *Essays in Zen Buddhism* [1927]).

As with so many other terms examined in this volume, it should by now be obvious that there is a great deal of slippage between theological usage and the so-called academic study of religion—between experience present and experience past. Once we define religion as based on an inner experience, something that can only be represented in some sort of inevitably flawed language, scholars of religion—with Mircea Eliade (1907–1986) providing a useful illustration—fashion themselves as the ones most capable of inferring the characteristics of this inward sentiment, and its ultimate object, by studying its outward or external manifestations. Since more empirically oriented disciplines (e.g., history, anthropology, sociology) are supposedly unable to understand the so-called dialectic between essence and manifestation, scholars of religion have often regarded themselves as uniquely qualified to study these relationships. In fact, this is the very argument upon which the North American emergence of the field, as an autonomous academic discipline in 1960s, was based. Though "religion" has, as of late, been critiqued as a colonial-era category that may be of little analytic viability today, "experience" is for many still considered to be a universal and privileged phenomenon (despite other languages often lacking equivalent terms). We witness this orientation in many of the classic theorists in the field, e.g., the US psychologist of religion, William James (1842–1910), in addition to theorists of mysticism, such as W. T. Stace (1886–1967) and Aldous Huxley (1894–1963)—all, despite important differences between them, distinguished between a universal experience and its subsequent culturally conditioned expressions. For while it was assumed that, for example, Jewish mystics might describe their experience using the religious language of their specific tradition, and Hindu mystics would do the same, the basic experience being represented and translated by each remained the same.

This also means that literary, artistic, and ritual representations are often seen as significant only in so far as they represent manifestations of this unquantifiable and undefinable experience. It is likely a mistake, however, for a critical scholar to approach such representations as if they refer or correspond to something other than the situation in which such claims are made. This deferral of meaning, wherein texts and objects are read as pointing back to something beyond themselves, pre-dating language and history, means that the term experience can be used for numerous ends, including highly ideological ones. There have certainly been critiques of this position (a stance sometimes called perennialism, which imagines all of the world's religious traditions as sharing a single and transcendent origin from which all knowledge and doctrine has developed). For example, Proudfoot, along with Steven Katz and Grace Jantzen (1948–2006), have all argued that, should such an inner state even exist, scholars cannot have access to unmediated mystical experiences, only to the texts or claims of authors that purport to have had them. So, rather than read these texts for a mystery that is presumed to inspire them, we would suggest that it is much more productive to examine the practical and public conditions that govern their production and circulation—seeing the rhetoric of experience, and its effects on social actors, as far more interesting to study than so-called experience itself.

Not all agree, however, so the term is alive and well in the study of religion today. Case in point: in his *Perceiving God: The Epistemology of Religious Experience* (1992), the philosopher William P. Alston (1921–2009) argues that religious experience is not purely subjective and that it can, in fact, function as a source of reliable grounds for religious belief. People who claim to have mystical experiences of God, he reasons, are rationally

Experience 93

justified in believing whatever they have mystically perceived. It is a circular argument, to be sure. Or consider that the *Journal of the American Academy of Religion* (*JAAR*) regularly publishes articles on the topic of religious experience. Thus we read that whitewater kayaking constitutes a religious experience in A. Whitney Sanford's "Pinned on Karma Rock: Whitewater Kayaking as Religious Experience" (75/4 [2007]: 875–895). We also find this discourse in use when Jason N. Blum, in his "Retrieving Phenomenology of Religion as a Method for Religious Studies," seeks to recalibrate traditional phenomenology with an eye toward reinterpreting religious experience (80/4 [2012]: 1025–1048); and, in Lexi Eikelboom's "Rhythmic Flesh: How the Regulation of Bodily Rhythm Contributes to Spirituality in the Jesus Prayer, Medieval Dance, and Africa American Preaching," where we are informed that the three disparate practices of the subtitle all form a body "capable of connecting with spiritual forces" (88/3 [2020]: 805–831). Moreover, in the subfield of Cognitive Science of Religion (CSR), we also find continued attempts to study religious experience, but this time from the vantage point of the scientific laboratory. For example, in his book, *The Neuroscience of Religious Experience* (2009), Patrick McNamara, a professor at Boston University's School of Medicine, argues that religious experiences involve activity in key nodes of the amygdala, large portions of the prefrontal lobes, and the anterior temporal cortex of the brain. Similarly, in an article titled "Neural Correlates of Religious Experience," and published in the *European Journal of Neuroscience* (13/8 [2001]: 1649–1652), the authors investigate the neural correlates of religious experience using functional neuroimaging. When self-identified religious subjects engage in religious recitation, the authors argue that a frontal-parietal circuit—composed of the dorsolateral prefrontal, dorsomedial frontal, and medial parietal cortex—is activated, concluding that religious experience *may* (their term, by the way) be a cognitive process which feels immediate. Such attempts within the domain of CSR are similar to earlier non-scientific accounts in the sense that material and other historical and social conditions of such reports are ignored so that the medical—as opposed to transcendent—source of the experience can be located, now in the brain rather than the heart.

All of these attempts to locate the actual source of such reported experience, or to explain religious objects and artifacts as grounded in such an experience, try to ascertain that which by definition is nonobjective, and because of this, that which is claimed to resist all signification. But curiously, at least in this one sense of the term (i.e., experience present), the word names something that is said to exist *beyond the world* but while using language to accomplish something *in the world*—otherwise why even talk about it? This indicates that, much as Donald S. Lopez claims in the case of the discourse on belief, claims of experience are an agonistic affirmation whose legitimacy is based in a discourse "that cannot be submitted to ordinary rules of verification" (in *Critical Terms for Religious Studies* [1998], 33). As such, it is better understood as an authorizing technique. For in positing a vague place prior to, or outside of, language but which anchors claims inevitably made from within the world, the rhetoric of experience posits an originary place where, as Sharf himself argues in the same volume (113), negotiation and signification come to an end and where "the really real" is said to be located. Finding such claims to be anything but examples of critical scholarship, we advise that scholars cease searching for experience's source or referent and that the term be retired from our scholarly vocabulary. They should instead begin to hear or see it as a word whose use provides evidence of an ongoing dispute in which one or more sides are forced to marshal the authority of the transcendent and the immutable in support of their obviously contestable position.

In this volume see: authenticity, belief, comparison, culture, definition, description, essence, history, religion

In *Religion in 50 More Words* see: conversion, emic/etic, founder, immanence/transcendence, initiation, liberation, meditation, mysticism, piety, spirituality, tradition

17 Explanation

"Knowledge of any set of phenomena, whether natural or cultural, comes about not primarily from the application and development of taxonomies, but from explanatory theorizing"—so we read in the entry on "Typology, Classification" in 1995's *The HarperCollins Dictionary of Religion* (1102). This quotation makes evident that, despite a tremendous effort placed on studying religions by assigning them into various types and subgroups—whether it is the earlier distinction between world religions vs. so-called national or ethnic religions or even the more enduring (but problematic, nonetheless) Eastern vs. Western as well as monotheistic vs. polytheistic distinctions—it is explanation, and explanatory theories of religion that derive from it, on which gains in knowledge are based. For only in the light of such theories do we know what we are studying, by determining *why* it exists, *how* it is different from other things, and *what* purpose it may serve or what effects it may have. Only then might we decide that we need to fine-tune the items that we are examining by looking for similarities and differences (using comparison) within the class of those things that our theory and thus our definition of religion has enabled us to designate *as* religion in the first place. Important to recognize, however, is that this basic role played by explanatory theories—a position shared across many of the human and natural sciences—has long been contested in the study of religion, all depending on what someone means by this term religion and how they think it ought to be studied.

The noun "explanation," often opposed in modern speech to the word "interpretation," comes into the English language somewhere around the fifteenth century and derives from the classical Latin *explānāre*, meaning to level, flatten, and to spread or roll something out (from the Latin *planus* for flat and even clear or plain). This derivation links the modern English verb "to explain" to the other modern verb "to plane" (as in to flatten or smooth a piece of wood, with a tool known as a plane or hand plane) as well as the modern noun "plane" (as in the term used to name a flat surface, as evident in the study of geometry) along with "explicate" (to express something clearly and in detail; to disentangle and make clear). This early sense of flattening or unfolding was eventually applied to the production of knowledge, such as coming to understand clearly a text or a topic of study or even to accomplish some desired end, such as the still used phrases "explain my meaning" and "explain yourself," the latter used to invite an accounting of one's actions. For instance, consider the Anglican clergyman, John Scott, and his 1647 text, *The Christian Life Wherein that Fundamental Principle of Christian Duty, The Doctrine of our Saviour's Mediation, is Explained and Proved* (5th edition), where we read: "for tho' the Spirit taught them no *new* Doctrines, but did only *repeat* and *explain* to them what our Saviour had taught them bfore . . ." (vol. 3, 68).

The modern technical or even scientific use of "explain" to identify the cause or function of something, in distinction from interpreting and thereby understanding the meaning of something, does not fully develop until sometime in the mid- to late eighteenth century. Perhaps not coincidentally, this period also witnessed the frequency of the term's use rise sharply in English writing. For example, in 1800 we read in a published letter on electrical conductivity from Alex Ander Volta (i.e., Alessandro Volta [1745–1827], the Italian scientist and inventor) that was written to the English botanist, Sir Joseph Banks (1743–1820): "The hypothefis of this learned and laborious philofopher . . . is indeed very ingenious, and is, perhaps, the beft theory that has been devifed to explain the phenomena of the torpedo [i.e., the electric eel], adhering to the hitherto known principles and laws of electricifty . . ." (*The Philosophical Magazine*, vol. 7, 310). We see here the association between theory—technically understood not just as a viewpoint or mere opinion but, rather, as a set of propositions about the world that has implications, such as leading to developing a testable hypothesis concerning some future state of affairs—and explanation. This, in turn, helps us to distinguish the traditional scholarly sense of an explanation from an interpretation, in that the former now comes to be associated with causal analysis. It does this by identifying the prior observable conditions and factors that either necessarily or sufficiently led to the origins or workings of something, such as an explanation of thunder making reference to the sudden pressure changes that result from the superheating and then cooling of the air along the path of the electrical discharge, resulting in a shockwave that then travels outward. It is precisely this sense of the term that we find in the Scottish financial author Robert Mishet, in his 1826 book, *An Attempt to Explain from Facts the Effect of the Issues of the Bank of England Upon Its Own Interests, Public Credit, and Country Banks*, such as in the following, which opens Chapter 7: "I shall now proceed to state the cause, which appears to me fully and satisfactorily to explain the theory

Explanation 97

of general speculation . . ." (91). This is a usage that one might further describe as deductive or nomothetic (from the Greek, *nómos*, referring to laws or customs), that is, studies that presume general laws that enable one to understand specific situations. Interpretations, on the other hand, concern the effort to decode what is popularly known as meaning, including authorial intentions of the author, namely, that which is presumed to be the inner motives and dispositions symbolized or encoded in a text, requiring a "close reading" to understand correctly.

This all takes on direct relevance in the study of religion, given that there are long-standing (and conflicting) scholarly traditions of what religion is and how to study it. Some conceive of religion (let alone the very designation of something *as* religious) as an ordinary element of human history and culture, thereby enabling one to determine its causes, identify its origins, and possibly write what an earlier scholar would have termed its natural history. We think here of the Scottish philosopher, David Hume (1711–1776), and his influential book, *The Natural History of Religion* (1757). There are also those who are more theologically and humanistically inclined. Such scholars counter that the thing that we call religion is unique and therefore uncaused by other items in the mundane human world. (Influenced or shaped, perhaps, but caused, no.) They argue that religion somehow resists explanation inasmuch as it cannot be the result of prior and more basic building blocks. They might then claim that more naturalistic explanatory accounts of religion are simplistic and attempt to "explain it away" by reducing religion to non-religious sources, leaving no core of essentially or inherently religious residue after such analysis is complete. Instead of "throwing the baby out with the bathwater," as opponents of such explanatory approaches once used to phrase their disagreement, they often opt for an interpretive approach, by claiming religion to be a species of human meaning-making, seeing meaning as a rather more ethereal and unexplainable quality than would, say, a semiotician (i.e., one who studies the workings of sign systems).

Even if we bracket out theological accounts, which might see religion's cause as a divine intervention in human affairs, this disagreement in the field has characterized pretty much all of its history to date, with scholars still lined up on either side of this debate. The one side argues that in order for the field to be truly scientific, its practitioners must be engaged in developing rigorous, causal frameworks that have predictive power (meaning that they can be tested empirically) and thus applicable to general laws of human behavior or psychology (harkening back to science being comprised of theory-based hypotheses). Those on the other side respond that religion, or more often something termed religious experience, utterly eludes all such naturalist frameworks and modes of analysis, with religion instead being seen as a far more emotive or qualitative sentiment than can only be inferred by studying its public expressions or symbols. As famously argued by Mircea Eliade (1907–1986) on the opening page of the foreword to the English translation of his book, *Patterns in Comparative Religion* (*Traité d'histoire des religions* [1949]): "it would be hopeless to try and explain religion in terms of any one of those basic functions [e.g., social, linguistic, or economic factors]." Relying on an interpretive model for the field, he then goes on: "It would be as futile as thinking you could explain *Madame Bovary* by a list of social, economic, and political facts; however true, they do not affect it as a work of literature." So too, explanations of religion in natural, causal terms, flatten out and erase the presumed nuance and even the mystery of religion, such scholars would surely add, inevitably failing to capture what they would simply phrase as the essential religiousness of religion. One also thinks here of the work of the still influential German Protestant theologian, Rudolf Otto (1869–1937), such as his claim that religion was an ineffable feeling of "the numinous" (Latin, *numen*, a nod, i.e., a power giving assent), recently cited by the US scholar of American religion, Robert Orsi, as an underappreciated theorist in the field and thus model for Orsi's own notion of "real presence"—something Orsi contends is inappropriately studied in explanatory scholarship. In fact, despite their effort to distance their work from a theological approach, we may even see traces of it in Catherine Michael Chin's more recent effort to describe what they name as historical radiance or "the force of alterity. It is the force of the past's otherness, an otherness that can never be entirely domesticated . . . [R]adiance is experienced as the unsettling force of encounter, rather than the reassuring process of explanation" ("Marvelous Things Heard: On Finding Historical Radiance," *The Massachusetts Review* 58/3 [2017]: 482, 484). The problem, though, is in devising a signifier that tries to name "the more" or that which is claimed to go beyond signification and thus knowledge—an approach that, as Matthew Baldwin rightly argues, adopts the uncritical position of a novel's all-knowing narrator or a god's eye view of history ("Objects and Objections: Methodological Reflections on the Data for Religious Studies," in Leslie Dorrough Smith's *Constructing "Data" in Religious Studies: Examining the Architecture of the Academy* [2019], 73–100).

Today, the divide between these two opposed positions continues, of course, with explanatory theorists being far fewer in the field than are their more humanistic counterparts. As some in the latter group might argue, the former, reductionistic posture jeopardizes the field as a whole, in that nothing truly religious remains to be understood after a nonreligious cause of religion is proposed. How, then, can departments of religious studies continue to exist in such a scenario—when, unless we assume an essentially religious kernel, its study might be sufficiently done in yet other parts of the modern research university? Moreover, reducing religion to its possible natural origins—whether religion in the singular (by identifying some prehistoric cause of the phenomenon) or the religiosity of a particular person (by identifying aspects of their biography that account for their beliefs and behaviors)—is said by some to demean and belittle, by dismissing or criticizing, the faith and thus value and dignity of the people whom scholars study. To fail to treat religion, and thus religious people, respectfully, perhaps even reverentially, is thus—or so some might claim—to fail to treat human beings with the dignity and respect that they deserve. That this is not how explanatory theorists understand the issue should be evident— think here of Bruce Lincoln's strong counterstatement in the last of his 13 "Theses on Method" (*Method & Theory in the Study of Religion* 8 [1996]: 225–227)—inasmuch as religion, like any other aspect of the human or the natural world as a whole, strikes them as being open to causal analysis rather than limited to mere description, appreciation, or amplification.

Despite the way that these opposed alternatives have defined the field, a third position is now possible, at least as outlined by Jonathan Z. Smith (1938–2017). While certainly not content with studying religion as inherently religious, he was also wary of explanatory reductionists who seemed overly confident in the realness (i.e., ontology) of the thing to which they were reducing religion (e.g., to the psyche or to the economy). Taking seriously scholars' own roles in defining domains of study, as well as their role in devising the very tools by which that work takes place (e.g., the categories that they use, such as religion let alone culture, society, economy, myth, ritual, etc.), Smith preferred to talk about translation. It is the scholar's job, he maintained, to translate the claims or actions from the conceptual system of the people under study to that of the research university, which, he argued, necessarily exists at a distance. Using the early sociological work of the French scholar Émile Durkheim (1858–1917) as an example, Smith argued that Durkheim did not so much explain or interpret religion but, instead, *translated* the language of religion into the language of sociology (as Smith phrased it in his essay, "A Twice Told Tale: The History of the History of Religions' History" published in *Numen* 48/2 [2001]; see 143–144). He did this, for example, by concluding that religious claims about a god can, once this translation takes place, be understood as symbolic claims about society itself, with claims about gods being among the tangible devices that members use to represent their group to themselves, as if they too are tangible.

The debate over explanation shows no signs of being resolved any time soon. This is probably on account of its links to wider and sometimes undisclosed assumptions about the field and its object of study, not to mention the wider role of scholars of religion and their relationship to the people under study. If so, then discussions over the possible cause of religion will

100 *Explanation*

remain an important way into understanding much about how the modern field works, but it may tell us little about the origin of religion.

In this volume see: comparison, culture, definition, description, essence, experience, function, history, interpretation, religion, theory, world religions

In *Religion in 50 More Words* see: animism, commentary, dialogue, emic/etic, understanding

18 Faith

Many scholars regard faith as an essential component of religion. Indeed, it is not uncommon to encounter religions frequently referred to *as* faiths (e.g., faith traditions and their members termed "the faithful"), this despite the fact that references to something akin to faith—especially as traditionally understood with its roots in Protestant Christianity—plays very little role in the claims or the literature of other groups known as religions. The cross-cultural use of this term as a synonym for religion is therefore yet another example of using a specifically Christian term, often with little or no reflection on what it is and how it has been used, *as if* it were a natural scholarly rubric that has comparative and therefore analytic rigor. Once again, we witness how a term with a very specific history is forced upon others; the result, as we have often seen throughout our critical approach to the vocabulary of the field, is a host of taxonomical and other problems.

The English word "faith" derives from the Anglo-Norman and Old French *feid*, *feit*, and *fait*, which in turn come from the classical Latin *fidēs*. The latter has a rather broad semantic range including everything from trust and guarantee to honesty and what we might today designate as belief. In post-classical Latin, especially by the fourth century ce, the term comes to denote a more specific belief within Christianity, namely, Christian doctrine, and thus becomes associated with a claim of membership within the Christian community. In English, early uses include a pledge or formal declaration, in the sense of "to give one's faith," as in Chaucer's fourteenth-century "Lo here my faith in me shal be no lak" (*Summoner's Tale*, line 431). It is, thus, fairly easy to connect this sense of belief to religion (at least as the latter is commonly understood to name an inner sentiment or feeling), and it is around the same time that faith comes to connote the belief in, and acceptance of, the doctrines of what comes to be known as the Christian religion (such as the belief in God and the authenticity of divine revelation in the person of Jesus Christ, etc.). Faith now becomes associated with the innate capacity of the (Christian) individual to apprehend or otherwise intuit

DOI: 10.4324/9781003140184-19

and respond to such divine truths, often imagined as being well beyond the realm of mere reason, argumentation, and empirical evidence. In this sense, faith is regarded as a capacity or even faculty of the human soul or the direct result of divine illumination (known as "the grace of God" in parts of Christianity). In Thomas Hobbes's still well-known work of political philosophy, *Leviathan* (1651), for example, we read that: "Faith is a gift of God, which Man can neither give, nor take away" (Part III, chpt. xlii, 271).

But in the seventeenth century we begin to see the term employed to refer not just to the "Christian faith," but also to other groups now known as religions. Thus in Charles Blount's *Great is Diana of the Ephesians, or, The original of idolatry together with the politick institution of the gentiles sacrifices* (1680) we read of the "Heathen faith": "for although they did not own themselves to be made after the Image of God, yet did they in their fond Imaginations make their Gods after the Image of men" (29). We also see attestations such as "the Religion of Moses and the Faith of the Jews" (1748) and "the Moslem faith" (1777). Such uses, still very much in evidence today, take what is known from one's own tradition—i.e., that the true Christian religion is predicated in "faith in Jesus"—and then assume that at the core or essence of other religions there must exist a similar concept (e.g., an inner affectation). This often coincided with the desire to demonstrate how other "faiths" lacked the authenticity of the Christian one.

Recent years have continued to witness this local and situated term expanded in a way that makes it seem synonymous with "religion." Thus, we now routinely hear of "the Jewish faith," "the Muslim faith," or "the Hindu faith" (and invariably always used with the definite article "the"). If the term religion is regarded as a European-derived construct that groups together the doctrines, behaviors, and claims of other peoples, both in other time periods and geographic regions, the term faith (or faiths) is even more problematic. For one thing, it assumes that an evidence-defying assuredness in something is a universal human trait. In so doing, it can transform the "religions" of others into (often inferior) versions of Protestant Christianity. Since the latter tradition puts little to no emphasis on ritual—which does not mean that they do not have plenty of rituals, of course, but that they are often seen as derivative secondary expressions of a prior and pure individual sentiment—then the moment we call a religion with a heavy ritualistic dimension (e.g., Orthodox Judaism) a "faith" or "*the* Jewish faith," scholars have repackaged it to suit their assumptions.

This gives way to the "faiths of men," a precursor to the modern world religions model. In 1906, for example, James R. Forlong (1824–1904) had his posthumous and idiosyncratic three-volume *Faiths of Man: Cyclopaedia of Religions* (which was subsequently reprinted in 1964) published. Or, again, we see this idea that all religions are ultimately faiths in Charles

Francis Potter's *The Faiths Men Live By* (1955). Lest one think that this is part of an earlier generation in the study of religion, we still witness books with the word "faith" in their titles that are not simply Protestant and theological. For example, consider the title of the edited collection, *Faith and Law: How Religious Traditions from Calvinism to Islam View American Law* (2008), which includes numerous denominations of Christianity, in addition to "new immigrant faiths" (Hinduism, Buddhism, and Islam). But again, note how "faith" in the singular and "religious traditions" in the plural are interchangeable, presumably because at the root of all religious expression is assumed to exist private faith. This idea that all possess faith is also behind those attempts to get people from various religions to converse with one another in, e.g., interfaith dialogue or multifaith dialogue—an attempt often taking place in the guise of scholarship on religion.

While one may maintain that there is little use for the word "faith" in critical scholarship on religion, it certainly has a place in the study of theology, particularly that of Christianity and, to a lesser extent, Islam, where there is a tradition of elucidating the "six articles of faith" (*iman*). Though, of course, a critical study might be interested in ascertaining whether Muslim and Christian concepts of faith are even the same, at least from an historical perspective. Regardless, claims about faith ultimately are truth claims, and the goal of critical religious studies is not to accept such claims at face value, but to ascertain how such claims are constructed, by whom, and for what purpose is social life individualized as if inspired by a unique sort of inner sentiment.

In this volume see: authenticity, belief, essence, experience, ideology, orthodoxy, pluralism, religious literacy, sacred/profane, world religions

In *Religion in 50 More Words* see: animism, church, commentary, conversion, idol, initiation, mysticism, nones, piety, prayer, salvation, soul, theology, tradition

19 Function

Function, a term that was especially popular when the academic study of religion originated several generations ago, refers to a theoretical approach that is interested in explaining the work that religion, or being religious, is imagined to perform in society or for the individual. Functionalist approaches to religion are therefore interested neither in metaphysics nor in uncovering either the characteristic or the source of the experiential or the sacred, and, because of this, today such approaches are criticized by some in the field as reductionistic (i.e., failing to "take religion seriously," as the criticism is sometimes phrased). In distinction from those scholars whom we today commonly refer to as a group as Intellectualists (late-nineteenth-century scholars who consistently focused on determining the origins of religion), the shift to functionalism was nicely summed up early on by the early Polish anthropologist, Bronislaw Malinowski (1884–1942), writing in the Introduction to his study of the culture of Trobriand Islanders (off the eastern coast of New Guinea), *Argonauts of the Western Pacific* (1922): "in historical science, no one could expect to be seriously treated if he [sic] made any mystery of his sources and spoke of the past as if he knew it by divination." Instead, as he recommended, writing an ethnography neither meant speculating on origins nor reading static documents but, rather studying "the behavior and in the memory of living men [sic]." Today, the functionalist approach continues to comprise a widely shared framework for the human sciences, not to mention those who maintain that religion defies scholars' usual methods, inasmuch as the latter work is also often interested in determining religion's function. Here it might be worth noting the ambiguity of the term in the study of religion, for even more humanistically or even theologically inclined scholars are content to attribute that role of purpose to domains well outside those usually adopted by critical scholars, such as seeing religion's function as allowing human beings to express meanings or as evidence of God's grace. Nothing could be further, however, from the functionalism that today characterizes much of the social sciences.

The English term "function" derives from the classical Latin *functiōn-*, *functiō*, meaning the performance or execution of a task, and by the fourteenth century it could be employed to refer to a specifically religious ceremony. Interestingly, the academic study of religion, probably on account of its close relationship to such academic disciplines as Sociology and Anthropology (at least at its beginning), has chosen, as we shall see, to employ the term in the former sense and not the latter. The primary meaning of function is to denote a person's role in life, society, or within an organization; hence, its relation to one's employment, profession, or calling. Thus we read Thomas More (1478–1535) in his *The second parte of the confutacion of Tyndals answere in whyche is also confuted the chyrche that Tyndale deuyseth* (1533): "the sayntes be all departed hense & dede and be no lenger of our funccyon" (Book viii, cccclxxiiii). In this sense it could also refer to a duty attached to a role or an office, such as an official duty (often used in the plural). Thus the evangelical reformer Richard Taverner (1505–1575), in *On Saynt Andrewes Day Gospels* (1542): "Ye shal morouer vnder|stand, that there be angels and also archāgels that is to saye, chiefe or principall angels, and they haue distincte officies and seuerall functions wherby god almyghty exerciseth hys wonders" (from the section entitled, "On Michelmas daye," xxxiii). In the modern field of Biology, a "function" refers to a specific action that is performed by an organ or any other part of the body of a living organism, while it also includes the activity that is special, normal, or proper to that organ or other part of its body. As early as 1565, we read in John Hall's (1529–1568) translation of the text attributed to the medieval surgeon, Lanfranc of Milan (1250–1306), *A Most Excellent and Learned Woorke of Chirurgerie* [and Old French word for surgery]: "Y^e wormlike processe, called *Vermiformis epiphysis* [possibly in the cerebellum]: whose function is chiefly, to stoppe and open the pore, by contractinge together, or distending it selfe" (vol. I, 39). Although a scientific term, it could also be used to refute science, as we read in the chaplain Richard Bentley's (1662–1742) *A Confutation of Atheism from the Origin and Frame of the World*, a sermon that he preached at the Church of St. Mary-le-Bow in London on December 5, 1692: "If our Air had not been a ſpringy elaſtical Body, no Animal could have exercifed the very function of Refpiration" (see the third part of the set of sermons [1693, 28]).

Early-nineteenth-century functionalists in those fields that would later be understood as members of the social sciences tended to adopt this latter, biological usage of the term, and chose to imagine human societies as akin to higher organisms, wherein all organs and body parts—now resignified as social institutions—were understood to fulfill specific and separate functions in maintaining the health of the overall organism (i.e., society). Societies, and we will see this especially in the writings of the early sociologist,

Émile Durkheim (1858–1917), below, are held together on account of, or perhaps better in spite of, their dissimilar (and often *very* dissimilar) parts, each of which in its own way contributes to the collective life of the individuals contained within. Functionalism (a term that, like functionalist, steadily gains more use in English beginning in the 1920s) thus refers to the idea that all aspects of a society serve a discrete purpose and are each necessary for the survival of that society and, by extension, the integration and wellbeing of the individuals that comprise it.

Ascertaining the specific function of that part of the social known as religion played a large role in the formation of the academic study of religion and is what differentiates anthropological and sociological approaches to religion from, say, theological or philosophical ones, the latter tending to be more interested in the creation and study of truth claims themselves. On account of their interest in understanding and describing the prehistoric origins of religion, many early functional theories attempt to show what role or practical work religion performs in a given society. Since they are interested in religion writ large (i.e., in the singular), as opposed to specific religions (in the plural, i.e., what are often known as the world, or the world's, religions), functionalist theories of religion—not unlike phenomenology—are interested in ascertaining what they consider to be universal characteristics of belief and practice across time and geography. Unlike phenomenology, however, functionalist approaches often begin with what is sometimes known as "a hermeneutic of suspicion" (a term closely associated with the work of the French philosopher, Paul Ricoeur [1913–2005], though actually little used by him) meaning that the critical scholar assumes that practitioners of religion (just as with members of any group) do not necessarily or fully understand what they are doing. As a result, the descriptions that practitioners (among which we count theologians) might provide, though they can indeed be articulate, detailed, and rational attempts to make sense of what they understand themselves to be thinking and doing, fail, by definition, to take into account a variety of deeper, more complex, or generally unseen causes and implications. We think here of a classic example of early functionalism, that of the analytic psychologist, Sigmund Freud (1856–1939), whose theory of the human psyche presupposed that human beings are necessarily unaware of the unconscious sources and meanings of their actions.

Many in the academic study of religion find this "hermeneutic of suspicion" to be problematic, however, on account of the fact that it makes data of the self-understandings of the practitioners—seeing not just their actions but their self-reports about those actions as being in need of scholarly explanation. As already noted, this not infrequently leads to the charge that those who follow in an intellectual tradition associated with a scholar such as Freud take neither religion nor religious people "seriously," a judgment that functions as code for being too critical or insufficiently sympathetic. The critical student of religion, however, should recognize that, while the accounts practitioners and theologians provide should therefore be documented and studied carefully, reproducing or paraphrasing such reports by no means exhaust our analysis. The voices of practitioners, then, and the detailed documentation of their own declared reasoning or rationale for their actions, should not be mistaken for the terminus of scholarship in religion. This stands in opposition to those, like the still influential Wilfred Cantwell Smith (1916–2000), who claim that it should be, when he famously argued that, for a scholarly statement about religion to be true, it should be able to find favor in the eyes of practitioners. See his "Comparative Religion: Whither—and Why?" in the essay collection, *The History of Religions: Essays in Methodology* (1959, 31–58). Instead, people's carefully recorded and studied self-reports constitute data or examples for critical scholars, used in the service of their curiosities and the questions they bring to their research.

Functionalist theories of religion therefore begin from the premise that practitioner accounts are not in competition with, nor a complement to, those accounts that are offered by the scholar. We see this on clear display in Durkheim's still influential early work, *Les formes élémentaires de la vie religieuse* (1912; English: *The Elementary Forms of the Religious Life*), wherein he argued that religion plays a crucial role in both the creation and maintenance of human society. Using reports on Australian indigenous groups as his data and engaging in what later scholars called armchair ethnography (from the comfort of his Parisian office), he argued that a study of people living in such small-scale societies would, if generalized, shed light not on the origins of religion at the dawn of humanity (as his predecessors had done) but also on the role it plays in all groups—our own included. Hardly a supersessionist or social evolutionary theorist—that is, putting Christianity at the apex of religions with all others juxtaposed against it by the act of comparison and found wanting—Durkheim maintains that religion, that is, *all* religions, are "eminently social" because "religious representations are collective representations which express collective realities" (as phrased in Joseph Ward Swain's translation [1915], 22). Using this approach, Durkheim argued that religion has three major functions in society: (1) it provides social cohesion (and thus social solidarity) by means of providing an interrelated and shared set of rituals and beliefs for all its members; (2) it establishes social control to enforce morals and norms that further contribute to this cohesion; and (3) it offers shared meaning and purpose to members. This notion of social function, especially the latter notion of providing meaning to a group, was further picked up by Peter Berger

(1929–2017), the American sociologist who argued, in his once influential book, *The Social Construction of Reality* (1966), that every society wants its members to see its particular (and, by necessity, arbitrary or at least idiosyncratic) set of rules and regulations (what he calls "nomos," from the ancient Greek for law or custom) as objectively right and authoritative, and therefore as part of what they perceive as the natural order of existence, and thus something in need of internalization, let alone following. Society, for Berger, is therefore based on members acting *as if* their shared beliefs are necessary and inevitable, and in such a manner that an objective reality beyond our own appears to them to exist, something we have no ability to change. Within this context, the main function of religion is to show a society's members that its nomos is eternal and not chaotic. We also see this functionalist approach in the theory of Rodney Stark and William Sims Bainbridge's *Theory of Religion* (1980), wherein they develop the notion of "compensators," what they describe as the promise of a future reward that, though it cannot be tested empirically, nonetheless is imagined as tangible by members of a group in lieu of desired and actual rewards in the present.

With Ricoeur's notion of a hermeneutics of suspicion in mind, there may be no better classic example of a functionalist theory of religion than that of the German political theorist Karl Marx (1818–1883), who argued that society was defined by the relationships that its members needed to enter into, in order to produce the means of their daily survival (food, shelter, etc.). Within this context, religion—a belief in a god, an afterlife, etc., all of which, he argued, was the direct product of human alienation, caused by relationships of dominance and subservience—provided a temporary but, ultimately, unsuccessful relief to people's daily suffering. Thus his famous quote from the Introduction to the "Contribution to the Critique of Hegel's *Philosophy of Right*" (1844): "Religion is the sigh of the oppressed creature, the sentiment of a heartless world, and the soul of soulless conditions, it is the opium of the people" (see Robert C. Tucker's edition of *The Marx-Engels Reader* [1978], 53). From this quotation alone we can see how religion, for someone in Marx's tradition, represents an ideology that masked what he considered to be the real nature of social relations—conditions of which members of the group are, by definition, unaware (a lack of awareness presupposed by the very workings of such a system). Like Freud, then, Marx deemed religion to be an unnecessary aspect of human culture, one that would disappear after the abolition of a class-based, capitalist society and its replacement by a system grounded in equality and fairness. And so we have what eventually came to be known as the so-called secularization thesis, whose advocates, throughout the mid-twentieth century, predicted the increasing irrelevance of religion in the modern world (a version of the theory that has far fewer followers today, however).

In their "Functionalism Reconsidered" (*History of Religions* 23/4 [1984]: 372–381), Robert McCauley and E. Thomas Lawson seek to make a renewed case for functionalism in our field—owing to what they call its "explanatory suggestiveness" (373)—by connecting it not to the field of sociology or anthropology, but to that of evolutionary biology. The two are, in many ways, responding to Hans Penner's *The Poverty of Functionalism* (*History of Religions* 11 [1971]: 91–97), which argued that functional explanations of religion, far from explaining the category, are based on a faulty "if-then" assumption, namely, that religion intentionally causes its function, say, social maintenance. Penner—an ardent critic of phenomenological approaches but also suspect of functionalism—further argued, by using an example, that a religious individual who believes that he has been bewitched does not believe that his "bewitchment" is the result of offending the social order or some social authority, but of his having offended the gods or spirits (95). Again, though, we return to the thorny issue of description, interpretation, and ultimately understanding in the study of religion: just because a religious practitioner does not admit to something, does not necessarily make it untrue.

Returning to the use of the term in biology, as seen above, McCauley and Lawson—themselves pivotal in the development of what is today known as the Cognitive Science of Religion (CSR)—argue that functional explanations have the utility of identifying the structures that "account for the fitness of the organism within the containing system at hand" with the ultimate goal of ascertaining "the causal laws which underlie the functional integration of the overall system" (377). Despite the suggestion by McCauley and Lawson, in addition to other theorists associated today with CSR, functionalism is, at least as strictly associated with its earlier, classic form, out of fashion in the study of religion. However, it cannot be gainsaid that the claim, on the part of many scholars of religion, that religion plays a crucial role in society is, to paraphrase the early anthropologist, E. B. Tylor (1832–1917), a "survival," or an idea that has been carried unwittingly into a new context. While perhaps not as obsessed with origins as earlier theorists, the idea that religion—though now often left amorphous, as opposed to defining it clearly and demonstrating how it actually works—defines a particular social group or gives society meaning is certainly related to much work taking place today. Left unqueried in such claims—as is so often the case—is the very term that is supposed to be the operative one, to wit, "religion." Undefined, imprecise—hardly exemplary of how earlier functionalists approached the task of definition—the term nonetheless is assumed to play an active role in both history and society. While the days of grand theories of religion that emphasize either their origin or even the function of religion in society at large may well be behind us, functionalism still provides a useful lens to examine how certain historical actors have used religious discourses, e.g., to justify any number of social acts, from the high-minded to the murderous, let alone how some now understand religion to be a source for resistance to such domineering tendencies. But perhaps most important, functionalism also reminds us that it is not the job of the critical scholar of religion simply to engage in description and mere paraphrasing of participant accounts, because there are a variety of other, more analytic, ways to engage data that people describe as "religious."

In this volume see: critical, description, explanation, phenomenology, society, world religions

In *Religion in 50 More Words* see: emic/etic, symbol, understanding

20 Gender

Inasmuch as some today understand the study of religion to be a field and not a discipline (the latter often presumed to have a unified method and object of study) it could also be described as an area study, i.e., a cross-disciplinary exercise focused on a specific topic, such as Latin American Studies or Asian Studies. Among the modern academic fields commonly grouped with other area studies is Gender Studies, suggesting that academic studies of gender, understood as an identity and traditionally distinguished from biological sex or even sexual orientation, can be considered to have something in common with the field commonly known as Religious Studies. This is especially the case given the fact that religion is also considered as an identity claimed by people in specific and negotiable situations. Given that human subjects are presumed to be sites of overlapping (and, at times, contesting or even contradictory) identities, drawing on studies of gender has, especially over the past few academic generations, added much-needed nuance to the study of religion. While this should be self-evident, we must not forget that, throughout much of the history of scholarship, men were not only the ones doing much of the research (and thus posing the questions that the research was designed to answer) but also the ones on whom much of the research was carried out (and thus the people answering the researcher's questions). Given the basic role that ascriptions of gender play in how members of groups classify and further subdivide themselves, a study of religion that fails to take gender into account, or one that fails to account for developments in Gender Studies, is likely one that is out of step with some of the most interesting contemporary scholarship.

But all of this begs the misleadingly simple question: what is gender? The noun itself derives from the Old French *gendre* (linked to the origins of the modern English term "genre"), broadly naming what is considered to be a class of items that are alike, whether objects or people, or even referring to offspring (e.g., the Middle French verb *genrer*, to beget or to engender, linked to the English "to generate" and "generation"). Eventually, its history can be traced to the Latin *genus* and the prior ancient Greek *génos*, naming what we today designate not just as kind, stock, or clan but also as what we moderns might now mean by race. Genus (plural genera) is also part of modern biological classification, subdividing the higher ranking of Families and itself further subdivided into Species. Sometime after the fourteenth century we find the French term *genre humain* used for what we might today name as the human race or simply humanity. The term "gender" entered the English language during the medieval Anglo-Norman era (twelfth century onwards) further specifying a difference between masculine and feminine traits within a couple of hundred years. We see, for example, in the medieval (mid-fifteenth-century) English dramas known as *The Towneley Plays* (in play 30, "The Judgment") the character Primus Demon who asks: "has thou oght Writen there / of the femynyn gendere?" (line 161). By the mid- and late twentieth century it had become routine for scholars to distinguish sex (also a term of French and Latin origin) from gender. The former becomes associated with what is understood to be biological and therefore anatomical traits, while the latter is linked to behaviors said to have been conditioned by society. This, of course, could lead to the possibility of a person being, for example, a biological male yet either exhibiting or adopting traits stereotypically deemed feminine, and vice versa. This makes plain the now common association, at least for many, of the terms "male/female" with the realm of sex while "masculine/feminine" are often used to denote gender, with only the latter thought by some to name contingent distinctions of social origin or consequence. Given the now close relationship between the terms sex and gender, though they are each used to name different aspects of the human, it makes sense that the frequency of their usage closely parallels each other, at least since the mid-twentieth century. However, the fact that individuals are routinely born with what was once called ambiguous sex characteristics (whether impacting their chromosomes, hormones, or even genitalia), placing them in a classification today known as intersex, indicates that even this modern complicating of our ideas of sex and gender does not adequately grapple with human variety. Intersex babies in some societies have routinely undergone surgery, often very early in life, so that their anatomy forcibly matches one of the two genders, while in yet other groups they are granted a privileged ritual status and understood as having "a third gender." This should make us pause to consider just how important traditional ideas of gender as well as sex have been in how human beings manage their populations.

The work of the American cultural anthropologist Margaret Mead (1901–1978) stands as a helpful example of research on sex and gender as carried out at a time when rather more weight was being placed on the human differences that each could name. Consider, for example, her two books *Sex and Temperament in Three Primitive Societies* (1935) and *Male and Female* (1949). The former work, based on research began in 1931, focused on the childhood to adult lives of people from three different groups in the Sepik river region of Papua New Guinea—the Arapesh, the Mundugumor, and the Tchambuli (now known as the Chambri), with each group exhibiting its own approach to the gender roles and all differing from the specifically American roles with which Mead (as well as her readers) was already familiar. In the preface to the 1950 edition, she writes: "I wanted to talk about the way each of us belongs to a sex and has a temperament, a temperament shared with others of our own sex *and* others of the opposite sex." Her interests concerned the long-standing debate between nature and nurture, as it is often phrased, i.e., the degree to which human characteristics and behavior are either innate or learned. Across the two books her conclusion is, simply put, both. Peggy Reeves Sandy, an anthropologist from the University of Pennsylvania, summarizes this in an *American Anthropologist* article entitled "Margaret Mead's View of Sex Roles in Her Own and Other Societies" (82/2 [1980]: 340–348). According to her, "Mead demonstrated the enormous variability in cultural definitions of maleness and femaleness" in the first book, whereas in the second she argued that "cultural variability in sex roles was founded on 'primary sex differences' conditioned by the reproductive functions and anatomical differences between the sexes" (340). In other words, Mead concluded that both biology (i.e., each sex's role in reproduction) and society (e.g., an adult criticizing a boy for "throwing like a girl") play a role, with variations and unforeseen possibilities resulting in behaviors (possibly extending well beyond just a so-called third gender), all due to the interplay between these two different constraints on the developing identity.

From this early work it is not difficult to understand how, in scholarship today, we frequently find research that complicates the once taken for granted binary between male and female, including the far too simplistic assumption that that gender and sex necessarily coincide. Two of the most influential books on this topic have certainly been Judith Butler's *Gender Trouble: Feminism and the Subversion of Identity* (1990) and *Bodies That Matter: On the Discursive Limits of Sex* (1993). Butler, following in the footsteps of Simone de Beauvoir and Luce Irigaray, argues that gender roles, i.e., presenting as masculine or feminine, are learned and therefore adaptable performances, filtering this through the lens of the drag performer, among others. This thesis pressed so-called second wave feminism of the mid- and later twentieth century considerably further, calling into question the long-assumed idea of an essential core of femaleness or femininity (for which one could advocate, for example), let alone maleness or masculinity. Gendered identity could now be understood as resting on a wide variety of factors that result in one identity among and intersecting with a variety of others, with those others linked to region, generation, race, and economic status, to name just a few domains. Butler's work goes even further, however, by questioning whether sex is a natural, biological constant, coming to see it, much as with gender, as an acquired and changeable performance. We witness this in contemporary debates on whether transgender women (people assigned a male identity at birth but who, for a variety of reasons, later come to identify as women) are "real" women. This oftentimes revolves around legislative action, e.g., to limit who can use which public restroom (with conservative politicians sometimes basing the law's assignment on the sex that was assigned to a person on their birth certificate). We also see this in athletic governing bodies that might require medical tests to confirm that a competitor is actually a biological female. Such examples make plain the continued relevance of this sort of scholarly analysis—not least because there is no single trait or empirical characteristic that settles the debate over one's sex or gender. In fact, the malleability of our ideas over sex and gender have shifted in recent years to the use of pronouns in the public sphere, e.g., whether one wants to be referred to as "he," "she," or "them."

Such critical analysis of gender is but one example of the more recent move toward seeing identity as an always negotiable and developing attribute, rather than a static and inner quality simply projected outward and into the world. Such an approach challenges a number of seemingly settled facts of day-to-day life that have long been authorized by their association to the traditionally opposed, but mutually defining, poles of the male/female binary. In the study of religion this trend in critical scholarship on sex/gender as an identity has had a significant impact, in part because of already-mentioned assumptions about the centrality of male leadership in the communities that are usually under study. That groups commonly designated as religious take full advantage of the same sort of gender stereotyping to assign and regulate their members' roles and spheres of influence further persuades some that religion is not privileged, ahistorical, and somehow set apart from its surrounding culture (as many have asserted) but, instead, is but one more element within it. This, in turn, has led increasingly to the study of subgroups other than those already authorized to speak on behalf of the group and its texts, practices, and traditions (often its elite men). We now therefore see a more common focus on studying underrepresented women and their roles within religions, which includes showing how assumptions and practices concerning both (or now, better put, all) genders help to structure the limits of the group itself. Contemporary work on gender and/in religion has, thus, proved to be a quickly growing area in the field. In fact, the once popular "add women and stir" model, one that was previously adopted as a way to increase representation, is itself now criticized for its failure to theorize the conditions in which members of groups are designated a sex/gender and how these designations are employed to police populations—with so-called third and, today, fourth wave feminism greatly complicating prior feminists' assumptions about merely empowering women politically. Thus work is now being done on how the very assumption of a gendered binary, let alone the once popular biology vs. culture division, makes certain sorts of social life possible.

The issue for the critical scholar of religion, then, is not simply amassing more studies of women and religion, a still popular course title. For as important as greater representation of the variety of social actors may be, approaches to studying women in Islam and women in Buddhism or, more generally, women's roles in worship services or within the religious community at large, can leave untheorized why the rest of the curriculum unproblematically focuses on men via studying *their* spheres and *their* cultural productions as if they were natural and therefore ungendered. In place of such an approach, we point to studies that integrate the wider findings of more recent identity studies to address the broad range of sometimes overlapping or even contradictory roles people play in their social worlds from situation to situation—including being designated and then treated and even managed *as* male or female and *as* masculine or feminine—always being careful to understand these designations as being strategic and situated techniques used by social actors for specific purposes (including what goes on in the scholar's own society and among members of their own field, of course). K. Merinda Simmons therefore asks the important question, in a review essay on resources for teaching the traditional Women and Religion course: "just what are 'women' and 'religion,' and do these tropes change when cast in the same conversation?" (*Journal of the American Academy of Religion* 78/2 [2010]: 543). Critical scholars can join her by answering, "what women and religion *are* is always a question of who is defining them" (561). This forces us to switch our gaze, once again, from seemingly stable persons or identities in the world to the way that people in discrete settings, including scholars themselves, strategically arrange, sort, and then value the contents of their world for practical effect.

In this volume see: classification, critical, definition, essence, function, identity, race, society

In *Religion in 50 More Words* see: emic/etic, sexuality, tradition

21 History

Arthur McCalla, the Canadian scholar of religion, once posed a question in the title of an article: "When Is History Not History?"—to which he responds: when it is the history of religions (*Historical Reflections* 20/3 [1994]: 435–452). The historical record has long posed a problem for the academic study of religion on account of the fact that history (i.e., the accumulated record of past events which left some tangible evidence of having taken place) has taken on a merely supporting role, subservient to what some scholars maintain should be the elucidation of the universal and thus ahistorical meaning of the sacred and its role in helping us to understand religious experience. But if the study of religion is itself understood as a human exercise predicated on other human exercises and productions, then the role of history and the historical record should play a far more prominent role. Despite how familiar this English word "history" has become, in that it is now a word of common vocabulary, it will therefore require more careful redefinition if it is to be a useful term in a critical vocabulary.

History, in its earliest sense, was a narrative recounting of events that could easily be akin to what we now designate as fiction—something to be distinguished sharply from writing a history, at least for many today. The word came into the English language from Latin (*historia*) and Old French (*istorie*), both of which have the sense of a story of past events comprised of a narrative account. In early English usage, history and story (derived from the same root words) were used interchangeably to offer accounts either of imaginary events or those thought to be true—the modern sense of history had obviously not yet developed. Unfortunately, however, some in the study of religion continue to use the term in both senses. It was only in the late fifteenth century that the two nouns diverge so that history came to refer to an account of past *real* or *actual* events (i.e., historical events), which would subsequently be associated with what would later emerge as the academic discipline of History that many of us today take for granted as part of the modern university. We arrive at a split in terminology and meaning, then, with "history" naming the organized and systematic knowledge of the past, and a "story" signifying less formal narrative accounts concerning imaginary or fictive events.

As McCalla agues, the field of religion has struggled with the notion of history. This is all the more remarkable since one of its major subfields is, after all, commonly called in English the "*history* of religions." Mircea Eliade (1907–1986), who popularized this term for North American audiences (and thus the name of the field as still practiced at the University of Chicago's Divinity School), seems largely uninterested in history—understood as chronological time and thus the domain of natural and contingent events. This is perhaps not surprising given the fact that history represents, for him, "profane" time on account of the fact that it is understood as linear and can therefore not be repeated—something that is imagined throughout his work to be the hallmark of archaic religion and thus the paradigmatic worldview of the so-called *homo religiosus* (i.e., the religious human). Time is meaningful, he argues, when it is sanctified and can thus be repeated by the believer—such as, he would argue, in a ritual that re-enacts a moment of origins, which enables the participant to enter into sacred time. In and of itself, however, linear time or history holds no significance and, if anything, its untethered, contingent nature leads to the phrase he uses in his 1949 book, *Le Mythe de l'éternel retour: archétypes et repetition* (translated into English in 1954 as *The Myth of the Eternal Return or, Cosmos and History*): the terrors of history. This is evident in the many writings of Eliade wherein we frequently encounter extended musings on the structure of the sacred, punctuated by the briefest of historical points, often selected from dramatically different periods and regions such that their context and specificity are not nearly as important as is his interest to generalize from what he saw to be their shared, essential character. Such examples from the historical and ethnographic record are meant to underscore his theory, but the former are usually so vague and decontextualized that they are of little analytical value. This is exemplified in his use of historical examples in his *Patterns in Comparative Religion*, first published as *Traité d'histoire des religions* 1948). His overwhelming emphasis, as it was for so many of the generation he trained, is on understanding the morphology (from the Greek for the study of shape or form) of hierophanies, theophanies, and kratophanies (i.e., manifestations of the sacred, gods, and powers, respectively), to wit, what he characterized as irruptions of the sacred into profane time. We see subsequent criticism of this emphasis in the works of those like his onetime doctoral advisee, Bruce Lincoln, whose later work, though equally interested in myth and ritual, for example, is much more attuned to and therefore concerned with historical and regional specificity of the items and peoples under study. Lincoln therefore argues, in his pithy but important "Theses on Method" (*MTSR* 8/3 [1996]: 225–227), that the categorical confusion endemic to the "history of religions" can be clarified if we remember that history is the method of study and religion the object of study. As he notes there, in the first of his 13 thesis statements: "The conjunction 'of' that joins the two nouns in the disciplinary ethnonym 'History of Religions' is not neutral filler." Instead, as he immediately goes on: "it announces a proprietary claim and a relation of encompassment."

Despite Lincoln's rigorously researched interventions, however, the academic study of religion continues, for the large part, to resist history. Instead, it replaces such a concern with an emphasis on determining the contours of non-historical essences and the subsequent deployment of a set of rather ahistorical terms and categories (i.e., using the term "myth" or "tradition" as if they name something unique in the item so designated rather than seeing them as the scholar's own tools that name something the scholar wishes to isolate in the items so designated). Despite Eliade's work seeming to represent a much earlier phase in the field's history, it is highlighted here as exemplary of continuing problems in the field because it is representative of what still takes place in many of its classrooms and publications. Juxtaposed against this, critical scholars might note that detail-oriented historical work that avoids taking sides in the apologetic debates (those in which the people we study are understandably engaged) provides an important antidote to such tendencies because such work forces us to localize and contextualize our data—purposefully seeing it *as* data, i.e., as something the scholar has decided to focus on, and thus not as the authentic expressions or instances of the lives or meanings of the people under study. Within this context, history, more than anything else in our conceptual toolbox, ought to prevent critical scholars from making overarching generalizations and invoking ahistorical categories that include theological or quasi-theological baggage (e.g., claims about a transcendent quality often known as human nature or the enduing human spirit). For instance, rather than examine the generic category, religious experience, it would be much more productive to understand the history and practical, contestable implications of making such claims in, say, the political sphere (e.g., taking seriously the practical utility of claims about a non-verifiable, private sentiment). However, instead of such attention to detail and material conditions, there is an unfortunate tendency, that yet continues, to assume that those groupings usually known as religions possess essences that move—Hegelian-like—throughout history, manifesting themselves in various times and places, in differing forms, all with some underlying unity that only the careful scholar can intuit. Such an already discredited phenomenological model, yet one still very much in vogue regardless of the approach's current name, potentially ignores the conflict and creativity that goes on as various actors and groups seek to define and legitimate themselves and others by appealing to concepts that they understand as "authentic religious teachings" or "perennial wisdom of the ages." The issue, of course, is not whether they are or are not authentic, as if a standard could be found to help us to judge which forms of Hinduism or Islam are truly extremist or orthodox, but, rather, the various ways in which they are *imagined* and then *authorized* to be—something always taking place in a competitive setting. Many in religious studies unfortunately confuse the former for the latter, judging by the way in which they continue to preoccupy their work with studying "mainline religion" as opposed to its marginal deviants or forms that have "hijacked their religion." (On the latter, see the helpful essay collection, *Hijacked: A Critical Treatment of the Public Rhetoric of Good and Bad Religion*, edited by Leslie Dorrough Smith, Steffen Führding, and Adrian Hermann [2020].)

This certainly does not mean that we should all be historical positivists—a once common stance which took its task to be the accurate and descriptively neutral representation of past events, without interpreting them—nor is it to deny that we should refrain from theorizing or analyzing our datasets. After all, some of the most interesting work in the past decades in the academic study of history, in particular the subfield that studies history writing itself (i.e., historiography), came on the heels of such scholars as Hayden White (1928–2018). He argued that it was not insignificant that the modern literary genre of the novel developed at roughly the same time in the nineteenth century as the modern sense of writing a histories, all of which came around a time when newly developing modern mass identities, known as nation-states, were in need of a development narrative that seemingly led directly to them (a way of authorizing the new by linking it to the seemingly self-evident past). This narrativization implied that the positivist view of writing on the past effectively hid the manner in which historians were themselves the ones who were making the selections from the almost limitless archive of past doings and crafting the narratives that linked items to each other as if they necessarily were in relationships of prior-cause-to-later-effect. We adopt the phrase "archive of the past" from the anthropologist Michel-Rolph Trouillot (1949–2012), especially his still influential *Silencing the Past: Power and the Production of History* (1995). Increasingly we see the necessity on the part of careful historians to recognize their own role in the creation and use of historical narratives, much like careful anthropologists now recognize that they pose the questions, representative of their own curiosities, that elicit the answers that eventually make their way into the ethnographies that they themselves write—seemingly about other people's culture. (In terms of the latter, see James Clifford and George E. Marcus's once groundbreaking essay collection, *Writing Culture: The Poetics and Politics of Ethnography* [1986].) The point that we wish to draw attention to is the problems that result when ahistorical and uncritical categories take precedence over historical (i.e., contingent and contestable) particulars. When, for instance, contemporary ecumenicists, for example (those interested in studying religion so as to identify universal sameness), appeal to the "Golden Age" of tolerance witnessed in a place such as tenth- and eleventh-century Cordoba in Muslim Spain, they are rarely interested in the specifics or the historical details of the interactions among those whom we today identify and group together as Jews, Christians, and Muslims (the so-called Abrahamic religions—yet another undertheorized and ahistorical term). If anything, the often-messy details often get in the way of a good interfaith story of mutual understanding and respect. Instead, we witness appeals to anachronistic categories that carry much valence in the modern world (such as "tolerance" or "interfaith dialogue"), but that clearly would have had little or no meaning in the time in question.

We should thus be aware that history is rarely just about the past, or whatever past we can infer something about based on the material items that happen to remain today. It is, instead, also about the present—or should we say the presents, in the plural, since each contemporary subject position may tell a different narrative of how some particular past led to them and just them today. It is also about a future that each of those presents anticipates, a tomorrow that supposedly exists in some sort of linear relationship with the past they have chosen to highlight. Witness, for example, those multi-volume "histories of the German People" produced by German historians during the Romantic period—a time when modern German national identity was being forged and local identities among various German-speaking groups were being merged into one via such grand historical narratives. In that context, history was what enabled diverse thinkers and their readers to imagine themselves *as* a nation—as if they were all the product of a common and uncontested past, something that, or so it was then argued, ought to lead to renewal in the present, and a glorious future. Despite claims to science (German *Wissenschaft*) and objectivity in the newly developing historical discipline, such works were rarely anything but disinterested.

Another genre of history writing that is seen as related directly to the present, perhaps one confined to the study of religion, is one that imagines a pristine past that has been subsequently corrupted by later generations. It is not uncommon to read, for example, scholarly accounts that try to show how, say, at the time of Jesus or Muhammad, there was gender equality, something that was subsequently rejected and excised from the tradition on account of later male elites, a variation on the once prominent, anti-Papal "nasty priestcraft" theme. In the subfield of Islamic studies, for example, virtually every single contemporary virtue (gender justice, gay-friendly, ecological, interfaith, to name but a few) has been projected backward onto the early Islamic community, in an apologetic effort to show that in order "to move forward" we need a roadmap from the "historical record."

Here, it might be worth distinguishing between history and what has traditionally been termed salvation history (once commonly known by scholars via the German term, *Heilsgeschichte*): the story of God's grace unfolding in history, as often studied by scholars of the Hebrew Bible and the New Testament. There is a deep-seated tendency in the study of religion to conflate the two so that stories found in, e.g., the Christian bible, the Hindu *Ramayana*, Buddhist Pali canon, etc., can be assumed to have actually happened the way they are recounted therein. We often see books and articles written as if their authors knew the motives and intentions of figures recounted in these texts, as if we today knew, from our careful reading of the historical record as we have it today, what they were thinking as they went about their affairs. Or, especially in the case with early Islam, as if our earliest sources (all of which are much later than the events in question) offered stenographic reports of things people really said. Indeed, we see this all across scholarship, e.g., in the field of Classics where modern editions or interpretations of works from antiquity sometimes fail to make evident that not only do originals to these texts often not exist but that the text as we know it today has come down through multiple fragments, sometimes in multiple languages, and often dating to several centuries after the supposed original, which has been lost, leaving us no standard whatsoever against which to compare our modern attempts at reconstruction.

The Cognitive Science of Religion (CSR) represents the latest subfield to sometimes ignore history. Since many therein argue that religion is a biological or a neurological phenomenon, they can maintain that there is little or no need to examine the historical or textual record and instead focus their interests on living subjects in the laboratory. Consider the current *Database of Religious History* (DRH), for example, which is described as "the world's first comprehensive online quantitative and qualitative encyclopedia of religious cultural history." Searches in the online DRH are done according to topic, name, or group, and the results are anything but historically specific. They reveal mere descriptions and unnuanced comments with little to no interest in history or the historical record. Once again, if indeed further proof was needed, we witness the shoddy use of history within the academic study of religion, presumably because the eternal subject matter—religion—is deemed to be more important than the methods that conjure it into existence.

There is a common practice in the study of religion to spend the first week of an undergraduate course reinforcing that what the students are about to engage in is the academic and historical study of religion and *not* theology. After the first week, however, this issue is often retired and replaced with detailed descriptions of what are portrayed as the obviously religious beliefs and practices of others, including the simple repetition of a salvation history (i.e., the participant's own self-narrative of their group's origins) as if it were history, often in ways that might prompt those students who might claim membership in a particular religion to nod their heads in assent. The last week of the class may then witnesses the reappearance of the phrase "academic" or "objective" once again, whereupon there is a repetition of the difference between theology and religious studies. This would be tantamount to historians saying to their classes that they study history, not salvation history, and then subsequently spending the rest of the semester reproducing the contours of the latter (such as studying the supposedly irresistible and inevitable development of specific nation-states in ways that their own members tell the tale), before subsequently ending the course emphasizing the former once again. This confusion of purpose and intent, to reinvoke McCalla's opening comments, means that, often, history is not historical, let alone critical, in the study of religion.

In this volume see: authenticity, critical, culture, description, essence, experience, phenomenology, politics, sacred/profane, theory, world religions

In *Religion in 50 More Words* see: commentary, creation/endtimes, emic/etic, founder, hagiography, tradition, understanding

22 Identity

We frequently encounter the descriptive study of identity in the study of religion—a linkage indebted for some to the influential work of the Jamaican culture studies theorist, Stuart Hall (1932–2014). However, theorizing on how those things commonly referred to *as* identities are possible—and thereby historicizing the situations in which something called an identity is produced and claimed, and, in many cases, eventually so authorized as to be seen and represented as an essential trait or quality—is often neglected in favor of describing the features or limits of something called an identity. Critical scholars' likely inclination to pursue the latter over the former means that they will probably approach some of the scholarship on identity as data in need of further analysis. We see this, for example, in the work of Kimberlé Williams Crenshaw, the critical race theorist who coined the term "intersectionality" (in a 1989 paper, "Demarginalizing the Intersection of Race and Sex"), and who saw identity as far more complex than just having a gender, *or* a race, *or* a class, etc.. Instead, identity comes to be seen as what happens when the prior structures that allow us to be any one of those things intermixes with all others, making any subject position a more complicated experience than previously assumed. Witness, for example, how the ill-defined adjective "religious" is often used to modify the noun, as if a supposedly religious identity could (or even should) be differentiated from other sorts of identities (i.e., economic, gendered, generational, racial, regional, etc.). The turn toward identity studies has, in recent decades, impacted virtually all fields in the human sciences, often with a focus on how group members already understand and represent themselves—both their commonalities with those seen as their peers and their collective differences from those seen by them as outsiders. Such scholarship often highlights marginalized groups that are often overlooked in scholarship by aiming to register their existence, their distinctiveness, and their worth, sometimes in the context of long histories of scholarship that was openly antagonistic to the interests of their members. The history of scholars

DOI: 10.4324/9781003140184-23

simply condescending toward various peoples or subgroups, notably those once seen by earlier scholars as being inferior or even deviant, is something that critical scholars will certainly continue to address. We think here of the once prevalent scholarly terms "primitive" and "uncivilized savages," not to mention how the designators "fundamentalist" and "extremist" are often used in descriptive scholarship today, though carrying out (often undisclosed) normative, socially formative work in which scholars themselves sometimes have deep investments. However, carrying out this work in any way other than taking all claims of identity seriously as always human and situated, and thus historical and cultural productions, strikes us as continuing a long history of taking a paternalistic stance toward the other—whether one happens to have affinities for the members of such groups or not. Instead, the critical scholar will probably be interested in studying identity (including scholarly efforts to establish a ranked system of identities by means of their own work, including how they sort and identify members of their own profession as well) as always being active and contingent processes of identification, carefully aiming to distinguish the outcomes of such procedures from the conditions and actions that made them possible. (This is argued, for example, throughout the essays collected in the volume *Fabricating Identities* [2017].)

It is with all of this in mind that the careful reader may now recognize that many of this volume's entries have specified that, as just noted above, people *claim* this or that as opposed to maintaining that, for instance, they *believe* something. The difference is not mere semantics. Instead, it signals two competing approaches to the study of identity and makes plain the side that this volume has adopted. For one phrasing focuses on the discursive object (i.e., a supposedly inner disposition or individual mental state called a belief or an experience) while the other takes seriously that all we have are actors making claims about themselves and others, and doing so from within practical, historical, and social settings. The latter focus, then, is on the observable actions of people in specific sorts of situations who respond to, and thereby impact, their context by making claims about a variety of things. Case in point: it is highly likely that anyone reading this is not, at this moment, self-consciously reflecting on their national identity (an identity, by the way, that is a fairly recent invention, given the span of human history). Yet, if placed in a situation where being, for instance, Irish or Chilean was not simply assumed or was being openly contested, then we might expect such things to become evident as demonstrations of what are often termed their national pride—from songs and styles of clothing to flag-waving, languages, and styles of cooking. Thus, by placing the emphasis on *claiming* to believe something, this nonempirical thing that we commonly designate as a belief is historicized and thereby redescribed as the outcome of a series of contingent events, with precursors and implications of their own that can also be studied. Or, making a turn back toward the identities that many of us commonly assume ourselves and others to possess and only subsequently to express in public, we could follow the French Africanist, Jean-François Bayart's *L'Illusion identitaire* (1996; *The Illusion of Cultural Identity* [2005]). "There is no such thing as identity," Bayart argues, no doubt somewhat counterintuitively for many of his readers, "only operational acts of identification." He then continues: "The identities we talk about so pompously, as if they existed independently of those who express them, are made (and unmade) only through the mediation of such identificatory acts, in short, by their enunciation" (92; the equally important work of the American sociologist, Rogers Brubaker [b. 1956], also comes to mind, as crucial for developing this alternative approach, e.g., his book *Ethnicity Without Groups* [2006]). To study such tactical, operational acts, or what Bayart also terms the enunciation of an identity, we must therefore study actors in settings where things are being negotiated and thus where something is at stake, rather than merely studying the products of their discourse as if, to repeat the above quotation, "they existed independently of those who express them." In this way the critical shift in identity studies benefits from a much earlier Marxist insight concerning the need to not mistake the finished good for an autonomous or inherently valuable commodity by overlooking the situated, human labor that made it, values it, and then exchanges it.

To make this shift we would benefit from considering how this noun "identity," and the related but slightly more recent verb "identify" (i.e., to demarcate, specify, or disclose), have changed over time. Entering English in the mid-sixteenth century, from the variously spelled Middle French *identité* but also from the earlier Latin *identitas*, the term was originally used to name the conclusion that two things not only shared a similarity but were, in fact, the same, as in the related adjective "identical," dating from the same period. Thus, identity's early synonym is sameness, as was evident in Rev. John Gauden (1605–1662), the onetime Bishop of Worchester, writing in his *Ecclefia, Anglicanæ Sufpiria: The Sighs of the Church of England* (1649): "So the reducing of Miniſters to ſome unity in their judgments, to uniformity in their Miniſtrations, to an identity or fameneſſe for their Miniſteriall power and ordination . . ." (445). Or again: "I cannot remember a thing that happened a year ago," wrote the Scottish philosopher, Thomas Reid (1710–1796), in an essay entitled "Of Memory" in his *Essays on the Intellectual Powers of Man* (1785), "without a conviction as strong as memory can give, that I, the same identical person who now remember that event, did then exist" (213, citing the abridged 3rd edition of 1852). This example nicely illustrates that a word that once named a trait or quality judged to be shared in common by, and thus constant between, two items. Here, we could also cite the English clergyman, Rev. Martin Fotherby (d. 1620), writing in his posthumously published treatise denouncing atheism, *Atheomastix: Clearing Foure Truthes, against Atheists and Infidels* (1622): "The soule is delighted with variety. It is dulled with identity" (Book II, chpt. xi, 325). Here, the term names that which is assumed to be the constant and thus defining trait of a person, regardless of changes in time and place. In this usage it is therefore easily equated with that which is presumed to be something's or someone's enduring substance or uniform essence. We certainly find the earlier usage when, in *Neeley's History of the Parliament of Religions and Religious Congresses at the World's Columbian Exposition* (1894), Rev. E. T. Rexford describes religious identity as the "[p]rimal unity where man appears as the child of God before he is a Christian or Jew, Brahman or Buddhist, Mohammedan or Parsee, Confucian, Taoist or ought beside" (205). However, the modern or likely more familiar usage of the term would conclude that in each of his examples there resides a distinct and possibly incomparable identity of its own, indicating that, as with beauty in the old saying (widely credited, by the way, to the Irish novelist, Margaret Wolfe Hungerford [1855–1897]), identity is not just in the eye of the beholder but is always a product of a comparative perspective that establishes similarities and differences in the items under consideration.

As Thomas Reid's above quotation makes plain, then, the now familiar act of gazing at an old photograph of a young child and then saying "That's me" entails a fairly complex set of assumptions and assertions regarding what we might now refer to as personal identity being a permanent acquisition of sameness, unaffected by obvious changes in time, appearance, or situation. Should this be the manner in which the term is used—and thus "to identify" means to determine the specific feature that distinguishes something from other things (e.g., being identified as a suspect by the authorities or "producing identification")—then identity remains a rather undertheorized, seemingly private quality that is simply assumed to be expressed outwardly or performed publicly. Apart from describing the supposed enduring features of that sameness, in sometimes rich detail, the only issue that may remain of interest to scholars approaching it in this manner is how one changes that identity, and thus, at least in the study of religion, we arrive at the common interest in studying conversion. If, however, this impression of permanence is seen as a social product itself, then studying identity implies examining the situations and wider structures that make it possible for someone to be seen and treated in this rather than that way—and thereby to self-perceive themselves as well. For to identify is now seen to be a form of labor, invested in moderating the inevitable differences of historical existence, all in order to produce the image of sameness and constancy. Thus, we arrive at the classic example of a retiree suddenly feeling aimless, lonely, and depressed, all linked to lacking the sense of self that they may have previously taken for granted, given that the once regular schedule, duties, and social setting that defined them (i.e., their career or job) is now wholly absent. Or, at the other end of spectrum, consider the tremendous focus and resources that modern universities place on what are now often called their divisions of student life, by means of which they hope to transform incoming undergraduate students, abruptly displaced from social networks and support systems at home, by helping them to craft a new sense of self in their new surroundings, often by means of encouraging them to get involved in various campus groups and activities outside class (thereby being integrated into new social networks). Returning to an aside from just above, conversion from one religion to another becomes an interesting topic but in new ways, such as studying how increasingly overlapping social networks account for how people gradually come to claim a new identity. This is all more complicated than, as participants themselves often report, making an instantaneous change in membership because of, at least as they represent it, a persuasive argument from an evangelist at their door or because of their agreement with some doctrinal issue or belief.

This shift to seeing self-reports of identity as evidence of the internalized remains of a prior series of public and always social processes (instead of approaching it as an individual and thus internal issue), is akin to the critical shift seen across many of the key terms included in this volume. We saw this, for example, in studying experience as a residue of a prior social situation rather than a pristine inner sentiment that is only later projected outward and expressed. Or it is akin to studying religion itself as a social designation created by the implementation of rule systems (which establish the sacred/profane zones—zones whose existence is left unexamined if scholars merely describe the so-called religious identities that they produce) rather than an inner affectation known only to the so-called believer. What we might term the personalistic model is so widely shared by scholars of religion that it likely accounts for why the sociologist Sean Everton finds that even "[s]ociologists of religion often treat social networks as an afterthought as well. A review of five leading introductory texts to the sociology of religion . . . turned up no mention of social networks in the table of contents or the indexes" ("Networks and Religion: Ties that Bind, Loose, Build Up, and Tear Down," in *Journal of Social Structure* 16/1 [2005] n. 2; see also his 2018 book by the same title). But the empirical research supports the social model, as in when Ronald J. Burwell, Peter Hill, and John F. Van Wicklin (in a study of people from southeast Asia seeking asylum in the United States after the end of the war in Vietnam) concluded, as far back as 1986, that:

> [t]he longer the refugees had been in the United States, the more likely they were to report that they had changed religious beliefs. On the basis of the kinds of changes that were noted above (e.g., becoming a Christian, going to church, etc.), it may be that the progressive religious change over time reflects gradual assimilation into American society.
>
> ("Religion and Refugee Resettlement in the United States: A Research Note," *Review of Religious Research* 27/4 [1986]: 360)

Claims of identity can then be studied by the critical scholar as the results of collaborative and always social acts and occasions, whereby a situated and invested identifier and an identified establish often ranked relations of similarity and difference between each other, whose sum result is reported by each as their identity. Following the French philosopher Louis Althusser (1918–1990), we may then examine this effect in more detail, such as the process that he termed interpellation, whereby authority figures, for their own purposes, insert others into structured roles. We see this in his well-known example of a police officer hailing someone with "Hey you!" thereby identifying them as a suspect and, in the wink of an eye, integrating them into a role, or perhaps even a fate, in the so-called justice system (see his influential essay, "Ideology and Ideological State Apparatus: Notes Towards an Investigation" in his book, *Lenin and Philosophy and Other Essays* [1971]). With this in mind, consider how an unexpected knock at the door instantly makes one into a potential host who is suddenly concerned about how messy the unannounced guests will find a place that, prior to the knock, struck the person as so generic as to be neither neat nor messy. Or, following the American philosopher Judith Butler, one might also examine how social actors perform themselves into being seen as having a certain sort of identity, specifically one that is seen as either masculine or feminine, as famously examined in her still important book, *Gender Trouble* (1990). Performance here is not considered a public exhibition of a prior or previously hidden, inner quality but, rather, part of the contextual setting that instills certain subjectivities into actors. This introduces another key term, "subjectivity," into our work (from the Latin for one who is subservient or under the control of another, hence its onetime use for those who are governed by a monarch), as a way to theorize explicitly how identity is the result of power relations. In both examples, identity is studied from the outside-in—and thus the preference to describe it as a process of identification—contrary to the common starting point whenever the adjective "religious" is paired with the term. The latter is clearly seen in Jenny McGill's 2016 book, *Religious Identity and Cultural Negotiation: Toward a Theology of Christian Identity in Migration*, in which we read that "religious faith is connected to the formation of individual and corporate human identity" (24). Her quick addition that "[r]eligious identity is also *colored by* a person's historical culture" (emphasis added) nevertheless reinforces the idea that so-called externals are mere "markers" of religious identity, rather than the practical means by which they are constituted in the first place (much as one's diet is portrayed as another such marker in the entry for "Food and Religious Identity" in *Food, Feasts, and Faith: An Encyclopedia of Food Culture in World Religions* [2017], vol. 1, 217). Then there are those who also represent religious identity as uniquely being the product of certain doctrines and thus beliefs (as argued by John F. McCauley in *The Logic of Ethnic and Religious Conflict in Africa* [2017], 36). All of these examples, however, should strike the critical scholar as far too meager an admission of the fundamental role played by history, setting, and social labor in enabling people to be seen, and even to see themselves, as being certain sorts of things.

In this volume see: belief, comparison, definition, description, essence, experience, gender, power, race, redescription, religion, sacred/profane, theory

In *Religion in 50 More Words* see: conversion, cult, emic/etic, initiation, liberation, meditation, nones, paganism, piety, sexuality

23 Ideology

As with other technical terms in the field, "ideology" is used in multiple ways and, much as with the term "critical," it is used in ways that are either sharp-edged or rather benign. Unfortunately, it is the latter alternative that often makes its appearance in the study of religion while the former is largely absent. This would seem to be the case on account of the fact that the status quo prevents scholars from making what is read by some as negative judgments about the religious content being studied (i.e., judgments that do not accord with what some participants say about themselves and their own social worlds). That the rather benign sense of the term, often used as a synonym for "worldview," comes with its own implicit judgment that the content is wholesome or somehow positive seems to be overlooked by those who use "ideology" simply to mean an overarching system of ideas or a viewpoint or even a mindset. The term, however, can and ought to do considerably more work than this for a critical scholar—something demonstrated throughout Terry Eagleton's still useful survey of the term's history and application, especially in literary studies, *Ideology: An Introduction* (1991; see the new edition of 2007).

Not unlike other terms, "ideology" has oscillated in its meaning over the years, from its earliest usage in the late eighteenth century to its more popular as well as technical uses today. As is widely accepted, *idéologie* was first coined in 1796 by the French philosopher Antoine Destutt de Tracy (1754–1836) in his desire for a new term to replace the more traditional metaphysics or psychology. He introduced it in his *Memoire sur la faculte de penser*, which he presented in installments at the Institut de France in Paris, and also used the term throughout his later five-volume work, *Éléments d'idéologie*. In that work, he proposed a science by this name, one that we might see as a forerunner to the philosophy of mind, with *idéologiste* and *idéologues* at first naming those who are like-minded, notably the Parisian intellectual circle which first proposed to develop and practice this new science. The term combines the French *idéo-* (itself of Latin origin), a term designating "idea," with the Greek *lógos* (often used as a modern suffix to signify the systematic or rational study of some topic, such as the English disciplines of biology, histology, or psychology). The science being proposed aimed to link seemingly immaterial ideas to physical bodies, inasmuch as so-called bodily sensations were seen as their source. Eventually the term came to designate one branch of the once popular field of philology (the early science of language, though linked more to the study of language as it appears in texts), along with, for example, phonology and etymology. As such, ideology was "the comparative study of the grammatical forms and idiomatic constructions of languages, by which we are taught to analyze and distinguish the different shapes in which ideas combine themselves in order to fix perceptions in our minds, and transmit them to those of others," as the term was later used by Peter Stephen Duponceau (the early French linguist, born as Pierre-Étienne du Ponceau [1760–1844]) in the *Transactions of the American Philosophical Society* in 1830 (vol. 3, 75).

But soon the term would take a more critical, even dismissive turn, generally credited to the French Emperor Napoleon Bonaparte (1769–1821). Having previously invited Destutt along on the French military campaigns in Egypt, he adapted the term *idéologues* to mean those holding ideas with which he disagreed, describing the Ideologists as "des rêveurs et des rêveurs dangereux" ("dreamers and dangerous dreamers") (as quoted from volume I of Charles Maurice de Talleyrand-Périgord's *Mémoires*). In fact, volume 5 of the 1901 edition of *A New English Dictionary of Historical Principles* provides an entry on "ideologue," which cites the English author and translator Helen Maria Williams (d. 1827), writing in her series of published letters of 1815, *A Narrative of the Events Which Have Taken Place in France, from the Landing of Napoleon Bonaparte On the First of March 1815 Till the Restoration of Louis XVIII*. She describes Napoleon there, upon his consolidation of power in late 1799, as leaving behind "the ideologues of his council to arrange what he calls their revolutionary rubbish, such as sovereign people, equal rights, &c." (see her Letter VII, May 1815). This is echoed in a July 13, 1813, letter from John Adams to Thomas Jefferson (recounting the former's pessimism that the French revolution would succeed in realizing its ambitious Enlightenment principles, given the vast majority of citizens were, at the time, uneducated): "Napoleon has lately invented a word, which perfectly expressed my opinion at that time and ever since. He calls the project *ideology* . . . [I]t was madness" (*The Works of John Adams*, vol. 10, Letters 1811–1825 [1854]). As this tradition comes down to us today, we might understand the description of one who is labeled an ideologue to name one who is considered to be irrationally and unreasonably in the grip of outrageous and extremist views.

It is from this pejorative sense of the term that we then arrive at what is surely the most influential use of the term in modern scholarship, that of the political economists Karl Marx and Friedrich Engels. In *Die deutsche Ideologie* [*The German Ideology*] (1845–1846) they put the term to new, critical use, retaining something of the earlier judgmental sense but, in the process, largely reframing it. Now the term takes on the meaning of a strategic or self-beneficial (i.e., class-based) misrepresentation of reality. In a crossed-out passage in their original manuscript, and sometimes appearing as a footnote in later editions' opening to part 1 of *The German Ideology*, they wrote: "almost the whole ideology amounts either to a distorted conception of this history or to a complete abstraction from it." Or, as they subsequently argued: "in all ideology men [*sic*] and their circumstances appear upside-down," such that what Marx and Engels understood as the material foundations of all human life (e.g., labor, ownership over resources and methods of production, etc.) are obscured. The result is that human products, whether ideas or commodities, are portrayed and experienced as primary or even natural, as if they were not the result of human labor and ingenuity, erasing their practical, manufacturing history along with who engaged in, let alone benefitted from, that work.

The Marxist redefining of ideology as a "false consciousness" that was alienated from its actual conditions presupposes a correct, unbiased, and therefore realist understanding of the world by which others' distortions can be identified and corrected. The result is that this classic Marxist use of the term becomes rather troublesome for a critical scholar who sees all knowledge production to be situated and therefore invested and, in a word, ideological. For this reason, the manner in which the term was fine-tuned by later Marxist theorists (we think here of Antonio Gramsci [1891–1937] in Italy, or Louis Althusser [1918–1990] in France), resulted in the term being used, along with the word "hegemony" in Gramsci's work, for the manner in which a ruling class's interests are naturalized within the ranks of those who are governed, leading to the latter's apparent consent to be ruled. And, according to Althusser, for the institutions and specific social moments in which individuals are defined so as to be governed, such as his term Ideological State Apparatus (an ISA, of which the education system counts as but one example). Here we see the particular utility of Althusser's term "interpellation," to name the mechanisms and situations by which an identity, or what we could more properly term a subject position (intentionally playing on the notion of being subjected to something), is not simply *adopted* by a social actor but, rather, *imposed* upon them from outside by other actors and institutions. This is nicely exemplified, he argues, in everything from a friendly "hello" (what he calls hailing) spoken to us on the street by a passerby (which affirms our existence and social relations as a peer to the speaker) to a police officer yelling "Hey, you there" at someone (an act by which the authorized actor integrates the person into a system of governance and oversight, thereby making them a suspect or perhaps even a criminal). In this more recent sense, then, subjects are best understood as being constituted by or simply inhabiting ideology, an approach that problematizes long-held assumptions about individualism and freedom of choice, inasmuch as, at least according to those in Althusser's tradition, "individuals are always-already subjects" (from his influential essay "Ideology and Ideological State Apparatuses" in *Lenin and Philosophy and Other Essays* [1971]). For, with contemporary gender reveal parties in mind—an example that reminds us that contemporary feminist scholarship must be added to the contemporary inheritors of ideology critique (e.g., see Marsha Eileen Hewitt's "Ideology Critique, Feminism, and the Study of Religion" in *Method & Theory in the Study of Religion* 11/1 [1999]: 47–63)—even prior to our birth we are each already hailed, and thereby interpellated, into identities not of our own creation, by being placed by others into specific systems of identity and governance. Thus, painting an expected baby's rooms blue or pink, and color coordinating their clothing in like manner, not to mention the names being entertained and the child's future already being imagined by the soon-to-be parents, are hardly neutral acts. Instead, they comprise the practical conditions into which the baby is born and within which they are raised and thereby shaped.

Given this history of the term's use, and given long-standing debates in the study of religion, it may come as no surprise that the latter, critical use of the term does not make nearly as much of an appearance in the field as does its earlier and more generic use (that is, simply to name the system of ideas that we all are said to possess). In this regard, saying that one has an ideology is akin to saying that one has a viewpoint or an opinion, something everyone is presumed to have. For this reason, and as suggested at the outset, it is likely that the term will be used in a way that complements the equally general term "worldview" or even "belief system," which are themselves often found in place of the word "religion." In this sense, it is assumed that those things designated *as* religions are but a subtype of the broader category, what in German might be termed one's *Weltanschauung* or philosophy of life. At least this was a position argued by the Scottish comparativist and phenomenologist Ninian Smart (1927–2001) and was the topic of one of his introductory textbooks, *Worldviews: Crosscultural Explorations of Human Beliefs* (1983). The critique of (i.e., historicization of) the category "religion" over the past few decades (for, among other things, its colonialist history) seems to have reinvigorated efforts to subsume "religion" within "worldview," a move that, we would argue, conserves and still studies those items formerly known as religions but while portraying them as akin to a variety of other mass movements and systems of thought (e.g., political worldviews, such as Communism or economic systems, like consumerism).

This is not to say, however, that the term "ideology" does not retain its critical edge in some parts of the current field. Here, we might note those who see religion as not something to appreciate or privilege, such as Tim Fitzgerald's 2000 book, *The Ideology of Religious Studies* (a political critique of the field's history and current shape) or the late Gary Lease's concluding chapter, "Ideology," in the *Guide to the Study of Religion* (2000). Lease cites the American sociologist Peter Berger (writing in *The Sacred Canopy* [1969]), who defined religion as the "audacious attempt to conceive of the entire universe as being humanly significant." Lease connects this statement with the work of the German sociologist Niklas Luhmann (in his *Funktion der Religion* [1977]), which argued that ideologies enable people to represent to themselves certain of their actions and their consequences as acceptable (or not). Lease thus concludes: "Religion is therefore not simply one ideological creation among others . . . but also a key node for the distribution of power or control over the texts and limits of consciousness" (442).

Finally, we think here of the current work of Naomi Goldenberg at the University of Ottawa, who argues that those social movements today known as religions are what she terms "vestigial states." By this, she means that they are once and always competitors to the universalist (i.e., ideological, at least in Lease's sense) aspirations of the modern nation-state, making them competitors for the affinity and allegiance of the members which they inevitably share—thus groups that the state must carefully manage so as to contain. The state does this by defining and governing such groups in a way that seems to privilege their members, providing them with certain legal rights extended to the so-called sacred sphere from the secular state, but which in effect cordons them off within a tightly controlled domain by means of that very sacred/secular distinction. Now, the designation "religion" names not a distinct feature of the items so defined but, as Goldenberg argues, is seen as the ruling power's classificatory technique to marginalize subgroups by setting them apart from the levers of power as distinct, spiritual, and, importantly, strictly personal. It does this, moreover, all the while reserving for itself those domains of practical consequence to its continued exercise of power, e.g., the so-called public domains known as politics, economy, the law, etc. (See, for example, Goldenberg's chapter, "The Category of Religion in the Technology of Governance: An Argument for Understanding Religions as Vestigial States," in *Religion as a Category of Governance and Sovereignty* [2015] as well as the essays collected in Kathleen McPhillips and Goldenberg's co-edited volume, *The End of Religion: Feminist Reappraisals of the State* [2020].) Although the term ideology is not necessarily one that she uses, the inversion of marginalization as a form of privilege places her work firmly within a rather more critical tradition of ideology critique in the field. She is not concerned, in other words, with identifying the correct form for a religion to take (as this term "ideology critique" might have once been used by an earlier historian of religions, such as the German scholar of Gnosticism, Kurt Rudolph [1929–2020], and as some in our field still use it today), but, instead, with studying the conditions that enable such judgments to operate and be seen by people as persuasive and therefore effective.

It is therefore not difficult to imagine a renewed, critical use of the term "ideology" to have analytic benefit, so long as it is defined and then used in a way that avoids seeing it simply as a pejorative claim—as an insult or as a way to minimize the ideas of one's competitors and opponents.

In this volume see: critical, definition, description, gender, history, identity, politics, power, race, religion

In *Religion in 50 More Words* see: civil religion, emic/etic, myth, piety, tradition

24 Indigeneity

As should by now be evident, the field possesses numerous technical terms that, despite at first appearing to describe a stable quality or obvious trait of a collection of items or a group of people, turn out to have more of a socio-rhetorical role than was previously recognized. Once we designate something by a name and thereby study it in a certain way, as if naturally related to other members of said class, the scholar ends up shaping the material under study in ways that may either privilege or even undermine it. This is the case with the now widely used term "indigenous," which is employed to name something thought (e.g., indigenous religions) to be shared in common by those considered to be local to, or the original or perhaps even natural inhabitants of, a region or a land. The term is problematic because of assumptions that the worldwide collection of past and present claims, practices, and institutions that it groups together, as if all members of the same family, are thought to somehow be inherently related. Even more importantly, this collection often evades being understood merely as religious and, instead, is seen as more ethereal and thus spiritual, and often uniquely in-sync with the natural world. As the US scholar of religion Greg Johnson notes in his 2005 *Encyclopedia of Religion* article, the term "indigenous" is ambiguous, in that it is "(1) a term of self-designation; (2) an analytic concept; and (3) a legal construction" (see "Law and Religion in Indigenous Cultures," vol. 8, 5339 [2nd ed.]). He further describes the term as "a self-referential metaphor" that becomes meaningful "precisely because of the gaps and overlaps between its assumed meanings." Should academic progress be linked to the precision of our vocabulary and the utility of its use—judged by the standards of the academy and not those of the people whom we may study—then "indigenous" certainly deserves closer attention before we proceed to make generalized claims about so-called "indigenous peoples" let alone their "indigenous religions" (two terms that we should not assume are coterminous, as argued by Suzanne Owen in her "Druidry and the Definition of Indigenous Religion," in *Critical Reflections on Indigenous Religions* [2013]: 81–92).

From the Latin *indigena*, literally meaning "in-born," the English adjective, "indigenous" has, since about the mid-twentieth century, increasingly replaced earlier use of the word "native." The latter term, from the post-Classical Latin *nativus*, referred at first to one who is born into bondage, though, by the twelfth century in English, it comes to mean one who is born into or at a particular place, in opposition to those who are not and who therefore arrived from elsewhere (i.e., by some form of immigration or conquest). By at least the seventeenth century "native" is also used to name the inhabitants of other, distant lands with whom Europeans had come into contact through their own exploration, colonial expansion, and trade. For example, consider the work of the English physician and once noted abolitionist Thomas Masterman Winterbottom (1765–1859), such as his *An Account of the Native Africans in the Neighbourhood of Sierra Leone, To which is Added, an Account of the Present State of Medicine Among Them* (1803):

> Nostalgia [considered as a disease since the Swiss physician, Johannes Hofer, coined the term in 1688, to name something from which Swiss soldiers suffered when away from home] . . . or an ardent desire to revisit one's native home, is a disease which affects the natives of Africa as strongly as it does those in Switzerland.
>
> (vol. 2, 174)

We see here how the use of the term simply to name someone who may hail from a certain place (i.e., "one's native home") easily slides into a more general usage for an entire group of people (e.g., "the natives of Africa").

Given common colonial-era assumptions (ones still in use to this day, by the way) about the ranked nature of human cultures and peoples, it may be obvious that terms like native, aboriginal, or indigenous have often been more than just descriptive terms. They instead have often implied more prescriptive judgments concerning the supposedly insufficient or inferior development of the people so named. This is evident even in the writings of an author from the era who supported the emancipation of slaves, such as Winterbottom's above-quoted sense that the people he studied in Africa were not as capable of coping with a longing for home as were Europeans (as his text goes on to claim). The frequency of use in English of the term "native"—as subsequently adopted by Europeans to name those who already inhabited what they once termed the New World, i.e., people also designated by settlers as "Indians," "American Indians," or even "red Indians"—has steadily declined since its height in the mid-nineteenth century.

In place of the term "native" (as in the term "native American," now also seen as problematic in that it brings the continent's early inhabitants under the umbrella of a later national identity) scholars have opted for a variety of alternatives—thus continuing to distinguish first inhabitants from newcomers. For example, in the study of religion's earliest years, in the mid- to late nineteenth century, we frequently find such words as "savage" (Latin *salvaticus* for untamed or from the woods), "primitive" (Latin *primitivus* for the first or earliest), "archaic" (from the Greek *archaíos*, for from the beginning or even old and also old-fashioned), or even the later preferred term "primal" (Latin *primus* for the first). It is not difficult to link each to once widespread Social Darwinist assumptions about the ranked development (i.e., evolution) of groups or even races along a hierarchy from seemingly simple societies to complex industrial civilizations—with European cultures of course portrayed (by the European authors who wrote these texts) as the pinnacle. Although such terms can be signified in other ways, of course (such as the nineteenth- and twentieth-century art movement known as Primitivism), sooner or later judgments about the progressive development of humanity, often along what is assumed to be a series of stages. We see this clearly in the development from magic to religion and then finally to science, as famously argued by the early comparativist James G. Frazer (1854–1941). Such models coincide with stereotypes of what early humans might have been like, or might have experienced, whether to demean that which is seen as earliest and unsophisticated or, in some cases, to romanticize its supposed simplicity (and thus we arrive back at the art movement just mentioned). It is easy to find, for example, contemporary, not to mention a wide array of historical, claims made by scholars about "the primitive *mentalité*" or "archaic man," such as the Jungian analyst Alfred Ribi: "For archaic man, the whole world reflects his psyche . . ." (see his "Demons, Psychological Perspectives," in *Encyclopedia of Religion*, vol. 4, 2282 [2nd ed.]).

Some have begun to employ the term "small-scale societies" as a way to be more precise, and as a way to offer a less prescriptive way to name and thereby distinguish the people who were once or are now members of societies that are seen as rather different from the scholar's own metropolitan, industrialized setting. Consider the anthropologist, Jean E. Jackson, who defines the term as referring "to either hunter-gatherer groups or horticulturalists characterized by low population density and absence of stratification and political centralization" ("The Impacts of the State on Small-Scale Societies," *Studies in Comparative International Development* 19 [1984]: 3). This allows scholars to describe those groups in which the division of labor was low and thus seen as being more homogenous as opposed to our own, which is seen as highly diversified. Then again, a different distinction was sometimes made instead, based not on social organization but on the invention and role of reading and writing, with the term "oral culture" serving as a designation for groups that either historically pre-date literacy or for contemporary groups that mainly rely upon verbal means to convey information and local traditions. In the latter sense the technical term "nonliterate" is preferred to the obviously judgmental sense of being "illiterate." That continual changes in terminology, which included sometimes significant changes in defining criteria, lead to each new term possibly collecting yet a new and different group of items and peoples within its net, seems not to have been carefully entertained by scholars who were intent on studying archaic or aboriginal religions. Indeed, this is indicative of the field at large, where general or meta-claims about religion are often made based on data derived from research that employs not only different but sometimes outrightly conflicting definitions.

Looking at historical examples from world religions textbooks over the years makes the development of this terminology all too apparent, at least once the canon of world religions was opened and started to include something other than just the so-called "big five" (i.e., Hinduism, Buddhism, Judaism, Christianity, and Islam). The inclusion of so-called native groups was often seen as challenging the long-standing discourse on world religions, as identified by Carol Cusack, inasmuch as such traditions often failed to resemble sufficiently either the implicit or sometimes explicit Christian prototype that is so often presumed by scholars (see her chapter in the collection, *After World Religions* [2016], 54). Despite the inclusion of terms like "native traditions" or "native spiritualities" to organize and identify such people and their practices, there is nevertheless a tendency to name a set of defining characteristics that supposedly names a coherent group—across time and geography—as being *different* from all other religions but enough *like* each other, and therefore *as* requiring different methods for their study. However, no matter how "they" are defined (e.g., as nonliterate vs. descendants of people local to a region) there is always a uniform group there to be named and studied. For instance, consider that so-called Australian aborigines (a once common term for Australia's pre-European inhabitants, based on the Latin *ab* + *orīgine* for the earliest or first inhabitants of a place [as in the current Canadian preference for "First Nations peoples"], though now replaced by Aboriginal Australians or Indigenous Australians). They have made appearances in a variety of resources throughout the history of the field yet often under different classifications—are such people primitive? Archaic? Primal? Natives? This should cause us to pause and ask whether the successive names are continually improved designators for a stable type or class of religions and peoples. Or, perhaps better, whether different generations of European and increasingly North American scholars have been continually searching for a new and, given the mores of their time, socially acceptable rationale and thus criterion to designate a changeable group of others *as* under-developed and simple—and, as is more often the case today, *as* more essentially connected to the environment and the natural world? All of these terms, and the classifications they imply, have provided scholars over the years with a seemingly acceptable way of saying "us and them," for a variety of effects, thereby indicating that this long-standing intellectual tradition is but another Orientalist trope by which a historically situated self is constituted in relation to a continually changing but always caricatured other.

The term "indigenous," or the modern noun "indigeneity"—the later thought to name a quality of the people under study—is now the currently preferred designation, of course, as in indigenous peoples, indigenous art, or indigenous ways of knowing. Case in point, Jacob K. Olupona's edited collection, *Beyond Primitivism: Indigenous Religious Traditions and Modernity* (2004). Moreover, as Johnson noted at the outset of this entry, the term is often self-adopted by the contemporary descendants of those who inhabited lands prior to the arrival of settlers. Regardless of the term used, the presence of a negotiation and possibly a conflict animates all of the terms in this discourse, inasmuch as not just a difference but a *ranked* difference between us and them provides the context in which scholars seek to identify and study such groups. This can then marginalize those being named or, more recently, to privilege them in an effort to address what are now understood by many as historical inequities and long traditions of outright persecution. The latter can be exemplified in, e.g., indigenous land claims now before the courts as well as recent efforts to enshrine "indigenous rights" in governing legal documents, such as the United Nations' Declaration on the Rights of Indigenous Peoples (adopted January 2007). When we make the claim that someone or something is indigenous, we see an ongoing contest over identity, place, and resources, carried out by sorting people by means of such binary alternatives as natural or unnatural, simple or complex, primary or derivative, local or imported, safe or dangerous and, finally, us or them. This could not be more evident than in a much earlier botanical usage, such as we find in the 20-page *Catalogue of American Indigenous Trees, Plants, and Seeds Cultivated and For Sale at the Linnaean Botanic Garden, Flushing, Long-Island, Near New York* (1820). Near the end, it notes that "a choice and extensive collection of *exotic* Trees, Flowering Shrubs, Bulbous Roots, &c. &c." were also for sale (emphasis added)—local plants are to be distinguished from exotic imports, we conclude, making plain the discourse in which "native," along with its various modern alternatives, has long been placed.

"Indigenous" is a useful category for those who are today understandably interested in examining the role of power in the history of field, so as to decolonize curricula and scholarship after centuries of presumed

Euro-North American and White superiority. Despite this, the term nonetheless remains part of what Johnson characterized as an ambiguous vocabulary of identification and contest, involved in an ongoing arm-wrestling match with contenders vying for privileges. It is for this reason that it may be wiser for critical scholars to study the term's historical and ongoing use, as a means to examine how these contests have been and are being waged by a variety of actors that often occupy very different social positions and thereby exercise a dramatically different sense of agency. This might prove more useful than assuming that it is a neutral descriptive designator that names an obvious quality or stable trait that transcends time and geography, thereby allowing observers to identify the traits of specifically indigenous religions. For though this one term is widely accepted now, the tendency of each successive generation of scholars simply to go looking for a "better" way to name "them" fails to theorize this habit of scholarship to name certain others in this way to begin with. As Zoe Alderton has rightly observed, "[t]he idea of indigeneity and its academic study is politically loaded on numerous levels," resulting in, at least according to Jack Tsonis writing in the same volume, scholarship that leaves a problematic, wider discourse in place whenever it is used (see *Religious Categories and the Construction of the Indigenous* [2016], xi and chpt. 4).

In this volume see: classification, culture, definition, description, power, race, redescription, society, world religions

In *Religion in 50 More Words* see: animism, emic/etic, mysticism, myth, paganism, shamanism, spirituality, syncretism, tradition

25 Interpretation

Interpretation is one of the most basic acts and important or long-standing methods in the study of religion. Importance, as we have seen with several of the key terms examined here, often means that the word is problematic, however, or, at the very least, highly ambiguous or contentious. The term, a noun of action, came into the English language from Latin (*interpretātiōn*) by way of Old French (*interpretation*) to refer to the action of what many scholars would today call the opposed operations of interpreting or explaining a text, with the aim of offering what was once known as an exposition, i.e., to identify or clarify, in detail, the meaning or purpose/role of a piece of writing, so as to understand it. It is probably no coincidence that one of the earliest texts to which the term was employed was in studying the Bible (even today we have the scholarly journals *Interpretation* [founded 1947] and *Biblical Interpretation* [founded 1993], both devoted to bible study). Hence, the long tradition of biblical exegesis (derived from the Latin *ex-*, "from," and the Greek *egeísthai*, "to lead" or "to guide," hence the idea of pulling meaning *from* a text, almost always associated with scripture). To interpret, then, comes to be commonly used to name efforts to decode a text or an artifact (such as a work of art or an archeological find), as well as a person's claims or actions (e.g., to read a person or to interpret their body language), as if they are all comprised of deeper or hidden symbols whose associations and setting (i.e., context) need to be uncovered and closely examined in order to arrive at that which is called their meaning (that is, their collective relationship or the unstated and unexhibited thing to which they are thought to correspond or the target toward which they may point). That there is much here that, for the critical scholar at least, needs to be unpacked should be clear.

To use an example to highlight the fundamental problem of interpretation, one from which it can never really escape, we might ask: whose interpretation of an item or event is the correct one? To rephrase: what qualifies as a "valid" or "persuasive" Roman Catholic interpretation of a biblical text, for example, and why might it look so different from, say, what a Greek Orthodox reader would claim to be proper or accurate? Both of these two interpretations at least share a fundamental Christology (the doctrine of the identity and role of Christ, a form of God and the presumed savior in Christian theology) and, in that regard, would certainly look very different from, say, a normative Rabbinic Jewish interpretation of the same text. If the Catholic interpretation of a particular verse in the text commonly known by some as the Old Testament is correct to Catholics, just as the Greek Orthodox interpretation is to members of that Church and, yes, the Jewish interpretation (but of what will now be known as the Hebrew Bible as opposed to the Old Testament) to Jews, then we again confront the question: whose interpretation is the correct one? Or, put another way, which standard or set of standards can be identified whereby the claims of competing interpretive communities might be compared and judged? Critical scholars of religion would likely argue that all of these interpretations are valid in their specific contexts and for their interpreter's discrete purposes, identifying the utter relativity and ambiguity of the matter. This alone would make opting for an interpretative approach—and pursuing it as if that was the ultimate goal of scholarship—somewhat troublesome for such a scholar.

This, of course, is where the problems begin to creep into this seemingly simple task of interpreting something or someone. For what—and, perhaps just as importantly, who—gets to decide the criteria for finding a, let alone *the*, correct interpretation? If there is a hectic economy of competing readings of even the seemingly simplest texts (e.g., some readers may recall the then US President Bill Clinton quibbling in his 1998 grand jury testimony over the meaning of the verb "is," concerning the possibility of his having had what were termed "sexual relations" with Monica Lewinsky) then the members of such groups will no doubt deploy their own devices to regulate the many possible meanings. For instance, perhaps they will authorize one as self-evident or transcendent, while denigrating all others as merely mortal, as in the Rev. William Reid, of Edinburgh, Scotland, in his 1874 work, *Everlasting Punishment and Modern Speculation*: "To interpret Bible words by classic usage alone would be to subordinate Divine revelation to heathen speculations" (47—note also his choice of the term "infidel" as the opposite of a "believer" [115]). If objective or universal criteria to decide among various interpretations are lacking, as the critical scholar would suggest is always the case, and if such strategies as Reid's are unpersuasive or ineffective, then interpretations, by definition, remain arbitrary, situated, and engaged in an endless deferral of meaning. Take, for example, a text or practice from an ancient culture that possesses neither the term "religion" nor even "ritual." A scholar working in the context of, say, the English language, and thus one undoubtedly familiar with both of these terms as what are imagined to be universal categories of analysis, might have no problem interpreting such an ancient text as "religious" or such a practice as a "ritual," since such admittedly local terms—at least to the historically and regionally situated scholar—are simply and unproblematically imagined to be everywhere because they are "our" terms. Indeed, as Brent Nongbri has argued in his *Before Religion: A History of a Modern Concept* (2013), this so-called presentist desire to show what *we* hold dear, namely, religion, coincides with the equal desire to search (and, of course, find) it in other times and places, even if the it that we settle on is not known by that name.

Further contributing to the problem is the idea that different scholars, with different methodologies and perspectives/locations, will interpret the very same act differently. A Marxist, for example, arriving on the scene with a very particular theory of political economy (i.e., how systems of valuation and exchange are interwoven with how societies regulate and use power), would surely offer a radically different interpretation of a particular story in some ancient or contemporary scripture than would, say, a psychologist or even a sociologist—all of whom would undoubtedly give us different interpretations than the actual person or group engaged in reading the particular passage. If explanations of religion are all agreed that religion or religious activities should be explained by reduction to a non-religious cause or origin—regardless of the explanation—then interpretations of religion, which presuppose that the things designated as religions possess a meaning which must be decoded or perhaps even appreciated, have the potential to be radically divergent, often agreeing on very little and sometimes even contradictory. We think here of the dramatic difference between, on the one hand, how a practitioner might read and understand the tale of Purusha and the creation of the universe from the ancient Indian text, later written down in Sanskrit, known as the *Rig Veda* (a collection of just over one thousand ritual hymns or chants) and, on the other, how a critical scholar might read it. According to the tale, this cosmic being is sacrificed and from its portions arise the entire universe—significantly with the ritual, priestly class (Sanskrit, *varna*), or brahmans, developing from its mouth, the ruling warrior class from its arms and torso, etc. (see the *Rig Veda* 10.90). The Canadian scholar of religion, Graeme MacQueen, applying a critical, socio-political reading, once concluded that, via the tale, the interests of the very ones who would have told, enacted, and benefited from the hymn are naturalized if their claim of primary, ceremonial status is accepted as fact by those witnessing such ceremonies. After all, "what is legitimized is not merely 'order' but a particular order" (see his "Whose Sacred History? Reflections on Myth and Dominance," *Studies in Religion* 17 [1988]: 148). That there is considerable distance between such an interpretation and other more generous readings should be obvious, such as those that, for example, portray the story simply as providing either an illustration of how central the institution of sacrifice has been to the Hindu tradition or how the Hindu philosophy presumes a unity to creation.

This relativity or, perhaps better, the fact that we can interpret anything in howsoever manner we please, is one of the fundamental problems besetting the Humanities in general and the study of religion in particular. Indeed, it is particularly acute in the latter since its object of study, religion, is often defined as a fundamentally meaning-making activity that therefore demands a nuanced, interpretive approach. Take for example, the treatment of homosexuality in Islam. In an academic monograph titled *Homosexuality in Islam: Critical Reflection on Gay, Lesbian, and Transgender Muslims* (2010), Scott Kugle writes:

> What matters is not the sex of the partner . . . as long as that partnership is contractual on par with legal custom. Rather, what matters is the ethical nature of the relationship one has within the constraints of one's internal disposition, which includes sexual orientation and gender identity.
>
> (3)

We see here how Kugle's interpretation of Islamic law and doctrine is presented as if it is somehow the correct one and representative of all of Islam. While it certainly may seem this way to him (and for any theologically and socially progressive Muslim who might agree with him), there is no getting around the fact that this is but interpretation of the Muslim legal tradition (and one that is certainly at odds with yet other interpretations of the tradition in question, whether historical or contemporary—a difference of opinion on the place of homosexuality, moreover, that is easily found across all of the so-called world religions). This latter example also shows us that if interpretation is portrayed, as it often is, as drawing meaning out of a text, a belief or an action, it is also necessarily a reading into a text, and thus also the traditional opposite of exegesis: an eisegesis (*eis-*, the opposite of *ex-*, meaning "in" or "into"). Despite the fact that interpreters often aim to erase their own choices and work by representing meaning as revealed by the act of drawing *out* the significance of a text, a truly critical stance on how texts and signification work involves a scholar (along with any interpreter) reading *into* or *onto* a text, a belief, an object or an activity (what an earlier generation of literary critics called reader response theory).

Within this context, interpretation is also very much related to the concept of "hermeneutics" (a seventeenth-century English term originating in either Latin or Greek), or the act of interpreting texts, especially associated with those working with scriptural ones. Unlike the cognate "exegesis," which in theory is interested in the practical exposition of texts, hermeneutics tends to be more interested in the *discovery* or *recovery* of spiritual truths, imagined as hidden or, as the historian of religion Mircea Eliade (1907–1986) would frequently write, camouflaged in the text. Explaining the term in his *Biblical Hermeneutics: A Treatise on the Interpretation of the Old and New Testaments* (1890), Milton Spenser Terry (1840–1914), whose specialty was described as "finding Jesus in every corner of the Old Testament" and who defines hermeneutics as "the science of interpreting an author's language," writes that

> this science assumes that there are divers modes of thought and ambiguities of expression among men, and, according, it aims to remove the supposable differences between a writer and his readers, so that the meaning of the one may be truly and accurately apprehended by the others
>
> (17)

Of course, when applied to the biblical text, as he proceeds to do, the act refers to the desire

> to establish the principles, methods, and rules which are needful to unfold the sense of what is written. Its object is to elucidate whatever may be obscure or ill-defined, so that every reader may be able, by an intelligent process, to obtain the exact ideas intended by the author.
>
> (19)

This idea, mistaken to be sure, that one can ascertain the meanings of texts, understood by their believers to be either god-given or divinely inspired, undoubtedly plays a crucial role in defining a religion for its participants. Judaism—or, at least that form known as Rabbinic Judaism—is all about, for example, trying to ascertain the meaning of the biblical and later texts through the act of interpretation, whose interpretive outcome is subsequently canonized in the commentary tradition, something that continues to this day. "The" Jewish response to, say stem-cell research, is therefore an act of interpretation between the religious tradition and science. This is the way those institutions known as religions work. Problems arise, however, when this activity simply crosses over into the so-called secular academy and academic scholars of religion engage in similar moves to offer their interpretations of religious texts, as we saw above with Kugle's desire to create a modern, gay-friendly Islam through his own act of interpretation. Although those like the much-earlier Terry, and perhaps even many today, seek to differentiate biblical (or scriptural) hermeneutics from other textual approaches, such as scriptural criticism, where the one ends and the other begins is anything but clear or obvious.

Coinciding with biblical hermeneutics is the activity of philosophical hermeneutics, broadly understood as the theory and methodology of interpretation. Perhaps most relevant to the study of religion is the influential Protestant theologian, Friedrich Schleiermacher (1768–1834), who distinguished between the literal or grammatical interpretation of a text, whether religious or secular, and its deeper or what we might today refer to as its psychological interpretation. For Schleiermacher, and this is still very much relevant today, understanding what someone means is less a *science* than an *art* involving the ability to grasp the mental processes of the person being interpreted. Interpretation, for Schleiermacher and indeed for many in the field to this day, begins with an expression or observed act followed by the desire to work backwards to reconstruct the intention and thus meaning (read: experience) of its author. Schleiermacher also maintained that meaning was two-sided, with the interpreter dealing with both the words written (or spoken), which were in the public domain and thus "objective," and the author's original intention, which was subjective and thus private. It was precisely this gap, between text and inner thought, that led him to emphasize the importance of understanding (German, *Verstehen*) the non-scientific ability to ostensibly reconstruct the thinking of another person, either in the past or a contemporary, through the mediation of written text. We see the vestiges of this in such recent scholars as Ninian Smart (1927–2001), the one-time influential scholar of religion who speaks, especially in his *Phenomenon of Religion* (1973), of the need for empathy on the part of the researcher. In suitably phenomenological fashion, Smart proposes that interpretation requires provisionally setting aside one's own cognitive and emotional commitments so as to be able to put oneself empathetically into the position of those one seeks to understand. "In order to understand what it is like to be say, a Winnebago [the name once used for the North American Ho-Chunk people]," Smart reasons, "one must really make-believe that one is a Winnebago, rehearsing the thoughts and attitudes of a Winnebago" (70).

Though the field of philosophical hermeneutics became an increasingly technical one, Smart's work illustrates that its less technical iteration may be found in the phenomenology of religion, wherein the goal is to grasp the meaning of texts through our experience of them as the author's experienced them. Thus we read in the noted scholar of Tibetan Buddhism Robert Thurman's (widely known as both a scholar and a practitioner) essay, "Buddhist Hermeneutics" (*Journal of the American Academy of Religion* 46/1 [1978]: 19–39) that Buddhism, far from being "non-rational," places supreme emphasis on "the role of the transcendent experience, wherein the transcendence of verbalization is approached not as a non-rational escape into mysticism, but as an affirmation of empiricism"; accordingly, as he goes on, "a rational acknowledgment of the fact that reality, even ordinary reality, is never, in the final analysis reducible to what we may say about it" (19). Responding to Thurman, some five years later, Peter N. Gregory, in an article titled "Chinese Buddhist Hermeneutics: The Case of Hu-yen" (*JAAR* 51/2 [1983]: 231–249), writes about "the Buddha's teaching style as well as the conditions in which he taught," arguing that "[t]he Buddha's career spanned half a century, during which he preached to many thousands of people, both world-renouncers and house holders, men and women" (231). Because of this, Gregory surmises, the Buddha spoke in a way that he knew would lead to the need for interpretation or a hermeneutical framework. The point we wish to draw attention to here is neither the validity nor the invalidity of Gregory's argument, but the fact that he so easily assumes that he knew "the conditions in which [the Buddha] taught" and that we actually know what the Buddha taught, since whatever the message may have been, after all, has been interpreted through centuries of Buddhist interpretative practices. Critical scholars therefore do not presume to possess unmediated access to distant times and places that provide them with some special access to others' minds and motives. If anything, they instead tend to focus on the analysis of the reading itself, seeing interpreters as engaged in an activity that seeks to derive the intention or intentions of a so-called author and thereby deriving the meaning that suits their own practical needs and present circumstance (building on what is generally known as "the death of the author" movement in such fields as semiotics and literary theory). Thus interpretation is actually historicized as a socially formative act rather than a mystical form of time travel and mind reading.

In the final analysis, what might interpretive work in the field look like? We could point, perhaps, to the work of the once influential anthropologist, Clifford Geertz (1926–2006), who, though focused on studying meaning, sought to move away from the interiority of so many interpretive frameworks and, instead, argued that meaning was something external and social, that is, residing "outside the boundaries of the individual organism as such in that intersubjective world of common understandings" (*The Interpretation of Cultures* [1973], 92). Unlike Smart and many others in the study of religion even today, who focus on a set of amorphous and inner experiences or feelings, Geertz is an example of someone focused on meanings derived from the spheres of social practices and social dynamics (perhaps his most famous example being the Balinese cockfight). While Geertz called his method "thick description," as opposed to interpretation per se, the important issue that he raised to the surface is the need to focus scholarly attention on the observable and the social as opposed to the hidden (by virtue of

Interpretation 149

it being internal) and the experiential. For interpretation to become a valid method in the study of religion it has to adopt precisely this social aspect and eschew the undocumentable internal, focusing attention instead on the practical conditions that make different meanings possible and persuasive as well as the effects of adopting this rather than that meaning. Thus, critical scholars are uninterested in which interpretation is correct; rather, they study the conditions that allow one of the many to be seen as legitimate along with the practical implications of its operationalization and use in daily life.

In this volume see: description, explanation, function, phenomenology, redescription, secular

In *Religion in 50 More Words* see: commentary, dialogue, emic/etic, symbol, theology, tradition, understanding

26 Law

Given the manner in which the modern nation-state shapes and directly manages the lives of its inhabitants—including the close association between the idea of law and the procedures established and policed by representatives of the nation (e.g., police, courts, licensing and regulatory agencies, etc.)—it should come as no surprise that the topic of religion and law has a quickly growing scholarly literature. Curiously, though, popular assumptions about those things designated *as* religion often assumes that these two domains are separate, even mutually exclusive, since religion is often presumed to name things of transcendental origin and thus ahistorical consequence. According to such a popular—and, for some, even scholarly—view, while the state may either *interact* with or *interfere* in religious affairs, it should properly remain aloof from religious matters. We could refer to this as the traditional "render unto Caesar" position, referencing the Christian's book of Matthew 22:21: "Render therefore unto Caesar the things that are Caesar's; and unto God the things that are God's" (quoting the English Revised Version)—a line attributed to Jesus when asked whether people should pay taxes to the then Roman government. We see this approach adopted in many modern nations' governing documents where it frequently goes by the name of "freedom of religion/religious expression." Yet there are those who would argue that the nation-state plays a far more fundamental role in the religious lives of its members, going so far as to question the utility of the apparently neat division assumed in such a traditional approach.

Based on an old English (and prior to that Old Norse) word that once signified something layered or set in place or a fixed position, an early sense of our modern term "law" seems to have been extended from this to denote a shared basis, even partnership or agreement between parties. Over time, the influence of earlier Latin and ancient Greek sources (e.g., *nómos*, meaning something akin to customary practices, from which the terms "nomological" and "nomothetic" derive, referring to laws or scientific principles that, for example, guide research) sends us in the direction

DOI: 10.4324/9781003140184-27

of the modern sense of a set of codified rules concerning what is right, proper, or true. The English word, in one or another form, has therefore been with us for over a thousand years, though it is now defined as "[t]he body of rules ... which a particular state or community recognizes as binding on its members or subjects" (*A New English Dictionary of Historical Principles* [1908], vol. VI, 113).

It is at this point that we return to religion, though not necessarily by focusing on the laws *within* groups designated as religions (though this is, of course, one use for the term and thus an area of study, for theologians and scholars like—such as so-called canon law in Christianity or, in Islam, the notion of *sharia*). Instead, we are interested in how the larger operating parameters of the nation govern a religion's members as they go about their daily lives. Such a focus prompts us first to consider competing approaches or theories of religion. If religion is presumed to be a pre-social and inner feeling or sentiment that is only secondarily expressed in the public domain then scholars will likely phrase the question as being one of "religion and law," that is, seen as two distinct domains that interact in ways that require negotiation. We see this, for example, in Benjamin Schonthal's preferred phrasing of "studying religion in the environment of law" (see his chapter, "Law," in *The Oxford Handbook of the Study of Religion* [2016], 365–381). This is certainly the dominant position in the field today, with scholars usually studying the adequacy (or not) of legal structures that impact on the expression and practice of what are usually termed a person's religious beliefs or their so-called faith. Governments and, eventually, their courts thus aim to discern which, among the many forms that religion might take, deserve protections or sometimes prosecution, with judges eventually needing to determine which are legitimate and, as is often said, "sincerely held" and which are not—though formal criteria for adjudicating all of this are often entirely absent from law.

But if religion is instead understood to be a secondary effect of prior historical, social, psychological, economic, etc., forces that create the conditions in which religion arises or even becomes an item of discourse (in distinction from things not designated as religion), then scholars may instead become interested in a very different set of question. Now the focus moves from how religion interacts with law to the way governing authorities in nation-states establish a sanctioned structure in which some of their members' many claims and actions are seen *as* allowable or not, in this or that situation. Given that it is usually a protected category in liberal democracies, the role that the word "religion" plays in all of this becomes rather interesting. Critical scholars of religion may now opt to study law—and the prior political debates and social interests that drive the establishment of specific regulations—a little differently: as providing the setting in which safe and dangerous, familiar and strange, private and public, and, ultimately, legal and illegal are managed and identified (often in favor of dominant interests, to be sure). Thus, the traditional nomenclature of "religion and law" hardly captures this latter sense of these two terms' complex relationship. Certain types of the latter are now understood to create the impression of the former—with those things failing to meet a government's often inarticulate (or at least strategically implicit) definition of religion eventually designated (and thereby constrained and controlled) as sects, cults, or dangerous and radical political or revolutionary movements.

The critical study of religion *in* law therefore starts from a premise rather less ambitious than that of, say, Winnifred Fallers Sullivan, who opens her chapter, "Reforming Culture: Law and Religion Today" (in Robert Orsi's edited collection, *The Cambridge Companion to Religious Studies* [2012]), by stating: "Law, like religion, is a virtually universal feature of human society" (319). Instead, following Peggy Schmeiser, at the University of Saskatchewan in Canada, scholars might want to examine "the ways that legislation and the courts participate in classifying, regulating, and privileging certain types of thought and practice" (see her chapter, "Vestigial State Theory and Law in Canada," in *The End of Religion: Feminist Reappraisals of the State* [2021], 99–100)—just some of which, in certain national settings and as a result of specific legislation, end up going by the name of religion.

In this volume see: belief, classification, faith, politics, power, sacred/profane, secular

In *Religion in 50 More Words* see: church, commentary, dialogue, piety, reformation, theology, tradition

27 Lived religion

Beginning in the later decades of the twentieth century a new subfield developed in the study of religion, aiming to correct what was seen as a traditional over-emphasis on the interpretation of texts and a preoccupation with studying (mainly male) elites. Emphasis was instead placed on how religion was experienced, as scholars might phrase it, and thus often overlooked in everyday settings, i.e., the role that it plays in a wider array of people's daily lives—case in point, consider Meredith McQuire's widely used book, *Lived Religion: Faith and Practice in Everyday Life* (2008). Rather than assume that religion is all about what elite practitioners think, do, and leave behind, the focus of attention shifted to, for example, a small home shrine and how it is incorporated into the day-to-day lives of the people for whom it is undoubtedly significant. This shift, or so it was reasoned, allows scholars to discover that, contrary to long-held assumptions in the field about the sacred being a unique or distinct domain, clearly set apart from the profane, religion is actually integrated into people's wider practices and self-understandings. Predictably perhaps, those now studied—primarily through ethnographic methods of participant-observation (methods long-employed by others in the field, to be sure)—often turn out to be members of the working or lower classes as well as women and members of minority groups, i.e., people who, although traditionally overlooked in much of traditional scholarship, now are said to be granted by scholars a new sense of agency and thus worth.

Although the word "religion" will be examined in detail as the subject of its own entry, its qualifier here, "lived," entered English from earlier Germanic languages, with variants of the now prominent modern verb "live" (noun: life) dating to Old English (i.e., Anglo-Saxon), going as far back as the early Middle Ages. It has had a range of meanings, such as to exist, to inhabit a place, or even as a metaphor for food and nourishment, as evidenced in slightly late terms such as "livelihood" or "make a living" and the adjectives "lively" (to be life-like or full of life, i.e., active or energetic)

DOI: 10.4324/9781003140184-28

and "alive" (to possess life). The past tense of the verb "lived" can also function as an adjective, as in "a lived reality" such as, for example, "the secret of a healthy old age is a wisely lived life that begins in the cradle," as quoted from a column on old age, entitled "Twilight or Sunset?" from *Friends Intelligencer and Journal*, the onetime Quaker magazine published in Philadelphia (August 3, 1889: v).

In the second half of the twentieth century the term "lived experience" gains considerable prominence, with the related term "lived religion"—once considered by some early representatives as an awkward term (such as the scholar of American religion, Robert A. Orsi, writing in an early chapter on the topic entitled "Everyday Miracles: The Study of Lived Religion" [1997])—then gaining frequency closer to the turn of the century. Given significant momentum by Harvard Divinity School's church historian, David D. Hall, in his edited collection, *Lived Religion in America: Toward a History of Practice* (1997), the approach is described in the opening sentence to Carl S. Dudley's June 16, 1998, review of the book (in *The Christian Century*, a so-called mainline Protestant journal) as "address[ing] the gap between academic theology and the diverse ways people of faith 'live religion' in their circumstances." The volume collected the work of such authors as Orsi (who contributed the above-mentioned chapter) along with the French sociologist of religion Danièle Hervieu-Léger, as well as Anne S. Brown, Leigh Eric Schmidt, Stephen Prothero, Cheryl Forbes, Michael McNally, Rebecca Kneale Gould, R. Marie Griffith, Nancy Ammerman, and Hall himself. Many of these individuals either were already or then went on to become well-known representatives of this approach to studying religion in daily life. This is especially the case with Orsi and his critically acclaimed *The Madonna of 115th Street: Faith and Community in Italian Harlem, 1880–1950* [1985]), along with Ammerman, who would go on to edit a book series at Palgrave Macmillan with the title, Studies in Lived Religion and Societal Challenges. This series describes religion not as being "approached . . . as a stable system of official positions, traditions, creeds, and structures but as a fluid and multi-layered practice of what people actually do, experience, think, and share" (see also her edited *Everyday Religion: Observing Modern Religion Lives* [2007]).

Influenced by the earlier French scholarly approach to "la religion vécue" (literally, lived religion, though also "religious vitality"), as identified in Hervieu-Léger's chapter to Hall's volume, this modern subfield is associated with, among others, the work of the French sociologist Gabriel Le Bras (1891–1970) on regional Catholicism in France. An early example of Le Bras's work being applied to religion in the United States is the Catholic historian Thomas T. McAvoy's (1903–1969) "The Le Bras Approach to the History of the Diocese of Fort Wayne," published in *The Indiana Magazine of History* (52/4 [1956]: 369–382). There, McAvoy described the importance of studying the effects of sociology, geography, economy, and government on a local parish's religious life and also the parish's own effects on the local region. The method is descriptive and interpretive, tightly focused on local people, with the scholar at times interested in seemingly mundane daily activities along with the participant's self-understanding of their own motives and their meaning. As described by the Columbia University scholar Matthew Engelke, "[t]he nature of . . . lived religion, depends on the particularities of time and place and the exigencies of tradition" (from an overview on material religion approaches in Orsi's own edited volume, *The Cambridge Companion to Religious Studies* [2012], 212). Lived religion— or what some, following Edward Bailey (1935–2015) in the late 1960s, might even call implicit religion, in that it is supposedly found all throughout people's lives—is therefore taken as a fundamental given among all other parts of common people's daily lives. Indeed, as McAvoy summed it up, "the emphasis is on religious practices and non-religious factors" (370) and not on accounting for *why* people are religious in the first place.

This subfield also has antecedents in the work of other French authors. Orsi, for example, credits (in his own chapter in Hall's volume) the mid-twentieth century existentialist, Jean-Paul Sartre (1905–1980). Orsi particularly notes the idea of lived experience (French, *le vécu*)—a concept no less central to philosophical phenomenology, which aims to study the conditions that allow experience to take place, i.e., the structures that permit things to be perceived *as* things. The scholar of lived experience therefore aims to reconstruct what the first-person experience of a person might be and might have been, e.g., how they perceive themselves as a subject, along with the world as understood and inhabited by them. For some proponents, such as Orsi, the approach is also an effort to correct the way in which the field has often exclusively (and uncritically) been modeled on Protestant Christian norms and assumptions, notably the long-standing priority of seemingly individual and private belief (or, as we might more accurately say, claims of belief) over practice and social organization, i.e., ritual and institution. This once common way of drawing a distinction between Protestant and Roman Catholic understandings of religion has roots in the movement generally known as the sixteenth and early seventeenth century Reformation, which took place across Europe, whereby the onetime hegemony of the Catholic Church was contested. This resulted not only in the rise of a variety of new Protestant denominations but, also, the early modern rise of new forms of government and mass social identity. When we combine this with such later factors as the coming centuries' so-called Industrial Revolution, we witness the rise of what we today understand as the modern nation-state. Pivotal in this was a model of the human as a free, lone actor who, only by means of some secondary act, chooses to join in subsequent social organizations, thereby laying the basis for a modern understanding of the subject upon which such systems as liberal and representative democracies are today based (i.e., one citizen, one vote). In the study of religion, the success of this model results in a widespread emphasis on ascertaining people's beliefs, seeing such things as creeds or ritual as a secondary expression of prior inner states. Focusing, instead, on the careful study of daily actions and local social networks was therefore seen as among the ways to up-end this taken-for-granted but problematic model of the field.

When applied historically, this new approach prompts scholars of lived religion to draw on sources outside those usually used by the historian, given that the social actors under study may not have left much of a trace in the usually authorized archives (e.g., official government documents or newspaper records). While there have been attempts to study "lived religion" in, say, the Middle Ages, the overwhelming tendency has been to focus on the present, particularly within the American context. Scholars interested in studying lived experience and, by extension, lived religion, must either engage in fieldwork when studying current instances or, when studying the past, different sorts of material artifacts that allow them to infer what it was like to inhabit a specific subject position that had usually been left unstudied and therefore unknown and silent. In this way the lived religion approach is related to another subfield, that of popular religion, although the latter (related to the notion of popular culture, as in the non-elite culture of so-called common people) can presuppose a class distinction that deprioritizes so-called popular forms as somehow less legitimate. While this does not characterize all studies of popular religion, of course, it certainly fails to capture the motivations behind the lived religion movement in the field.

Inasmuch as such scholars write of lived religion being manifested in various practices, it is possible to also see the connection to the earlier approach known as the phenomenology of religion, which was popular among an earlier generation of scholarship (though, for some decades, the focus of much critique). The new subfield also proposes a method akin to Mircea Eliade's (1907–1986) so-called New Humanism. In the inaugural issue of the journal *History of Religions* (1961), he argued that the existential situation of previous people, encoded in the items we study, are to be re-experienced by scholars themselves, so as to be conserved and thereby experienced anew. The connections between the discourses associated with lived religions and these earlier approaches deserve more critical attention than they have so far received. The result is a subfield that focuses on more than just elite social actors, something that is also helpful when it comes to understanding that binary concepts that usually guide scholarship (e.g., the sacred/secular distinction) are far more negotiable or even ambiguous than previously seen. However, it is not difficult to read works in lived religion as a new generation's attempt to reassert a rather traditional position in the field regarding the supposedly unique nature of religion, understood more specifically as a private experiential state of deep meaning that expresses a pan-human yearning.

The American historian, Joan Wallach Scott, wrote in an essay entitled "The Evidence of Experience" (in the journal *Critical Inquiry* 17/4 [1991]: 773–797) that grounding scholarship on the category of experience is itself a problematic move. Adopted as the starting point by those who later came to be seen as inhabiting a subfield of History known as Social History (writing the history of marginal groups, "from the ground up," as it was often described), as the way to get around the absence of certain groups in the historian's traditional archive, this notion of experience, she argues, "depends on a referential notion of evidence which denies that it is anything but a re-flection of the real" (776). Scott here entertains that larger historical, contextual, and thus contingent structural conditions determine *what gets to count as* an experience, let alone one that is seen to be worth a scholar recovering and supposedly re-experiencing and publicizing. Imagining the scholar's work as something other than neutrally conveying observed facts, let alone approaching a social actor's experience as far more complex than simply conveying to others their own authentic and subjective realities, Scott builds on the work of such prior writers as the French historian, Michel de Certeau (1925–1986). The latter's own book, *L'invention du quotidien* (vol 1. [1980]; English: *The Practice of Everyday Life* [1984]) focuses on the seemingly mundane aspects of daily life, such as walking the city, but in a rather different way than the lived religion movement. Instead, he seeks to theorize such practices rather than try to describe them from the participant's point of view. Scott therefore proposes that studying the conditions that enable the generation of things narrativized and then reported *as* experiences should instead be the scholar's aim. As she writes: "the evidence of experience . . . reproduces rather than contests given ideological systems," such as those that produced the so-called experiences in the first place. The problem with such work, then, is that "the project of making experience visible precludes critical examination of the workings of the ideological system itself, its categories of representation" (778).

Concluding that the word experience is itself a term of common speech that fails to examine the conditions of its own production, Scott makes plain that research that is based on experiential claims is far removed from critical scholarship. Instead, it is complicit scholarship, though sometimes complicit with systems of governance with which scholars may agree or, perhaps, unknowingly inhabit themselves. Experience, the basis for the lived religion movement, therefore turns out to be a discursive product requiring its

158 *Lived religion*

own historicization, allowing scholars to study it always as a claim made by a social actor and *not* as a generalizable or authentic display of some sort of pure, inner sensation that is only secondarily expressed publicly into the world. Following Scott, then, a critical revision to the lived religion movement would entail seeing claims of experience not as something to record and then affirm and transmit via scholarship—something Orsi does in his later work on what he calls the experience of "real presence" (e.g., in *History and Presence* [2018])—but, instead, as either strategies or tactics devised and deployed in situated identity production—a practice that it is up to the scholar to explain as something other than natural.

In this volume see: authenticity, belief, culture, description, essence, experience, explanation, identity, interpretation, material religion, religion, sacred/profane, theory

In *Religion in 50 More Words* see: dialogue, emic/etic, hagiography, icon, idol, immanence/transcendence, nones, ritual, sacrifice, shamanism, spirituality, theology, tradition

28 Material religion

As is the case with the just examined term "lived religion," the related material religion approach represents a fairly recent attempt in the study of religion to switch the focus from texts produced by elite (and, indeed, often male) classes to other members of society. It does this by studying seemingly mundane objects, spaces, and images (again, often associated with items produced or used by lower classes or what is sometimes broadly referred to as "people on the ground") that are assumed to play just as important a role—though one that is largely overlooked by the scholarly tradition—within religious communities. This approach highlights interactions between religion and culture, aiming to document how religious beliefs are, for lack of a better term, "materialized." It is worth noting, however, that, as is the case with other compound terms with either the noun "religion" or adjective "religious" in them (e.g., embodied religion or religious practice), the emphasis is often on the other word or, in this case, the adjective modifying it. It is "material," in other words, that is assumed to give the noun, "religion," its meaning—in distinction, we suppose, from immaterial religion, or what is likely assumed to be the previous norm of studying supposedly disembodied beliefs as expressed in texts. Because of this emphasis, the noun, as is so customary in the study of religion, can be and often is left vague, open-ended, and subject to any number of interpretations.

It may therefore be no coincidence that the etymology of "material" derives from the Latin *materia* (i.e., matter) and the suffix *-alis*, and used as early as the fourth century by Augustine (354–430) to differentiate something claimed to be from the spiritual or ethereal world. Though the word today is employed in the study of religion to talk about how religion, still so easily assumed to be concerned mainly with otherworldly concerns, is found in everyday objects and the manner in which the human body and the senses react to such objects, one important historical use of the term was in theological circles to denote an outward form as opposed to an inner intention. John Norris (1657–1712), Anglican clergyman and philosopher,

DOI: 10.4324/9781003140184-29

for example, could write in his *Christian Blessedness; or Discourses upon the Beatitudes of Our Lord and Saviour Jesus Christ* (1690): "the Defiring material Righteoufnefs, by a direct Act of the Will, actually makes a Man formally Righteous" (vol. 1, 79, quoting the 1707 edition). Or, again, consider George Smalridge (1662–1719), once the Bishop of Bristol and Dean of Christ Church, Oxford, in a sermon from 1713 informing his congregation that "the heathen and the Christian may agree in the material acts of charity; but that which formally makes this a Christian grace, is the spring from which it flows" (*Sixty Sermons Preached Upon Several Occasions*, vol. 2, 26, citing the 1852 edition).

The critical scholar might be concerned here, as these two early examples, as well as the preference of some for the term "material religion" in the study of religion today, both suggest a tension between external and observable form and internal feeling or meaning. The priority of the latter is then assumed, inasmuch as it is often thought to drive or motivate the significance identified in the former—some prior thing, after all, is being materialized or embodied (literally, to put something into the body). Such a dialectic reminds us of the traditional assumptions of the phenomenology of religion, wherein the sacred—taken to denote religion's heart or essence, writ large—is graspable or knowable only insofar as it manifests itself in objects, be they natural (e.g., trees or rivers) or created (e.g., material objects). Recall, for example, Mircea Eliade's comments in his once widely read book, *The Sacred and the Profane: The Nature of Religion* (1959): "a sacred stone is venerated because it is *sacred*, not because it is a *stone*; it is the sacrality *manifested through the mode of being of the stone* that reveals its true essence" (118; his italics). Since this connection between the stone and the sacred "is not arrived at by a logical, rational operation," Eliade maintains that it is incumbent upon the careful scholar of religion to ascertain—presumably through intuition and feeling—the dialectical relationship between the essence and its various manifestations. Although the vocabulary has certainly changed, there is something reminiscent of the once dominant (but often criticized) approach in today's emphasis on religion being embodied, lived, and materialized.

The term "material religion," however, pre-dates even Eliade. In his *Whole Works* (1822), the Right Rev. Jeremy Taylor, D.D. (1813–1892) connects the term to the public service in the Church of England, discussing how God "overcame the difficulty in defiance of all such pretences, as were made even from religion itself to obstruct the better procedure of real and material religion" (vol. 6, 432). And the English poet and philosopher Hannah More (1745–1833) writes:

> But, if material bodies are the sources whence general knowledge is derived, why is every thing to be incorporeal which respects religion?

If innate ideas have no existence in the human mind, why are our religious notions not to be derived from external objects.
(vol. 7, 251, citing the 1835 edition of *The Complete Works of Hannah More*)

In addition to such early usages, "material religion" could also be used pejoratively to differentiate the lesser corporeal as opposed to the greater metaphysical. For instance, from her 1813 book, *Germany*, the Baroness Staël Holstein (1797–1838) adopts a once prominent developmental association between the two: "the progress of the human mind has been characterized in every different manner, passing from material religion to those which are spiritual, from nature to Deity" (vol. 1, 305). Similarly, we read in an article, "Modern Deities Worshipped in the Dekkan," by the Rev. J. Stevenson, D.D. that appeared in the *Journal of the Royal Asiatic Society of Great Britain and Ireland* (7 [1843]: 105–112):

> The subtility of argument and flights of imagination the Brahmans in former times have exhibited in expounding an ethereal philosophy and a material religion, ought to encourage the hope that when philosophy has been brought down from heaven to earth, and religion directed to the worship of that Spirit who requires to be worshipped in spirit and in truth, a new race of Hindu philosophers and divines will yet be seen adorning their respective walks of literature.
>
> (112)

That there is often an implied, though sometimes quite explicit, racist valence operating in this vocabulary should therefore not go unnoticed.

If, prior to sometime around the year 2000, the term tended to be used in this manner, to differentiate the prior spiritual from the mundane material, after this date the term is transformed and now used in such a manner that the way to access the spiritual is through the material. For instance, in his *A History of Religion in 5 1/2 Objects: Bringing the Spiritual to Its Senses* (2014), S. Brent Plate—a scholar closely associated with the material religion movement today—informs the reader that the book they hold in their hands is "about a religious love, though not necessarily the love of a god" (3). "This book tells the story of a human half body," he continues, "such as we are, and some of the objects we connect with in our quest for religiously meaningful, fulfilling lives" (3). Some may read these as curious claims for an academic book (even for one directed at a wide readership, as is this volume) devoted to history (at least given the fact that this term appears in the title). However, in suitably phenomenological fashion, Plate goes on to differentiate between the sacred and the profane, listing types of objects (e.g., stones [in rather Eliadian fashion], incense, drums, crosses, and bread) that, though "ordinarily common, basic, profane," can become "extraordinary" by means of "religious experience" (4). In a passage reminiscent of Eliade—a scholar whose now often critiqued work remains curiously influential in the analyses of Harvard's Charles Stang, such as his essay "Digging Holes and Building Pillars: Simeon Stylites and the 'Geometry' of Ascetic Practice" (*Harvard Theological Review* 103/4 [2010]), which seeks to "move Eliade from the margins [of scholarship on this fifth-century Syrian ascetic] to the center of our interpretation" (465)—Plate notes that "the strangest part of all this is the assertion, for example, that a rock can have character, agency, power, and not just when it trips us on the sidewalk" (10). The goal for Plate, as indeed it is for many others engaged today in the now popular study of material religion, is to examine more closely the role of the senses in this experience, all in order to come to a richer documentation (and perhaps even appreciation) of it. As with the phenomenological tradition in the field, however, the prior and presumably motivating religious experience is simply assumed, taken for granted, or otherwise passed over in silence—it exists solely because both practitioners say, and scholars infer, that it does. There is no critical effort expended on the practical social and historical conditions that might lead people to claim that they have had such an experience in the first place, let alone the effects of making such claims.

The material religion approach now begins to sound remarkably like its cognates, such as lived religion or embodied religion, all of which emphasize an awareness of the human body as an overlooked but still secondary site of religious manifestation. We learn more about religion, according to those who promote this understanding, from the kinesthetics of a body in prayer than we do from the authorized liturgy that informs the prayer as ritual. It is not just the body of the religious practitioner that becomes the focus or object of study, however, but also the body of scholars as well, as they participate in or watch the movements in question. This means, again like lived religion, that the primary way to collect information is through participant-observation and ethnography, sometimes to such an extent that studies in this genre can border on "auto-ethnography," basically the inserting of oneself, as a scholar, into a larger narrative, often by focusing on oneself and one's actions and responses. Thus, we read in Manuel A. Vásquez's introductory chapter in the *Wiley Blackwell Companion to Religion and Materiality* (2020):

> As contributors to the turn towards materiality, we . . . embrac[e] the embodiment of both the religious practitioners and the scholars who study them. This embodiment involves a material being-with,

being-amongst, and being-through materiality that has binding consequences for how we practice religion and how we study it.

(7)

Vasquez here builds on his own study, *More Than Belief: A Materialist Theory of Religion* (2011), wherein he sought to show how Latino immigrants to the United States were, and indeed still are, less interested in high Church doctrine than they are in trying to make sense of their new lives in their new homes through the material culture that they have brought with them. "How," he asks, "can the heavily textual approaches that are still dominant in religious studies explore the full force of glossolalia, exorcism, and divine healing among Latino(a) Pentecostals and Charismatic Catholics"? Accordingly, the critical study of religion needs a theoretical attunement to the embodied ways that knowledge—religious and non-religious—is acquired and transmitted.

This "turn towards materiality" can be witnessed in a wide variety of works from just the past few years. To cite a short but representative list of books: Fabio Rambelli's *Buddhist Materiality: A Cultural History of Objects in Japanese Buddhism* (2007); E. Frances King's *Material Religion and Popular Culture* (2009); David Morgan's edited volume, *Religion and Material Culture: The Matter of Belief* (2009), with chapters on such topics as dolls as the locus of the spiritual in Japanese homes (by Inge Daniels) and clothing as the site of embodied experiences of belief (by Anna-Karina Hermkens); Tracy Pintchman's *Sacred Matters: Material Religion in South Asian Traditions* (2015); Plate's own edited resource, *Key Terms in Material Religion* (2015), with entries on, among other topics, body, display, icon, masks, medium, smells, and sound; Timothy W. Jones and Lucinda Jones-Matthews's collection, *Material Religion in Modern Britain: The Spirit of Things* (2015), with chapters on objects of transcendence (by Joseph Webster) and Irish Catholic cathedrals (by Ann Wilson); Bruce M. Sullivan's edited *Sacred Objects in Secular Spaces: Exhibiting Asian Religions in Museums* (2015); and David Chidester's *Religion: Material Dynamics* (2018). Then there is also the Bloomsbury Studies in Material Religion book series, now numbering ten volumes, including Charles Orzech's *Museums of World Religions: Displaying the Divine, Shaping Cultures* (2020) and Natalia K. Suit's *Qur'anic Matters: Material Mediations and Religious Practice in Egypt* (2020). We could also point to events such as the "Materiality, Mediation, and the Study of Religion" conference held at Utrecht University (in October 2012) and the "Material Religion Embodiment, Materiality, Technology" interdisciplinary conference held at Duke University (in September of 2015). There also exists Concordia

University's Material Religion Initiative (a working group of the Centre for Interdisciplinary Studies in Society and Culture), whose website describes the context of the research group as follows:

> the study of religion has undergone an important shift, as a growing number of scholars foreground the role of diverse forms of media, technology, material culture, embodiment, and the senses in research on religious experiences, practices, affiliations, and forms of public-making.

Of course, we must also not overlook the peer-reviewed journal, founded a decade earlier, that helped to establish this now thriving subfield, *Material Religion: The Journal of Objects, Art and Belief*. The journal, as described on its website, examines "how religion happens in material culture—images, devotional and liturgical objects, architecture and sacred space, works of arts and mass-produced artifacts." And further: "Ritual, communication, ceremony, instruction, meditation, propaganda, pilgrimage, display, magic, liturgy and interpretation constitute many of the practices whereby religious material culture constructs the worlds of belief." Despite the claims of those engaged in material religion, critical scholars may be cautious of the apparent reintroduction, as already mentioned, of phenomenological method into the study of religion and thus the possible repackaging of the old idea that the sacred is *manifested*—though now opting for the terms materialized or embodied—in the profane along with the purported importance or religious experience, re-articulated for a new generation. While "material" conditions—by which we can signify capital, economic, political, and other practical conditions—are certainly important for the critical scholar of religion, those engaged in the study of material religion use this term in a rather different manner, prompting one to ask just what is being materialized and embodied. Most often, it appears to be the illusive term "meaning" (if not religious experience itself, of course) which is thought to be placed into or found within artifacts which are themselves sometimes studied as if they have a motive force, or agency, of their own. We see this, for example, in Colleen McDannell's important early contribution to this subfield, *Material Christianity: Religion and Popular Culture in America* (1995). This amounts to reporting what participants say in response to the observer's questions—an approach that broadens our descriptive understanding, to be sure, inasmuch as more than just the leadership of a group is queried, but what is lacking is a theorization of these descriptive reports. For such an approach may assist us to document how meanings are, as McDannell phrases it, "directed and articulated" (17) but they do not go much distance toward helping us to explain meaning and experience as all too human and thus historical productions.

While there are certainly gains to this so-called turn to the material, such as broadening the scholar's sense of what counts as legitimate data, as well as who scholars should be speaking with as part of their studies, there is nonetheless a nagging sense of the unexplained ethereal throughout this subfield. We can also see the way this subfield seeks to complicate a prior generation's almost exclusive emphasis on the written and therefore codified reports of elite practitioners concerning their beliefs. This emphasis is often criticized as too closely mirroring Protestant assumptions and practices (e.g., see the opening page of Matthew Engelke's "Material Religion" in *The Cambridge Companion to Religious Studies* [2012]). Yet, what seems to have been overlooked is that all we have ever had to study were items of material culture. It is just that many of our peers too quickly went from reading a tangible thing called a scroll or a text to assuming that it was merely an "expression" of a prior, animating force—whether called an intention, a belief, meaning, or that old nugget from the British philosopher Gilbert Ryle (1900–1976): the supposed ghost in the machine. It is this jump, this attribution of agency, self, and meaning, that really ought to be attracting our attention—whether attributed to people, texts, or stones. So perhaps a better way to approach all of this would be to say that whatever we call "a culture" or "a religion" is itself the evidence of prior or current flesh and blood human beings engaging in observable actions (i.e., producing, sorting, contesting, etc.), making plain that "material culture" (the term that pre-dates "material religion" by about a century) is itself a redundant term. To the critical scholar, there is no prior, non-empirical thing called culture that only later somehow manifests itself in teapots or clothing. Instead, "culture" itself is a sound that we make or a script that we write, not unlike "religion," and one that acts as a placeholder in our efforts to collect, organize, signify, and thereby make sense of a situation—something that the contributors to the once influential book, *Writing Culture: The Poetics and Politics of Ethnography* (1986) certainly understood.

Culture, let alone this thing that we call religion, is therefore always and already material. Prefacing it with the adjective "material" tells us nothing new, other than that the person doing so more than likely acts *as if* there's some prior or long-lasting ethereal thing floating out there or in here somewhere, that somehow manifests itself, under its own steam, first here and then there. And, at least for critical scholars, that sort of action is something that needs to be studied rather than just engaged in ourselves. For only if we presume that the things we designate *as* religion were something and somehow other than thoroughly historical and inevitably material (and thus constituted by some mysterious surplus that defies eyes, noses, and tastebuds)—as evidenced in Engelke's surprisingly frank claim: "[m]ateriality is the stuff through which 'the religious' is manifest" (213)—would we proceed as if adding this particular qualifier tells us anything that we did not already know.

In this volume see: culture, essence, experience, interpretation, lived religion, phenomenology, practice, religion, sacred/profane, society

In *Religion in 50 More Words* see: church, emic/etic, hagiography, icon, idol, piety, prayer, renunciation, ritual, sacrifice, symbol, theology, totem, tradition

29 Method

Often distinguished from theory, and just as frequently used in combination with it (i.e., the now common term "method and theory"), the word "method" signifies the approach one takes to a topic of study, along with the tools that one uses in going about scholarship. These can include, for example, the comparative method or the participant-observer method (when carrying out research that will result in writing an ethnography). If the ideal of the sciences is to study our material systematically and as part of a replicable step-by-step procedure, such that the analysis of some topic is the same regardless of where it is carried out or by whom, then a preoccupation with careful method, both following one and reflecting explicitly upon its use, should be a characteristic feature of any scientific pursuit (understanding this term "science" more broadly than just its current close association with the natural sciences, of course). It is for this reason that, as each generation comes of age in the field, new works on method in the study of religion are published, in which long-standing issues in the field are renegotiated, such as the two-volume *New Approaches to the Study of Religion* (2004), with essays on such topics as comparison, translation, etc., or as also seen in the many multi-author handbooks and companions that now exist in the field, with survey essays on various approaches to the study of religion (e.g., Michael Stausberg and Steven Engler's important volume, *The Routledge Handbook of Research Methods in the Study of Religion* [2012]).

The modern noun "method" is derived from the Latin *methodus* and, prior to that, the ancient Greek *méthodos* naming a way of investigating a topic or the procedure and approach one adopts. It also names a medical tradition in late antiquity, such as Chapter 3 of Galen's (d. 210 CE) *On Medical Experience*, which differentiates between such early Methodists and those who we would today refer to as the Dogmatists as well as the Empiricists. (This is not to be confused, of course, with the Protestant denomination, Methodism, established in England in the mid-nineteenth century.) Apart from more generic uses simply to name a way of proceeding or a plan of action, and thus a way of attaining some particular end, by the early seventeenth century the term had come to mean a classification system or an organized procedure, evidenced early on in William Shakespeare's *Hamlet*, written around 1600, such as in Act 2, Scene 2, when Ophelia's father, Polonis, says of Hamlet (who is pretending to be insane): "Though this be madness, yet there is method in't." This sense of a systematic or eventually even rational procedure colors much of the word's modern usage, such as Thomas Hornby's later book, *A Treatise on the New Method of Land Surveying, with the Improved Plan of Keeping the Field Book, Designed for the Use of Schools, and For Those Who Wish to Be Practitioners of the Science* (1827). However, in the modern theater the term is closely associated with the Russian actor and director, Konstantin Stanislavski (1863–1938), naming an approach that some actors use to identify viscerally with the role that they are playing, sometimes inhabiting the character all throughout a play's run or while shooting a film, with Marlon Brando (1924–2004) still being among the most cited examples of a so-called method actor.

Perhaps one of the most famous uses of the term as a scholarly mode of analysis is René Descartes' (1596–1640) 1637 *Discours de la Méthode Pour bien conduire sa raison, et chercher la vérité dans les sciences* (English: *Discourse on the Method of Rightly Conducting One's Reason and of Seeking Truth in the Sciences*). The work is, in part, concerned with ascertaining a non-theological foundation upon which a system of human knowledge could be built, something that he claimed to have found in his ability to doubt everything *but his own existence* as a thinking subject. Hence his famous declaration, "*Je pense, donc je suis*" (I think, therefore I am). There also exist explicitly theological uses of the term, especially in the Christian tradition of systematic theology. We see this in the work of Bernard Lonergan (1904–1984), the Canadian Jesuit theologian, especially his *Method in Theology* (1973), which argues for a unified approach across theological fields, one that could then be used as the basis to judge whether any progress in these fields had been made.

More narrowly, both "method" and "methodology" have often been used in the academic study of religion, to name both the approach that one adopts in studying religion as well as the work of those who examine the tools and methods that bring the study of religion into existence in the first place. A prime example of this is Jonathan Z. Smith's book, *Drudgery Divine: On the Comparison of Early Christianities and the Religions of Late Antiquity* (1990), ostensibly a work in Christian origins. Despite the topic of the work, Smith engages in a subtle but nonetheless significant change of view so that it can also be read as making a significant contribution to methodology by illustrating how scholars have traditionally gone about making comparisons (i.e., searching for sameness) while arguing for an alternative approach (an

Method 169

emphasis on both difference and illustrative analogues). Smith's work thus shows the difference between data and method, and in such a manner that the latter should be of significance to any student of religion no matter what religion or period they happen to work in.

This reflection upon and refinement of method has played a large role in the study of religion, not just by those critical of earlier approaches. It has also been done by those who have argued that religion was unique and therefore something that could not be reduced or explained. We think of the so-called Chicago school of thought from the late 1950s onward, associated early on with the work of Joachim Wach (1898–1955) and then Mircea Eliade (1907–1986) and Joseph Kitagawa (1915–1992) but, more recently, exemplified by the well-known work on myth by Wendy Doniger. What helped to define this group *as* a school of thought was their shared interest in developing and using a common method, capable of tackling the unique experience that they all agreed defined religion. This resulted, early on, in Eliade and Kitagawa's influential, co-edited volume, *The History of Religions: Essays in Methodology* (1959), which included chapters by, among others, the Canadian Islamicist, Wilfred Cantwell Smith (1916–2000), the Italian historian of religions, Raffaelle Pettazzoni (1883–1959), and the German theologian and scholar of religion, Friedrich Heiler (1892–1967). A variety of other edited books on method in the study of religion also emerged out of Chicago: e.g., 1967's *History of Religions: Essays on the Problem of Understanding* (edited by Kitagawa, Eliade, and Charles H. Long [1926–2020]); 1985's *The History of Religions: Retrospect and Prospect* (edited by Kitagawa); and, in 2010, *Hermeneutics, Politics, and the History of Religions: The Contested Legacies of Joachim Wach and Mircea Eliade* (edited by Christian Wedemeyer and Doniger). Writing in the Preface to the 1959 volume, theologian and historian of Christianity, Jerald C. Brauer (1921–1999), then the Dean of the Divinity School, home to Chicago's program in the History of Religions, states that the volume shares both Wach's and Eliade's common "concern that the discipline develop and exhibit a method adequate to its own content, problems, and materials" (x). Translation: although psychologically or sociologically reductive approaches had, by then, developed their own systematic approach for studying religion as a secondary effect based on prior and natural causes, such work was not deemed adequate by historians of religion. The latter was the name for the field adopted by Chicago, instead of the more customary Religious Studies, based on the German *Religionswissenschaft*. The History of Religions, as articulated at Chicago, began with the assumption that religion was *sui generis* (Latin for self-caused), and predictably concluded that only a unique method could properly grasp religion's unique essence. It makes sense, then, that the method they settled on was interpretative, aiming to understand the presumably deeper and often hidden meaning of religion by the scholar, in a word, re-experiencing the existential situation that led to the religious expression to be experienced in the first place (whether it be manifested in a text, a symbol, a ritual, architecture, etc.).

This interpretive method—one that assumes a stable meaning to a text, object, or act, if read in the *correct* manner—remains a popular option for some scholars today, notably those committed to engaging in what is commonly referred to as "a close reading." Yet, for others, the terms "method" and "methodology," especially when used in conjunction with the word "theory," name a rather different stance on the character of religion and the approaches needed for its study. Instead of assuming that a unique method is required for its proper study, from the late 1980s onwards others engaged in "theory and method" argue quite the opposite to Eliade et al. Rather than imagine religion as unique, we begin to see the adoption of the same methods used to study other human behaviors and organizations. This includes even the category religion, which can be studied as historically specific efforts to name, organize, and manage aspects of the natural world. This more critical focus on such long-standing categories as religion, myth, ritual, canon, magic, pilgrimage, superstition, primitive, sacred, etc., hardly exhausts the work today that is understood as methodological—work that is often surveyed early on in required courses in graduate school, making the "method and theory" class almost a rite of passage for many as they enter the field. This more critical interest in method drives both novel and interesting work in the field on the one hand, along with a variety of more conservative responses from those still interested in studying the essential or privileged meaning of religion on the other. The latter still retains the notion of having respect for participants' own self-understandings, something evidenced in the rise of recent subfields like lived religion or material religion.

While often critiqued as the domain of "dead white males" (such as those still covered in the typical method and theory survey course, from Marx to Frazer, Tylor, and Freud, etc.), today this more critical tradition of work in the field is being carried out by a far wider and more varied group of scholars, trained not only in traditional subfields of the study of religion (e.g., New Testament, Asian Religions, Religion in America, etc.) but also in such fields as social theory along with gender and race studies. Allow us to give two recent examples. The first is Leslie Dorrough Smith, whose work applies methods from social theory to study the techniques used by groups to manage membership and identity—among both so-called religious people as well as the scholars who study them (e.g., her book, *Righteous Rhetoric: Sex, Speech, and the Politics of Concerned Women for America* [2014]). The second is Richard W. Newton, whose work takes a method devised initially to study both origins narratives and how texts are authorized (and turned into something popularly known as scriptures) and applies it to the analysis of other texts, such as widely read works of literature (e.g., *Identifying Roots: Alex Haley and the Anthropology of Scriptures* [2020]). Both Smith and Newton count among a new generation of scholars focused on studying religion as a human act and institution while paying careful attention to the tools that they use. This latter is a form of self-consciousness that Jonathan Z. Smith (1938–2017) described as a scholar of religion's "primary expertise" in the influential Introduction to his *Imagining Religion: From Babylon to Jonestown* (1982).

Like other critical terms examined throughout this volume, method and methodology are equivocal, in that they have each been adopted by parts of the field that are sometimes diametrically opposed. Wilfrid Cantwell Smith famously characterized as his "revolutionary" methodological rule for the field: "that no statement about a religion is valid unless it can be acknowledged by that religion's believers" (from his now classic 1959 essay, "Comparative Religion: Whither—and Why?" included as a chapter in the above-mentioned methodology volume edited by Eliade and Kitagawa). We could then juxtapose this with the peer-review journal founded in 1989 by graduate students at the University of Toronto and now published with Brill of the Netherlands, *Method & Theory in the Study of Religion* (*MTSR*), which has become a leading journal interested in history, sociology, economics, race studies, and so on. The difference between these two traditions can be seen as an issue of theory, given that one can argue that a scholar's theory of religion prompts their choice of method and, finally, their selection of data on which to use said approach. A Marxist scholar, for example, will surely not adopt a Jungian method in their studies of religion—making for a rather different understanding of the so-called scientific method discussed earlier. It would seem that—all depending on how one defines "theory," of course—only the latter group of scholars (i.e., those associated with *MTSR*) have a theory (whether derived from sociology, psychology, economics, literary studies, critical race studies, etc.). The former, however, seem only to possess what might be better characterized as a rough intuition about how that which they designate *as* religion somehow transcends or defies all attempts to study it as something thoroughly human and thus inherently historical, sociological etc. In this way, work such as Cantwell Smith's method is *not* grounded in theory—an organized set of propositions about aspects of the world that can be applied and tested at discrete sites, about such general things as how groups form or how cognition works. It would instead seem to be based in the sort of folk knowledge that is often shared among those whom the scholar of religion might study, people who, understandably perhaps, claim that or act *as if* their actions and institutions are legitimized in ways that defy human understanding. Often the word "approach" has been preferred to "method" by those Humanists who find the latter's frequent association with the word "theory" to be too closely associated with work carried out in the social and natural sciences. As such, and contrary to the noted Chicago scholar of myth and ritual, Bruce Lincoln, those using such interpretive methods to study religion's uniquely deep meaning "speak of things eternal and transcendent with an authority equally transcendent and eternal." Such an approach, as Lincoln argues in the second of his "Theses on Method" (published in *MTSR* 8 [1992]: 225–227) is better understood as religious and not as historical and therefore not as critical scholarship.

In this volume see: classification, comparison, critical, experience, explanation, interpretation, theory

In *Religion in 50 More Words* see: commentary, dialogue, emic/etic, initiation, ritual, symbol, tradition, understanding

30 Methodological agnosticism

Methodological agnosticism is the name for a stance, attitude, or approach that scholars of religion have often employed, as they would say, to suspend (often said to be linked to the Greek *epochē*, "holding back") their personal judgments about religion while they are engaged in their academic work. Their methods, in other words, are considered to be agnostic—a term coined by the writer Thomas Huxley (1825–1895) in the late 1860s, as an Anglicized version of the ancient Greek *ágnostos* (from *gnósis* for knowledge), naming one who claims to possess no privileged knowledge on a given topic. Or, as he phrased it:

> Some twenty years ago, or thereabouts, I invented the word agnostic to denote people who, like myself, confess themselves to be hopelessly ignorant concerning a variety of matters about which metaphysicians and theologians, both orthodox and heterodox, dogmatize with the utmost confidence; and it has been a source of some amusement to me to watch the gradual acceptance of the term, and its correlate agnosticism.

The quotation comes from an 1884 letter of Huxley that was first published in *The Agnostic Annual* and quoted in a column in the *Sacramento Daily Union* (18/150 [February 16, 1884]). By 1885 *The Agnostic: A Monthly Journal of Liberal Thought* had been founded, bearing quotations from Huxley along with the early sociologist, Herbert Spencer (1820–1903) and the biologist, Charles Darwin (1809–1882) on its masthead. Included in the contents of its first edition was a short poem with the line: "No mortal mind can reach the mystic *Why*" (6). As applied to the tools and approaches used in the study of religion, the approach—to be distinguished from personally adopting such a stance in one's own life, of course—advocates avoiding so-called truth questions that the historically based scholar just cannot answer. One such question, for example, might be: did Siddhartha Gautama really become an enlightened Buddha? As phrased by the once influential philosopher and mathematician, Bertrand Russell (1872–1970), in his 1953 essay "What is an Agnostic," an agnostic is one who "suspends judgment, saying that there are not sufficient grounds either for affirmation or denial" (*The Basic Writings of Bertrand Russell, 1903–1959* [1961], 577). It is, then, a skeptical attitude that, in theory, has traditionally differentiated the academic study of religion from theology. In the latter, insider privilege and thus special forms of knowledge—sometimes called belief or faith—are routinely drawn upon in making or authorizing claims. However, we say "in theory" because, despite appeals to the contrary, some have argued that the field of religious studies is still very much interested in the articulation of broad (but not necessarily denominationally specific) truth claims, in ascertaining the nature and validity of religious experience, and then trying to determine the relationship between religion and a higher or deeper reality.

The term "methodological agnosticism" was coined by the phenomenologist of religion, Ninian Smart (1927–2001) in his 1972 book, *The Science of Religion and the Sociology of Knowledge*. He did this in direct response to the sociologist Peter Berger's (1929–2017) proposal for a methodologically atheistic study of religion, as outlined in his once influential book, *The Sacred Canopy: Elements of a Sociological Theory of Religion* (1967). It is perhaps coincidence that these two books, both concerned with the "proper" way to study religion in a public university, appeared in the immediate aftermath of the US Supreme Court case, *School District of Abington Township, Pennsylvania v. Schempp* (1963; popularly known as *Abington v. Schempp*). While preventing such things as Bible readings and prayer in public schools, on account of what is popularly known as the separation between Church and state, the Court acknowledged that it was certainly legal to teach *about* religion in public schools, so long as it was carried out in a secular and non-theological manner. As the majority decision famously put it (famous at least for that generation of scholars looking for a rationale by which the study of religion could find a place within US public universities):

> it might well be said that one's education is not complete without a study of comparative religion or the history of religion and its relationship to the advancement of civilization. It certainly may be said that the Bible is worthy of study for its literary and historic qualities. Nothing we have said here indicates that such study of the Bible or of religion, when presented objectively as part of a secular program of education, may not be effected consistently with the First Amendment.

The following year the US National Association of Bible Instructors (NABI, coincidentally the Hebrew term for "prophet") changed its name—originally founded in 1909 and called the Association of Biblical Instructors in American Colleges and Secondary Schools until 1933—if not its overarching methodology, to the American Academy of Religion (AAR). So-called secular departments of religious studies at state universities (e.g., Indiana, Iowa) were soon established around the country. This is, of course, a particularly North American narrative, to which could be added others, such as the field's longtime presence in Britain, where it often existed (and continues to exist) as a subcomponent of larger theology programs. A pressing question was thus: how to define this new study—both its object of study and its method—and, just as importantly, how can both be differentiated from classical (and now unconstitutional, when practiced in a tax-funded school) theological approaches?

The main term in Berger's preferred "methodological atheism" has a much lengthier history in English, of course. It entered the language in the sixteenth century from the French *athéisme*, itself from the Greek privative particle "a" (to denote absence or negation) + *theós* (God), hence atheism meaning the denial of God. The term in English, not unlike French, therefore, signals the disbelief in, or denial of, the existence of a god—whether used as an accusation and thus criticism of someone else or, instead, as a self-identification used as a badge of honor. Thus, Francis Bacon (1561–1626), in his *The twoo bookes of Francis Bacon: Of the proficience and aduancement of learning, diuine and humane* (1605):

> And therefore there was neuer Miracle wrought by God to conuert an Atheift, bycaufe the light of Nature might haue ledde him to confeffe a God; But Miravles haue beene wrought to conuert Idolaters, and the fuperftitious becaufe no light of Nature extendeth to declare the will and true worfhip of God.
>
> (22)

Or consider that Eliezer Cogan (1762–1855), an English scholar and teacher (of, among others, the Prime Minister Benjamin Disraeli), published in 1800 a book with the title *Christianity and Atheism Compared in a Discourse Delivered in the Meeting House, Carbunkle Street, Cheshunt*; his argument was that

> fpeculativ atheifm, is therefore principally to be dreaded, becaufe it may, and probably *will*, conduct to atheifm of practice; a fpescies of atheifm, I am forry to add, not confine to thofe who deny in form the being of a God. Multitudes there are who bear the Chriftian name, who live without God in the world.
>
> (21)

Though the term "atheism" has a fairly lengthy history in English where it could be neatly, if conveniently, used to distinguish true and proper belief from its opposite (which might be termed heresy), its connection to the adjective "methodological" dates, seen above, to the late 1960s. Berger coined the term in order to show, as he wrote in *The Sacred Canopy*, that "every inquiry into religious matters that limits itself to the empirically available must necessarily be based on a 'methodological atheism'" (100, citing the 1990 edition)—something that necessarily involved bracketing "the ultimate status of religious definitions of reality." This means that, according to Berger, religion has to be seen by scholars as a human creation, nothing more. This reinforced the idea that secular scholars of religion ought to adopt a theologically neutral, value-free position (i.e., objective) with respect to the study of religions. At issue in these early methodological debates is what the study of religion should be, in addition to framing its object of study. It can be, as many desire, an interpretive field where the scholar sifts through manifestations of religious experiences in a never-ending quest to track down the unique characteristics of the sacred. Or, it can be like other disciplines throughout the human sciences—such as anthropology, psychology, or sociology—that is, a field wherein scholars seek to understand and explain, through observation and description, aspects of human behavior known as religious, but doing so without affirming their truth or eventual and ultimate value.

The desire to take metaphysics out of the equation was certainly challenged. The Canadian theologian, Charles Davis (1923–1999), argued against this "methodological atheism" in his 1980 book, *Theology and Political Society*, stating: "When applied to religion this method excludes, as all modern science does, any appeal to God and keeps therefore intact the principle of methodological atheism"—a principle that he there called "the cornerstone of all modern science" (129). In this context, it might also be worth mentioning the spirited debate over the proper way to study religion that Davis had with another Canadian scholar, Donald Wiebe, in the pages of the Canadian scholarly journal *Studies in Religion/Sciences religieuses* (*SR*). In an article titled "The Reconvergence of Theology and Religious Studies" (4/2 [1975]: 205–221), Davis remarked that "the distinction between theology and religious studies has served its purpose. It is now outdated" (205), and that a "reconvergence" between the two approaches would introduce "greater clarity and honesty into the procedures of both." Wiebe, well-known as occupying quite the opposite position in the field, retorted in a response with the title "Is a Science of Religion Possible?" (7/1 [1978]: 5–17) that, if we were to take Davis's position seriously, then to study religion one would need to be "in some sense at least, religious, for there is a *uniqueness* in the religious experience that is impossible to capture

Methodological agnosticism 177

in rational, scientific concepts" (5, italics in the original). Wiebe argues here that the methods used in the academic and ostensible secular study of religion unfortunately have a propensity to fall back on the language, assumptions, and categories of theology, ones that a methodological atheism had sought to avoid. Though scholars in religious studies desire to be seen as an accepted academic field, Wiebe maintains that its default position is often one that is interested only in studying the external expression of what are presumed to be highly subjective and thus non-empirical inner experiences.

As already noted, among the main criticisms of Berger's proposal came by way of the Scottish historian of religion Ninian Smart, who is credited with helping to lead departments first at the University of Lancaster and then, later, at the University of California at Santa Barbara. Perhaps somewhat like Davis, he was bothered by the term "atheism" associated with the study of religion. He was therefore critical of Berger's assumption of God's non-existence for the purpose of studying religion. In his aforementioned *The Science of Religion and the* Sociology *of Knowledge* (1972), Smart argued that the term "methodological atheism" implies that scholars must deny the possibility that the objects of religious faith are true or real— itself a truth claim of dubious basis. After all, as Smart argued in his 1983 textbook, *Worldviews: Crosscultural Explorations of Human Beliefs*, "the agnostic has not decided whether God exists; the theist and the atheist have" (149). According to him, we know and study religion only through what he referred to as its various "dimensions" or manifestations; as he listed them, they were: the ritual, mythological, doctrinal, ethical, experiential and social dimensions. Though these manifestations may well vary from culture to culture and time to time, an essence, called religion, was nonetheless presumed to exist (making evident his phenomenological assumptions) and features of this essence can then be inferred, or so it is argued, from observing particular cultural and social dimensions, especially in comparative perspective. As a result, Smart—and then many others, throughout the past 50 years, or so—preferred the phrase "methodological agnosticism," allowing them to defer, or bracket out, questions of transcendental value and ahistoric origin. As the sociologist of religion Rodney Stark has phrased it in his *The Rise of Mormonism* (2005), "whereas only methodological agnosticism represents good science, both methodological atheism and theism are unscientific" (34). Whether explicitly recognized or not, this stance today informs much of the work being carried out in field, such as the still widely present world religions paradigm evidenced in publishing and school programs for the study of religion.

Criticisms of this still dominant view continue, however. For instance, Elizabeth Arweck, writing in her *Researching New Religious Movements: Responses and Redefinitions* (2004), has observed how difficult such an approach is to maintain. After all, it has always balanced on a tightrope, according to Mary Keller (in *The Hammer and the Flute: Women, Power, and Spirit Possession* [2002], 233 n. 13)—especially when the once strong boundary between researcher and subject has broken down, as it has for many who now see the onetime goal of disengagement and objectivity as illusory at best and, at worst, a disguised means of imposing the scholar's own point of view under the guise if disinterest. For instance, Tim Fitzgerald, in his critique of the field, *The Ideology of Religious Studies* (2000), argues that scholars of religion have long used the notion of "methodological agnosticism" as a way to support their traditional theological claims that religion somehow comprises a distinct and thus special category for study. This leads to the claim that the study of religion requires a unique set of methods that protects it from the sort of critical assessments that might attend studying the many other claims that social actors regularly make about the world. According to Fitzgerald, then, what most scholars of religion take to be distinctive is a transcendental referent (whether God, the sacred or some other unverifiable and unanalyzable object or sentiment). Thus, while claiming to be "agnostic" when it comes to the approaches it uses to study claims about this transcendental referent, such careful bracketing nevertheless assumes religion to be set apart (Latin *sui generis*, of its own kind) and thus stakes a claim on its existence or, at the very least, treats the topic more carefully than does the study of almost any other human topic. Fitzgerald concludes that this returns us to the realm of theology, from which the secular and academic study of religion ostensibly sought to differentiate itself. This circularity, based as it is on presumptions of the irreducibility of the sacred, means that the study of religion continues to be based on principles akin to those of the people the scholar studies—with the protestations of many to the contrary.

Other critiques of such approaches have emerged from the so-called postmodern turn in the field, at least as it has been adopted by some writers. Consider an article entitled "The Study of Religion and the Return of Theology" (*JAAR* 72/1 [2004]: 195–215), in which Gavin Hyman argues that the way to reframe the study of religion is *not* to engage in the sort of critical and genealogical study that is suggested in this volume but, rather, to engage in what is represented as theoretical pluralism. The way to do this, he suggests, is to embrace the so-called postmodern idea that we can never actualize neutrality, that once hoped-for Archimedean point from which to examine other cultures, one that seems to be suggested by both methodological atheism and agnosticism. Instead, according to Hyman, this goal of neutrality is "highly particularistic, being indissolubly linked with a modern scientific canon of rationality" (199). His solution? "[R]eturn to the adherent's particular tradition, which then serves as the criterion of truth for that individual and that community" (202), advice that ostensibly means that everyone sees their own religion as true, so scholars ought to as well (a position that makes it a challenge to study groups with which one disagrees, we should note). Hyman's odd use of the postmodern turn here, to return scholars to the question of truth, would seem to be little more than a replacement of critical theory for a liberal form of theology, something we have already witnessed above in the much earlier debate between Davis and Wiebe.

Despite being seen by some as a *passé* issue, this debate continues to comprise one of the field's main points of debate. We see this, for instance, in Sara J. Fretheim and Elias Bongmba feeling the need to note that much African Christian scholarship on religion today is "distinct from methodologically agnostic approaches to the study of religion in Africa" (as quoted in their volume, *Kwame Bediako and African Christian Scholarship: Emerging Religious Discourse in Twentieth-Century Ghana* [2018]). Their effort, such a difference notwithstanding, to include such voices is shared by the contributors to Karen Lauterbach and Mika Vähäkangas's recent volume, *Faith in African Lived Christianity: Bridging Anthropological and Theological Perspectives* (2019). Another recent attempt to address the problem in this same fashion may be found in another article published in the *JAAR*, by Michael A. Cantrell: "Must a Scholar of Religion be Methodologically Atheistic or Agnostic?" (84/2 [2016]: 373–400). Like Hyman, Cantrell also invokes postmodernism as a way to reintroduce theological concerns into the study of religion, with claims that Berger originally formulated his concept in a decade defined by positivism and that, since then, we know better that truth and objectivity have been called into question. He then goes so far as to declare that "methodological atheism fabricates and trivializes religious experience and renders religious belief and commitment inexplicable" (375). The critical scholar, of course, would respond that, while trivializing is not the goal, always historicizing and studying such claims as thoroughly *human* claims is precisely the point of critical study.

Despite such attempts to dislodge Smart's methodologically agnostic stance, it still plays a crucial role in the academic study of religion. We see this in Religious Education classrooms around the world, along with university lecture halls, where students are encouraged to withhold judgment and empathetically understand the worlds of the people under study. The appeal is surely linked to the fact that, as historically and culturally situated scholars, we are unable to know what, if anything at all, exists beyond the empirical world, let alone which claim about such things is most persuasive or true. All that we have to study, then, are human behaviors, actions, and institutions—many of which happen to make their own authorized claims about just such things. Given criticisms of the methodologically agnostic stance—notably, from our point of view, that of Fitzgerald rather than many

180 Methodological agnosticism

of its other critics—it may therefore be wise to follow Bruce Lincoln's lead. He carefully distinguishes truths from truth claims and regimes of truth (see the last of his "Theses on Method" in *MTSR* 8 [1996]: 227)—with the last as the contingent and always changeable structured conditions which enable the second to be made and debated, and, if heard as persuasive, the first to then be asserted.

It is not so much that critical scholars bracket out or suspend the issue of truth, as Smart might have once recommended, but, instead, that they study its establishment and inevitable contestation as historical acts carried out by social actors who always come to the dispute with practical interests and goals. So, while probably finding considerable interest in the detailed work of such a scholar as the anthropologist Tanya Luhrmann, whose work is "agnostic about the ultimate source of the event" (*How God Becomes Real: Kindling the Presence of Invisible Others* [2020], 83), the critical scholar's work has only begun once we have established a thick description of some act of claim. In fact, they may even end up siding with Craig Martin in his essay, "Incapacitating Scholarship: Or, Why Methodological Agnosticism Is Impossible" (in Jason Blum's volume, *The Question of Methodological Naturalism* [2018], 53–73).

In this volume see: belief, description, experience, explanation, interpretation, method, orthodoxy, phenomenology, pluralism, religion, sacred/profane

In *Religion in 50 More Words* see: commentary, emic/etic, evil, idol, magic, piety, theology, tradition, understanding

31 Origin

Why would the Prime Minister of India, Narendra Modi, go to the city of Ayodha, in northeast India—long held to have been the birthplace of Rama (along with Krishna and various others, said to be an avatar, or incarnation, of the great god Vishnu)—as he did in August of 2020, to give a speech on the ruins of a sixteenth-century mosque that had been destroyed in Hindu nationalist riots back in 1992? Well, not just to give a speech but to engage in a series of public Hindu rituals orchestrated around a groundbreaking ceremony for the construction of a new temple on the site, proclaiming, as part of his speech: "The wait of centuries is coming to an end." With the COVID-19 virus ravaging India's people and its economy at the time, the event's references to what many there would no doubt describe as the nation's glorious Hindu past provides for us an initial example of the powerful nature of discourses on origins. In this case we witness what some there claim to be the origins of the Indian nation—a nation-state thoroughly modern, of course, but which, on occasions such as this, makes strategic use of a discourse on a lost—but apparently now regained—golden past. As reported in the *New York Times* on August 5, 2020, "Mr. Modi's Ayodhya ceremony was a captivating distraction. It symbolized Mr. Modi's 'total domination over India,' said Arati Jerath, a political commentator." Tales of origins, far from an idle narration of where something came from, are thus socially formative devices that therefore require more from the critical scholar than just their repetition and paraphrasing.

The word "etiology" (also spelled aetiology, from the ancient Greek *aitía* for cause) was once used as a technical term to name a family of tales that narrate the origin of something. A prime example is a cosmogony, i.e., a myth on the origins of "order" (from the ancient Greek *kósmos*), a story that tells how the system of order that we call the cosmos came into being. Yet, there is an ambiguity between the modern English terms "cause" and "origin," which suggests a semantic range that, once again, might prompt

DOI: 10.4324/9781003140184-32

confusion if used uncritically in scholarship. While some ways of talking about causes (e.g., temperatures of 100°C or 212°F *cause* water to boil) are historically situated, empirical, and therefore at home in the university classroom, there are yet other ways of talking about origins that are imagined to pre-date history (e.g., "In the beginning . . ." that opens the Bible's Book of Genesis) and therefore removed from all forms of evidence, suggesting that the two discourses need to be distinguished. Generally, in the study of religion, origins tales refer to the latter type of narratives, usually classified by scholars as myths and mostly told by members of groups when situating themselves in their world. However, the manner in which narratives of origins are sometimes treated by scholars as if they have historical veracity is troubling and in need of closer attention.

Based on the ancient Latin *orīgō* for source or beginning, the modern word "origin" continues to imply ancestry or lineage and thus even the provenance and legitimacy of something. Entering from French, we see the term used in English from roughly the fourteenth century onward, along with the adjective "original," the later noun, "origination," as well as the related adjective and noun "aboriginal" (for those people or things considered to have existed somewhere from the earliest times). The term is often used with regard to the place or time from which something is said to have first arisen or been created. In this latter sense, it occasionally coincides, as noted, with the word "cause," which names either the source or the reason and thus motivation for something to be or to be the way that it is. Consider the title of the book by the Reformation-era German Anabaptist, Balthasar Hubmaier (1480–1528): *Reason and Cause why Every Man who was Christened in Infancy is Under Obligation to be Baptized According to the Ordinances of Christ, Even Though He be One Hundred Years Old* (1527). The assumption is that to identify a source is also to identify the reason for something's existence, as may be seen in the title of the book by the dissenting English minister, Israel Worsley (1768–1836): *An Enquiry Into the Origin of Christmasday: Shewing that this and the Other Festivals of the Christian Church are Continuations of the Heathen Feasts of Antiquity. Together with Remarks on the Celebrated Number Three, which Has Been Made Sacred by Pagan Superstition* (1820). Throughout the nineteenth century "origin" gains considerable prominence, especially in scholarship and notably for those influenced by Darwinian evolutionary theory to account for the perceived changes in entire species—or in the case of some, groups of people—over time. Thus, we have the title of Charles Darwin's (1809–1882) own influential book, *On The Origin of Species by Means of Natural Selection Or The Preservation of Favoured Races in the Struggle for Life* (1859). Implicit in the title is that if we can identify something's origin, we can then somehow understand its *raison d'être*.

Origin 183

Applied to the study of religion, notably in the later nineteenth and early twentieth centuries, the term is most often associated with early theories of religion's cause. This is associated with a variety of naturalistic and therefore explanatory theories of religion that sought to trace religion's origins to an error in reasoning among early human beings. We see this, for example, in E. B. Tylor's theory of animism (a term for belief in spiritual beings), as argued in his then influential book *Primitive Culture* (1871), or in the British anthropologist, R. R. Marett (1866–1943) and his subsequent theory of mana (a term adapted from Melanesia to denote a primal and pre-animistic sense of power), as elaborated in his entry in James Hastings's once well-known *Encyclopaedia of Religion and Ethics* (1915, vol. 8, 375–380). By the first decades of the twentieth century, such attempts to trace the origins of religion, with little or no prehistoric evidence, were tantamount to speculation. While it might result in a gripping story, such theories increasingly were of dubious scholarly value since there was no way either to confirm or disconfirm such assertions.

The early twentieth century instead saw a move toward functionalist approaches, which were more concerned with studying religion's observable social, political, psychological, economic purpose or role. This meant moving away from studying prehistoric time to conducting fieldwork among contemporary groups. Despite the shift, scholarship continued to be shaped by an interest in ahistorical origins—something argued persuasively by Tomoko Masuzawa in her book, *In Search of Dreamtime: The Quest for the Origin of Religion* (1993) as well as her entry "Origin" in the *Guide to the Study of Religion* (2000), not to mention Willi Braun's critique of scholarship on Christian origins, e.g., his essay collection *Jesus and Addiction to Origins: Toward an Anthropocentric Study of Religion* (2020). Despite the increasing focus on fieldwork with contemporary groups by means of the participant-observer method, scholars would still fall into the temptation of drawing untestable conclusions on the distant and even prehistoric past based on inferences from their current observations. It took quite some time for scholars to realize that people living elsewhere in the world did *not* correspond to a living artifact of humanity's supposedly common evolutionary past. Thus, nineteenth-century references to our historical predecessors as being the supposed "childhood of the species" found their counterpart in later references to "the primitives." For instance, consider the French Catholic, Alexander Le Roy (1854–1938), and his *The Religion of the Primitives* (a book based on his long career as a missionary in Africa, beginning in 1877), where, representative of his time, we read that "[t]he primitives that our theories deal with are barely disengaged from animality" (1922, 284). We also see this in the much later *The Cambridge Ancient History, Vol. 1 Prolegomena and Prehistory*, from as recently as 1970, where we find unproblematized, descriptive claims made about "primitive ways of life," "primitive man," "primitive languages," and "primitive occupation." There also exists an entire chapter, the third, devoted to "Primitive Man in Egypt, Western Asia, and Europe," which is concerned with the earliest record of human habitation in these regions. While this latter may well lack the overt chauvinism of Le Roy's earlier book, it nonetheless participates in now rather troublesome assumptions about the presumably universal or inherent qualities of early human populations, in distinction from what was usually just referred to as "modern man."

What might be apparent by now is that origins tales can be understood in two rather different ways, only one of which strikes us as critical. The first understands them as narratives that are exclusively concerned with saying something factual about their object, such as a tale concerning how the nation was founded. The second, in contrast, understands them as narratives that use some object, such as the nation's past, as an opportunity to authorize the speaker's own position. Since the time of origins is lost to historical research, then claims about it cannot be studied with an eye toward how accurate they are or are not. Even more recent historical events, such as founding the nation or how one's grandparents came to move from there to here, have many possible causes, all somehow working in concert with one another. However, there also exist many possible viewpoints such that each one inevitably selects items from the archive of the empirically knowable past by subsequently connecting those items into a narrative that makes sense to, and suits the interests of, the contemporary speaker. Recognizing this complexity suggests to us that origins discourses are not actually concerned with their purported topic—how some past thing came into being—but instead seek to legitimize or benefit the position of the one who is telling or hearing the tale. This shift in how we study origins tales takes seriously recent work in historiography, which argues that claims about the past implicate the historian far more than previously recognized. In our own field, we see this approach in those like Jonathan Z. Smith, who argued that, for example, the thing that scholars today designate as "the archaic" is actually something devised in the modern era, to satisfy contemporary curiosities (see his essay, "Scriptures and Histories" in *MTSR* 4/1 [1992]: 100). Returning to narratives of national origins, it is not difficult to find dramatically different tales within the same nation-state, each drawing upon different items from the archive of a nation's past. This archive contains dramatically different events and actors, often held together in tension with one another, some of which are authorized by the nation's leadership while others are dear to marginalized subgroups within. The tales that result sometimes explicitly conflict with one another, given that they are in the service of contesting

Origin 185

positions in the present, despite both supposedly narrating the story of how the same group arose.

Because origins tales can be neither confirmed nor rejected, they are particularly convenient for entrenching a wide variety of contemporary interests *as if* they were each eternal, obvious, and justified. For this reason, we need to be careful in how we treat such accounts in our work. Even the supposed simple task of describing a group's narrative of its own past risks uncritically reproducing and thereby legitimizing it. While this tendency might be obvious when used to describe the tales of groups that are widely seen to be controversial, it is often more difficult to detect when descriptive scholarship passively recounts an origins narrative shared by the members of groups seen to be uncontroversial. Consider scholars of Christian origins who wish to study the ancient social world from which what we today call early Christianity arose. They are understandably suspicious of the common story told by Christians, which involves a fairly linear narrative concerning Jesus's birth, teachings, and eventual crucifixion followed by the ardent work of disciples. Such a narrative, however, strikes critical scholars as being the refined product of later writers, back-projected in time, in an effort to suit later purposes and self-understandings of what it meant to be a Christian. Oftentimes, these purposes and self-understandings may be radically different from those who are later considered to be the tradition's founders. That we could cite yet other examples should be obvious, especially those tales contained in each chapter of a world religions textbook, often differing very little from the story told by the group's own members.

To gain some more precision we can cite the distinction between origins and beginnings, as offered by the literary critic Edward W. Said (1935–2003), in his collection of essays, *Beginnings: Intention and Method* (1985). While origin claims imply for him a passive origination, as if something springs forth out of nothing (e.g., the old Latin doctrine of *creatio ex nihilo*, as applied to God creating the world from nothing), Said argues that claims made about something's beginning presupposes the agency or at least effect of a precursor of some sort, as in A was the beginning of B—which was itself the effect of yet another prior cause, and so on. This distinction implies that beginnings, as well as claims made about a beginning, take place in a world of historical cause/effect relationships, a world of choice, contest, and consequence, rather than what Said characterized as the privileged world of origins. This is a helpful distinction for those wishing to study the past but in a way that avoids the authorized voice of the origins tale. As the historian of religions, Bruce Lincoln puts it, the historical voice constitutes "that discourse which speaks of things temporal and terrestrial in a human and fallible voice, while staking its claim to authority on rigorous critical practice" which he distinguishes "in the sharpest possible contrast" from the discourse of our object of study, what we term religion, "whose defining characteristic is its desire to speak of things eternal and transcendent with an authority equally transcendent and eternal" (see the second thesis in his "Theses on Method," *MTSR* 8: 225).

Simply put, discourses on origins is what Braun has characterized as "a prominent (and troublesome) point of preoccupation, even devotion" for scholars, given "the possibility that origins are retrospective constructions" (*Jesus and Addition to Origins* [2020], 69). Discourses on what he calls absolute beginnings therefore should constitute data for the critical scholar of religion. They can be studied as rhetorical techniques, always of socially formative effect should they be heard or read as persuasive and legitimate. Rather than being understood as benign references to some bygone or distant era, we can instead analyze them as techniques that are invariably situated in the present of the speaker or the writer, who uses the narrative's supposedly timeless object as an opportunity to shape a particular representation of a past that will be understood to lead irresistibly to a present, all of which supports a specific set of interests and choices that shape our possible futures.

In this volume see: classification, description, explanation, function, history, method, power, theory, world religions

In *Religion in 50 More Words* see: creation/endtimes, emic/etic, founder, hagiography, nones, paganism, sacrifice, theology, tradition

32 Orthodoxy

Orthodoxy, not unlike its synonym "normative" or even its antonym "heterodoxy," has what a critical scholar might conclude to be a problematic history in the study of religion. For if they regard those beliefs or claims so-named as historical products, invariably produced by a set of situated and often highly ideological and thus contestable discourses (including those of the scholars who designate them *as* authoritative), then there is a tendency to designate only certain practices, traditions, or subgroups *as* normal or *as* proper, as if such designations were the result of a disinterested description or neutral statements of fact. For example, consider when someone says that orthodox Buddhists do not engage in violence or that mainline Christians believe in the separation of Church and state, thereby implying that those Buddhists who *do* commit violence or those Christians who do *not* subscribe to this distinction are somehow illegitimate or inauthentic. Even if these value judgments, which effectively function to rank and privilege certain subgroups among others, are not recognized by the scholar as such, they are often offered in scholarship, providing a useful examples of how, in the words of the American scholar of religion Steven Ramey, so-called "accidental favorites" are often selected and advanced in seemingly descriptive work. (See his Afterword to the edited collection, *Claiming Identity in the Study of Religion: Social and Rhetorical Techniques Examined* [2015].) Such favoritism is well out of bounds in the critical study of religion.

Tellingly, the noun "orthodoxy" derives from the Greek *órtho-* (meaning straight, rectangular, upright, perpendicular or, in the case here correct, right or proper) and *dóxa* (for opinion or belief). The latter term is also used in the Christian theological term "doxology," naming a short statement in praise of God used in worship services, such as the brief song, dating from 1674, that is sung collectively at the conclusion of a service in some Protestant denominations: "Praise God, from Whom all blessings flow . . ." Orthodoxy thus usually names the belief in or agreement with those doctrines and opinions that are held to be right or correct. The critical question in need of asking, of course, is: "As held by whom?" Indeed, the Eastern Christian Church is so sure of the correctness of its own doctrines that, in order to differentiate itself from its Roman Catholic counterpart (i.e., the self-proclaimed universal church [from the Greek], centered in Rome), it refers to itself simply as the Orthodox Church (with local specifications, such as the Greek Orthodox Church, the Russian Orthodox Church, etc.). That the term functions as part of a discourse of social contest for rank and thus authority therefore begins to become apparent. And, despite so-called Orthodox Judaism's emphasis on correct practice, oftentimes at the expense of an explicit focus on proper belief, it nevertheless refers to itself as Orthodox, implying that other forms of Judaism are less authentic and somehow not in accord with what are claimed to be traditional and thus authoritative Jewish teachings. (In this latter case, it is also worth emphasizing the cognate term "orthopraxy," which is the performance of what are believed to be correct practices, especially evident in ritual performance.)

The word "orthodoxy" seems to have come into use in English primarily in the aftermath of what is widely known as the Protestant Reformation, which took place in Europe beginning in the mid-sixteenth century, presumably as a way not just to name but to thereby demonstrate to others that new religious teaching were somehow more aligned with the original teachings of Jesus and thus the doctrines of the New Testament. Protestants maintained that these had been corrupted by the mediated layers of Catholic tradition and institution—again, making evident the term's role in normalizing options within a contest. For example, in the work entitled *Anti-Arminianisme* (1630) William Prynne (1600–1669), the English pamphleteer, lawyer, and prominent Puritan critic of Anglican Church policy, writes: "Dying men, especially of such orthodoxie, worth, and fame as he, speake truth." Or, again, in the English poet and politician, Andrew Marvell's *Rehearsal Transpros'd* (1673), wherein we find: "His Sermon is extant . . . some Heads and Points of it I gave you . . . as a Pinne-paper of your modern Orthodoxy" (vol. II,70). Theologians and religious practitioners therefore have no problem determining what is "orthodox" belief in their communities and for their believers. In fact, one could go so far as to say that making and policing such judgments is among their primary roles, all in their attempts to manage the ever-changeable limits of group identity.

Here we should keep in mind Ramey's point that critical scholars of religion must be prepared instead to examine and uncover just how that which is represented *as* orthodoxy is constructed, disseminated, and, at times, overthrown and replaced, hearing claims of ortho- and heterodoxy as strategies social actors use. For example, constructions of orthodox

Orthodoxy 189

positions or practices are often based on showing, often retroactively, the errors of others. This is because the members of the class who are usually responsible for framing religious and theological doctrine, whatsoever we choose to call them (e.g., legists, jurists, theologians, clerics, ideologues, propogandists), find it necessary to create epistemological and ontological space for what they are doing while simultaneously showing how that which came before or that which currently threatens this new domain ideologically went astray or was just plain wrong. In antiquity we see this as early as the *Theodosian Code*, commissioned by the Emperor Theodosius and compiled between 429 and 438 CE, and which represented a compilation of all the laws of the Roman Empire under Christian emperors since 312. In so doing, the Code, among other things, divvyed up the social world it encountered into communities according to an orthodoxy/heterodoxy binary. This binary, not unlike the east/west one familiar to us today, means that the first item needs the perceived negative traits of the second, heterodoxy, for both its own definition and functioning. The identity of one is necessarily contingent upon the subsequent elucidation of the other. Without social groups that can be imagined and then portrayed as "wrong" or "incorrect," that which is constructed as orthodox ultimately remains adrift in its own lack of clarity.

Positions claimed to be orthodox do not simply appear, as previous generations of scholars assumed, wholly formed, and in such a manner that various heterodoxies only emerge after the fact to challenge its rightful supremacy. It was long held, for example, that so-called early Christian heretical groups (from the Latin, for a school of thought, later for that which is wrong), such as the Gnostics or Monophysites, were deviant movements that departed from what was, in opposition to them, represented at the time as mainstream belief. The tendency now is to acknowledge that such groups only later became understood as heretical, at which point the position that had slowly developed into Christian orthodoxy could be imagined as its opposite. The assumption that orthodoxy precedes heresy and that true teachings necessarily existed before before heretical ones is therefore a political one that often involves taking the writings of later theologians (e.g., Early Church Fathers, early Muslim thinkers, the Rabbis, even the ancestors) at face value, thereby authorizing them via a hindsight discourse on origins. When, as Ramey correctly noted, scholars simply describe such positions, they risk merely retelling the stories already recorded in their sources and told by their informants, thereby overlooking the disputes and ideological battles that went into the construction of what only later emerged as the seemingly authoritative orthodox belief or normative practice.

Whenever they find claims of orthodoxy/heterodoxy, scholars should therefore see the deployment of a set of discourses that are meant to organize and subsequently classify and rank often messy social worlds in which there are always a variety of options for group members. This would seem to me more profitable that simply presuming the existence of a supposedly pristine and true normative faith that is only subsequently undermined by those "heretics" who reject or distort the orthodox mainstream. Discourses around orthodoxy, then, manage boundaries and thereby establish the limits of identity for a community, defining who is in and, just as importantly, who is outside. For instance, although no introduction to the study of Buddhism is complete without identifying the later Mahayana tradition from the prior Hinayana tradition (of which Theravada Buddhism is considered to be one of the few remaining schools), learning the Sanskrit roots of these terms betrays that they are themselves evidence of such a contest, in that the former, naming the so-called Great Vehicle or Way, is distinguished from the latter, understood as the Smaller or Lesser Vehicle. It therefore makes sense not only that the latter term does not exist much in the earliest sources (that is, one would not expect it to be a term of self-designation), but also that the later Mahayana sources will use their own self-description as synonymous with what we might today designate as Buddhism itself. Using these seemingly innocuous descriptive names in scholarly work can therefore overlook—and by overlooking erase—a much earlier dispute, with the designations themselves being among the means by which the contest was waged and, presumably, won. In much the same way, claims of orthodoxy emerge subsequent to and function dialectically with competitors that are only retroactively labelled as lesser or wrong (i.e., heterodoxy). Since purveyors of orthodoxy dislike that which appears to be different (in terms of belief, doctrine, membership, and so on), they seek to ostracize, excommunicate, or otherwise put an end to what they consider to be "heterodox" or "heretical" belief and/or praxis, all in the service of solidifying their own group's position and influence.

Alternative positions represented as heterodox are therefore often reduced to taint and/or portrayed as infiltrated from external and thus impure sources. On account of this, they are often associated with claims of syncretism (or improper intermixing and thus impurity), producing a fear among those charged with ascertaining and maintaining orthodoxy and, because of this, they label such beliefs as "incorrect" all that compromises what they imagine as "correct." Heterodoxy—again, noting the ideological work this term is performing—undermines from within and risks destabilizing a community, as some understand it to properly function, notably those priding themselves on the possession of divine truth or seeing themselves as being in-step with the ways of their ancestors. Correct belief/practice, not surprisingly, is therefore articulated as the inverse of those beliefs/practices imagined to be in opposition to it.

Orthodoxy 191

Whenever scholars uncritically write or say, for example, "Muslims believe [x]," "Neo-pagans do [y]," Hindus maintain [z]," let alone the more recent claims that some scholars make about the so-called self-identified Nones voting in this or that way in an election, such descriptions unwittingly participate in and thereby reproduce this discourse of orthodoxy. This would be painfully obvious only if, following the unremarkable opening "Hindus believe . . ." one then included, matter of factly, a feature of a subgroup widely understood in so-called orthodox circles to be marginal to or even as a dangerous deviation of what was considered the proper, or we might say textbook, form of Hinduism. In such a case it would be evident to many within the academy that a mere part was being misportrayed as the whole, to the ideological benefit of those who identify with that part. Yet ultimately such misportrayals occur in all discourses on orthodoxy/heterodoxy. It is certainly no coincidence that the part usually claiming the central and thus superior position coincides with the interests of the one offering such unelaborated descriptions. Or, as another example, consider a roundtable in the pages of the *Journal of the American Academy of Religion* (84/1 [2016]) devoted to the topic of "normativity" (read: orthodoxy) in Islamic studies. Therein the reader is presented with Muslim perspectives on the environment, interfaith dialogue, gender, and other issues—all of which are written by scholars but from the perspective of Sunnī Islam, which, though but one among other branches, is just assumed to be the position from which a supposedly unified Muslim perspective is properly derived. There are, for example, no Twelver Shiʻi, Ismaʻili, Ibadi, or other Muslim voices represented—all of which, the critical scholar would no doubt conclude, are just as much as part of the Islamic tradition as those championed by the contributors. Accordingly, without debate or defense, but one type of Islam is simply imagined as normative, orthodox, and thus the only type of Islam worthy of consideration—thus its orthodoxy is established in the very act of seemingly disinterested description. Implicit as well as explicit claims of orthodoxy connote and thereby produce the impression of mainstream religion, irrespective of any particular tradition. In his "Religious Orthodoxy and Premarital Sex," for example, the sociologist Richard R. Clayton uses the concept of religious orthodoxy to refer to "the degree of commitment" of a wide variety of religions, including Catholics, Protestants, and Jews (*Social Forces* 47/4 [1969]: 469–474).

The problem with all of this is that uncritical descriptions or outright assertions of orthodoxy imply that there is a "right" or "correct" way to be religious, regardless of past or ongoing disputes within the group itself. Whatever does not conform to this ideal is then imagined to be "wrong" or "incorrect." That participants within groups engage in this behavior and make such normative claims should come as no surprise, of course, since the group is theirs to define and contest. The discourse on orthodoxy is therefore part of an insider's contest, with the critical scholar keen to chronicle the dispute, tracking the techniques employed by the various social actors involved in the dispute (something studied in detailed by the French sociologist Pierre Bourdieu [1930–2002], such as his book, *Outline of a Theory of Practice* [1977]). Participating in it, by uncritically adopting the position of one of the disputants, is something that ought to be avoided, as it is surely not our goal to pass judgment on the correctness or incorrectness of diverse people's beliefs, doctrines, or practices. However, given the fact that presumed essences (e.g., mainstream Jainism is defined by this and spirituality is best understood as that . . .) play such a large role in the history of the field, jettisoning the term as an analytic category will likely prove to be a difficult task. Regardless, the goal of the critical scholar is not to weigh in on matters of orthodoxy and heterodoxy, but to study the discourse and the implicit contest itself, to show how such concepts are always constructed and negotiated, historically, socially, and materially.

In this volume see: authenticity, culture, definition, description, environment, identity, lived religion, material religion, origin

In *Religion in 50 More Words* see: atheism/theism, church, east/west, emic/etic, fundamentalism, monotheism/polytheism, mysticism, paganism, reformation, theology

33 Phenomenology

Phenomenology names a method of study in mid-twentieth-century European philosophy. It was then adapted and proposed as the proper way to study religion, lending support to the idea that the study of religion was a unified academic discipline and not merely a cross-disciplinary and therefore polymethodic field. Within this latter context it might be worth pointing out that the discipline vs. field debate is still present, with European scholars often preferring the former, in part due to how university funding works in places on the continent, though adopting the phenomenological method is no longer the defining trait of those who today understand our studies to comprise a discipline. In the last decades of the twentieth century, however, phenomenology of religion became the focus of considerable critical debate, and though its dominance has now been dislodged, many of its basic assumptions about religion continue to inform how religion is studied.

Entering English from classical Latin around the sixteenth century, the modern word "phenomenon" (plural, phenomena; adjective, phenomenal; and sometimes abbreviated, as in popular speech today, to phenom) ultimately derives from the ancient Greek term *phainómenon*, that which appears to the senses or in the mind's eye. Sometimes it denotes a specific reference to the heavenly bodies, e.g., the ancient work, *Phaenomena*, said to have been written by Eudoxus of Cnidus (408–355 BCE), which, though no longer extant, is referenced in later writers such as Aristotle (385–322 BCE) or Diogenes Laertius (180–240), a Greek biographer writing some 400 years later. By the seventeenth century the word names an object of scientific analysis, as in the Scottish scientist, Joseph Black's (1728–1799) *Lectures on the Elements of Chemistry* (1807): "Let [the chemist] notice every general fact in the phenomenon . . . and carefully note the substances which are the subjects of these general phenomena" (vol. 1, 271). The term also names something noteworthy, unexpected, or extraordinary, such as the anonymous promotional booklet in the British Museum's collection,

DOI: 10.4324/9781003140184-34

Some Account of the Celebrated Madame Girardelli Known Throughout Continental Europe and in England, Scotland & Ireland as "the Wonderful Fire-Proof Phenomenon" (1818). Therein, a circus performer is presented as a "phenomenon" whose act is said to have included her being unharmed while swishing dangerous chemicals in her mouth or while placing red hot metal or flames on her skin and hair. It is in this latter sense that the word is used in common speech when something is described as wonderful or tremendous. The term is also used today in its abbreviated form, often reserved for describing particularly noteworthy individuals, such as the small book by children's author Valerie Bodden, aimed at teen fans: *Justin Bieber: Musical Phenom* (2012).

The word "phenomenon" can sometimes be used in current scholarship in its rather generic sense, as simply naming an item being studied, in which case it functions as a synonym for datum (plural data), a word that is regarded by some as controversial in the study of religion on account of the assumption that it dehumanizes the people under study. More specifically, though, when the term "phenomenon" is associated with the intellectual tradition of designating things as religious phenomena, it usually implies a particular sort of theory and thus definition of religion, along with an approach that is portrayed as required if such phenomena are to be studied properly. Because of this, critics avoid using the term altogether, while there are yet others who continue to freely use it when, for example, describing religious symbols, even despite the critiques.

Although for some the phenomenology of religion might simply designate a descriptive method (i.e., providing an account of the world as participants themselves reports experiencing it, free of commentary or analysis by the observer), the phenomenological method in the study of religion is rather more than this. It involves the use of what has been called *epoché* and eidetic vision—respectively: the suspension, or so-called bracketing and thereby setting aside, of all assumptions in order to neutrally or objectively describe items in the world as they present themselves to the observer. In this sense the term *epoché* derives from the Greek word of the same name, meaning the suspension of judgment, as first developed by ancient Greek skeptical philosophers. *Epoché* also implies the ability to infer, by using inductive reasoning after observing numerous discrete manifestations, something about the essential traits of a collection of similar items that are under study. The latter term, eidetic, derives from the Greek *eídos*, meaning form, shape, image, or appearance. Taken together these two operations—disinterested observation of particulars followed by inference to an otherwise non-observable, general principle—are so central to the phenomenological method, as classically practiced in our field, that the English translator, the Welsh Hegelian philosopher John Evan Turner (1875–1947), decided to highlight both in his English translation of the once influential Dutch phenomenologist Gerardus van der Leeuw's (1890–1950) famous *Phänomenologie der Religion* (1933) as *Religion in Essence and Manifestation* (1938). Indeed, the translation even bears the telltale epigraph from a poem by Johann Wolfgang von Goethe (1749–1832): "All things with God a changeless aspect wear," which one later commentator rephrased as follows: "It does seem that religion is experienced as bringing down to changeable man the experience of the immutable world" (see the essay by the Spanish Indologist, G. Gispert-Sauch, "The Dynamics of Cultural Pluralism and Worship Patterns," *The Journal of Dharma* 3/4 [1978]: 350).

Van der Leeuw's book outlined the method as it was used by subsequent generations of scholars who agreed that religion was so distinct from all other human operations and productions that it required an equally distinct method, one that avoided improperly reducing the *sine qua non* of religion to some non-religious source or cause. Setting aside for the moment whether this starting point ought properly to be even called a theory, such a conception of religion—often reflected in a definition of religion that made reference to the participant's experience of the sacred, the numinous, the holy or simply, as in van der Leeuw's preferred term, Power (with the uppercase intended)—led to the need for a scholarly method that would do no harm to what was seen as the uniquely meaningful object of the study. It was also presumed to be an object that existed only in the participant's own subjectivity—their experience of an otherwise ineffable source. Turning to Edmund Husserl's (1859–1938) philosophical phenomenology, those who later fashioned themselves as phenomenologists of religion found here (and in other sources as well) just the tools they needed, notably their reading of Husserl's interest in studying so-called things in themselves, that is, their essence or substance. In the words of the Irish philosopher, Dermot Moran, writing in the Introduction to volume one of Husserl's *Logical Investigations* (first published in 1900–1901) phenomenology constitutes "the efforts to inquire . . . back from the categories of objectivities to the subjective acts . . . in which the objectivities . . . come to be objects of consciousness" (2008, xxiv).

If philosophical phenomenology is concerned with how we come to experience the world, it would seem to differ dramatically from its later misapplication in the study of religion, the latter of which is focused on decidedly non-empirical characteristics. (See, for example, Jonathan Tuckett's 2018 essay "Prolegomena to a Philosophical Phenomenology of Religion: A Critique of Sociological Phenomenology," in *MTSR* 30/2: 97–136.) The phenomenology of religion can be likened to a theologically liberal approach, in which historically and regionally discrete items are of interest only inasmuch as they can be read as instances that betray something about a shared and enduring essence. We think here of the late-nineteenth-century and even mid-twentieth-century comparativists who placed decontextualized water, sun, or moon symbolisms and references side-by-side in order to conclude something about the sacred. This tendency, however, is still evident, not least in the field's long-established world religions paradigm—whether seen in the common introductory course and its textbooks (often still divided between Eastern/Western religions) or the manner in which this approach also structures much of the field's research (with specialties largely based on discrete religions). Consider, for example, the cover art to the first edition of the still widely used textbook (in its fourth edition as of 2019), *Sacred Paths: Understanding the Religions of the World* (1996), written by the onetime missionary and later Professor of Theology, Theodore Ludwig (1936–2020). The earlier cover offers a kaleidoscopic image that resolves into one distinct, central cell, an approach to the one and the many that hearkens back to van der Leeuw's use of the quotation from Goethe. Although Stephen Prothero is a notable current example of an author trying to resist this tendency (e.g., his book *God is Not One: The Eight Rival Religions that Run the World* [2011])—in its opening pages he calls the view that all religions are essentially the same "wishful thinking" and "naïve theological groupthink" that "has not made the world a safer place." Yet, sooner or later the temptation to identify an essential unity amidst the diversity, even if only as an organizing principle for our work, proves even too much for him, as in his later world religions textbook, *Religion Matters: An Introduction to the World's Religions* (2020). The Introduction to the latter work settles on grouping them all together as powerful story systems after attempts to identify them collectively as belief systems, ritual systems, or ethical systems fail to do justice to each of them. Apparently, we just agree that, after all, they are all religions.

Among the most prominent critiques of phenomenological method as it was adapted to the study of religion came from Dartmouth University's historian of religion, Hans H. Penner (1934–2012), such as his essay, "Is Phenomenology a Method for the Study of Religion?" (*Bucknell Review* 18 [1970]: 29–54). Apart from identifying the inconsistent use of the methods of their philosophical forerunners, Penner argues that taking phenomenologists of religion seriously means finding a contradiction between the two major operations of their work—the effort to study manifestations in detail in order to later infer features of their common, transcendent source. This is what van der Leeuw had phrased, in volume 2 of *Religion in Essence and Manifestation*, as "obtain[ing] ... its reflection in experience" (680). If, as someone like Rudolf Otto (1869–1937) once famously argued, this source is "wholly other," then, by their own admission, it is quite unknowable—even knowing whether "it" is indeed a unified or common thing that is conveniently illustrated in its supposed historical instances. As the British mathematician Frank Ramsey (1903–1930) is said to have once put it, in reply to the work of the philosopher, Ludwig Wittgenstein (1889–1951), especially the concluding lines of the latter's *Tractatus Logico-Philosophicus* (English edition 1922), "Whereof one cannot speak, thereof one must be silent": "What we can't say we can't say, and we can't whistle it either"—i.e., there's no artful way of getting around claims of ineffability and thus unknowability. Penner therefore concludes that a science of religion, at least as practiced by phenomenologists of religion, is an impossibility. (See also his still important article, co-authored with Edward Yonan, "Is a Science of Religion Possible?" *Journal of Religion* 52/2 [1972]: 107–133).

These debates continue to the present day of course. Though few who argue that scholarship needs to resist reductive, explanatory theorizing on religion's cause still openly claim to be phenomenologists, given the critiques levelled at the method. Instead, such active subfields as lived religion or material religion, to name just two, could be argued to employ much the same presumptions by imagining religion to be comprised by an inner uniformity that can be inferred only from studying local instances or so-called materializations. Although designating this core as the sacred or the numinous is far from common today—with Robert Orsi's work to rehabilitate Otto as a so-called theorist of the holy being a notable exception (see, for example, his chapter "The Problem of the Holy" in *The Cambridge Companion to Religious Studies* [2012])—the presumption that some enduring and universal sense of deep meaning is indicated by examining discrete items remains popular for many scholars of religion. For instance, consider Brent Plate's book, *Religion in 5 ½ Objects: Bringing the Spiritual to its Senses* (2015), with chapters on stones, incense, drums, crosses, and bread, which asserts at one point, in rather phenomenological fashion, that "[s]tones can be manifestations of a divine force" (doing so in a style that's reminiscent of an earlier phenomenological classic, Mircea Eliade's *Patterns in Comparative Religion* [1949]).

In this, phenomenology is no less reductionistic than the approaches its supporters criticize by this label. The method, in other words, reduces a wide variety of historically and regionally specific claims, practices, symbols, and institutions (i.e., manifestations), to a universally shared subjective state (i.e., an experience). This reduction, judging by its continued prominence in the field, offers an appealing model for anyone trying to overlay their own grand narrative onto history or present-day humankind. It offers a way to understand and manage what yet others would name as difference and possibly even a contradiction that defies easy understanding. Phenomenology offers what the critical scholar would characterize as an ahistorical response to the situatedness of history and culture, that is, when happenstance and contingency continually defy our efforts to make sense of the world as regulated and sensible. The phenomenological presumption concerning our ability to bracket and set aside our own subjectivity, while observing others, constitutes yet another dehistoricizing technique, for the world, lacking agency, does not "present itself" to us so much as we fashion a world in a variety of ways. Having said this, we should recognize that the effort to make the situation in which we find ourselves, filled with what can be seen as diverse and often competing elements, into a holistic environment that can be represented as predictable and therefore habitable is persuasive and effective for many—both within and outside of the university. This suggests that we should expect that such approaches will not go away any time soon (case in point, *The Sea Can Wash Away All Evils: Modern Marine Pollution and the Ancient Cathartic Ocean* [2006], by the Harvard scholar of religion, Kimberley Patton)—which means that a critical re-contextualization of the claims made in such scholarship will continue to be needed as well.

In this volume see: definition, description, environment, experience, explanation, lived religion, material religion, method, power, sacred/profane, theory, world religions

In *Religion in 50 More Words* see: emic/etic, immanence/transcendence, symbol, theology, understanding, value

34 Pluralism

While pluralism can be argued to be a beneficial thing, problems arise when the academic study of religion is imagined to be the place to both promote such a concept and such a social end, something that is unfortunately all too often the case. While certainly the study of religions can aid in understanding the diverse and pluralistic social worlds that humans create for themselves, such an approach should not be an end in and of itself for the critical scholar. Yet many go about their work as if the study of religion's classrooms and publications are home to a form of interfaith dialogue that nurtures understanding religious "worldviews" different from our own. There is a tendency to appreciate religion and diverse religious expressions, in much the same way, perhaps, that some art appreciation courses train students to respect or even savor something called "art," and often doing so with very little interest in the material and social conditions that lead to its creation let alone its changing valuation over time.

The word "pluralism" combines the Anglo-Norman adjective (spelled variously, e.g., *plural, plurell*, and meaning more than one or many) with the common suffix *-ism*. It derives from the German term *Pluralismus* and the Latin adjective *plūrālis*, which initially had two primary meanings in English, one ecclesiastical and the other philosophical. The former denotes the system or practice of one person occupying two or more offices or positions, especially with regard to offices within the church hierarchy and governance. Thus, W. Pennington's *A Free Inquiry into the Origin, Progress, and Present State of Pluralities* (1772)—a book concerned with refuting, among others, Henry Wharton's (1664–1695) previous *A Defence of Pluralities, or, Holding Two Benefices with Cure of Souls as now Practifed in the Church of England* (1692)—and thus a volume much concerned with the many different versions of the Christian church had arisen since "its firft inftituion under the government of the Apoftles and their immediate fucceffors" (1). Pennington opens his Preface with the following: "The Permiffion of Non-refidence and a Plurality of Benefices with Cure of Souls has always been the occafion of many fcandalous abufes" (iii). Such "scandalous abuses," while on clear display to some in the Church at that time, nevertheless often went unpunished. As he goes on:

> We are fure from hiftoric facts, they could fee the turpitude of Pluralifm, when it prevailed among their inferiors, and fpeak of it with feverity they could underftand well enough that every falary was a reward to enforce the laws againft delinquents of a lower order.
>
> (54)

Likewise, in the 1885 autobiography, *The Life of Sir Robert Christison, Bart.* (edited by his sons), the baronet and Scottish author (1797–1882), onetime physician to Queen Victoria and among the founders of the study of nephrology, complains that "Pluralism was at this period (1822) in the ascendant in the Scottish Church" (vol. 1, 411). In the realm of philosophy, on the other hand, pluralism can refer to the theory that the world is made up of more than one kind of substance or thing, as opposed, say, to the stance known as monism, which reduces the world to but one substance. Classically this is exemplified in those ancient Greek thinkers known as the pre-Socratics, whom we now term materialist monists, who debated what exactly was that one substance (e.g., air, fire, or water). In the history of philosophy this has posed a problem for many, especially the later Neoplatonists, from the third century onward, who had to try to explain how what was one and simple could produce the complexity of the sublunary world. In fact, even as late as the early twentieth century, the distinction between pluralism and monism posed a problem for many philosophers. In his *The Realm of Ends, Or Pluralism and Theism* (1911), based on his prestigious Gifford Lectures delivered between 1907 and 1910, for example, the English psychologist and philosopher James Ward (1843–1925) opined "that pluralism has equally failed to reach a satisfactory of the problem of the One and the Many" (47–48). This leads, according to Ward, to "the pendulum of human thought swing[ing] between the two extremes of Individualism (or Pluralism) leading to Atheism and Universalism (or Absolutism), leading to Pantheism and Acosmism" (46).

While today in most liberal democracies—itself a form of government, traced to eighteenth-century Europe, that, like others, could be understood to be founded on a specific way of navigating and thereby managing this very issue—the term pluralism is often employed as positive thing for society. This is because a so-called healthy liberal democracy is supposed to be able to account for and include, at least in theory, all of its minority and ethnic groups. Such was not always the case, however. In the *Pluralism and Non-Residence: Unnecessary, Injurious, and Indefensible; and Their*

Entire Prohibition Practical and Indispensible to the Security, Extension, and Efficiency of the National Church; with Statistical Tables Founded on Public Documents (1838)—significantly penned by the anonymous "A Clergyman" and, as the Preface opens, written to "the friends of religion in every class and especially those in parliament"—we learn that the work is "directed to devise and promote such measures as will strengthen, enlarge, and perpetuate the *apostolical church*. Which the providence of God has planted in the land; and thus render it actually, as well as constitutionally, *the national church*" (iii; italics in the original). At risk to this enterprise, our unnamed author informs us (and who here sounds not unlike some contemporary neoconservative, nationalist demagogues), are those things designated as "pluralism" (i.e., those unlike "us") and "nonresidents" (i.e., those who do not live "here") (8). Our author seems to be worried that, if this situation should continue, the established Church, to wit the Church of England, would no longer be the religion of the majority—again, words not at all unfamiliar to current political debates in a variety of national settings.

Only in the early twentieth century, with the frequency of the English term's use rising sharply from the 1950s on, does the term come to denote the presence of a tolerable amount of diversity of ethnic or cultural groups within a society or state. This also includes the advocacy of toleration and acceptance of the co-existence of differing views, values, and cultures. This is evident in the sociologist Edward William Strong's (1901–1990) chapter "Civilizations in Historical Perspective" (1959), which, though using now outdated assumptions by which just some large-scale social groups are known as civilizations, nonetheless argues for a heterogeneous enough understanding of inter- as well as intra-variety among groups that "[o]ur description of civilizations remains pluralistic" (93). That Strong later had to resign as the Chancellor of the UC Berkeley campus due to the controversial handling of the so-called free speech student protest movement of 1964–1965, along with later mass arrests at sit-ins, introduces an important dose of irony concerning just how far tolerance for pluralism can often go.

In circles associated with the study of religion, however, pluralism often means—in the words of the late liberal Christian theologian John Hick (1922–2012)—that we ought "to think of the religious life of mankind as a continuum within which the faith-life of individuals is conditioned by one or other of the different streams of cumulative tradition" (as phrased in his once influential book, *God Has Many Names* [18, quoting the 1982 edition]). This pluralism can lead to a type of relativism, as it does for Hick and many in the field who do not see themselves as theologians, in that all religions are presumed to be essentially one, because religion, as a universal spiritual force, unites them all. To cite Hick again, "the different religious traditions, with their complex internal differentiations, have developed to meet the needs of the range of mentalities expressed in the different human cultures" (21). Or, going to the other end of the spectrum, this same pluralism can be seen as a threat to true belief when, for example, Harold A. Netland—a missionary-turned-academic, onetime student of Hick's, and later Professor of Philosophy of Religion and Intercultural (often just another name for "pluralism") Studies at Trinity Evangelical Divinity School—disagrees with his former teacher. According to him, "other religious systems can be regarded as forms of unbelief in so far as they explicitly reject what Christian faith affirms or they embrace teachings incompatible with Christian faith" (see his *Encountering Religious Pluralism: The Challenge to Christian Faith and Mission* [2001], 17–18). Thus pluralism, not unlike the views of the much earlier authors quoted above, "emerges from and serves humankind's sinful tendencies," something of which we are aware only "from the special work of grace by the Holy Spirit upon our hearts" (18). While such a view, let alone Hick's positive but nonetheless theologically inspired assessment, is surely beyond anything that ought to pass for the critical and secular study of religion, we do nevertheless see such sentiments at work throughout the field. Consider, for instance, the former president of the American Academy of Religion, David Gushee, a professor of Christian ethics at Mercer University and who is ordained by a Southern Baptist church. While initially opposed to LGBTQ+ civil rights, he subsequently changed his mind, something on display in his 2015 book, *Changing Our Mind: A Call from America's Leading Evangelical Ethics Scholar for Full Acceptance of LGBT Christians* (2nd ed.). While many would no doubt congratulate him on changing his mind to a more liberal perspective by now arguing for a plurality of voices and lifestyles within his own church, critical scholars would contend that the study of religion is *not* an avenue to achieve religious reform—whether one authorizes one's speech on contemporary issues from either a so-called liberal or a conservative theological position. Instead, it is concerned with examining and always historicizing the social worlds that humans make for themselves by using a set of discourses that they (sincerely) imagine to be divinely sanctioned.

Sometimes scholars of religion are called to weigh in on matter of civic pluralism, within their own social group, to defend it in light of detractors. We think here of the debates after the attacks of September 11, 2001 in the United States—debates which continue today. That the attackers flew planes into buildings in New York City and Washington (and crashed in rural Pennsylvania) in the name of religion in general, and Islam in particular, posed countless problems for the field of religious studies, many of whose members had long been in the business of representing religion as a force for all that is good, peaceful, and spiritual in the world. For religion, using the language that still largely defines the field (and perhaps even more so in recent years), is often portrayed as being fundamentally about achieving social justice, gender justice, racial justice, etc. According to this paradigm, religion is all about freedom, and rarely, if ever, about coercion or, regardless whether one agrees with or supports its use or not, about violence. And so, when it *is* about the latter, it ceases to be about religion, which, by definition, is quite often claimed to be immune from so-called politics or culture. A veritable post-9/11 cottage industry therefore emerged among scholars, not to mention journalists, to demonstrate how Islam was, like all others, essentially a religion of peace that had, in this case, like some others, been "hijacked" by "extremists." However, complicating all of this was the long-standing chorus in the field for scholars of religion to take participant self-disclosures *seriously*, as it was often phrased, by—as members of the phenomenological tradition in the field had long advocated—suspending scholarly judgments on the claims and actions. It soon became clear that the perpetrators of the events of 9/11 regarded themselves as not just being Muslims but, instead, as being the best and most pious Muslims, just as do those associated with such other contemporary militant movements as Boko Haram, ISIS, and al-Shabaab. (The problem, then, is with the limits of any pluralist stance.) Indeed, members of the field even adopted a relatively new category to more closely associate (what was then represented as mainline or orthodox) Islam with the other so-called Western or monotheistic religions, i.e., the mid-twentieth-century designation "Abrahamic faiths" or "Abrahamic religions." The latter term is certainly a strategic way of establishing the unity of Judaism, Christianity, and Islam while also taking into account a certain degree of pluralism and thus diversity. This is perhaps best encapsulated using the words of Leonard Swidler, Professor of Catholic Thought and Interreligious Dialogue at Temple University and the founder of the *Journal of Ecumenical Studies*; he writes:

> the three Abrahamic faiths have many more things in common, such as the importance of covenant, of law and faith, and of the community . . . But just looking at the list of commonalities already briefly spelled out will provide us with an initial set of fundamental reasons why it is imperative to engage in serious, ongoing dialogue with Muslims.
>
> (*After the Absolute: The Dialogical Future of Religious Reflection* [1990], 123)

Such works—obviously and unapologetically written from a liberal theological perspective yet understood by many in the field today to comprise a legitimate example of the study of religion—are attempts to get certain members of the various religions talking to one another for the sake of ascertaining their shared commonalities, since, according to this approach, all (authentic) religions are believed to be equally grounded in the sacred.

Another approach, one less theological but no less based on a similar liberal vision, is the study of religious diversity (recently also described by some as promoting a form of religious literacy among the general population). Take the case of Lori Beaman, who works at the University of Ottawa and who holds a Canada Research Chair in Religious Diversity and Social Change. Her work uses the idea of so-called "deep equality" to explain the micro-processes whereby people in a pluralistic society can work out their differences and accept one another as fellow citizens (e.g., her book, *Deep Equality in an Era of Religious Diversity* [2017], 2–3). In her scholarly quest to develop what she might represent as a true equality of others, Beaman and a team of international experts have gone even further and developed a grant-driven project that they call "Non-religion in a Complex Future" (with a wide variety of partners but funded by the Social Sciences and Humanities Research Council of Canada [from 2019 to 2025]) and which seeks to examine how non-religious and religious people can coexist in an increasingly diverse and complex world. The project is described on its website as taking into consideration "nonreligious populations," namely, the majority of people with no religion and who "are often absent in discussions about living well together in diversity." A more critical approach to such diversity was offered by Matt Sheedy, who, in an October 2015 post at the *Religion Bulletin Blog*, titled "The Niqabis Are Coming," argued that, rather than promote such diversity in multicultural societies, such as Canada, it is more appropriate for the scholar to examine the internal political debates over pluralism and multiculturalism (i.e., their limits and the interests that drive and benefit from them). He persuasively demonstrated how the then prominent discourse over the possible banning of the *niqab*, or full Muslim face covering, in the Canadian province of Quebec was less an issue of pluralism and more one of reacting against the federal government by appealing to the province's strong anti-clerical sentiment, its long-standing self-identity as a "distinct society" (i.e., from the rest of English-speaking Canada), and its preference for a variation of French secularism, i.e., *laïcité*. Rather than regard the issue as many others do, i.e., framed around the potentially competing issues of women's rights vs. religious freedom, Sheedy therefore encouraged critical scholars to imagine the debate as one that concerns the role of the state in defining what is or what is not a religious sign under the law, all in order to exercise a specific type of governance on its citizens. (See his book, *Owning the Secular: Religious Symbols, Culture Wars, Western Fragility* [2021].)

The critical scholar more than likely realizes that the goal of the study of religion is not to make normative positions on pluralism (even one with which, in their life away from their scholarship, they may in fact support). On the contrary, our role as scholars is to understand the rhetoric of pluralism in the modern world—its context, limits, and effects. Certainly, North Americans and Europeans live in highly pluralist societies, which most scholars would probably agree to be a beneficial thing—nonetheless, laws formally, and social conventions informally, continue to dictate the limits of the allowable. However, the goal of the critical study of religion ought not to be about promoting or celebrating that, for the study of religion is not the place to engage in religious appreciation or to promote respect for different viewpoints or understanding different "worldviews." Obviously, the critical scholar must, of course, take seriously the requirement for careful and nuanced descriptive work when it concerns documenting the self-representations of the groups they study. While those same scholars will undoubtedly draw upon a variety of tools and approaches when going about their work, there is little room for promoting either liberal or conservative views on so-called religious pluralism in the critical study of religion, at least insofar as it has come to be defined in the modern period. If, however, we want to shift the ground and examine the rhetoric of pluralism, the way that it excludes and includes, along with the ways that it can be curtailed or expanded and thereby used for various political and other ideological purposes, then surely it belongs to the data of the field.

In this volume see: authenticity, culture, phenomenology, politics, religion, religious literacy, sacred/profane, secular

In *Religion in 50 More Words* see: dialogue, emic/etic, fundamentalism, nones, syncretism, theology, understanding, value

35 Politics

The inclusion of the term "politics," along with our particular approach to it, perhaps best signals the volume's editorial stance. Many in the field, both past and present, regard this term as relevant solely to the externalization of religious faith, since religion is imagined as either pre-political or inherently apolitical on account of its perceived intimate relationship to private experience. We understand politics less as party politics, such as being a member of or voting for a particular party, and more broadly as the ongoing contest over who retains the authority to use power (whether coercive or persuasive). This latter understanding has unfortunately long been considered as secondary by many members of the field, many of whom prefer to see politics as a corrupting influence separate from the purer and original realm of sacred feeling and dispositions. Although writing for a popular audience, the British author, Karen Armstrong, nicely represents this tradition when, in the Preface to her *Islam: A Short History*, she flatly states: "The spiritual quest is an interior journey; it is a psychic rather than a political drama" (2000, ix). While those who hold this position certainly acknowledge that religions have what she goes on to characterize as "a life outside the soul," so-called power struggles are generally considered, as she concludes, "an unworthy distraction from the life of the spirit." This pose was especially evident in the aftermath of the events associated with 9/11, when so many scholars of religion tried to argue that the perpetrators of the attacks were not really "religious," but instead "hijacked" the real Islam for "political" (i.e., nefarious) ends.

Politics therefore enters the scholar of religion's analysis often only as part of the broader context of the expression of religious faith, something that is also termed piety. In her rightly influential book, *The Politics of Piety: The Islamic Revival and the Feminist Subject* (2005), Saba Mahmood (1962–2018) challenged traditional understandings of liberal secularism's division of faith from politics by offering "ethnographic examples [from Egypt] in which [pious Muslim] women may be seen as resisting aspects of male kin authority" (175). The subfield known as religion and politics has therefore been invigorated recently, not only following Mahmood's lead by examining the political ramifications of so-called embodied religion, but also in studying how political systems worldwide do (or, more likely, do not) promote so-called religious freedom. The latter can be seen, for example, in the influential work of Winnifred Fallers Sullivan, such as her *The Impossibility of Religious Freedom* (2007). Despite the importance of such recent work—notably refocusing attention on the agency of social actors who had traditionally been ignored by scholars along with the attempt to begin to understand practice as formative of belief—what is still common and worth considering, though, is the continued presumption that the public stage is where sentiments are either enacted or regulated.

We instead prefer to see politics as the contingent, i.e., historically and socially situated, contest for the right and ability to exercise power in the service of a set of practical interests. This understanding is considerably different from the aforementioned notion of "religion" and "politics." Such nomenclature generally signifies two separable domains that more or less interact with one another at the point where they meet, i.e., the "growing influence of religious factors on international relations and domestic politics" of which Hubert Seiwert writes (see "Politics" in *The Oxford Handbook of the Study of Religion* [2016], 431). Instead of adopting this admittedly prominent view, politics is here understood not as one domain interacting with others but, rather, as the operating condition for all social life and thus not merely the public stage on which faith is, at some point, displayed or acted out. Understood in this way, politics envelops day-to-day life, including not just those aspects designated *as* religious, since we understand religious identity not as an inherent quality, but also those classified and either protected or regulated *as* private. This means that the private/public binary, invoked so casually by Armstrong and so many others throughout the field, must itself be an object of study. It also inhabits the conceptual and institutional tools by means of which such designations are made and reproduced. We have in mind here the definition and use of such categories as religion itself, not to mention the sacred/profane binary or calling something a myth as opposed to a legend or a fairy tale, along with the rest of our scholarly vocabulary. Indeed, as the anthropologist Talal Asad has reminded us, "definition is an historical act" (see "Thinking About Religion, Belief, and Politics" in *The Cambridge Companion to Religious Studies* [2012], 39). We start from a position that argues that there is nothing other than the virtually limitless social and historical contexts which must be demarcated and delimited in order to become meaningful, and therefore useful, to social actors. All of this is accomplished through participating in an economy of signification (recalling Jonathan Z. Smith's theory of ritual;

see his "The Bare Facts of Ritual," *History of Religions* 20/1/2 [1980]: 116–117), whereby attention is concentrated or distracted, and action is carried out or suspended. Although managing such an economy is inevitable, because necessary in order for life to proceed in any fashion at all, there are innumerable ways to establish and regulate a ranked division of the social (us vs. them) and the historical (now vs. then), making the way that things happen to be arranged now hardly a natural or necessary occurrence. This ongoing negotiation over signification, which provides the structured situations in which force can be seen as legitimate or illegitimate, is what we mean to convey by the term politics.

Contrary to those approaches that cordon off negotiation and conflict by seeing them relevant only in studying (later) expressions of a pure faith, the world-making process that we have in mind is political through and through. We think here of the British Marxist literary critic Terry Eagleton, who once remarked about readers who noticed that his *Literary Theory: An Introduction* (1983) lacked a separate chapter on political readings of literature. "There is no need to drag politics into literary theory," he commented, in reply. Why? Because "it has been there from the beginning" (169, citing the 1996 second edition). By politics, then, Eagleton meant how social life was organized, and the power relations that are fundamental to it. This is not too far off from what we have in mind by seeing politics permeate all of social and historical existence, though we aim for a greater degree of precision by distinguishing power (i.e., the use of force) and authority (the legitimacy of the use of force) from politics (the ongoing negotiation over who retains, and what counts as, legitimacy in the use of force). Such distinctions help us to make sense of such modern developments as the idea of a "police force" or the "power of attorney," i.e., both naming the ability to act in ways that are represented as legitimate, at least according to the current ruling order, in order to further certain interests. In this regard, this very volume is itself political in that it seeks to identify and then contest some of the long-established assumptions about the structure and purpose of the field, and thus the practices within it. Whether its argument will be authorized by readers and, through their actions, participate in a force that effects some degree of change remains to be seen, of course.

Some might object that we have merely substituted a previous generation's use of "the religious" let alone "the sacred" for these three interrelated technical terms (i.e., force, authority, and politics), thereby making our approach just as theological as any other. However, we maintain that a key difference is that, siding with Bruce Lincoln, we are merely attempting to clarify his term "fallible," as in his definition of history as "that discourse which speaks of things temporal and terrestrial in a human and fallible voice." The precision that we hope our proposed clarification helps to make possible is itself an effort to carry through on Lincoln's further claim that the persuasiveness of this work is based on "rigorous critical practice" (see the second of his "Theses on Method," *MTSR* 8 [1996]: 225).

Before proceeding, however, it might be worth considering the etymology of the term. The noun "politics" (and thus the later adjective "political" and the noun "politician," and related to such modern words as polity, policy, as well as police) derives from the French *politique*, the much earlier Latin *politicus*, and well as the ancient Greek *politikós* (itself from a word for citizen, in turn from *pólis* for community, city, or city-state). The noun enters English in the early fifteenth century, steadily gaining in use from the mid-eighteenth century onward, and implies everything from a sensible, practical, and judicious person to a prudent system of oversight and regulation in civil, public affairs (i.e., the governance of the city). Thus we have historical examples ranging from John Skelton's late-fifteenth-century translation of the ancient Greek historian, Diodorus Siculus's (c.90–c.30 BCE) *The Bibliotheca Historica*: "The beneficiall and pollitike envention of oxen in the plough to tille the lond" (vol. IV, 313, quoting the 1956–1957 two-volume edition). From the same era, "They polytyk philosophyrs & poetes were," from "The Banquet of Gods and Goddesses" (part of the anonymous poem, "The Assembly of Gods" [line 1742]). Or, in the Scottish historian, John Gillies's (1747–1836) description of Aristotle in 1813, in words attributed to the early political theorist, John Locke, as "'a mafter in politics;' furpaffing in perfpicuity and precifion every writer ancient or modern in explaining how 'civil fociety is formed into different models of government' . . ." (*Aristotle's Ethics and Politics, Comprising His Practical Philosophy*, vol. II, Book VI, 317 [3rd ed.]). *The Annual Register Or a View of the History, Politics, and Literature, of the Year 1827*, published in 1828, describes the declining health of George Canning, then British Prime Minister (1770–1827) in the following terms: "It was not the mere ordinary contests of politics that now claimed his attention . . ." (chpt. VII, 189). Today, the term often popularly signifies—as already suggested—the particular system of participatory government (i.e., party politics) as well as being a pejorative term for those considered to be overly strategic or too cautious, even deceitful (being political, playing politics, or criticisms of so-called political correctness). The latter is related to the adjectival use of the term, as in someone being described as politic (i.e., careful and wise), as in artfully broaching a controversial topic. Traditionally it has also been used to name the group being governed, i.e., the collective or corporate body politic (a medieval legal concept that anticipated the modern understandings of business corporations as persons under the law). For instance, Charles Knight writes in volume 2 of his *Popular History of England* (1856): "The king of 'so tender age' [i.e., Edward VI (1537–1553), son of Henry VIII, who was crowned at the age of nine] was taught to consider these unhappy people [beggars and vagabonds] as weeds to be rooted out. He speaks of them as the 'filth' of the body politic" (469). Note here Thomas Hobbes's (1588–1679) book, *Leviathan or The Matter, Forme and Power of a Commonwealth Ecclesiasticall and Civil* (1651), whose frontispiece's etching famously pictured the giant, crowned sovereign looming over the landscape and whose body and arms, upon closer inspection, were pictured as comprised of his subjects, all facing toward the monarch.

While there certainly has been a range of meanings, we take seriously that both the individual and collective uses of the term generally presuppose the sort of strategic negotiation that we argue inevitably takes place in the social groups of which humans have no choice but to participate. Saying "people have social interests," for example, seems redundant, since the contestable social and the historical are the necessary operating condition of all human beings, even those who attempt to renounce the groups of which they were members, inasmuch as our very conception and rearing, let alone language and culture, all presuppose it. To be deemed prudent, judicious, or well-managed presupposes a judgment that, depending on who was making it, could have gone any number of other ways. This leads us back to what was argued earlier: politics denotes the contingent arena and the techniques used to contest the right to enact such judgments (i.e., to exercise authorized power). It is an arena that is in place whenever people work to make an alliance or aim to confront perceived difference, whether with regard to identity, status, or access to desired resources. It is also the grappling with the differences that become apparent when confronting the new or the unknown—a moment when techniques must also be deployed to understand (i.e., to manage and domesticate) the new situation. Understanding itself is therefore hardly a benign activity—as anyone can tell you if they have studied the linkage between the age of European expansion, colonialism, and the birth of the academic disciplines that today comprise the modern research university. This process involves local frames of reference being extended, as far as possible, to encompass the distant and the alien, searching for analogues and familiarities, thus making evident that intellectual no less than behavioral and institutional mechanisms come into play at the boundary of the strange and the unfamiliar.

It is not that religion and politics are intertwined, as argued by, along with many others, the political scientist George Moyser (see his "Religion and Politics" in *The Routledge Companion to the Study of Religion* [2005], 423–438]), and so it is therefore not that, as he then goes on to suggest, "religious phenomena . . . influence the whole system of governance" (423). This religion *and* politics model is unfortunately the default position throughout the field. Instead of seeing politics as the subsequent context onto which uniquely private religious hopes and dreams are projected, we instead recommend that critical scholars question the management that is taking place in that very phrasing and framing of the issue, doing so by paying careful attention to the effects of, for example, the rhetoric of privacy. It is this rhetoric that, upon closer inspection, may be seen to be all too public, as in the ongoing debates and negotiations in government, as well as court cases over what should count *as* private and therefore *as* beyond most people's reach for most of the time. Within this context, we must not forget that even so-called private residences can be broached, and private property confiscated by the authorities, for what they try to demonstrate as persuasive reasons, while citing privacy rights can be a handy strategy for authorized individuals to keep tax or medical records away from the public's prying eyes. Making this shift, we suggest, will prompt scholars of religion to begin to see a structure of politics entailed by the significations that make daily life, as well as their very scholarship on those lives, possible—but always doing so with an eye on the need to be self-reflexive. We must therefore keep ever-present in our minds that the domain in which scholars' judgments are consequential is a rather limited one, i.e., academia, along with its classrooms, conferences, and publications, where our expertise is authorized because it has been credentialed there. Scholars are often tempted to move beyond this self-authorized, because self-policed, domain, to inhabit the role of the so-called public intellectual or media pundit. While in some cases this merely requires the translation of technical research to far wider audiences (what some today refer to as the public humanities) when that research has direct bearing on matters of the day, in yet other cases we find that scholars trade on their credentials from one area in domains that are far removed from that recognized expertise. This, we advise, should be avoided since the person is a scholar, apart from whatever other roles they may play in other parts of their social world, precisely because of their specialty which, by definition, means that there are numerous domains in which they have no training and thus no expertise whatsoever. We hope that recognizing this, and then responding, when needed, by means of self-limitation, will introduce a dose of moderation to the expert's voice—a quality that the ancient Greeks named and valued as *sophrosýne*.

In this volume see: belief, classification, gender, identity, power, race, religion, sacred/profane, secular

In *Religion in 50 More Words* see: civil religion, dialogue, east/west, evil, idol, piety, reformation, sect, sexuality, spirituality, theology, tradition, understanding

36 Power

Power is a critical term related to issues like politics and authority, yet scholarship explicitly addressing the concept is surprisingly absent in much of the field. It is certainly invoked in surveys so as to include the functional theory of Karl Marx (1818–1883) as an early (though sometimes portrayed as no longer important) example of how to study religion, one that puts emphasis on the means of production and systems of exchange/valuation and thereby highlights, among other things, the suppression of the proletariat (i.e., the working class of laborers). Typically, it is implicitly invoked in his famous definition: "Religion is the sigh of the oppressed creature, the sentiment of a heartless world, and the soul of soulless conditions, it is the opium of the people," which seeks to call attention to (and, indeed, redress) the power imbalance in society in general and religion in particular (from the Introduction to *A Contribution to the Critique of Hegel's Philosophy of Right* that was published separately in 1844 in the only issue of the journal *Deutsch-Französische Jahrbücher* [*German-French Annual*]). A question we might well ask is: why, for much of its history, has the academic study of religion moved away from such concerns and has instead been decidedly uninterested in issues of power (understood as a type of agency, i.e., the ability to exercise persuasive let alone coercive force), not to mention the related term "authority"? This, despite the fact that religious discourses are easily understood among the most useful means to authorize one's right to exert power over others so as to either maintain the current social structures of, and access to capital by, the status quo or, in some cases, challenge it.

To this question one might be tempted to answer that a field whose members are often interested in determining the nature and features of the sacred, i.e., its essence/manifestations, and the experiences to which they give rise, will more than likely be uninterested in, or unattuned to, the power dynamics, and concomitant material conditions, that create such discourses in the first place. The field's interest in the ostensible meanings *behind* human discourses, behaviors, and institutions therefore often translates into an unwillingness to understand the acts that make such things as meanings possible. If influential members of the field assert, as has been done for so long, that the sacred cannot be reduced to anything else, including the political, this means that issues of power will more than likely largely and inevitably recede into the background.

The English term "power" is a borrowing from the Old French *pooir* by way of the Anglo-Norman *poer* and its many derivatives (e.g., *poere, poeir, poir, poier*). Early, twelfth-century, usage denoted authority (hence the still present connection between power and authority in English) and one's physical strength or vigor. By the thirteenth century, the term begins to take on an even greater political valence in the sense of referring to a jurisdiction or other administrative area, so that, by the eighteenth century it can also designate the strength of either a political or national variety. Thus we read in William Wood's (1679–1765) *A Survey of Trade: In Four Parts* (1719):

> *Great Britain* can be only confiderable, and hold the Balance of *Europe*, while fhe is Rich and Powerful; and we can only be faid to be Rich and Powerful, as our Riches and Power bear Proportion with our Neighbour Nations; and that nothing can more effectually eftablifh our Profperity, than an *Excefs and Predominancy* of *Foreign Trade*.
>
> (11–12, quoting the 1722 edition)

However, when the word "power" is used in the study of religion—or at least in its more traditional variations—it can be employed as a descriptive term for that which is claimed to emanate from the sacred. This once again showing the long-standing slippage in the field between theological and academic usage. We get a relatively early glimpse of this use of the term in John Hunt's (1775–1848) *The Power of God: A Sermon on Psalm LXII:11* (1808), which seeks to differentiate the power inherent in humans and that found in God. Thus we read:

> By the power of a creature we mean, either delegated authority, or physical strength; mechanical force, or intellectual energy. But by the POWER OF GOD we do not mean the first of these; it cannot be the second; it is infinitely superior to the third; and if the last come any thing nearer to it in its nature, yet this, and indeed all these together afford but a faint idea of omnipotence.
>
> (8)

Likewise, we read in a *Sermon Delivered on the Ordination of the Rev. Thomas Ruggles* (from August 31, 1809), preached by Aaron Dutton (1780–1849), a graduate of Yale and subsequent minister in the New Haven area: "The Gospel is the instrument, by which the power of God prepares men for glory" (5). Or further: "We have no reason to expect, that a single soul, in Christian lands, will ever be saved, but by the power of God, in the gospel" (14). Power, in this sense, is largely undefinable, unverifiable, and exists beyond the human sphere. This would change dramatically in the later German philosophical tradition, of course, which connected power to much more mundane and political concerns, something that is on clear display in the writings of Marx, writing about a generation after Hunt and Dutton.

Power, in theology not unlike some parts of the study of religion, tends to refer to God's power, largely avoiding any investment in either politics and/or ideology. This, of course, makes sense, given prominent distinctions throughout the history of the field between the practical and often messy domain of human affairs and the presumably more rarified air of the religious. We see this most clearly early in the field's development in Rudolf Otto's (1869–1937) *Idea of the Holy* (1917), wherein we read about what Otto called the *mysterium tremendum*, Latin for what he also described as the essence of religion: the experience of a compelling yet repelling force. According to him,

> It has its wild and demonic forms and can sink to an almost grisly horror and shuddering. It has its crude, barbaric antecedents and early manifestations, and again it may be developed into something beautiful and pure and glorious. It may become the hushed, trembling, and speechless humility of the creature in the presence of—whom or what? In the presence of that which is a *mystery* inexpressible and above all creatures.
>
> (13, quoting the 1958 edition of John Harvey's translation)

This is precisely the type of power that many in the field of religious studies continue to be interested in. It is also exemplified early on in the once influential work of the Dutch phenomenologist of religion, Gerardus van der Leeuw (1890–1950), for whom the term "power" was fundamental, signifying being overpowered: "The religious man," he writes, "desires richer, deeper, wider life: he desires power for himself . . . seek[ing] something that is superior" (*Religion in Essence and Manifestation* [1933], 679, quoting the 1986 edition). This can lead to statements that power *emanates* from sacred objects, such as the Torah in Judaism, the saints in Islam, or relics in medieval Christianity. Such statements, however, do not get the critical scholar very far inasmuch as they return us to a circularity witnessed in so many of the other terms examined here, notably those that emerge from vague and underdefined referents as opposed to more mundane analyses of the political, historical, social, economic, and ideological forces that can help to explain the rhetorical utility of vague circularity for social actors.

Or, alternatively, we might read about the "power of religion," such that Ross Douthat, a contemporary op-ed writer for the *New York Times* can write in a February 28, 2018 column titled "The Edges of Reason" that claims the world inhabited by religious practitioners seeks to venture out

> in search of answers in an intensely experimental spirit—trying to see what people or prayers or situations recreated the initial religious experience, trying to discern what remedy or diet or program might actually make them feel, not just alive, but well.

Religion here offers a different explanatory map from secular empiricists, but one that nonetheless gives people power to act or believe in alternative ways. And in his *The Significance of Religious Experience* (2011), Howard Wettstein argues that even though a person may not actually believe in the literal account of creation found in the book of Genesis, an observant Jew is nevertheless able to recite the liturgy of Sabbath observance on account of the "religious power" that the biblical narrative holds on him or her (49). This amorphous power, it would seem, is simply interchangeable with other amorphous concepts that define the field (e.g., experience, the sacred). Less extreme, but equally problematic, are the comments of Meerten ter Borg (1946–2017), in his contribution, "Religion and Power," to the *Oxford Handbook of the Sociology of Religion* (2011). He writes that "religious power in its pure form is rare. It is *always* connected to other forms of power" (205; emphasis added). He here subscribes to the still popular autonomy of religion thesis, though one always tempered by the admission that religion is diluted or potentially polluted by the historical and cultural media in which it must necessarily be manifested, materialized, or embodied. But—or so the critical scholar might inquire—if it is *always* connected to other forms of force, as ter Borg admits, then *there can be no such thing as a strictly or inherently religious power*. Power that is imagined to be religious is therefore efficacious only inasmuch as it is associated with mundane authoritative structures (e.g., politics, economics, etc.). Again, the adjective "religious" would seem to be doing *very little* analytic work and, instead, signifies a purely imagined quality that is somehow thought to pre-date the historical.

Juxtaposed against such treatments is the work found in critical theory, and which has been applied in the study of religion for the past few decades. Perhaps nowhere is this on clearer display than in the work of the French scholar, Michel Foucault (1936–1984). His *Discipline and Punish: The Birth of the Prison* (1975), for example, provides a genealogical study of the very idea of criminality as a quality of people by means of examining the modern practice of isolating and imprisoning criminals, as opposed to the public torturing or killing of them, as was more customary in the premodern world. Though seemingly more humane, on one hand, this new mode of punishment (by which the governing authority defines the conditions in which it is legitimate to exert force on people's bodies) could then be used to control an entire society, on the other, with many institutions (e.g., factories, hospitals, schools, etc.) modeled on the modern prison. Foucault argues that this system of society-wide, disciplinary power, by which certain sorts of individuals are made possible, is predicated on hierarchical observation and knowledge that subsequently combines into a unified whole, or what he terms "the deployment of force and the establishment of truth" (184). This echoes his often-quoted association of power with knowledge (what he sometimes writes as power-knowledge, i.e., "that power and knowledge directly imply one another" [27]). We also see a related approach at work in writings of the anthropologist Talal Asad with his focus on studying the conditions that make it possible for moderns to imagine, and then put into practice, the secular. Rather than assume, like many in the field, that "religion" has some kind of content, his *Genealogies of Religion: Discipline and Reasons of Power in Christianity and Islam* (1993) argues, among other things, that religion is *not* a universal category. Both in the past and outside Europe, it would have been configured and operated in ways that we today would neither define nor recognize as "religion" or "religious." The ability to think and act in ways that are understood as religious, for Asad, is thus a by-product of the unique historical and political circumstances of modern European (and now North American) modernity (e.g., 39–43). Central to his analysis is the notion of power at the place where religion and the secular meet, with the boundary between them frequently redrawn, but always in a manner that the formal authority of the premodern Church remained central. However, the rise of the modern nation-state, including the effects of industrialization and urbanization, etc., witnessed a division of social labor, and thus spheres of force, with the Church retaining its *ecclesiastical* power (which is largely persuasive) by shifting "the weight of religion more and more onto the moods and motivations of the individual believer" (39). This new, privatized concept of religion, for Asad, then serves a variety of modern political ends, not least of which was reserving all other forms of power (often coercive and practiced in the public domain) for the exclusive use of the state, which converges, he writes, "with the liberal demand in our time that it be kept quite separate from politics, law, and science" (1993, 28). Asad elaborates on this idea of secularism in his later book, *Formations of the Secular: Christianity, Islam, Modernity* (2003), wherein he argues that secularism, far from making the world a better place (as the common narrative has it), instead rearranges the premodern rules of the socio-political game: "A secular state does not guarantee toleration; it puts into play different structures of ambition and fear. The law never seeks to eliminate violence since its objective is always to regulate violence" (8). This sentiment is explored further in the writings of the anthropologist Saba Mahmood (1962–2018), especially her *Politics of Piety: The Islamic Revival and the Feminist Subject* (2011). Building on the work of such writers as Foucault and Asad, she argues that power is not solely about domination, but should perhaps more correctly be seen as a strategic relation of a variety of forces that produce in subjects a set of desires and discourses (wielded by those marginal to dominant structures as well). Such discourses succeed in actually producing subjects, she argues, as opposed to just being produced by them. Such statements about the discursive features of power, and its varied exercise at a diversity of centers, has the potential to radically subvert traditional notions of human agency, i.e., who qualifies as an actor with the authority to act.

Unfortunately, Asad's and Mahmood's far more nuanced discussions of power and related concepts rarely cross-over in a meaningful or elaborated way into the field of religious studies. We read, for example in Carl Ernst and Richard C. Martin's book, *Rethinking Islamic Studies: From Orientalism to Cosmopolitanism* (2010), what may strike the critical scholar as a tactically simplistic reading of Asad, in that he is described as "argu[ing] forcefully that Muslim societies must be understood on their own terms and not a superimposed Western model" (9). Such an invocation of Asad, though highly problematic, would seem to be used as a way to provide intellectual legitimation to projects that seek to identify and then legitimate a specific aspect of a larger tradition *as if* it were the unquestioned, authoritative center. Here, once again, we witness the selective use of what is ostensibly critical theory to make a set of points that are often removed from being either theoretical or critical.

One of the most prominent scholars in the field of religion to consistently draw attention to issues of power and authority in a sophisticated manner is Bruce Lincoln. Having been a doctoral student of Mircea Eliade

(1907–1986)—who, it eventually came to light, had what many argued to be a politically tainted past, with earlier twentieth-century right-wing political groups in Romania—Lincoln's work became increasingly uneasy with the ideologies of power and domination implicit to both the practices that he was studying and, increasingly, with the various theories and methods many scholars of religion employed to study them. In his *Death, War, and Sacrifice: Studies in Ideology and Practice* (1991), for example, he shows how so-called religious discourses possess "very real and considerable persuasive power" to justify numerous acts, including murder. "My goal in studying these constructs," he then goes on, "is first to see how and why these discourses were so effective, and second to demystify them, revealing the consequences that they entail and rendering visible the social and material interests that they serve" (xv). Rather than conceive of religious texts as inherently special or sacred, or as containing a mysterious abundance dimly perceived by the scholar, Lincoln instead regards such texts, like all texts, as implicated in and supportive of patterns of class, gender, and ethnic hierarchy. That he then devotes not just further essays but an entire book to this—i.e., *Authority: Construction and Corrosion* (1994), which explores the social nature of authority and the role of those governed in legitimating those who govern them—tells us much about how different his work is to many now in the field.

It is unfortunate, then, that the default position of power in the study of religion involves either elucidating the feelings and experiences that the sacred supposedly invoked or invokes in religious practitioners, on the one hand, or entering into debates within the communities we study so as to empower certain players on certain sides of the issues, on the other. While critical scholars will certainly wish to retain the word "power" in their vocabulary, they will likely do so in much the same manner that it is used in some adjacent disciplines, where the term—along with its cognate, authority—allows us to study force as exercised in the complex and dynamic, though often unapparent, set of networks that govern the interaction between different elements within a social group (i.e., what we might term politics). Within this context, power becomes the ability to influence and control that which is of value to self and others, thereby either persuading or coercing others to do what they might not otherwise do. The term power, in other words, ought to be used in a way that understands the various conditions—political, economic, racial, gendered, and, generally speaking, ideological, etc.—that legitimate the structures of day-to-day life. This seems a much more critical and analytic way to use the term than by connecting it to, or anchoring it within, the ostensible power that various manifestations of the sacred instantiate. For if the latter is imprecise and forever unanalyzable, the former is always readily apparent for the critical scholar.

In this volume see: critical, definition, experience, gender, ideology, method, orthodoxy, politics, race, religion, secular, theory

In *Religion in 50 More Words* see: church, commentary, cult, dialogue, emic/etic, reformation, sacrifice, spirituality, tradition, understanding

37 Practice

Adopted from the broad field of social theory, the term "practice" (sometimes spelled "practise," outside of American English) has recently been favored in scholarship on religion over more traditional words like "action" and even "behavior." This preference is likely because the former carries with it, at least for many, assumptions about the creative intentionality of the person involved as opposed to what might be characterized as the more mechanistic and thus impersonal implications of the latter options. Consider, for example, the 2015 article published in the journal *Climate Change* entitled, "Habitual Behaviors or Patterns of Practice? Explaining and Changing Repetitive Climate-Relevant Actions" (6: 113–128), which hinges on whether scholars should understand actions that fail to address climate change as the result of deliberative processes (and thus classified as practices) or unthinking "habits and routines embedded in everyday life" (113). In like manner, there are those who would never consider re-naming the occasions designated as rituals as just being the result of mere habit, given that such scholars would more than likely maintain that the latter term minimizes or fails to acknowledge the motivations and deep meanings of the participant. Since the above-cited article defines habit as "an intra-individual psychological construct that sustains ingrained behavior patterns in stable setting" (113), many who study "ritual" would prefer to see it as closer to ceremony or performance, and thus practice, than to mere behavior or other more generic doings. As a result, the choice of term by which scholars in our field categorize bodies in motion—whether practice, action, or behavior—brings with it a theory of the human, making this about so much more than, as some might say, mere semantics.

This volume has often opted for the term "social actor," with sympathies for Christian origins scholar Will Braun's frequent choice of "human doings" as a rough translation of the subtitle of volume 1 of Michel de Certeau's *L'invention du quotidien: Arts de faire* (1980), translated in English as *The Practice of Everyday Life* (1984). While not wishing to minimize the importance of taking into account human agency—the conscious calculations and decision-making that constitutes a good part of social life—the study of religion has long overemphasized the role of the intentional individual, which functions as the site of the supposedly private religious experiences that are manifested in outwardly observable symbols. This usually comes at the expense of taking into account the many non-agential structures that, in many (often unnoticed) cases, govern human life, from such seemingly mundane examples as the rules of grammar that enable readers to make this text seem meaningful to them while reading it and the unspoken rules that we call table manners or those for standing in lines at the movie theater. From these rather simpler and perhaps obvious examples, we could also point to far more consequential ones. The latter could include the implications of the hierarchical class system or the explicitly ranked nature of racial or gender identity in much of the world today, often enforced by laws sanctioned by the state let alone also being policed by physical violence. Much like a degree program's requirements or the rules of the road, none of these systems emerge from the ground fully formed and of their own accord. Instead, they all represent the products from previous human agency—not individual, but *collective* human agency, over time and generations, in which individual intentions (of which there no doubt were many) were amplified, contradicted, and often just cancelled out and forgotten, all in ways that could never have been anticipated by any one agent. Politicians, to use another example, who carefully crafted and passed laws could never anticipate how their statutes would be interpreted and used by others, in the years to come. For this reason, laws are continually revised, and new laws are proposed in response to what had once been unanticipated situations. It is along this continuum, from the idealized example of a freely choosing agent (i.e., the creative and intentional individual), on the one end, to the impersonal governance of non-intentional structures, on the other, that we must locate terms such as practice, behavior, and action. Where a scholar positions him- or herself on this spectrum, and what theory of the human they use in their work, will be evident in how they refer to the *arts de faire* that they happen to study.

The etymology of the modern English noun "practice" derives from the slightly older verb (to practice) which itself comes from the Middle French *practique*, sometime in the fifteenth century. The English term can also be traced to the post-classical Latin *practizare*, therefore overlapping with the derivation of other modern words as "practical," "practitioner," and "practicum." The word thus carries a variety of connotations, from simply implying generic activity, i.e., to do something (such as the old saying, as found in Charles Dickens's novel, *The Old Curiosity Shop* [1841, 302]: "Doctors seldom take their own prescriptions and Divines do not always practice what they preach"), to performing a role in a specific and prescribed way (as in "The practife or cuftom of the church of God," from *A Retentive to Stay Good Christians in the Trve Faith* [1580, 38]). To this, we could also add the modern sense of a repetitive act in order to train and, eventually, acquire a skill, e.g., practicing an instrument; or the common saying that dates back to at least the sixteenth century, as in "For practices makes perfect, as often I've read" (from an unattributed "poetical essay," printed in the monthly *The Gentlemen's Magazine and Historical Chronicle* [May 1766, 233]). The term has also named the accomplished and confirmed skills that one possesses after sufficiently preparing, as in the English physician, Thomas Denman's (1733–1815) two-volume work (which went on to have seven editions), *An Introduction to the Practice of Midwifery* (1794).

The sense of practice as an acquired, disciplined skill that has taken place over time—something that takes planning, dedication, consistency, experience, focus, craft—makes it somewhat akin to an art. This certainly sets "practice" apart from the term "behavior," which would seem to connote an unthinking human action. The latter term is more akin to reflex or even instinct. We get a glimpse of this in Alix Woods's contemporary children's book, *Animal Handler*, a volume in "The World's Coolest Jobs" book series: "Any action an animal does or any response to a stimulus is a behavior" (2014, 6). It is perhaps also worth noting that while scholars in the so-called Behavioral Sciences (e.g., psychology or sociology) might also use the term "stimulus," those in other fields, perhaps trying to elicit an opinion or viewpoint from an interviewee, might prefer "prompt." This is not unlike preferring to employ the word "practice" over "behavior," since the former denotes intentionality and thus a theory of the human as a creative meaning-maker. Thus, we arrive at, for instance, Rabbi Isaac Klein's book *A Guide to Jewish Religious Practice*, published by the Jewish Theological Seminary, which was "the product of, and intended for the vibrant Jewish community which continues to flourish in the United States" (1979, xxi)—a book whose foreword, by the Jewish historian, Rabbi Gerson Cohen (1924–1991), notably begins with: "Classical Judaism has no word for 'religion' ... It is for this reason that Torah is often called a way of life, for its purpose is to teach Jews how to act, think, and feel." Predictably, perhaps, we also find "religious behavior" as a favored term in such subfields as the cognitive science of religion, such as its use throughout Mladen Turk's book, *Being Religious: Cognitive and Evolutionary Theory in Historical Perspective* (2013), not to mention how it is sometimes used by scholars when studying groups who strike them as puzzling or alien. We see this, for example, in the chapter on "Theological Beliefs and Religious Behaviors Among Evangelicals" included in the political scientist Corwin Smidt's book, *American Evangelicals Today* (2015).

Practice 223

Most influential of all in the modern preference for the term "practice" is the work of the late French sociologist, Pierre Bourdieu (1930–2002), especially his *Esquisse d'une théorie de la pratique* (1972), known in Richard Nice's English translation as *Outline of a Theory of Practice* (1977). To this work, we could add the British sociologist Anthony Giddens's *Central Problems in Social Theory: Action, Structure and Contradiction in Social Analysis* (1979). Such works make readers aware that the distinction between practices and acts owes much to the philosopher and psychoanalyst, Julia Kristeva's earlier disagreement with the philosopher John Searle, concerning his theory of speech-acts (words that accomplish something, such as a pledge of allegiance or swearing an oath in a courtroom). In her reply Kristeva argues that these ought instead to be understood as signifying practices, involving language that, for her, was a "socially communicable discourse" and thus one that, as described by the Canadian scholar of religion, Dawn McCance, requires the speaker to draw upon its different modes, based on the speaker's intentions and the needs of the situation. Kristeva also argues that there is a correlation between types of signifying practices and the various types of subject positions occupied by a speaker (see McCance's entry for "Signifying Practice" in the *Encyclopedia of Contemporary Literary Theory* [1993, 628]; Henry Louis Gates's *The Signifying Monkey: A Theory of African-American Literary Criticism* [1988] provides an excellent example of this approach, with regard to African, Latin American, and Caribbean literature and reading traditions). In Kristeva's 1974 book, *Revolution in Poetic Language*, for example, she argues that adding human practice to Marx's notion of "human sensuous activity" is "a first step in removing the notion of practice from its subordination to a consciousness present to itself" (199, quoting the 1984 English edition). In this sense, the classic Marxist term "praxis," understood as a combined form of theory and action, begins to reveal what is at stake for many in opting for the slightly less Marxist-inflected term "practice" over the potentially directionless implications of "behavior."

Thus, we come to what, in the last third of the twentieth century, becomes known as practice theory. In her *Anthropology and Social Theory* (2006), the cultural anthropologist Sherry Ortner describes this as a response to symbolic anthropology's emphasis on meaning (closely associated with the once influential work of Clifford Geertz [1926–2006]), Marxist political economic analysis, and the structuralism of Claude Lévi-Strauss (1908–2009). All three of which she describes as theories of constraint, i.e., approaches emphasizing the impersonal role of prior structures on human affairs. "But a purely constraint-based theory," Ortner argues, "without attention to either human agency or to the processes that produce and reproduce those constraints—social practices—was coming to be seen as increasingly problematic" (2). Here, she emphasizes Erving Goffman's (1922–1982) early work on symbolic interactionism and the anthropologist Marshal Sahlins (1930–2021, such as his book, *Historical Metaphors and Mythical Realities* [1981]) to a list that already includes the likes of Kristeva, Bourdieu, and Giddens. In the process, she arrives at an approach that, from the 1970s on, aimed to "conceptualize the *articulations* between the practices of social actors 'on the ground' and the big 'structures' and 'systems' that constrain those practices and yet ultimately are susceptible to being transformed by them" (2). *Structure* and *agency* now become understood as being in, as she phrases it, a *dialectical* and therefore mutually informing, rather than the traditionally conceived *oppositional* or *binary*, relationship (something explicitly proposed in Giddens's own theory of structuration).

It is certainly the case that not every use of the term "religious practice" today presupposes such a nuanced theory of agency/structure. Oftentimes, especially in the study of religion, it is used exclusively to emphasize individual agency and competency. However, it should be clear that the category may indeed signal a very specific scholarly tradition and thus theory of the human that takes the non-intentional mechanisms of governance into account. It does so, moreover, by also taking account of human planning and acting, such as the manner in which speakers both work within the pre-established rules of grammar while simultaneously changing it in their very use (often in unanticipated ways), thereby constituting yet a new version of the rules that are subsequently taught to the next generation. In so doing, the differences in historical usage of a single word (something that has been evident throughout this very book) offer but one example of just how dynamic human practice can be.

In this volume see: affect, experience, gender, identity, orthodoxy, power, race

In *Religion in 50 More Words* see: idol, liberation, meditation, piety, pilgrimage, prayer, renunciation, ritual, sexuality, shamanism, tradition

38 Primitive

This term "primitive," whether used as an adjective (e.g., primitive practices) or noun (e.g., the primitives), has performed a tremendous amount of intellectual labor in the study of religion, just as it has done in the adjacent field, Anthropology, not to mention across several hundred years of modern European writing. The generic type of person, social configuration, aesthetic style, religious life, or whatever else the term "primitive" supposedly qualifies—whether denigrated, romanticized, constructed in the distant past, or imagined to inhabit some far-off land in the present and thereby said to be representative of what late-nineteenth-century scholars regularly called "the childhood of the species"—has played a large role in theorizing and generally thinking about religion within the academy. However, the supposed primitives never speak, but are only spoken for by the scholar; nor do such scholars recognize them to have any agency or even names and individual identities. In this way the term, but one element of a larger Orientalist discourse dating to at least the seventeenth century, is frequently used similarly to much earlier uses of such terms for others as "the heathens" or "the pagans." Instead, people so designated, whether long past or present, have functioned as passive play pieces, protagonists that can be moved around, often from the safety of the scholar's armchair, and thus as a site to apply and perhaps prove a theory correct or to demonstrate the superiority of Christianity or, at the very least, monotheism.

The word enters English sometime in the late fourteenth or early fifteenth century, partly a borrowing from the Middle French adjective, *primitive*, and also from the much earlier Latin noun, *primitiae*, both of which have the same basic semantic range of "original, first, early, or ancient." It is therefore from these same roots that we also derive "prime" as well as "primary," along with such related terms as "primeval," "primordial," and "primogenitor." Though now largely obsolete, one of the early usages of the term was to designate an early Christian who was believed to have belonged to the primitive, i.e., original and thus pure Church, such as the early fourteenth-century French *église primitive*. Though, of course, one still finds today congregations self-named in this manner, such as either the Primitive Church of Jesus Christ (an off-shoot of the Latter-Day Saints, established in the United States in 1914) or the Tuscaloosa Primitive Baptist Church in Alabama—a title that makes a not-so-camouflaged claim concerning the presumed authenticity of their creed and practice. Thus, we find a 1609 reference, in a text written by Henry Ainsworth (1571–1622), who led an English dissenting church in Amsterdam, entitled *A Defence of the Holy Scriptures, Worship, and Ministerie, used in the Christian Churches separated from Antichrist*, which claims that "the primitive Apostolik institution" was different from the mistaken governance of "the Englifh affemblies" at the time (121). We also read in Matthew Stevenson's (b. 1685) poem, *Bellum Presbyteriale Or, as much said for the PRESBYTER As may be. TOGETHER WITH THEIR COVENANTS CATASTROPHE. Held forth in an Heroick Poem* (1661). Writing at the time of the Restoration of the Church of England after the return of Charles II to the United Kingdom, Stevenson romanticizes the primitive in the following manner:

> Thus, *PRESBYTERS*, ye see what ye have done,
> Brought *CHURCH* and *STATE* into Confusion.
> *EPISCOPACY* (as it well appears)
> Has prosper'd in this *Church* a thousand years.
> Look back upon the *Church*, you may derive
> Its Institution from the *Primitive*.
> In sacred Scripture no where it appears,
> *Titus* and *Timothy* were *PRESBYTERS*.
>
> (7)

This rhetoric conveniently allowed early Protestants of the era to claim that initially the "primitive" Church was true to the teachings of Jesus (as they themselves understood them, of course) before the Roman Catholic Church co-opted them to deprive Christians of the original message. We also read in *Primitive Truth, in a History of the Internal State of the Reformation, Expressed by the Early Reformers in Their Writings; And in which the Question, Concerning the Calvinism of the Church of England, is Determined by Positive Evidences* (1807), published under the pseudonym "Clericus," who declares: "Where the Substance of any thing is most perfect, there the accident must be most perfect. But, the substance of true Religion was most perfect in the Primitive Church, and yet there was no Archbishop" (26). Or, immediately going on: "in the primitive Church, God raised up Apostles and Prophets, and gave them power extraordinary, as the gift of tongues, the gift of healing, the gift of government, &c."

Relatedly, primitive could also be used in the sense of an original inhabitant, what we might now better designate as an indigenous person, or someone belonging to a pre-literate, non-industrial society with a low division of labor. It is in this manner that "the primitive" largely figures in the literature found among the founders of our field, all of whom date to the late nineteenth or very early twentieth century, an era when various applications to the social of Darwin's biological theory of evolution (i.e., the long discredited approach known as Social Darwinism) resulted in widespread speculations on what was presumed to be the unilinear development of the entire human species from the so-called "lower races" to what was then considered "advanced civilization" (work carried out in the context of an explicit colonial exercise, to be sure). Before examining this once predominant use, however, it is worthwhile to detail some other uses of the term, since it has been used in a variety of other ways as well. For instance, in terms of art and aesthetics primitive or "primitivism"—a term for an art movement that is rarely in use today on account of its now widely agreed upon negative connotations—was until just a few years ago still used to designate pre-Renaissance European art, thereby registering what was once believed to be its admired (though highly Romanticized) simplicity, sincerity, and power of expression, terms that were subsequently used to refer to contemporary non-European art (e.g., deriving from peoples in Oceania and Africa). In either of these uses, "primitive" took on yet another inflection, offering a prized alternative to what was then believed to be the decadence of the modern world and its art forms. Despite the fact that the term is now out of favor, it is still alive in the sense that many North American and European museums continue to categorize art on a quasi-evolutionary spectrum that is no less informed by a notion of the "primitive." For example, in the Metropolitan Museum of Art in New York City, one of the world's premier museums, the "Arts of Africa, Oceania, and the Americas" (tellingly all grouped together, despite the fact that they are all very different parts of the globe with histories and cultures of their own) are on the bottom floor, near the back of the building (and thus difficult to get to), whereas "European Painting (1250–1800)," which includes the still much valued works of the so-called Renaissance, is upstairs, at the very heart of the second floor. The term, also used as an adjective, can have a pejorative sense, especially where politics is concerned. This can occur when one person charges another with holding "primitive" ideas, with the implication being that such a viewpoint is imagined as either backwards or reprehensible. Regardless, though, whether used Romantically or pejoratively, the term is extremely relative (i.e., primitive as compared to what and whom?) and thus devoid of any meaningful content, something that, as we see in such other binaries as East/West or sacred/profane, can be used by anyone not just to name things but to elevate or denigrate them at will.

It is within such contexts that the idea of "the primitive" took shape in the imaginary of earlier generations of scholars associated with the study of religion along with sociology and anthropology. As David Chidester has argued in his important book, *Savage Systems: Colonialism and Comparative Religion in Southern Africa* (1996), it was certainly no coincidence that a field once known as comparative religion emerged at the height of the colonial period, on the frontiers of European empires, where unfamiliar peoples and customs were grouped together and designated not just *as* religious or heathen but also *as* savage, uncivilized, let alone primitive, all of which was done in comparison to those things familiar to European sensibilities. In order to be understood, in other words, the different had to be taxonomized, necessary also for colonial governance and manipulation. Reports from the frontier would then be sent back to metropoles—e.g., Amsterdam, Vienna, Paris, London—where, sooner or later, they could be employed in what were then the latest theories of religion. The category "religion" has thus long played a central role in an understanding of "the human"—the latter category central to understanding those encountered for the first time via imperial expansion, e.g., it was only in May 29, 1537, that Pope Paul III issued a statement that the local people of the Americas were in fact fully human beings and thus should not be enslaved, only converted. "The Indians are truly men" (Latin *veros homines*, i.e., real people), it reads in English translation, "and that they are not only capable of understanding the Catholic Faith but, according to our information, they desire exceedingly to receive it."

Moreover, in their quest to uncover forms of universal human behavior that could be associated with religion, many settled on studying contemporary "primitives"—often code for indigenous traditions in places such as Australia, North America, or Africa—as a way to understand humanity at the earliest stages of its development. For it was claimed that the study of these chronologically proximate "primitives" would reveal features of what scholars assumed to be our species' earliest stages of cognitive and social development. On account of what was understood as their simplicity and since their oral traditions struck observers as untheologized or unphilosophized, so-called primitives were believed to offer simpler expressions of the religious life of humankind, for it was assumed that they might offer a glimpse of the shared, developmental past and origins of the so-called "high" or civilized religions.

There may be no better early example than Edward Burnett Tylor (1832–1917), the English comparativist, who argued in his once important book, *Primitive Culture* (1871), that studying such survivals holds the key to unlocking our understanding of the past. There he defines these survivals as those aspects of culture that

> have been carried on by force of habit into a new state of society different from that in which they had their original home, and they thus remain as proofs and examples of an older condition of culture out of which a newer has been evolved.
> (15)

Survivals thus function as modern conduits that lead directly into ancient practices. In his own words:

> the savage state of mind in some measure represents an early condition of mankind, out of which the higher culture has gradually been developed or evolved, by processes still in regular operation as of old, the result showing that, on the whole, progress has far prevailed over relapse.
> (28)

We also witness a focus on contemporary primitives in the work of another giant in the early field, Émile Durkheim (1858–1917), but who studied the religion of the Australian Aboriginals of his time, albeit via reports of others and thus from the comfort of his own armchair, as was the case with most scholars of this generation, with the idea of ethnographic fieldwork still a generation away. However, he did so not in order to see the evolutionary origin of higher religion (as did his contemporaries, such as Tylor) but, instead, in order to provide a study of the social function of religion that was based on what he understood to be a more controlled example, from which findings could then be generalized to other groups. Thus, in the opening paragraph of his *Elementary Forms of the Religious Life* (1965 [1915]), for instance, he writes: "In this book we propose to study the most primitive and simple religion which is actually known, to make an analysis of it, and to attempt an explanation of it." He elaborates:

> A religious system may be said to be the most primitive which we can observe when it fulfills the two following conditions: in the first place, when it is found in a society whose organization is surpassed by no others in simplicity; and secondly, when it is possible to explain it without making use of any element borrowed from a previous religion.
> (13)

As someone engaged in the early "positive science" of sociology, Durkheim undoubtedly was also a product of his times, thus still seeking to understand and reconstruct earlier forms of civilization, despite his interest in observable function. Thus, we read him writing that it may seem strange that "one must turn back, and be transported to the very beginnings of history in order to arrive at an understanding of humanity as it is at present" (14). He subsequently compares this to the discovery of unicellular biology, which has "transformed the current idea of life since in these simple beings, life is reduced to its essential traits, they are less easily misunderstood" (19). Obviously, despite his functionalism, there is still an implicit evolutionary model here that interlocks with his comparative method. For religions are assumed to develop structurally over time, and to be complicated on account of subsequent theologizing. Comparing later forms—presumably the "world" or even "our" religions—to contemporary "primitive" forms, even if a controlled study of a setting seen to have fewer variables, still seems to enable scholars to see what the former would have looked like at an earlier stage of its slow but steady development. Thus, in studying "them," Durkheim implies, we study ourselves—itself yet another useful example of the invariably Orientalist nature of scholarship using such categories. Eventually many other writes enter the race to "discover" the most "primitive" social and religious forms, each offering new and competing theories on progressively earlier and simpler forms that are found on yet new imperial frontiers. If not the aboriginals of Australia then is it the Inuit of Northern Canada, or maybe the inhabitants of the islands in the Melanesian islands, or perhaps even the indigenous populations of the Americas?

Regardless which group is identified, it is always assumed that "primitives" have simple religious forms. Going against the grain of this approach we may point to the work of the later and once influential Italian historian of religions, Raffaele Pettazzoni (1883–1959), who offers yet another example of the use to which "primitive" could be put in an earlier era of our field. In his *The All-Knowing God: Researches into Early Religion and Culture*, the translation of his 1955 *L'Onniscienza di Dio*, he sought to break ranks with the scholarly consensus of his time, that had maintained that monotheism was the original form of religion (the once so-called Urreligion, with the German *ur-* prefix, to denote original or oldest), as described by the likes of the early Scottish anthropologist, Andrew Lang (1844–1912), as well as the Austrian ethnologist, Wilhelm Schmidt (1868–1954). Their claims, perhaps in good Christian fashion, were that monotheism had been the original form of human religion before "degenerating" into the multiplicity of polytheism. While Pettazzoni found evidence of monotheism in so-called primitive societies, including the recognition of a supreme being, he subsequently argued that there was little evidence to suggest that such beings were worshipped to the exclusion of a variety of other spiritual entities. He thus

Primitive 231

challenged the notion that these supreme beings were in fact monotheistic gods. In fact, Pettazzoni claimed that the basic thesis of the existence of "primitive monotheism" conflated theology and history, something the critical scholar might conclude happens far too often even in the current field, and he instead argued that monotheism is but a recent development. Despite his pioneering historical researches into the topic, however, Pettazzoni's method is today generally seen to be related to the phenomenological method, an approach that is considered by many to be notorious for ignoring historical specificity in favor of making what are often seen as superficial generalizations based on often unrelated data taken from various sources (many of which were second or even third hand removed from the original).

From these many highly dubious uses of the term, it seems safe to say that "primitive" has no place in the modern, critical study of religion. Its primary use today should therefore be illustrating the manner in which a trope has been used and to whose benefit, and thus to what ends it has been employed throughout the history of the field. Such a genealogical approach has the advantage of showing the excesses of the field at some of its most formative moments. Though the term is rarely in scholarly use anymore, the way the field was structured around the assumptions that informed it—monotheistic vs. polytheistic religions, East/West religions on the one hand and indigenous heathenism but then later spiritualities on the other, all placed on some sort of evolutionary grid—means that the ramifications may remain in some surprising places.

In this volume see: authenticity, comparison, culture, function, history, indigeneity, origin, race

In *Religion in 50 More Words* see: animism, cult, east/west, idol, magic, myth, paganism, ritual, sacrifice, shamanism, totem, tradition

39 Race

If identity is the larger category around which much scholarship now revolves, race—a word with a variety of meanings in the history of the English language—is arguably among the most prominent ways in which modern social identifications are assumed to be signaled and subsequently studied by scholars. The latter term is often used to name a group defined by a claim connected to origins and thus heredity and supposedly essential traits. However, it is also a term that can often determine a group's material circumstances, social status, and even safety and well-being. Whether as a self-designation or, more frequently, as a way to identify others and what are portrayed as their differences from the self, scholars of religion cannot afford to exclude this term from their critical vocabulary—especially should we follow Theodore Vial's argument in his book, *Modern Religion, Modern Race* (2016), which sees both religion and race as concepts that have been paired from the Enlightenment to today.

Derived from the fifteenth-century French term *rasse*, akin to the earlier Italian *razza*, it is currently unclear from where the English term arises. Some maintain that it is either an abbreviation of the ancient Latin *generātiō* (action, procreation, begetting offspring, as well as kind and group of people) or perhaps initially from the Latin *ratio* (proportion, calculation, as well as reason or calculation, thus the modern "rational" as well as "rationale"). Its modern adjectival form, "racial," gains in use from the later nineteenth century, perhaps not coincidentally the same period in which the world religions paradigm is launched and spreads. Racial is commonly used as a synonym for the more recent "ethnic" or the noun "ethnicity" (itself from the ancient Greek *éthnos* for kind, group, or even foreigners, or what we might today generally call a nation or type of people). While the noun "racialize" has become more prominent in recent decades, the use of the related adjective "racist" in addition to "racism" have increased since the middle of the twentieth century. The former term designates people or practices that claim one race as superior to others, while the latter names this general attitude or institution. Over the past 60 years, with dramatically increased usage in just the past decade, the designation "white nationalism" has come to name one version of the long-standing intersection of race and nation, comprising what Damon T. Berry characterizes as "a complex dynamic of racial activist thinking in America after World War II" (*Blood and Faith: Christianity in American White Nationalism* [2017], 10).

Given Europe's imperial and certainly Orientalist penchant for determining whether or not a group was religious, it is difficult not to understand the various ways in which large-scale populations have been classified, ranked, and governed as all being closely interconnected and therefore supportive of each other. We see here the practical impact of this in David Chidester's *Savage Systems: Colonialism and Comparative Religion in Southern Africa* (1996), in addition to his *Empire of Religion: Imperialism and Comparative Religion* (2014). Christopher M. Driscoll and Monica R. Miller have even gone so far as to argue, in their co-written book, *Method as Identity: Manufacturing Distance in the Academic Study of Religion* (2018), that the historic and even contemporary connection between the concepts of "religion" and "race" is "impossible to disconnect, untether, and disassociate" (132).

The now explicit emphasis on the role of race in the study of religion should be welcomed by the critical scholar. Despite its importance, of the many field-wide handbooks now in print, only in Richard King's 2017 volume do we find articles on race, but in a separate section of the book entitled "Religion, Coloniality, and Race." Instead of cordoning the term off in a separate domain or genre of scholarship, however, we instead need to see it as a long-standing, under-studied, and field-wide issue throughout the history of a field that was concerned from the start with establishing a universal designation and ranking of all peoples. This is a point made by Malory Nye, the social anthropologist and scholar of religion and culture, in his recent efforts to argue for the decolonization of the study of religion (e.g., see his "Race and Religion in the Post-Colonial Formations of Power and Whiteness," *Method & Theory in the Study of Religion* 31 [2018]: 1–28; we think here also of the work of the anthropologist Aisha Beliso-DeJesus and the scholar of religion and ethnic studies, Professor Natalie Avalos, as well). Both "religion" and "race" have circulated for hundreds of years, in popular culture, government, and scholarship, as part of mutually informing and authorized discourses on human similarity and difference. Establishing and managing sentiments of affinity and estrangement, as phrased by Bruce Lincoln, can probably be understood as a basic mechanism of identification within all human populations, something that is undoubtedly accomplished in a wide variety of ways, along a complex spectrum of inclusion/exclusion. While scholars will no doubt continue to be interested in categorizing populations for their own analytic purposes, the discourse on natural and thus essential racial differences has historically been a highly valorized way of accomplishing this. Perhaps this was most notable in the hands first of Europeans, as they and their local systems made their way throughout the world during the colonial era, and then, later, for dominant North Americans during the rise of their global political and economic influence. This longtime discourse on race has had (and continues to have) fundamental practical consequences in the lives of those people who are *overtly* (i.e., via racist practices on the part of individuals) or *covertly* (i.e., via what was once termed institutional racism but which many now name as structural racism) deemed to be members of a common group. (We borrow this distinction from the early work of the onetime US civil rights organizer, Stokely Carmichael [1941–1998]—who subsequently adopted the name Kwame Ture—and the political scientist, Charles Hamilton [b. 1929], author of *Black Power: The Politics of Liberation* [1967].) Thus, individuals or groups can be portrayed as being lesser, inferior, uncivilized, under-developed, or primitive based on certain biological characteristics that can be (i) generalized to an entire group and then (ii) employed as a point of leverage in the regulation of their place, status, and access to resources.

We frequently see academic studies on gender and religion, in which university courses and publications on "women *and* religion" have sometimes been assumed both to satisfy an interest in gender as well as to address past inequities based on an identifier equally tied to long-standing social and political inequities. We see something similar with race. There is the temptation for scholars of religion to document and address problems linked to the racialization of populations or to study race by continuing to participate in the discourse on race, though adopting a dramatically different position within it. Such approaches produce works on the role played by religion in the history and lives of those commonly seen to be marginal to the traditional exercise of power, e.g., studying racial minority groups. During the past few decades this focus has resulted in an explosion of publications generally understood as inhabiting the genre of religion *and* race. Over just the last decade alone we think of such important works as: Suzanne L. Marchand's *German Orientalism in the Age of Empire: Religion, Race, and Scholarship* (2010); Bettye Collier-Thomas's *Jesus, Jobs, and Justice: African American Women and Religion* (2010); Junaid Rana's *Terrifying Muslims: Race and Labor in the South Asian Diaspora* (2011); Edward E. Curtis's *Islam in Black America: Identity, Liberation, and Difference in African-American Islamic Thought* (2012); Joshua Paderson's *American Heathens: Religion, Race, and Reconstruction of California* (2012); Jonathon S. Khan and Vincent W. Lloyd's edited volume, *Race and Secularism in America* (2016); Max Perry Mueller's *Race and the Making of the Mormon People* (2017); Thien-Huong T. Ninh's *Race, Gender, and Religion in the Vietnamese Diaspora: The New Chosen People* (2017); Judith Weisenfeld's *New World A-Coming: Black Religion and Racial Identity During the Great Migration* (2017); Alexander Jun et al.'s *White Jesus: The Architecture of Racism in Religion and Education* (2018); Harold D. Morales's *Latino and Muslim in America: Race, Religion, and the Making of a New Minority* (2018); Eric L. Goldstein's *The Price of Whiteness: Jews, Race, and American Identity* (2019); and Stephen C. Finley, Biko Mandela Gray, and Lori Latrice Martin's edited collection, *The Religion of White Rage: Religious Fervor, White Workers and the Myth of Black Radical Progress* (2020).

While critical scholars will certainly welcome new descriptive work on previously unstudied or under-studied and thus poorly understood groups, they may also be just as interested in examining the very functioning of the discourse that enables such work to be carried out. Such an approach will not just produce more studies on the religious practices of the members of so-called different races but, instead, work on the conceptual and institutional preconditions, procedures, and implications of these very identifications. The very word "race" itself will therefore require closer examination before we proceed to study the myths, rituals, and symbols of different "races" of people. For, as Raymond William has already pointed out, in his entry on "racial" in his *Keywords*, "the very vagueness of race in its modern social and political senses is one of the reasons for its loose and damaging influence" (1983, 250). However, the problem, as we have seen with so many other critical terms in the field, is that within scholarship imprecise terminology is put to all sorts of uses. What is more, Williams immediately goes on—and as exemplified in the merely partial list of above recent works in the field—the category has been used to name and thereby manage virtually every group against which self-perceived dominant groups have defined themselves. We see this in those who often present themselves as if they have no ethnicity and are thus represented as white or what was once widely termed the Caucasian race. As with so many designators in the field today, this latter term was initially a rather benign geographic classifier, pertaining to the region around the Caucasus Mountains in modern-day southeastern Europe, that was only later linked to what were presumed to be not just the uniform but, predictably, also the superior status of all those claimed to have originally derived from this region. Thus, as evidenced here, the idea of "the races" has, from the outset, been the basis for a system of distinction intimately associated with ranked judgments of origins and present-day value.

This specific linkage of geography, origins, and presumed racial identity can be dated rather precisely, in fact: to the third edition of the German physician and naturalist, Johann Friedrich Blumenbach's (1752–1840) *De Generis Humani Varietate Nativa* (1795; English: *On the Natural Variety of Mankind*). "I have taken the name of this variety from Mount Caucasus," he writes, "both because its neighborhood, and especially its southern slope, produces the most beautiful race of men, I mean the Georgian; and, because all physiological reasons converge to this, that in that region, if anywhere, it seems we ought with the greatest probability to place the autochthones [i.e., the progenitors] of mankind" (269, citing the 1969 edition of Thomas Bendyshe's 1865 translation). What should be clear is that, as is evident to anyone who studies how comparison actually works, discussing racial identity in this way not only presupposes determining stable similarities within and differences between populations, across time and space, but, more importantly, it also requires us to overlook that such acts of identification are themselves always situated and interested. This is a crucial point that we often bypass, thanks to such things as the authorized designation, if not sheer assertion, of the "natural," as in the very title of Blumenfeld's book or as assumed in the even older saying, "what's bred in the bone will out in the flesh" (e.g., a version of this can be found as early as the English playwright and poet, John Heywood's 1546 collection, *A Dialogue of Proverbs* [166, line 2318, citing Rudolph E. Habenicht's 1963 edition]). For such statements as "A is like B" and "B is unlike C" presuppose a nimble comparativist with a way to comb through the always innumerable possible similarities and differences between any two generic items so as to arrive at just those now isolated features that enable one to make seemingly definitive determinations of identity and distinction.

For instance, take Blumenbach's thoughts from well over 200 years ago on "the most beautiful form of skull, which in my beautiful typical head of a young Georgian female always of itself attracts the eye . . ." (300; he is said to have possessed up to 240 skulls in his collection). The situated and always local nature of the relative interests that inform such a judgment are likely pretty obvious to most modern readers of that passage. Quoting earlier writings by Blumenbach, the German scholar Norbert Klatt (1949–2015) argued in a self-published article that his judgment was likely motivated by the once widely shared, Romantic-era assumption that ancient Greek art set the standard against which to judge a contemporary sense of beauty (see the final chapter to Klatt's *Kleine Beiträge zur Blumenbach-Forschung* [2008; English, *Brief Contributions to Blumenbach Research*], 90).

Such an assumption, we should not forget, is not uncommon to this day. Consider the online backlash and threats against the University of Iowa ancient historian, Sarah Bond, after she published a June 7, 2017 online article, at *Hyperallergic*, on her work on the once colored/painted artifacts that remain from antiquity, where she concluded that "the equation of white marble with beauty is not an inherent truth of the universe. Where this standard came from and how it continues to influence white supremacist ideas today are often ignored." Such a statement troubled contemporary racist assumptions (those that are not far off of Blumenbach's own) that a statue's whiteness was a permanent feature and thus signified a universal and timeless ideal of beauty represented today by those who consider themselves to be white. Among the lessons to be learned from this admittedly ugly episode is that no less local and idiosyncratic interests and self-beneficial judgments drive all such generalized comments on timeless human similarity or difference, *and not just those dating from the late eighteenth century.*

While it is likely fair to say that most scholars of religion interested in race aim to document previously under-studied groups, there are a small number of critical scholars in the field who, as suggested earlier, wish to pull the camera back still further. Drawing partially on critical race theory—a late-twentieth-century, cross-disciplinary "collection of activists and scholars interested in studying and transforming the relationship among race, racism, and power" (as defined by Richard Delgado and Angela Harris in the 2nd edition of their *Critical Race Theory: An Introduction* [2012], 3)—and thus sharing an interest in, for instance, historicizing the tenets of liberalism (i.e., individualism) that had previously framed the actions of the US civil rights movement. Such scholars also draw on the broader field of social theory, e.g., that of French theorist Jean-François Bayart and his 1996 book, *L'illusion identitaire* (English translation, *The Illusion of Cultural Identity* [2005]), with the aim of situating identifications based on race *and* religion within a far wider historical and political context. We see this in some of the contributors to Katheryn Gin Lum and Paul Harvey's edited collection, *The Oxford Handbook of Religion and Race in American History* (2018), such as those by Sylvester Johnson, K. Merinda Simmons, and Michael Altman, especially the latter's interest in the linkages to a much earlier Orientalist era in American scholarship. Simmons' work starts from a place outlined by the American historian, Nell Irvin Painter: "[R]ace is an idea, not a fact" (from the preface to her *The History of White People* [2010], ix), and, as nicely phrased by Richard Newton (in a paper entitled "Signifying '*Der Rassist*' in Religious Studies and the Axes of Social Difference," presented to the 2018 annual meeting of the North American Association for the Study of Religion [NAASR]), "race does not exist at the level of essence but discourse . . . Race is a symbol system." Taking a cue from such scholars—among whom we must also mention Charles Long's (1926–2020) influential work on signification in the study of religion (e.g., his collection of essays, *Significations: Signs, Symbols, and Images in the Interpretation of Religion* [1986], notably the four chapters in Part II, Religion and Cultural Contact)—one's interest might then be focused on how these ideas are transmitted and instantiated by anyone, paying particular attention to their practical effects in all people's lives, including the conditions that lead to a people's formation as even having such a thing as a race. Thus, quoting Simmons: "The future of scholarly work [on] the identifications of race and religion relies upon analyzing them as exactly that: identifications." Invoking Michel Foucault (1926–1983), she then terms "a certain functional principle by which, in our culture, one limits, excludes, and chooses" (from his 1969 lecture, later published as his influential essay, "What is an Author?"). Examining such principles, in the case of both religion and race, helps us to examine "the wizard behind the curtain," as she puts it, by "calling attention to how the terms become wielded differently across various historical contexts and by different groups" (36). Whether or not this constitutes the sort of culture critique sometimes associated with those who work in race studies (see Victor Anderson's "Black Cultural Criticism, the New Politics of Difference, and Religious Criticism" in *Religion, Theory, Critique: Classical and Contemporary Approaches and Methodologies* [2017], 573–578), it nonetheless "goes some way in reorganizing sociopolitical realities," as Simmons rightly concludes. Indeed, as Newton makes plain near the end of his above-cited paper: "What is at stake in these formations are the very terms by which people are signified as at home, out of place, and even members of the human race" (see Rebekka King's edited volume, *Key Categories in the Study of Religion: Contexts and Critiques* [2021]). Thus, historicizing the devices of human difference that are taken by some to be essential, hereditary, and authoritative necessarily means making plain that things could have been otherwise. Now it will be clear that there are contingent and therefore always changeable factors that keep people identified and associated with one another in precise ways. For this reason, the issue should not be the effort to refine the terms of reference for, and thus ways to study, the religions of various members of different races but, rather, to answer two related questions. *Why* it is that the wider public and scholars alike so easily, almost naturally, think and act *as if* there are different races that each require distinct names and specific methods for their proper study? And then *how* does the circumstance established by the interrelated discourses on religion and race impact people's lives and the fate of the social formations so constituted? Inquiring into these questions is the challenge for the next generation of critical scholars.

In this volume see: classification, comparison, culture, description, gender, identity, origin, politics, power, status

In *Religion in 50 More Words* see: dialogue, east/west, piety, sexuality, spirituality, syncretism

40 Redescription

The act of redescription—taking an initial folk or idiosyncratic description and then reframing it in a different and more analytic register—is central to the academic enterprise of the Humanities and should, in theory, be especially so within the study of religion. At its most basic level, it means not taking at face value what the people we study, as well as their texts, report. Instead, it involves using such data as a way to uncover other, and sometimes initially unapparent, aspects of human creativity. Within this context, a valid redescription ought to involve transforming often personal ideas, beliefs, and practices into themes or topics that can be objects of cross-cultural, scholarly analysis by means of connecting original descriptions to a more critical vocabulary and set of methods. Despite the analytic utility of this act, something that ideally provides broad and comparative frames of reference, redescription is sometimes mistrusted or even completely avoided in the academic study of religion. The reason for this is that, based on the scholar's framework and curiosities, the redescription recodes or otherwise "changes" the stories of initial beliefs that religious practitioners may tell themselves and others, transforming such understandably untheorized accounts into data for the purposes of scholarly study. Despite the fact that this is the way that the majority of disciplines in the Humanities and Social Sciences actually work—a procedure that does not conflate participant reports and productions with scholarship on those same reports and productions—those in the field of religious studies often have other ideas. Many scholars of religion are often unwilling to reframe the initial description of a so-called religious claim or act because, or so it is maintained, they imagine it as their goal to chronicle such primary self-reports, with an eye to shed light on a hidden and unverifiable wellspring—such as the so-called sacred or even features of what is held to be a universal and enduring human spirit. Redescription is then resisted because, too often, the field works with the default position that religious acts, beliefs, and texts provide direct access to these otherwise unseen sources and, accordingly, they ought to be protected from disinterested scrutiny so as to be appreciated or conserved as somehow innately or inherently "special." If the method of phenomenology still casts its shadow over the field today, despite a general awareness of its excesses, then the idea of religion's irreducibility means that that which is constructed as religious should not, by definition, be reduced to something else, including of course non-religious terms and categories of analysis.

The term "redescription" is a uniquely English one that gained use across the twentieth century, formed, by derivation, from the noun "description." The latter refers to a statement that reports on the contours or presentation of some item or person by offering a partial or detailed list of what are seen as its central or telling aspects and details. The term description enters English in the late fourteenth century, derived from the French *descripcioun* and, prior to that, the Latin *dēscriptiō*—along with the common prefix *re-*. The key to the newly formed noun resides precisely in this prefix, which denotes an action—in this case, description—that is performed a second time with the implicit understanding that the initial act or its results can either be undone or reversed. It is within this sense that a redescription is a renewed or repeated description, oftentimes giving the original a new or different description inasmuch as it is now framed in a different way.

In legal contexts, a redescription designates something that must move beyond the original description for it to be valid or legally binding. Thus, we read in the ruling on *Barksdale* v. *Barksdale* in the Supreme Court of Mississippi (February 10, 1908) that involved a land claim, and which subsequently set precedent for a number of later cases that "while a particular description, following a general description, controls the general description, and the latter will be rejected, to do so the particular description must not be a mere redescription, but must be a second granting clause" (*The Southern Reporter*, vol. 45 [1908], 616). We are more interested in the term, however, in the context of scientific method, where things in the natural world are redescribed as more data and information comes to light, an act that alters our original estimation or understanding of the item, such as its function or relation to other things (i.e., its similarities or differences). Most germane in this sense is an article titled "The Composition of Taxonomic Papers" appearing in the *Annals of the Entomological Society of America* (4 [1911]), in which the zoologist, Richard A. Muttkowski (1887–1943) writes that "taxonomy is the most important incident of Science—things must be named before we can write them" (194). A key to this enterprise, he informs us, is redescription: "How a redescription should be formed depends on the original description. If the original was carefully drawn, the other may be a summary of the first with possible new points of variation, etc., discovered." However, as he goes on:

> if, as very often is the case, the original was insufficient, the redescription should be carefully formed; in fact, the author should aim to replace the first with the second description. Even though his name stand not as the sponsor of the species, the task of redescribing is not a thankless one, as need hardly be explained.
>
> (198)

This passage is interesting for a number of reasons. Most important from our perspective is Muttkowski's articulation of the fact that an original description—that is, what it is and how it is imagined to function—is often *insufficient* to the task of scientific analysis. For the latter takes the original and then reframes it with the aim of taking that which is potentially inaccessible to a larger community of scholars on account of its various idiosyncrasies and making it accessible. This makes something classifiable in the light of instances derived from other settings that the scholar finds to be akin or no less exemplary of some topic or problem being studied. Scholarship, or what might have once been termed higher knowledge, in other words, is only possible through such acts of redescription and classification. In this sense, then, redescription is not simply changing the way in which one describes or names something, as in Isaac Lea (1792–1886), writing on the classification of shells in the *Transactions of the American Philosophical Society* (1839) and lamenting why a colleague "does not mention why he changed the name on redescription" (vol. 6, 129). Redescription can indeed be based on the accumulation of new information, so that there are now changes in the original description, but it is also evidence of a recalibration in one's assessment of the item, its cause or function perhaps, or its relationship with other items—relations that were likely not initial apparent upon its first, initial, or passing, description. Here the implication is that we do not live in a static and unchanging world, one wherein meaning is somehow locked in original (or originary) descriptions. Accordingly, we read in the title of an article from the *Journal of Paleontology*: "Redescription of the Type Species for the Genus Notogoneus (Teleostei: Gonorynchidae) Based on New Well-Preserved Material" (2008).

When redescription is not used in the study of religion, we are afforded little more than accounts—often straightforward repetitions or mere paraphrases—of what the people under study themselves think they do or mean as they go about their so-called religious lives. Think of all those times when one hears or reads in the religious studies classroom that, for example, Muhammad received the Quran from Allah through the archangel Jibril (Gabriel) or that the descendants of Abraham migrated to what is today Egypt, where they lived under Pharoah's bondage before the Passover and Exodus. We have no eyewitness accounts, of course, let alone archival or historical evidence for either of these accounts. Instead, they are longstanding stories of origins that, respectively, Muslims and Jews tell themselves about how their groups arose, how, and for what reason—stories that are parts of narratives that thereby say something to members about who they themselves are today and where the group might be going in the future. Surprisingly, though, scholars often tend to treat the referents and events of such stories as if they are part of history, despite the fact that they have no way either to confirm or disconfirm such claims. Yet, mistaking what yet other scholars would designate as myth (a technical term used here very differently than its often-common sense of a false tale or lie) for history, or description for either analysis, explanation, or understanding, should make us pause. The scholarly key to such stories resides not in their descriptions, or so the critical scholar would likely argue, but in the ways that they can—and indeed should—be studied and, in a word, redescribed in scholarship. In the first example, that of the Prophet Muhammad, we might say that the character of the archangel Gabriel provides either those devising the tale or retelling it with a way of framing the new social movement with a certain legitimation linked to older and thus already established social forms (e.g., Gabriel is an angel from the Hebrew Bible). As for the second example, a redescription might begin from the premise that such stories were necessary because, given recent theories of the emergence of the ancient Israelites, it seems that they did not come from without (i.e., Egypt or Mesopotamia), but actually formed a subtribe of Canaanites. In both cases the redescription is more akin to an analysis, a reframing, as noted earlier, of the previous account that is offered in the light of a theory on how, in these two examples, origins accounts function for groups.

It is worth noting that redescription can, of course, be used poorly or for other than academic ends in the study of religion. We see this, for instance, when some scholars of Islam try to "redescribe" the time of Muhammad and thus earliest Islam as one of social or gender justice judged by contemporary standards. Such redescriptions, the critical scholar could conclude, are not based on a careful reading of the sources or comparanda (as Jonathan Z. Smith [1938–2017] recommended, as we shall see shortly), but, rather, on what seems mainly to be wish-fulfillment and present need (not dissimilar to how origins tales work for groups in the present). We see something similar in Louis Stulman's *The Prose Sermons of the Book of Jeremiah: A Redescription of the Correspondences with the Deuteronomistic Literature in the Light of Recent Text-critical Research* (1986). Though the word "redescription" is found in the subtitle of the work, the monograph does very little to reframe the sermons found in the biblical book for an academic audience. Instead, the redescription to which Stulman refers is one wherein the texts are, in the usual manner of theological commentaries on scriptures, situated in the light of yet other biblical texts, as opposed to doing so with regard to other second- or third-level order categories and questions.

We could here juxtapose such uses of the term to that supplied by the scholar of Christian origins, Burton L. Mack, such as his programmatic essay, "On Redescribing Christian Origins" (*MTSR* 8/3 [1996]: 247–269). In this study, Mack argues that the traditional scholarly account of the beginnings of Christianity ought neither simply to echo the gospel accounts as found in the New Testament or those of early Christian commentators (e.g., the influential developmental narrative offered by such early writers as Eusebius in the third and fourth centuries). "It is as if," Mack writes, "the emergence of Christianity cannot be accounted for any other way" (248). This is in opposition to simply assuming the veracity of such accounts, and then using them as the basis for subsequent scholarly studies—as, we recall, the sociologist of American religion, Rodney Stark, did in his book, *The Rise of Christianity: A Sociologist Reconsiders History* (1996). There, Stark presumes the traditional resurrection narrative—though bracketing out a judgment on the miraculous—by writing "on the morning of the third day something happened" (44). This prompted J. Z. Smith to comment, in a review of Stark's book, "Stark has not questioned the dramatic myth of Christian origins canonized by Luke and Eusebius" (*American Journal of Sociology* 102/4 [1997]: 1164). Juxtaposed against this, Mack seeks to "redescribe" Christian origins by accounting for the emergence of the gospels themselves, seeing the texts as "products of early Christian thinking instead of letting them determine the parameters within which all of our data must find a place to rest" (248). With this one seemingly subtle but significant shift, Mack transforms the gospels (along with traditional Christian origins accounts) from being considered as primary sources, as they usually have been by scholars, into secondary ones. Now such sources become indicative of distinct historical and other material conditions that allowed social actors to conceive of and write about their already forming groups in certain ways. This means that the gospels are less works of history or historiography and more ones of what Mack and others refer to as myth-making, which are inevitably grounded in what he calls "human investments and inventiveness" (264).

In proposing such a revision to how scholars study the earliest Christianities—a proposal that led to various multi-year scholarly working groups and a variety of publications, all devoted to carrying out the project—Mack acknowledges his debt to the work of J. Z. Smith. It is the latter who has perhaps done more than anyone to promote the importance of redescription in the academic study of religion. See, for example, Smith's early essay "The Social Description of Early Christianity" (*Religious Studies Review* 1 [1975]: 19–25 or the chapter "Sacred Persistence: Toward a Redescription of Canon" in his *Imagining Religion: From Babylon to Jonestown* [1982]). According to Smith's approach, the first thing that anyone working in the field must do is (i) define and then identify the data upon which they wish to carry out their work (e.g., a text, myth, ritual genre, practice, institution, or some other such socio-historical datum). This is then followed by (ii) a full and detailed description of it (e.g., contexts, forms of documentation, social and historical occurrences, etc.). The latter is necessary to ensure that we have noticed and accounted for the details as opposed to having simply assumed that we already understand what it is that had caught our attention. Following this, according to Smith, we must then (iii) look for an example (an "e.g.," Latin *exempli gratia*) of something that, for the scholar's purpose of analysis, can be judged to be either similar or different, in some regard and from some other cultural or historical context. This is necessary for the task of making a comparison, which he argues aids our ability to notice, once it is placed in relief, things about the original datum that were not apparent in the initial descriptive phase when it was first classified and defined. If the comparison is done properly—that is, not based on a series of hunches or merely superficial similarities or differences—we then learn more about each example, along with the larger category or interest of which we consider them both to be illustrations.

It is at this point that the issue of redescription comes in, according to Smith. The comparative aspect of our analysis forced it into a previously unforeseen and more interesting set of details and relationships, ones that just examining the initial item alone could not. At this point, we now begin to understand the similarities and differences between our comparanda. Such insights then, in a final methodological step, (iv) offer us a new way to look at the material with which we began our analysis in the first place. For, as Smith put it, "the 'end' of comparison cannot be the act of comparison itself" (citing his Epilogue to the edited collection, *In Comparison a Magic Dwells* [2000], 239). At this point, our original descriptions, in other words, require a redescription in light of our comparative work, and the previous manner in which we classified and studied the initial item may need to be rectified. This is something that Smith first outlined in his 1987 book, *To Take Place: Toward Theory in Ritual* (103). In the study of religion, this means being prepared to redescribe data in ways that can be diametrically opposed to the accounts offered by the religious practitioners themselves. It also means a willingness to compare so-called religious or sacred things to any number of previously unanticipated mundane examples. Thus, the traditional terms used to identify the items that our field often studies—whether terms used by practitioners or scholars—can be seen to be either problematic or so heavily invested in folk or parochial customs that they prove unworkable for scholarly analysis. And so, in this way, what might at first be described as a uniquely religious ritual, once compared to other rule-governed ceremonies taking place in yet other social situations, can be translated into the language of social theory. Within this context, Smith often used the theoretical framework provided by the early work of Émile Durkheim as an example of translation between first- and second-order languages—and thereby redescribed as a technique that members of groups use for a variety of socially formative purposes.

If this four-fold method helps to produce new knowledge in the case of Christian origins, then why should it not be the case for pretty much every other datum in the study of religion? Why, framed somewhat differently, should scholars not be willing to see the items that they study as comparable to a wide array of human claims and actions? For everything that scholars study can—and, as the critical scholar might be tempted to say, ought to be—subject to such an act. If we leave our scholarly analyses simply at the level of description, as detailed and rich as they may be, we fail to grasp either its nuance or appreciate the sheer human ingenuity and creativity that went into its production. Moreover, purely descriptive work presents the world as self-evidently interesting, as if it calls out for scholars to repeat others' claims and highlight how other people already arrange the world for themselves. Redescription, which uses such reports as the starting point for producing new knowledge about human culture, does not reduce the products of religion, but, rather, reveals social actors at their most creative. And unlike those who emphasize cognition, and who think they can reduce "religion" to various aspects of evolutionary biology or evolutionary psychology, and who may indeed use redescription in their analyses, the understanding of the term proposed here emphasizes its social aspects. In fact, understood in this way, redescription (along with the subsequent categorial rectification) has the potential to construct a more humanistic and cultural theory of religion, or at the very least contribute to a much more systematic study of religion, as well as naming anything as religious, as but one element of the human.

In this volume see: classification, comparison, definition, description, explanation, history, method, phenomenology, religion, theory

In *Religion in 50 More Words* see: commentary, dialogue, emic/etic, symbol, understanding

41 Religion

Certainly, the most central term of the field, the very word "religion," is taken-for-granted by most scholars. This includes those of a more recent generation who have gone through the rite of passage that the so-called method and theory course has become in many graduate programs. The prominence of such required courses, something almost completely missing from programs just 25 years ago, signals an irony at the heart of the field, for amidst increasingly close attention to the tools that the scholar uses there remains a widespread comfort in not explicitly defining our most central term. While there are many who favor the formula once offered by the Protestant theologian Paul Tillich (1886–1965), explicitly defining religion as faith in an ultimate concern, sometimes this also means proceeding in the spirit of the oft-quoted statement by US Justice Potter Stewart, "I know it when I see it" (from a 1964 obscenity case, known as *Jacobellis v. Ohio*, in which the manager of a movie theater was found not guilty for airing the then controversial French film, *Les Amants*). Yet other times it means opening a study by quoting Jonathan Z. Smith's (1938–2017) equally famous (at least in our field) line from the Introduction of *Imagining Religion: From Babylon to Jonestown* (1982):

> while there is a staggering amount of data, phenomena, of human experiences and expressions that might be characterized in one culture or another, by one criterion or another, as religion—*there is no data for religion*. Religion is solely the creation of the scholar's study.
>
> (xi)

Though, perhaps ironically, many then proceed to go about their work as if Smith had never written these sentences. To talk about religion as a social fact or a discursive object, rather than a brute fact of life, is seen as counterintuitive. As Yale University's Kathryn Lofton, a onetime undergraduate student of Smith's at Chicago, put it in her review essay on Christopher

Lehrich's edited collection of Smith's writings on pedagogy, *On Teaching Religion* (2013), "there is something dazzlingly absurd about such a claim" (*Journal of the American Academy of Religion* 82/2 [2014]: 536). As much as we may disagree with her on this point, we do indeed agree when Lofton then elaborates: "This passage could seem utterly idiotic, argumentatively important, or perfectly axiomatic, depending on your own relationship to religion as a problem for humanistic inquiry." As exemplified in the entry on interpretation, how someone reads Smith's statement (perhaps better phrased as a provocation?), let alone how they treat the word "religion" in their own work, tells us much about their stance on far wider issues in the field today. This includes everything—from the role of definition and classification to the ongoing legacy of early modernity and the colonial era, from which the current sense of "religion" came into focus. This focus assumes to name a pure, inner, and personal affectation only later expressed via claims, actions, and symbols that are set apart from all other aspects of the public world. Prior to this time, just several hundred years ago, versions of this Latin-based term did not signify believing in a god or having faith in things unseen. The terms "religious" and "secular," for example, once named a division of labor within the Roman Catholic Church. Those who were ordained and worked out in the community as opposed to those taking vows and remaining secluded (in convents, monasteries, etc.). Thus, Henry Bradshaw's *Lyfe St. Werburge* (1521): "After the translacion of Chestre monasterye From secular chanons to monkes religious . . ." (177, Book II, 195, line 1360, quoting the 1887 edition).

While the term's precise origins are a matter of continued debate, scholars are agreed that the noun "religion," spelled in various ways over time (e.g., relygyun in Middle English or ralegioun before the seventeenth century), entered English from French sometime around the twelfth century. It derives originally from one or more ancient Latin terms, and thus we find a version of it in other Latin-based languages, e.g., Italian, German, Dutch, Swedish, Danish, etc. Modern usage is anchored in the notion of a private belief that is only later expressed in practice, but its earliest English uses are linked with public behavioral situations, e.g., devotion, reverence, and conduct such as being pious (Latin *pietās*), a word once naming the quality ascribed to a person who is seen to properly defer to an authority (whether a god or a social superior). Thus, an ancient reader of Plato's *Euthyphro* (written sometime between 390 and 380 BCE) might reasonably conclude that the dialogue's namesake is impious not only because he brags and instructs Socrates, his elder, but also because he tries to occupy a position superior to his own father. Terms such as "piety," however, are those that, as J. Z. Smith argues, have today been "evacuated of [their earlier] ritual

Religion 249

connotations, and [now] seem more to denote a state of mind" ("Religion, Religious, Religions" in Mark C. Taylor's *Critical Terms for Religious Studies* [1998], 271). The premodern, Latin roots of "religion" signified something else entirely, though: either paying close or careful attention (Latin *relegere*, as in the contemporary, though dated, sense of doing something religiously, i.e., regularly and with attention to detail) or the act of binding together (Latin *religāre*). Thanks to a critical tradition stretching from Sarah F. Hoyt ("The Etymology of Religion," *Journal of the American Oriental Society* 32/2 (1912): 126–129) to Ernst Feil (1932–2013) in Germany (such as his essay "The Problem of Defining and Demarcating 'Religion'" in his co-edited book, *On the Concept of Religion* [2000] as well as his four-volume German work on the category, whose title we might translate as *Religion: The Story of a Modern Category* [1986–2012]) including the Canadian scholar of Islam, Wilfred Cantwell Smith (1916–2000), among many others, the complex etymology of the term became more relevant for scholars. In his *The Meaning and End of Religion* (1962), Cantwell Smith recommended against conflating what he claimed as two distinguishable things: faith in transcendence for one, and, the other, the secondary, cumulative tradition (i.e., the expression of that faith). In fact, although the term "religious tradition" pre-dates Cantwell Smith, once naming specific customs within a religion (e.g., self-denial is a religious tradition for Jains), the preference for renaming religions as religious traditions is in part due to his influence in the second half of the twentieth century (e.g., Byron H. Earhart's [b. 1935] once widely used textbook, *Religious Traditions of the World* [1992]).

Notable is the way that this now common synonym for religion presupposes the basic phenomenological assumption about a tangible form (i.e., the tradition) that an ineffable essence (in this case, faith) takes. This use of "religious tradition," even to this day, both within and outside of the academy, owes much to how it conserves rather than problematizes popular assumptions about being religious. This includes many scholars, for whom their own so-called religious training undoubtedly informs much of their studies and thus conception of religion, especially those working in fields outside the academic study of religion. Here, we might note the rather rudimentary manner in which religion is sometimes conceptualized—for example, as a moral force for good or a deeply personal feeling—by those who are otherwise noted specialists in other domains in the Humanities or Social Sciences. What this preference for "religious tradition" also makes clear is the large number of descriptive synonyms for the world "religion" which are in wide use, again both within and without the academy, from the already mentioned faith and ultimate concern to belief, including, of course, worship, devotion, religious experience, spirituality, and even worldview.

Given its place in the field, i.e., as the identifier of our primary object of study (a role played by such terms "cell" and "organism" in Biology or "particle" in Physics), the surprisingly wide semantic range of terms that are, for some, merely interchangeable with "religion" indicates that there is a form of fuzzy thinking that informs at least parts of the field. This is the same sort of fuzzy thinking that has animated other academic fields that have tried to retool a vernacular term into a term of technical precision— we think of "text" in various literary studies, "language" in Linguistics, or even "culture" in Anthropology, all terms that have been the focus of heated debates within these fields. One might reasonably expect such terms to be marked by a high degree of specificity that scholars consensually use to name the people or items under study. While this could certainly be understood as a shortcoming for the field, if indeed its proper object of study was religion, it actually tells the critical scholar much about the practical classificatory and social utility of this term. Regardless of who uses it or to what purposes it can be put, perhaps we may be less interested in studying religion than in shifting the ground and, instead, studying *the act of calling something religion*. The latter would involve understanding the discourse on religion and thus the practical conditions that create the impression of this now widely understood social fact. For while scholars are, of course, free to define the term explicitly in any number of ways, and then to use it as the basis for their studies of human communities, the common view that there are such things in the world to study *as* religions becomes, for some, a new object of study.

Two recent examples of this shift come to mind, as illustrations of what critical scholarship in this new key might look like. We leave aside a long list of scholars already associated with this critical turn, over the past few decades, from J. Z. Smith himself to an international group over the past 30 years, noting merely Brent Nongbri's *Before Religion: A History of a Modern Concept* (2013) and Daniel Dubuisson's *The Invention of Religions* (2019), the last two being highly accessible book-length models for this work. The first example of this shift involves an "e.g." from a specific place for which this local, Latin-derived designator "religion" is alien, while the second involves an analysis of the socially formative function played by the discourse on religion.

Regarding the first, consider the following list of recent publications: Jason Ananda Josephson Storm's *The Invention of Religion in Japan* (2012); Jun'ichi Isomae's *Religious Discourse in Modern Japan: Religion, State, and Shintō* (2014); Trent E. Maxey's *The "Greatest Problem": Religion and State Formation in Meiji Japan* (2014); Mitsutoshi Horii's *The Category of "Religion" in Contemporary Japan: Shūkyō and Temple Buddhism*

Religion 251

(2018); and Jolyon Baraka Thomas's *Faking Liberties: Religious Freedom in American-Occupied Japan* (2019). What is noteworthy is that none of these books are on religion in Japan, now a well-established subfield on account of the work of an earlier generation. The latter might include Joseph Kitagawa's (1915–1992) once important collection of essays, *On Understanding Japanese Religion* (1987), or be represented by the articles in the peer-reviewed *Journal of Religion in Japan* (founded in 2012), along with the presentations made at American Academy of Religion's annual Japanese Religions program unit. Unlike these latter works, the ones previously mentioned offer historical and ethnographic analyses of how a modern nation-state grappled with what was for its inhabitants an utterly alien governing category. (Concerning the Chinese effort "to accommodate the new generic term for 'religion'" [as she phrases it in the first item to follow (52)], see Francesca Tarocco's "The Making of 'Religion' in Modern China" in the edited volume, *Religion, Language, Power* [2008], and the piece that she co-authored with Tim Barrett, "Terminology and Religious Identity: Buddhism and the Genealogy of the Term Zongjiao" in the edited collection, *Dynamins in the History of Religions Between Asia and Europe* [2011].) In so doing, they provide case studies of how the category religion— understood as naming an interior disposition in stark distinction from such other aspects of daily life as those designated as political or economic— functions as a legal mechanism of state governance. Japanese scholars and government officials aimed to identify domestic and therefore familiar analogues that could be retooled to function as religion, something that the victors expected in the aftermath of Japan's defeat in World War II, followed by American occupation and the creation of a US-influenced Constitution, formally adopted on May 3, 1947. In the case of Japan, the term *shūkyō* was settled upon to name a so-called sectarian teaching, in distinction from state-sanctioned civic teachings, the latter of which would fall under the domain of official state action and control. However, as argued by Hans Martin Krämer, in his essay "How 'Religion' Came to Be Translated as '*Shūkyō*: Shimaji Mokurai and the Appropriation of Religion in Early Meiji Japan," *Japan Review* 25 [2013]: 89–111), this local concept was ideally situated to play this role because a previous generation of Buddhist scholars, during what is known as the Meiji era in Japan (1868–1912, the period in which the 1890 Constitution of Imperial Japan was developed) had already used the term "to come to terms with the role of Shinto within the modern polity, i.e., a purely domestic concern hardly affected by Western cultural dominance" (89). Thus, there was a ready-made concept able to distinguish what we would call beliefs from practices, a distinction of convenience should a government aim to curtail certain forms of action and association by idealizing them, while not seeming to discourage freedoms of belief. Or, as Horii concludes with regard to post-World War II Japan: "what became reclassified as religion [and thus as *shūkyō*] under the Occupation was the value orientations which were different from [the newly established] liberal democracy" (61).

The study of religion reframed as the study of the discourse on religion, or religion as a social fact, finds in modern Japan a helpful case study, one that can be generalized to how the category religion functions in other liberal democracies. This suggests that the term, defined in its widely accepted, interiorist manner, plays a central role in establishing the modernity that many of us today take for granted, what with our presumption of conscience as being an internal dialogue that the state cannot control. This analysis argues that what little remains within that seemingly private domain is not worth the state's time or attention. This is precisely where we move to our second example of what a reframed scholarship on "religion" might look like: the recent work of Naomi Goldenberg, from the University of Ottawa. Although known earlier in her career for her work as a feminist scholar of religion, Goldenberg increasingly applies political theory to the modern category religion. Drawing on a wide number of examples, she argues that the governance of modern nation-states depends upon having the category religion to name and thereby contain and rule social formations that are potential competitors to the state. Calling these "vestigial states," she argues (as in her 2013 essay, "Theorizing Religions as Vestigial States in Relation to Gender and Law: Three Cases" in *Journal of Feminist Studies in Religion* 29/1 [2013]: 395–2 or, again, in her chapter in the edited collection, *Religion as a Category of Governance and Sovereignty* [2015]) that the designation religion is, what she calls, a technology of modern statecraft, by which subgroups that the state has domesticated are designated a place which curtails their further competition with the state. In this analysis, much as in the case study of Japan, that which is called religion is not, as long assumed in that political philosophy that we know as liberalism, inherently separate from the state (as in the so-called doctrine of the separation of Church and state in modern, secular nations). Rather, it is a site of state governance inasmuch as whatever is so named must, by law, remain apart from the day-to-day operations of the state, which include such things as how power (i.e., politics) along with value and resources (economics) are negotiated and allocated. As Goldenberg summarizes:

> I am proposing an alternative to imagining religions as systems embodying an essence that require special interpretation ... Instead, I suggest that religions be thought of as "vestigial states"—that is, as the cultural

remnants of former sovereignties that persist within current . . . governmental jurisdictions.

(2013, 40)

"These vestigial states," she continues, "are subject to limitations within the territories of Western democracies and benefit from certain privileges"—which nicely encapsulates the freedom of belief that is gained at the cost of losing the freedom to organize and act in the above-named domains where state grants to itself exclusive control.

Goldenberg's work implies that, contrary to a long tradition in the field which suggests that the nation-state ironically has religion-like features (e.g., the concept of civil religion, as popularized in the late 1960s by the American sociologist, Robert Bellah [1927–2013]), the elite members of virtually all large-scale social formations can instead be understood to draw upon a relatively small and stable number of techniques and rhetorics to authorize certain versions of the group (in competition with other types). This makes so-called religions and other supposedly secular social formations different only inasmuch as the former have already been domesticated and are now being governed by the latter, part of which entails naming and policing them *as* bounded domains known as, and thereby treated as, religions. Goldenberg recommends that, when it comes to studying so-called religious versus secular law, it would be best "if both types of regulation were comprehended to be products of similar social motives and processes" (2013, 52).

Should this be the move made by a critical scholar of religion—shifting from studying religion to the discourse on religion—then the goal of the critical scholar is not to determine the correct or best way to define religion. Rather such debates themselves become the main data for the critical scholar. This hearkens back to J. Z. Smith's argument that the category religion is not just the modern scholar's category but the category of those who, defining it as they wish, seek to govern others, thereby aiming to marginalize and cordon off potentially efficacious or consequential competition. For this reason, and somewhat ironically perhaps, it is willingly then adopted by those so designated, working to organize and identify themselves within a larger system of governance. Given these disputes, which now stretch well beyond esoteric definitional debates among scholars, Laurie L. Patton is quite correct to conclude in her *Who Owns Religion: Scholars and their Publics in the Late Twentieth Century* (2019) that "[p]erhaps a small subfield might emerge where the dynamics of controversy and analysis of the public spaces and spheres might become a new scholarly goal in the study of religion" (268). This would be one to which a critical scholar would make a significant contribution.

In this volume see: belief, classification, comparison, definition, description, experience, explanation, function, history, interpretation, method, phenomenology, politics, power, practice, redescription, secular, text, theory, world religions, worldview

In *Religion in 50 More Words* see: afterlife, animism, atheism/theism, civil religion, conversion, cult, emic/etic, founder, liberation, meditation, monotheism/polytheism, mysticism, myth, nones, paganism, piety, prayer, reformation, renunciation, ritual, salvation, soul, spirituality, theology, tradition

42 Religious literacy

Many in the international field contend that what some have recently termed religious literacy ought to be a focus and goal of the academic study of religion—whether carried out in its classrooms or in its wider public outreach. By this term they tend to refer to students', as well as the wider public's, ability to describe and understand both religion in general and, more specifically, historical and contemporary details of the world's religions. The idea behind this would seem to be that a knowledge of individual religions will play a constructive role in daily social life by enhancing people's mutual understanding for their neighbors—whether near or far—and thus their tolerance for those who are different from them. However, many works promoting religious literacy often seem to assume a fairly static notion of history, presuming that religious ideas and practices exist in a manner that is somehow immune from historical change and regional variation. There is also a tendency to imagine that many or even all members of a particular religion believe or do the same thing (e.g., Jews do "x"; Buddhists believe "y"). In many ways this is not unlike the earlier Orientalist distinctions between East and West, including the desire to identify and manage problematic concepts and groups, such as once prominent discourses around the so-called "Muslim or Arab mind." What is different today, however, is that those who promote the idea of religious literacy predicate its importance on the fact that we increasingly live in a multicultural and multiethnic world, and, as mentioned above, understanding religious diversity will aid in facilitating dialogue between various groups, both within the modern nation-state and between nations more generally. Although used in pursuit of liberal political ends, religious literacy is part of a discourse of human management and governance nonetheless—a function that may not strike everyone as being immediately evident, or at least as apparent as when yet other identifications of us/them are employed in the service of more conservative purposes. In typical fashion, religion within this discourse is maintained to be something that uniquely defines groups of people. It does this by either determining such things as their thought patterns, their social forms, their epistemological and political categories—instead of the other way around, i.e., that religion is merely a product of such factors. Certainly, religious literacy initiatives, and the result of having more self-identified religious actors talk to one another in forms of interfaith dialogue, has a place in our increasing small, globalized world, including in the daily life of a liberal democratic nation. However, the critical scholar may well argue that such activity should take place in settings distinct from the academic study of religion, especially given what are now well-established critiques of the history and the current place of the world religions paradigm in the field.

Unlike many of the words examined in this volume, "literacy" has both a modern and a distinctly American provenance to it. The term comes into usage in the beginning of the nineteenth century, with the specific term "religious literacy" gaining prominence only in the past few decades—leading to its general absence in most of the major resources that survey the state of the field. The term derives from the adjective "literate" added to the accompanying suffix -*sy* to produce the abstract noun meaning the quality, condition, or state of being able to read and write. Its meaning can also be extended to refer to this state in a given community, region, or period; for instance, by identifying a pre- or non-literate culture, or one that lacks the invention of a written alphabet. Eventually the term takes on a wider use, to name those members within a larger group who have competency within or command over not just reading and writing but a range of information or skills—a usage that links judgments over such capacities to a form of gatekeeping or boundary maintenance, determining membership eligibility or status. For example, in an extended debate entitled "The Literacy Test for Immigrants," appearing in the *Central Debating League* of the Delta Sigma Rho Chapter of the University of Chicago, against the University of Michigan and Northwestern University (1916), we read of the need to "advocate the literacy test as a further means of improvement and selection of immigration" (5). To be considered for immigration, or so the debate went, one must prove one's literacy (whether or not it is identified as such, reading, writing, and speaking in English is part of the US national citizenship processes to this day). Interestingly, what that literacy consists of is never specified. Even if narrowly confined to literally being able to read and write we can still inquire about what this skill of reading and writing would consist of. Is it literacy over the vocabulary related to baseball? Protestant Christianity? American history? Its history of systemic racism? Implicit in the term, then, is that people (in this case potential immigrants to the United States), need not just to be able to read and write but they will need to know how to read and write *about* something in particular, such as details concerning their new country of residence, all in order to be so-called productive members of society. One can only be productive, so the thinking goes, if one is familiar not only with specific abstract information (e.g., how many states are there?) but also with certain *mores* and customs (e.g., what are the responsibilities of a citizen)—or else, as it was argued then, illiteracy will produce more criminals. These debating clubs seem to have been responding to the US House of Representatives' Committee on Immigration and Naturalization hearings and report of the same year, revolving around what was by then the familiar issue of trying to administer precisely such a test to possible newcomers. After all, or so it was argued in the debate, as early as 1908 the American Federation of Labor convention "endorsed the literary test by a unanimous vote" (4). The result of that national discussion? Literacy was included in the 64th Congress's Immigration Act of 1917, which, in a subsection entitled "Illiterates," excluded from eligibility to enter the United States "[a]ll aliens over sixteen years of age, physically capable of reading, who can not read the English language, or some other language or dialect, including Hebrew or Yiddish" (House Resolution 10384 [February 5, 1917], 877).

As already noted, in its extended use (often with modifying adjective) the term can refer to the ability to "read" a specified subject, thereby denoting one's competence or knowledge in a particular domain. For example, we read in the *American Magazine*, which was published between 1906 and 1956: "To help many of the poverty-stricken peoples to set their feet on the path of education, manual dexterity, and economic literacy" (103/1 [1943]). Familiarity with economics, it is here assumed, will help people in lower social classes improve their lot. But even the public at large possesses "a general ignorance of elementary economic facts and principles" which can lead to disastrous outcomes for the nation, or so argued the education professor, Harold Florian Clark (1889–1947). He instead opted in favor of "raising the general economic literacy of the people" in the National Council for the Social Studies' periodical, *Economic Education* (11 [1940]: 35, 64). Within this same general context, we also see the rise, especially since the 1980s, of publications with titles such as *Cultural Literacy: What Every American Needs to Know* (1988); *A First Dictionary of Cultural Literacy: What Our Children Need to Know* (1989); *Cultural Literacy & Arts Education* (1991); *Achieving Emotional Literacy* (1999); *Sound Thinking: Developing Musical Literacy* (1995); *The New Dictionary of Cultural Literacy: What Every American Needs to Know* (2002); and *Cultural Literacy for the Common Core: Six Steps to Powerful Practical Instruction for All Learners* (2014). All of these titles share the desire to demonstrate to their readers that a lack of understanding of a particular topic deprives them of the ability to understand and to participate properly in the world and among the groups in which they live.

We can certainly extend this latter usage to the academic study of religion, and thus we return to the concept of nurturing a specifically *religious* literacy, as in the recent special issue of the scholarly periodical, *Journal of Beliefs and Values: Studies in Religion and Education*, guest edited by the British scholars, Adam Dinham and Stephen Parker, and entitled *Religious Literacy: Spaces of Teaching and Learning About Religion and Belief* (41/2 [2020]). This term was used with some degree of regularity in the late 1950s and early 1960s, before taking off—not unlike the term "Abrahamic religions" and its effort to promote a specific vision for the proper relations among Judaism, Christianity, and Islam—in the post-9/11 world. But as early as the 1951 *United States Full Committee Hearing on H. R. 2821 and Miscellaneous Matters* in the House of Representatives Committee on the Armed Services, for example, we read that "during the first 8-week period (initial trainee phase) the trainee will be counseled by a chaplain of his own faith. The purpose of this period of counselling is to enable the chaplain to gather the religious data and background of the individual and to ascertain his level of religious literacy," whose purpose was "to counsel relative to the place of moral and spiritual values in his own life" (2482). Religious literacy, it is worth pointing out here, refers not to literacy in other religions (as it comes to signify later), but refers solely to the knowledge that an individual has of his or her own religious tradition. In like manner, Mordechai Kaplan (1881–1983), the founder of Reconstructionist Judaism and creator of the Jewish community center concept (sometimes called "a shul [i.e., synagogue] with a pool"—see Kenneth Libo's essay in *American Jewish History* 88/2 [2000]: 303–305)—as well as being the first person to give his daughter a Bat Mitzvah (a coming-of-age ceremony for females), wrote in a volume called *A New Zionism* (1959) that

> if we cannot subscribe to the historicity of the miracles recorded in the Bible, including the theophany on Mount Sinai, *the only way to become God-conscious is to acquire religious literacy. This is a new human requirement which has arisen out of man's recent intellectual progress.*
>
> (158; his italics)

Influenced by the early sociologist, Émile Durkheim's (1858–1917) notion of the social aspect and function of religions, especially its ability to promote social cohesion, Kaplan further acknowledges that this religious literacy—of Jews and for their own tradition, Judaism—would promote a sense of the collectivity.

Many who today advocate for religious literacy are interested in teaching the study of religion at the pre-university level—what in parts of Europe might generally be termed Religious Education (RE) within the publicly funded school system. In her 2007 *Overcoming Religious Illiteracy: A Cultural Studies Approach to the Study of Religion in Secondary Education*, for example, Harvard's Diane L. Moore points out the consequences of American high school students not knowing about religion: "fueling the culture wars, curtailing historical and cultural understanding, and promoting religious and racial bigotry" (3). Her proposed solution? Promote a curriculum in the K-12 classroom that will promote an understanding of religion with the aim of creating "engaged, informed, and responsible citizens of our democracy" (4). This is not unlike what Boston University's scholar of American religion, Stephen Prothero, sought to do in his own 2009 book titled *Religious Literacy: What Every American Needs to Know—And Doesn't*, which is written for a popular as opposed to an academic audience. Here it might be worth showing his indebtedness to the aforementioned (and once controversial) 1988 book *Cultural Literacy: What Every American Needs to Know* by E. D. Hirsch, and which presents the reader with over 5,000 "facts" (e.g., dates, names, places, grammatical punctuations, etc.) that every so-called literate American should know (and which later resulted in a dictionary and curriculum that he developed for teaching these facts in schools). Like Hirsch, Prothero's intended readership is not so much the pre-university classroom, as it is *all* Americans. His rather bold (and, to some, perhaps alarmist) goal is that unless Americans learn about other religions then they will be unable to confront the domestic and foreign challenges facing this country today. Such a linkage between knowledge about religion and geo-politics hearkens back to Huston Smith's (1919–2016) own concerning comments, in the preface to the first edition of his longtime bestselling textbook, originally entitled *The Religions of Man* (1958), on the enthusiasm of the military of his time for learning about other people's religions: "they were concerned because someday they were likely to be dealing with the peoples they were studying as allies, antagonists, or subjects of military occupation" (7–8). Prothero's proposed solution was to provide the core tenets of the world's major religions. He does so, however, in an often highly essentialized, non-historicized, and rather monolithic factual fashion, with the aim of showing how these religions are similar to as well as different from one another. Implicit in his argument, it seems, is that a knowledge of Christianity and Islam might have helped to prevent the tragedies that happened in such places as Waco, Texas (i.e., 1993's violent conflict between the US government and the Branch Davidians, a subgroup of the Seventh-Day Adventists founded in 1955) and 9/11 respectively. Prothero relies on this essentialism again in his 2010 *God Is Not One: The Eight Rival Religions that Run the World—and Why Their Differences Matter*. Though, to his credit, he refuses to make the case as made by so many others: that religions share a common essence. Yet, his reified notion of each of the religions will nevertheless surely strike the critical scholar as problematic, not least because of the manner in which the colonial-era world religions paradigm is so well-established as to now be a commonsense, descriptive fact. In his desire to get lay audience to understand the world's religions, he uses a four-part schema to examine each world religions. As he frames it, each religion poses: (1) a problem; (2) a solution to it; (3) a technique; and (4) an exemplar. Thus, applying this formula to, say, Buddhism, we learn: (1) suffering; (2) nirvana; (3) Eightfold Path (e.g., meditation); and (4) Bodhisattvas or lamas. With this misleadingly simple knowledge in hand, akin to the sort of information some students wish to acquire so as to memorize for the test, readers are then expected not only to understand the world's religions but also to better grasp the nature of the world around them.

But as may be evident already, there is a problem with this approach. Most basic is that it assumes that, should students complete an "Introduction to Islam" course at the university level and suddenly find themselves transported to, say, Morocco, such students would somehow understand not only the new culture in which they find themselves, but what the actors with whom they are interacting are "thinking." This problem lurks within the world religions paradigm, of course, upon which so much of the field has been built. That which scholars designate as religion, in other words, is not something so well bounded and defined that it can be removed tidily, let alone at all, from the many mundane social and cultural activities that populate daily life—despite what the world religions textbooks suggest to their readers. Yet, for some reason or set of reasons, the field rarely seems equipped to teach, let alone analyze, these other activities.

Like any compound word with the adjective "religious" in it (e.g., religious community, religious experience, religious practices, etc.), we should perhaps pause to understand the intellectual work that it performs. If "religious" is, as we have seen with so many of the terms examined here, a purposefully vague referent, pointing to other equally vague referents (like "the sacred"—such as Elaine Peña writing: "There is no one set path toward the sacred," and then defining "the sacred" as "a dynamic, organic, and complex impression of one's spiritual world" [in the conclusion to her book, *Performing Piety: Making Space Sacred with the Virgin of Guadalupe* (2011), 145, 148])—then we have to ask what does gaining literacy in such an ambiguously and, very often, circularly defined domain even mean? Obviously, we understand what many people *think* it means. Recall Prothero's idea that we need to understand the various religions to understand our world and, by implication, live in it responsibly. A critical scholar might be tempted to counter, however, that we would be better informed about the world if we understood the ways in which social groups make their worlds meaningful by means of discourses imagined to be transcendent and thus beyond history and circumstance. Going even further than those who promote religious literacy, it would then be important to realize how religion functions as precisely within such an authorizing discourse, one that helps the members of social groups to arrange their worlds in certain ways (and not others) while legitimating these on only these sorts of arrangements. If, rather than theorize religion in this way, we simply focus on the descriptive contents of religion—e.g., Hindus believe "a," "b," and "c"; and Muslims do "d," "e," and "f"—we leave in place those dehistoricizing mechanisms that could have instead attracted our attention. Religious literacy initiatives may certainly help citizens to better understand and inhabit the worlds in which they live, thereby allowing them to conclude that they now better understand their Shinto neighbor and their Greek Orthodox classmate. Yet, this approach in no way introduces them to complexity of religion, let alone the taxon "religion" itself, as a modern system of classification and rank, a system that *cannot* be separated from the various cultural, social, and intellectual worlds they inhabit.

This discussion then raises the larger question of what should the place of religious literacy be—if any—in the academic study of religion? As should be clear, critical scholars may conclude that it has very a limited place. Here we might quote, as we have done several times already, from the onetime University of Chicago scholar, Bruce Lincoln's "Theses on Method." In his seventh thesis, he writes:

> Beyond the question of motives and intentions, cultural relativism [and, we would add, the current religious literacy initiative] is predicated on the dubious—not to say, fetishistic—construction of "cultures" as if they were stable and discrete groups of people defined by the stable and discrete values, symbols, and practices they share.

As Lincoln then observes, this approach is well-known for placing what the critical scholar will surely conclude is an undue importance on the appearance of continuity over time and uniform homogeneity of social membership within groups whose inevitable contradictions and local contests go unnoticed and unstudied. As such, it is an approach that "risks becoming a religious and not a historic narrative: the story of a transcendent ideal threatened by debasing forces of change" (*MTSR* 8/3 [1996]: 225–227).

While critical scholars certainly understand, and perhaps cherish, that they live in diverse multicultural, multiethnic, and multilingual societies, establishing and conveying this recognition should not be confused with the goal of the academic study of religion. In this respect, we do well not to confuse such academic study with efforts to cultivate interfaith dialogue, whose goal is to learn about the other so as to find common ground among various religious groups, all for the sake of trying to make the world a better place. The critical study of religion, on the contrary, is about studying the manner whereby social actors who participate in the discourse on religion represent and legitimate their ideas, their interests, and their associations, thereby justifying their actions and their access, all the while working to keep ahead of competitors for those same limited privileges.

In this volume see: belief, classification, comparison, definition, description, essence, experience, history, interpretation, phenomenology, politics, practice, text, theory, world religions

In *Religion in 50 More Words* see: civil religion, commentary, dialogue, emic/etic, understanding

43 Sacred/profane

There are surely few other paired words in the study of religion that are more prominent than sacred and profane. This, of course, pertains to the domains that their coupling establishes, and into which any number of items can be placed and thereby ordered and distinguished. While each word functions as a noun, often with the addition of an opening definite article (i.e., *the* sacred or *the* profane, along with sacrality and profanity or even sacredness and profaneness), they also function as adjectives, naming anything from sacred texts to sacred space, along with their opposites. It is therefore no accident that swearing (i.e., blasphemy [Greek *blasphaméo*, to slander, hurtful speech]), whether sexual or so-called religious profanity, has been known as "the greatest of all vices . . . a depraved and evil habit of mind," "as impolite as it is sinful" (from the June and also the July 1835 issues of *The American Magazine of Useful and Entertaining Knowledge* [415, 478]). Such profanity was also associated with "leudneffe" [lewdness] in Alexander Henderson's (1583–1646) *The Government and Order of the Church of Scotland* [1641, Part 1, 3]—notably, this claim is made in its explicitly anti-Catholic opening pages.

The terms "sacred" and "profane" thus constitute what we might call a binary pair, whereby they work in tandem, mutually informing one another, and in such a manner that neither needs to be defined explicitly as long as it can be understood as *not* being its opposite. This is evident in Robert Kemp Philips's (1819–1882) description of ancient lower Egypt "being celebrated both in sacred and profane history" (see the entry for "Africa" in *The Dictionary of Useful Knowledge*, Part III, 72). Perhaps this is no better exemplified in the field of the study of religion than in the scholarship of Mircea Eliade (1907–1986). In the Introduction to his once widely read book, which was written for readers outside the academy, *The Sacred and the Profane: The Nature of Religion* (1957): "The first possible definition of the sacred is that it is the opposite of the profane" (10, quoting the 1961 edition of Willard Trask's 1959 English translation from the German edition).

In some ways this is a rather sophisticated statement, for this is precisely how binaries actually work and would be the way to approach the issue if studying the binary itself were one's goal. For each pole can be utterly empty, so long as we think the other means something, hence the classic scientific definition of cold as the absence of heat, or kinetic energy. But this was not Eliade's goal, and it certainly is not the goal of most scholars today who discuss this thing that some frequently still call "the sacred" or those who use the adjective to qualify (or should we say enhance?) any number of things. Their aim instead is to develop a vocabulary capable of naming the presumably unique features of those things called religious—and thus the reason why they are set apart from all else. While this may indeed be the way that some, or even many, of the people we study happen to talk about their world—whether or not they use these actual two terms—for the critical scholar, such an approach accomplishes nothing other than describing or paraphrasing what people are already saying and doing for themselves. Instead, our scholarly language ought to satisfy curiosities that scholars themselves have about how something in the world works, such that after having described what we happen upon we are then able to say something new about what we have found. It is for this reason that the widespread use of the words "sacred" and "profane" may strike the critical scholar as items in need of study rather than merely as the way to describe yet other things in the world.

The historic derivation of these two terms, especially when compared to how they are commonly used today, confirms that studying their use in ordering social worlds may be far more interesting than merely using them to name things. "Sacred," entered English from the earlier French *sacre* around the twelfth or thirteenth century, originally deriving from the ancient Latin verb *sacrāre* and the related adjective *sacer*. We also see these roots in other common English words, such as "sacrifice" and "consecrate," both of which signify a process or act whereby the quality associated with being sacred is said to be established in something. The word was therefore traditionally associated with situations in which something was dedicated (i.e., set apart or marked for a specific use), thereby denoting its status as being different from other things, akin to the modern verb "to sanctify." In this way we see a curious link to the related modern noun and verb "sanction" (from the Latin *sancīre*), today naming a set of rules or prohibitions, along with enacting them ("to sanction"), such as modern nation-states imposing punitive limits, i.e., penalties, on each other (e.g., trade or diplomatic sanctions) so as to enforce certain sorts of relations between them.

What is curious is that the quality claimed to result from *setting* something apart, and thereby *marking* it as sanctified (all human actions that result in the appearance of qualities), eventually comes to be so closely associated with this term "sacred" that the supposed quality is eventually taken to be an autonomous and self-evident feature of the item. Once signified in this manner, we tend to lose sight of the practical, social procedures that led to the appearance or institution of the trait in the first place. That practitioners slip from one to the other is understandable, of course, inasmuch as overlooking the practical, manufacturing history of the quality surely enhances the presumed authenticity and thus authority of the item in question. However, that scholars also employ the terminology in this manner—as if the so-called sacred item is just naturally religious and thus obviously distinct from other items in its environment—is surely problematic. For example, in his little book in the onetime Fifty Key Words series, *Comparative Religion* (1971), Eric Sharpe (1933–2000) opens by defining "sacred" as "that which belongs to the sphere of the deity or the supernature . . . qualifying persons, places or objects in which the supernatural world interpenetrates with the everyday world" (57). He then goes on to cite the German Protestant theologian, Rudolf Otto (1869–1937), as exemplary of this use of the term. Sadly, all we find here is a description of its popular use, with no historicization, and thus no analysis of the practical (and thus contestable) human choices, actions, and institutions which create the conditions in which such a quality can be ascribed to people, places, or objects.

Looking at the history of our word "profane" further confirms this. This term's frequency in English parallels the rises and falls of the frequency of the early modern use of "sacred." Until the early- and mid-eighteenth century, however, when the use of the latter, now associated with the holy quality and not *the act to establish it*, is far more prominent. Curiously, this is just the time period when, as Jonathan Z. Smith (1938–2017) has already argued, a series of other words that we today associate with religion-as-belief were modified into what he describes as elements of a state of mind. At this point, their previous associations with social, ritual, and thus institutional settings were all but lost. For example, contrary to a variety of sources from the sixteenth and seventeenth centuries, where we find our term religion to have been closely associated with other words such as ritual, custom, deeds, and ceremony, Smith then cites Samuel Johnson's *Dictionary of the English Language* (1755) as now defining religion as a form of virtue along with the 1771 edition of the *Encyclopedia Britannica* indicating that religion means "To know God, and to render him reasonable service . . ." (see Smith's "Religion, Religions, Religious" in *Critical Terms for Religious Studies* [1998], 270–271). Apart from these later idealizations, the word "profane"—whether as noun (e.g., profanity), adjective (e.g., profane language), or even verb (e.g., to profane)—enters English a few centuries earlier, around the same time as the forerunners of our word "sacred," from Old and Middle French and, ultimately, from the Latin *profānus*, literally signifying something that is outside (*pro-*) the temple (*fānum*). That which is profane thus named something that was in the opposite location or position from that which is marked to its new status as set apart and thus sanctified.

Two important issues should attract the critical scholar's attention at this point. First, what Smith calls the "shift to belief as the defining characteristic of religion," which he argues is evidenced with the increasing frequency of associating religion with faith. Second, and with this idea of making a positional shift still in our minds, the agential and spatial aspects that result not in sacredness but, rather, ascriptions of sacredness only become apparent when we look into the word's derivation over time. For only then is it apparent that a word now commonly used as if it names an inner trait, often understood as essential, can instead be understood as being but the tip of a practical and inevitably situated process of signification. We witness the logical extension of this tradition resulting in later writers coining "the sacred" as if it is a mysterious, causal force or presence of its own, as in Baidyanath Saraswati's *The Spectrum of the Sacred: Essays on the Religious Traditions of India* (1984)—a book obviously influenced by Eliade's own prior work in the field.

It is for this reason that, despite the understandable problems we would today find with work that was carried out over 100 years ago, many critical scholars continue to return to the early French sociologist, Émile Durkheim (1858–1917) and his influential *Les formes élémentaires de la vie religieuse* (1912; English translation, *The Elementary Forms of Religious Life*). Here we see an early example of a scholar refusing to idealize our vocabulary, let alone idealizing the people and social situations that we study. Durkheim thought about religion in ways that were contrary to what was the already well-established tradition across Europe of defining religion as the outward expressions of prior private experience or individual feeling or sentiment, and in a way that is important to distinguish from the Eliadean preference for the noun "the sacred." (On this see William E. Paden's still important article, "Before 'the Sacred' Became Theological: Rereading the Durkheiniam Legacy" in *Method & Theory in the Study of Religion* 3/1 [1991]: 10–23.) Betraying his sociologist interests, Durkheim instead opted for the adjective when defining religion as a rule system enacted by people in groups—suggesting that Philip Mellor and Chris Shilling's claim, in the Introduction to their *Sociology of the Sacred: Religion Embodiment, and Social Change* (2014), that Durkheim "examine[d] how the sacred can be manifest[ed] in different, religious and secular, forms" is well off the mark. Instead of "the sacred," whatever that may actually be, manifesting itself, he instead studied the reported quality of sacrality as being a by-product of human action. As he famously wrote in the closing lines of Book 1, Chapter 1, "Definition of Religious Phenomena and of Religion":

> A religion is a unified system of beliefs and practices relative to sacred things, that is to say, things set apart and forbidden—beliefs and practices which unite into one single moral community called a Church, all those who adhere to them.
>
> (47, quoting the 1964 edition of Joseph Ward Swain's 1915 translation)

Given the wide number of scholars today who continue to focus their work merely on belief, Durkheim's words from more than a century ago are worth reconsidering. However, the growing influence of lived religion and material religion studies today, and their refocusing on practice, does not detract from the continued importance of his definition, in that it makes abundantly clear that these behavioral complexes not only have practical, rather than ethereal, sources and effects, but that they provide the all too mundane conditions from which such supposed qualities as sacredness or holiness result. Taking etymology seriously, Durkheim's definition places front and center the presumption that human actors are the signifiers and that devising and then enacting their rule systems is what quite literally sets things apart and thereby makes them seem to be sacred to members of such groups. The quality now clearly associated with something being "in place" as opposed to "out of place," whether that means inside versus outside the temple or, say, the ancient Hebrew character Moses being told (in Exodus 3) by a disembodied voice not to approach the burning bush because the ground is *qodesh*, often translated as holy but more properly, perhaps, also understood as set apart and therefore forbidden—a quality transgressed to one's own danger, or, we should add, to one's titillation, as in the romance author Torrance Sené's independently published *Sacred & Profane: Priest Erotic Romance* (2017), a collection of "stories of clergymen stepping outside their vows."

For the critical scholar this should all be rather illuminative, of course, for we now find a way to move from work that comprises mere repetition (even if detailed) of certain participant self-reports, such as scholars immersing themselves in documenting and describing everything from a people's sacred stories to their sacred stones. A recent example of this would be Robert Orsi's call for scholars to forgo explanatory studies and, instead, study the experience of the holy as a real presence in people's lives (see "The Problem of the Holy," in *The Cambridge Companion to Religious Studies* [2012]). Instead, we can carry out scholarship that studies those very claims about presence—as sincerely as they are no doubt made by many people—as always being historically situated and as socially consequential human acts. No longer content simply to discuss the features of such things as already designated sacred rites, the scholar will start to pose what Bruce Lincoln once described (in #4 of his "Theses on Method") as "destabilizing and irreverent questions." These include for whom is something sacred or profane while also inquiring into when, for how long, and in what circumstance can either status be granted, and, thinking back to Durkheim, by what practical technique is something "set apart and forbidden" (and again, at whose disposal are these mechanisms of separation)? Finally, with Lincoln's own list of irreverent questions in mind, we can also ask: "What are the consequences if this project of persuasion should happen to succeed?" Thus, returning to our opening, the lack of content to the sacred/profane binary (so nicely but, perhaps unwittingly, identified by Eliade himself) is thus not an impediment to such a scholar for there is now an understanding that such terms' individual content can be arbitrary or utterly unspecified. Instead, what is important is the ability for social actors to devise and employ an ordered system of opposition to organize (by which we mean not just to differentiate but also to rank and prioritize) the contents of their world, from its people to its objects, its remembered past to its present and imagined future—an imposed organization that accomplishes something for them in relation to their peers.

The critical scholar will likely approach claims of sacredness or profaneness as interrelated elements of a much larger social system of designation and allocation (whether it is resources or identities and status that is being governed). It is a system that sorts, privileges, and demotes, all according to the changeable (and therefore contestable) interests of those who are in the position to set whatever they wish apart. Ann Taves prefers to call this setting apart "special"—as in things, places, or people *deemed* special (see her *Religious Experience Reconsidered: A Building-Block Approach to the Study of Religion and Other Special Things* [2009]), all the while ensuring that the actions of others are policed in conformity with the authorized system of distinction and identification (i.e., the second part of Durkheim's phrasing is as important as the first: "set apart and forbidden"). This critical approach, perhaps somewhat ironically at least to traditionalists, will be more attracted to those items that seem to defy such designations, the so-called boundary cases which any system based on this opposed pairing fails to adequately designate or contain within one of the two mutually exclusive spheres. It was precisely such a scenario that the influential British anthropologist, Mary Douglas (1921–2007), examined in her work on identities that are produced by means of classification system, not simply conceiving of ambiguity as a temporary middle phase between two sequentially arranged statuses. These include the boundary moments between child/

adult or single/married (as do those scholars of ritual, for example, who sometimes study the so-called liminal [Latin *limen*, or threshold or edge] stage in a rite of passage, exemplified early on in the work of the folklorist, Arnold van Gennep [1873–1957], and, later, the cultural anthropologist Victor Turner [1920–1983]). Instead, for scholars influenced by Douglas's work, ambiguous status and thus identity is a necessary and therefore permanent feature of the world—and not, as the University of Kent's Gordon Lynch seems to argue, evidence that one's theory of the sacred is open to criticism (*The Sacred in the Modern World* [2012], 26). If we understand systems devised to designate the world, such as sacred/profane, as having themselves been devised from *within* that same world, then we understand how they cannot anticipate nor manage all cases and are thus bound to fail, leaving the people, objects, or places that confound them undesignated—or, better put, designated in yet new ways, i.e., as dangerous, anomalous, impure, hybrid, and generally out of place. It is therefore the ambiguous cases, evidence of where systems of conceptual and social governance have failed, which make most apparent the regulatory systems that are up and running and which, when unchallenged and therefore working properly, often appear to us as invisible or self-evident. Simply recounting, regardless the level of detail, that something is either sacred or profane tells the critical scholar nothing other than that their work to understand the people who are using these, or related, terms to try to arrange both their world and their own place within it, has only just begun.

In this volume see: authenticity, belief, classification, comparison, definition, description, essence, experience, interpretation, lived religion, material religion, phenomenology, religion, text, theory, world religions

In *Religion in 50 More Words* see: atheism/theism, church, civil religion, emic/etic, nones, paganism, piety, reformation, sacrifice, spirituality, theology

44 Secular

As the modern and ostensible opposite of the most important term in the field, religion (or religious), secular (and, by extension, secularity and secularism) plays no less a significant role, whether in the field or in society at large—something evident in the widely influential work of the Canadian philosopher, Charles Taylor (1931), such as his *A Secular Age* (2007). For, not unlike the sacred/profane or even the East/West, the religion/secular binary functions on account of the two words that, in their mutual pairing, give definition to the other, often in such a manner that neither needs to be defined explicitly as long as it can be understood as *not* being its opposite, though, paradoxically, all the while being defined by it. The secular, in other words, is imagined as the opposite of the religious, just as the religious is regarded as its opposite. This is the manner whereby the definition of the term, and its subsequent understanding, proceeds, with non-scholars and scholars alike casually and quickly differentiating, often all too neatly, between these two, for lack of a better term, "spheres." As has been the case with so many of the terms examined here, however, critical scholarship cannot simply paraphrase and reproduce—without critical comment, interpretation, or explanation—the way that the people and texts that they study understand and describe their reading of their world and its contents. Too often the default definition for the secular/religion distinction is akin to that provided in a verse from Matthew 22:21: "Render unto Caesar the things that are Caesar's, and unto God the things that are God's"—with the assumption that what belongs to Caesar represents all that is secular and somehow non-religious while that which belongs to God is then defined as its opposite, i.e., as that which is somehow "religious." This is done, moreover, despite the fact that there was no term for "religion" in our modern sense at the time that the Gospels were written. When we simply describe what our data say or do, without any sort of overlay or redescription grounded in scholarly method and/or theory, we fail to understand the social worlds that humans make for themselves—and the ways in which they do this and inevitably contest each other in the process. Our scholarly vocabulary, then, ought to describe, compare, and then always redescribe our datasets. It is for this reason that the widespread use of terms like "secular" and, by extension, "secularism," let alone "religion" or "religious," may strike the critical scholar as items in need of further investigation. All of this should be done, moreover, with an eye to seeing what sort of intellectual and practical work they may be doing, as opposed simply to describing things in the world as our sources phrase them. And so, rather than try to uncover or discover what the secular is or really ought to be, it might be more productive for critical scholars to see what sort of taxonomic or discursive activity it produces, both among our data and those scholars in the field who study it. After all, it is not that long ago that members of European or North American groups represented themselves (as some still do, of course) as inhabiting "a Christian nation" or "a Christian civilization," prior to making the shift to the discourse on the secular (e.g., see Sam Brewitt-Taylor's "The Invention of a 'Secular Society'? Christianity and the Sudden Appearance of Secularization Discourses in the British National Media, 1961–4" in *Twentieth Century British History* 24/3 [2013]: 327–350).

Like so many of the terms scholars today use, the English term "secular" derives from the Old French *seculer* (compare with modern French *séculier*), itself from the Latin *saeculāris*, referring to a "generation" or an "age." We see this, for example, in John Dryden's (1631–1700) "The Secular Masque," a turn-of-the-century poem about a turn of an era play, which opens with the Roman god Janus saying:

> Chronos, Chronos, mend thy pace,
> An hundred times the rolling sun
> Around the radiant belt has run
> In his revolving race.

In so-called Church Latin, the term designated "the world," especially as that which was imagined as in opposition to and thus outside of the Church. In its earliest usage, then, the term "secular" had what some today would refer to as a religious dimension to it—if one were to read our modern term religion backward onto this period—because it referred to not so much as the opposite of the religious, but, instead, to members of the clergy who *lived out* "in the world" as opposed to those who *lived in* a convent or a monastery. So, more correctly than attributing so-called religious origins to the term (as many scholars today do), a more careful reading might instead identify how the distinction was used early on within a once dominant institution to allocate its own leadership roles and duties. We thereby see the notion of a lay or "secular" abbot or abbess to refer to a person who was not a monk or nun, respectively, but who nonetheless had the title for governing a monastery or a convent and thus a share of the revenues, but none of the functions of a "religious" abbot or abbess. As such, it would be an error to assume that the term, at that time, had anything to do with the modern meaning it was only to acquire much later. Or, as we read in the *Chronicle of Robert of Gloucester* (c. 1325): "Canons þer were Seculers"—with the understanding that the individuals employed as Canons, a role of leadership in Roman Catholicism, for example, and in the Church of England, were those who lived "in the world." At the end of the sixteenth century, the term also comes to be associated with that which refers to common and/or unlearned people. It is in this sense that it subsequently became associated with "laity," a word that enters the English language at roughly the same time, from the adjective "lay" meaning "people" plus the suffix "ity," and which was related to the ecclesiastical Latin *lāicus*, itself derived from the Greek *laikós* (with the meaning of to "not be in orders"). To this day, in Romance languages, it is this root that is used to designate the "secular," such as the French noun *laïcité* (i.e., secularism), and the Italian adjective *laico/a*, "secular."

Even as late as the early nineteenth century we continue to witness this use of the term "secular" as naming a division of labor and identity within the institution of the Church—or, at the very least, in a manner that does not envisage the religious and the secular as two spheres that are completely cordoned off from one another. In his *Collection of Scarce and Valuable Tracts* from 1809, the Scottish novelist and playwright Sir Walter Scott (1771–1832) lists the "The Names of Romish Priests and Jesuits now resident about the City of London, March 26, 1624," with several of them described as secular. For example: "F. Musket, a secular priest, lodging over-against S. Andres church in Holborne, a frequent preacher, and one that hath much concourse of people to his chamber" (90). The term, however, gradually seems to have taken on the meaning of its now current usage, as that which is *distinct* from the religious. In the Dutch scholar Phillippus can Limborch (1633–1712) *Historia Inquisitionis* (1692), translated and abridged into English as *The History of the Inquisition, As it has subsisted in France, Italy, Spain, Portugal, Venice, Sicily, Sardinia, Milan, Poland, Flanders, &c. &c* (1816), we read:

> The inquisitors are commanded to pronounce the sentences against heretics, and to leave the condemned persons to the secular powers present, to be punished according to their dessert. Although this command requires the secular judge to be present at the pronouncing sentence, yet the sentence of condemnation against heretics, pronounced when the secular judge is absent, is valid, provided there be all other things essential to it.

(458)

Or, again, we see how it can be used polemically in David Simpson's (1745–1799) *A Plea for Religion and the Sacred Writings, Addressed to the Disciples of Thomas Paine, and Wavering Christians of Every Persuasion* (3rd ed., 1804) where it is synonymous with "superstitious." We read, for example:

> The secular and superstitious conduct of the *Heathen Priesthood* brought ruin upon the *Pagan* nations: the secular and superstitious conduct of the *Jewish Priests* brought ruin upon the *Jewish* nation; the secular and superstitious conduct of the *Catholic Priests* hath brought ruin upon the *Catholic* nations; and the same kind of secular and superstitious conduct of our *Protestant Bishops and Clergy* will involve us in similar destruction.
>
> (164)

His solution?

"Ecclesiastical reform" (164)!

So thus we arrive at the contemporary understanding, of terms that designate separate and opposite domains, as in Samuel Sharman's collection of poems, *Jottings in Verse, Sacred and Secular* (1889)—with poems on the Holy Spirit or the Communion of Saints in one section and others on birthday greetings, love poems, and one entitled "Why the Men Don't Propose" in another. We also see this in Charles Watt's (1836–1906) and George William Foote's (1850–1915) *The Secular Review & Secularist*, a so-called freethinkers weekly journal in England with its first issue on June 9, 1877, bearing the lead quote from the English theologian, John Henry Newman (1801–1890): "False ideas may be refuted by argument, but only by true ideas can they be expelled." The Newman quote, of course, sets a tone that equates secularism with freethought or, as it came to be known, agnosticism, and marks a moment when the term had not quite achieved it modern connotation. In fact, in a short essay in the first issue of *Secular Review & Secularist*, by H. V. Mayer (who also contributed to *The Secular Chronicle* in those same years), we read the following: "Secularism refuses to regard anything as sacred save the useful and good" (2). Just as some today use the term "critical" in the field, so-called religious writings could easily be included so long as they were considered rational and liberal, as in the latter periodical whose subtitle read: "a weekly journal established to promote free inquiry into social, political, and theological questions." But the opposed nature of the two realms was also being considered during this period, exemplified in the dispute over the credibility of the narratives in the Christian gospels that took place via dueling manifestos distributed in

England by the National Secular Society (established in 1866), on the one hand, and the older Religious Tract Society (founded in 1799), on the other. This dispute was narrated by Charles Bradlaugh (1833–1891), the former society's founder, in the second edition of his *When Were Our Gospels Written?* (1873, 5ff.).

Jumping ahead about a hundred years (when the binary is firmly established), in the contemporary field of sociology of religion the "secular" is now seen as a domain opposed to the religious. It increasingly becomes associated with what was widely known as the secularization thesis, something that is often associated with the so-called death of religion movement of the time. In this sense it was imagined that the irresistible force of modernization, especially after the Reformation and Renaissance, would eventually lead to the gradual disappearance of religion, except perhaps in the inner realm of the private. At least this was the thesis of the American sociologist C. Wright Mills (1916–1962) in, for example, his *The Sociological Imagination* (1959). This was a theory picked up by the American sociologist Peter L. Berger (1929–2017), who also predicted the increased secularization of the modern world—a trend some might even find evident in just the changes in the term "secular" itself. He subsequently changed his mind, however, when he wrote:

> The world today, with some exceptions . . . is as furiously religious as it ever was, and in some places more so than ever. This means that a whole body of literature by historians and social scientists loosely labeled "secularization theory" is essentially mistaken.
> (See, e.g., his *The Desecularization of the World: Resurgent Religion in a Pluralist Age* [1999], 2)

Such sociological examinations, however, seem to conceive of the secular—and indeed the religious—as if it is a natural part of the world, and thus as if it actually names something long established, instead, perhaps, as imagining it as part of a discourse and thus a system of classification that constitutes our modern world (by means of its internal divisions of labor and identity).

In many ways this latter sense is the way that it is used in the academic study of religion. In a recent zoom lecture series (on account of the COVID-19 pandemic) at McGill University in Montreal, devoted to the topic of "ReOrienting the Global Study of Religion: History, Theory, and Society," there was a lecture by Florian Zemmin, from the University of Leipzig (and senior researcher with the international collaborative "Multiple Secularities: Beyond the West, Beyond Modernities" project), on "The Secular in the Middle East and Islamic History." While the goal of the lecture was to show how contemporary Islamic thought conceptualizes the secular, again with the assumption that it names something distinct from the religious, the speaker subsequently sought to do this by showing the relationship between religion and politics. Once again, there is the assumption that the two terms name two separate spheres, with the secular obviously connected, in some way, to the so-called political. This presumption of natural alignment among domains may not be surprising, of course, given that the aim of the above-mentioned research program is, according to its self-description on its website, to "transcend the isolated issue of the transcultural applicability of the term 'religion' by focusing on the processes of differentiation between 'the religious' and 'the secular' or related distinctions." The problem, here, is that a distinction of obvious utility and thus importance initially to what became the European world is simply assumed to be natural and found in all historic periods, and subsequently exported to various places around the globe. Such an approach, however, may strike the critical scholar as data, inasmuch as it provides ironic evidence of just how successful this way of organizing a social world has been, given that the domains and associations that the religious/secular distinction generates are assumed to constitute a basic feature of the human. This tendency seems linked to how successfully this distinction has created the presumption of religion as a unique yet universal personal experience, something that is set apart from all other aspects of the social. This, in turn, leads to the conception that religion—whether called faith or spirituality—pre-dates the invention of the secular some centuries ago. Thus, the idea of religion, itself a product of the binary, is assumed to precede it. To the critical scholar this may be seen to indicate that the distinction, and the presumption of a specific human domain being permanently distinct and thus naturally set apart, likely plays a fundamental role in managing this modern world that is today taken for granted by most of its inhabitants.

While a great many imagine a simple dichotomy between the religious and the secular, some scholars have recently tried to demonstrate how much more complicated the actual situation is. The anthropologist Talal Asad, for example, has spent considerable time examining the various material conditions that have made it possible for members of modern, liberal-democratic nation-states to imagine, and then put into practice, this concept of the secular. For instance, in his still influential book, *Genealogies of Religion: Discipline and Reasons of Power in Christianity and Islam* (1993), he argues that "religion," far from being a universal category, has often been configured and has operated in ways that we today would neither define nor recognize as religious. What we think of in the so-called modern West as secular (or even as religious for that matter) is, for Asad, nothing more nor less than a by-product of larger political configurations and compromises that are, in many ways, unique to modernity. This has created a certain intersection between those domains demarcated *as* religious and those *as* secular. Though the line that bifurcates them has been consistently redrawn or remapped over the centuries it has been done in such a way that the identity and authority of the socio-political institution known as the Church remains intact, if increasingly regulated. Rather than dismantle this bifurcation, the rise of the modern nation-state over the past few hundred years took full advantage of it by deferring the power of the Church as purely ecclesiastical, thereby transforming the discourse on religion from one of membership and action (e.g., ritual performance and social status) into an interior sentiment said to reside within the individual believer. Thus was born a new conception of religion, both individual and private, that was unintentionally captured in Clifford Geertz's (1926–2006) famous anthropological definition of religion as being comprised of "moods and motivations." Religion could now be used for a host of modern political ends, not least of which was reserving all other forms of power to the modern state (e.g., of taxation, of the ownership and distribution of resources, of coercive violence, etc.). The secular state—as Asad further argues in the essays in his *Formations of the Secular: Christianity, Islam, Modernity* (2003)—thus retains the structure of the premodern Church by rearranging the power structures that regulate daily life.

The critical scholar may come to redescribe such historical events as the sixteenth-century's so-called Protestant Reformation as not being about religion, theology, and beliefs, as it is usually described. Instead, it functions as an early modern contest between a dominant system of governance (commonly called the Roman Catholic Church) and a wide variety of what were then emergent institutions across Europe (from regional monarchs and rulers to far more local groups), a contest that was waged by redefining what counted as authority and who counted as authoritative. In its wake the religion/politics distinction took on greater significance, across Europe first but then as part of what the colonial period exported throughout the world, as a way to name and thereby manage what Naomi Goldenberg has aptly called vestigial states within an emerging nation-state working to consolidate its authority by governing its potential competitors.

In a similar vein, in his *Discourse on Civility and Barbarity: A Critical History of the Religion and Related Categories* (2007), the English scholar Timothy Fitzgerald sought to connect the emergent discourse surrounding the category of religion in the early modern European period to the parallel formation of "non-religion" or the "non-religious." This distinction, he argued, is related to other such dichotomies that appeared at roughly the same period, such as those between Church/state, sacred/profane, private/public, ecclesiastical/civil, spiritual/temporal, supernatural/natural, and irrational/rational. Each part of these coordinated binaries needs its opposite for its own existence and ultimate clarification. As such, and in terms of religion, one can only clarify what it is by giving definition to what it is not, and it is that job that increasingly fell to the "secular," and it is within this context that we begin to see the semantic shift in the term, as mentioned above. For as "the religious" was increasingly imagined as a private belief in the supernatural, requisite conceptual space was needed for the simultaneous imagining of "the secular," such as those practices and institutions claimed first by the monarch and later by the newly forming nation-state. Fitzgerald's discussion here is an important one because, unlike so much recent scholarship on the secular, he does not see it as an actual space or definite realm, but, instead, as an authorizing discourse, connected to such related material concepts, such as culture, power, politics, and society.

We thus should be careful—or, at least, cautious—of those discourses, whether popular or in the academy, surrounding the term "secular." In this regard, it is important to note that what has been constructed as "the secular," to wit, the opposite of religion, cannot simply be assumed to name a clearly defined domain that is somehow obviously separate from the religious, and from which it is hermetically sealed. Indeed, the semantic twists and turns of the term over the centuries reveal that it has been used dialectically to both think about and subsequently define what religion is and what ideas, beliefs, practices, and institutions can, by extension, be labelled as religious—that is, identified as, set apart as, and thereby regulated as. Of course, this dialectic also works in the opposite direction, as well, since so-called secularists ultimately need the religious in order to define and articulate, simultaneously, what constitutes the so-called secular. But in order to avoid this mutually defining circularity, it would be more profitable for critical scholars to approach their studies of the secular as an always contestable authorizing discourse—a rhetoric, if you will—that, in bringing those things called religion into focus, simultaneously makes possible and persuasive certain ways of arranging and legitimizing certain people, ideas, things, and social spaces.

In this volume see: classification, comparison, culture, definition, description, essence, explanation, interpretation, politics, power, redescription, religion, sacred/profane, society

In *Religion in 50 More Words* see: atheism/theism, church, civil religion, emic/etic, nones, piety, reformation, theology, tradition

45 Society

Given the prominent role played by social theory in the work of many of those who are today engaged in the critical study of religion, the current volume would not be complete without paying attention to this word "society," since this term constitutes the ground upon which much of this work stands. Despite the long tradition of scholars who study "religion and society" as if they are separable things that sometimes interact in certain ways, the term is more complex than it at first appears. This complexity is linked to it generally being understood as the product of prior individuals' labors (the result of what the political philosopher, Jean-Jacques Rousseau [1712–1778] famously called their social contracts) yet one that is simultaneously also the basis for not just their very existence, but also for such individuals' own agency and identity. Society—a unified collectivity once designated as the commonwealth (e.g., common in the seventeenth century or even today, such as naming the reconfigured associations between former colonies of the British Empire)—is therefore the basis for the scholar's work as well as being the object of study, indicating that some care should be taken when we discuss it, describe its features and history, or study its effects. These very acts can, in a rather self-reflexive manner, also be understood to constitute the social world within which scholars carry out their own work.

In its various early spellings, the noun "society"—a term of increasingly prominent use across the second half of the eighteenth and first half of the nineteenth century—entered into English in the fifteenth century from the French (modern spelling: *société*), which in turn was from the much earlier classical Latin *societās*. Both terms designate an association of people for a shared purpose or joint venture, whether an alliance, a partnership, or even a friendship and thus a group of companions. It is related to the adjective "social," which arrived from French around the same time and which is used to describe both agreeable people (to be sociable) as well as military alliances, once even naming disputes between allies ("the Social War"

[Latin *Bellum Sociale*] between Rome and other cities on what is today known as the Italian Peninsula [91–87 BCE]). Related words are the later adjective "societal" as well as the verb "socialize" (to prepare for entry or participation in the group or the act of participating) and the noun "socialization" (naming the process of entering a group, akin to being enculturated), each dating to the eighteenth century and nineteenth century, respectively. Also from the early nineteenth century is the noun "socialism," naming a form of economic and political organization and thus government. This latter term was first used (in French) in 1835, according to the American clergyman and political activist, Charles Henry Vail (1866–1925), writing in his book, *Modern Socialism* (1899), to name a position "affirming altruism as the principle of social action" and thus entailing "the abolition of private property . . . and the substitution of collective property" (9, 10). It is thus proposed as the opposite of an individualist economy. Despite an apparently rather focused series of meanings (companions and the human collectivity), the word "society" (as well as those related to it) still had a rather wide semantic range. It certainly identified what we would today term sociability—as in the English dramatist James Kenney's (1780–1848) work, "Society, A Poem in Two Parts" (1803), whose opening analysis describes its theme as being concerned with "the causes and evils of Solitude" along with "the positive advantages of Society" (1803).

Yet, it has also been used to designate a specific collection of people. For example: the Society of Friends, the so-called Quakers, a dissenting group splintered off the Church of England in the mid-seventeenth century; the Society for the Propagation of the Gospel in Foreign Parts, a Church of England missionary organization founded in 1701 by the English clergyman and abolitionist, Thomas Bray (ca. 1657–1730); or even the current Society of Biblical Literature, the US-based professional organization for bible scholars, founded in 1880 with the clergyman and academic, Daniel Raynes Goodwin (1811–1890) as its first president. Like the words for collectivities, "culture" or "class," it also developed an inflection of hierarchical value, conveyed by its association with words that indicated height (e.g., high culture or low humor). This latter sense signifies that portion of the group which was seen to be more or less desirable and thus worthy of place. Thus, we arrive at "the temptations to error in high society are great and frequent; the heart is there more susceptible and more alive to the impressions made by those elegant and alluring habits" (in an October 1823 essay, signed only by the initials SH, entitled "High Life" in *The European Magazine*, 323). We also witness its opposite: "their common traits of low society, vulgar dialect, and intemperance" (from the 1822 entry for "History" in George Ramsay's *A New Dictionary of Anecdotes*, 282). More recently, we even find "the great society" used as the name for a series of social reforms in the United States under President Lyndon Johnson in the mid-1960s, aimed at economic and racial equality.

Despite this variation, modern readers are likely familiar with the term's use to designate the community or group at large and thus somewhat akin to "the public." We see this, for example, in the Welsh social reformer, Robert Owen's (1771–1858) essay collection, *A New View of Society: or, Essays on the Principle of the Formation of the Human Character and the Application of the Principle to Practice* (1813). The first essay outlines his "new view" that context shapes character, with the claim that "the governing powers of all countries should establish rational plans for the education and generation formation of the characters of their subjects" (19). His essay aimed to "pervade society with a knowledge of its true interests, and direct the public mind to the most important object to which it can be directed," to form proper character in its citizens (22). This usage is close to the collective good implied by "civil society," a term in political discourse since at least the late fifteenth century, such as "The Influence of Christianity on Civil Society," a sermon that Rev. George Horne (1730–1792), then President of Magdalen College, preached at St. Mary's in Oxford, England, on March 4, 1773 (and published soon thereafter in a pamphlet).

The challenge, however, once the term was so expanded and used as a collective noun is in understanding that any group is comprised of a variety of components, which can themselves often be in competition for resources, whether immaterial (such as rank) or material (such as access to and use of goods). Early on we see "a company or society of men" used—for example in Joseph Caryl's (1602–1673) 1648 commentary on the Hebrew Bible's Book of Job (368). This should make plain to the contemporary reader, inasmuch as the exclusive emphasis on the association of (more than likely land-owning) males was hardly accidental. Such divisions within the social were apparent to commentators early on, of course, hence the claims that were made about the differences between so-called high vs. low society, including those specific and isolated groups that required membership, such as the Society for the Reformation of Manners founded in London in 1691. There was surely no early theorist more influential for a close focus on differences within groups than Karl Marx (1818–1883), given his and his patron and sometime co-author Friedrich Engels's (1820–1895) focus on economic status. Such a status, they argued, was established by whether or not one owned what they termed the means of production, that is, the manner in which commodities to be later exchanged were first manufactured. This allowed one to benefit from the profit of those sales—i.e., surplus value, leading to the accumulation of capital—or whether, to earn a living one had no choice but to sell one's own body and skills, that is, one's labor. Society's hierarchical class differences were so ingrained, due to the prevalence of the economic system known as capitalism, that Marx advocated revolution in order to address what he saw as such inequities and oppression. Whether that would have led to his anticipated classless society is, of course, open to debate, especially given the likelihood that yet other internal and no less stratified divisions would have resulted.

Given that society is widely agreed to contain a number of factions and thus is understood to be comprised of ongoing frictions and fault lines, the question, then, is why are they often not more apparent? Or, to rephrase, how is the idea and long-term existence of a large-scale society even possible, given such internal dissent? Scholars interested in such questions argue that those institutions commonly understood as religious, among others, play a fundamental role in fashioning the group and providing it with cohesiveness. This view can be traced back to the earliest years of the subfield known as the sociology of religion, with perhaps no better example than the work of one of its founders, Émile Durkheim (1858–1917). One could argue, however, that for such scholars the study of religion was not the primary interest since it tended to be regarded as a secondary feature that offered them solutions to the problems they studied. None of these theorists imagined religion as unique and deserving of study for its own sake. Instead, each focused on the function of religion: maintaining economic relations under capitalism (Marx); offering a means for making collective life possible (Durkheim); or as way to manage the inevitable challenges that attend individuals who have no choice but to live within groups (Freud). None worked in the subfield that is today commonly referred to as "religion *and* society" since each presumed "religion" to be a basic element of the social world rather than as something set apart from or pre-dating society, only interreacting with it periodically.

Even within the work of those who see these two domains as separate but nevertheless intertwined, we still see evidence of this approach. For example, Robert T. Parsons, the former department head of Ethnology and Missions at the Kennedy School of Missions, a onetime division of the Hartford Seminary, in the United States, argued in his *Religion in an African Society* (1964) that religion among the Kono people of Sierra Leone organizes "the several parts of society into a harmonious whole" (201). Subsequent theorists would certainly complicate such a view by reminding us that the impression of a "harmonious whole" is often the result of series of ongoing ideological strategies and contests by which the inevitable presence of difference, disagreement, and outright dissent are minimized and thereby managed. We therefore cannot overlook the importance of early to mid-twentieth century scholarship that helped us to understand that anything called society is *not* and *never has been* monolithic, uniform, or static—whether over time or at any one given moment. Instead, the abstraction and generalization necessary to produce statements about society are always done from a specific viewpoint, which encourages readers to overlook any number of stratified or even happenstance differences, such as those between the subgroups known as classes, cultures, races, genders, geographic regions, etc. It is thus worth remembering that as early as 1968 the American anthropologist Bernard S. Cohn (1928–2003) could write: "The study of social change and acculturation has become over the last 35 years one of the anthropologist's major activities" (*Structure and Change in Indian Society* [2007], 3). To be sure, we must add to this the rise of the discipline of sociology during this period—a term first used in the early nineteenth century by the French philosopher Auguste Comte (1798–1857). An academic field going by this name did not result until the turn of the twentieth century, however, widely acknowledged to have started in Europe with Durkheim in France, and his founding and editorship of the journal *L'Année sociologique* in 1898 and his appointment, in 1913, to a university chair formerly known as "Science of Education" at the Sorbonne, in Paris, but now renamed "Science of Education and Sociology." Also significant in this development was the equally influential scholar Max Weber (1864–1920), who established the new discipline in Germany in 1919 at Ludwig Maximilian University of Munich. Interestingly the first chair of Sociology was founded even earlier in Japan, at Tokyo University, in 1893, "ten years after publication of the first general sociological treatise by a Japanese author" (see Ronald P. Dore's "Sociology in Japan," *The British Journal of Sociology* 13/2 [1962]: 116). The field subsequently spread throughout universities throughout Europe and North America over the subsequent decades (e.g., McGill University's Department of Sociology was established in 1922 and Harvard's in the 1930s).

There may be no better, more important work for the study of religion in this broad area from the past academic generation than political scientist Benedict Anderson's (1936–2015) *Imagined Communities: Reflections on the Origin and Spread of Nationalism* (1983). As earlier work in the field had already suggested, the idea of the group, let alone subgroups, is just that, *ideas* in the minds of individuals, who are themselves the products of yet prior social situations. We thus need to be attuned not just to how parts are represented as wholes, but also in how ideas of social membership are communicated, instantiated, and reproduced. As Anderson made clear, citizens of a country, despite never actually meeting the vast majority of other citizens, are still able to conceive of themselves and these others as belonging to the same country through a shared, but certainly imagined, identity. Anderson argues that this was, in part, based on the role of literacy and printing presses, both of which enabled people far removed from one another to participate in a shared *imaginaire*, making possible large-scale "imagined communities" that we today call nation-states. This enabled tens of millions of people who have never met (nor will ever meet) one

Society 283

other—people who often inhabit sometimes dramatically different regions and circumstances—to all claim membership in the same group, as if all sharing an enduring identity that stretches across not just geography but also time. Case in point, consider the misleadingly simple statement made in a course on the introduction to European philosophy: "Immanuel Kant was a German philosopher." Such a statement is interesting because, despite seeming to state a descriptively obvious point, it nevertheless normalizes a specific sort of modern German national identity. It does this moreover by dehistoricizing such an identity and back-projecting it. Though Kant lived his entire life, from 1724 to 1804, in the city of Königsberg (today part of Russia and known as Kaliningrad), which was in the Kingdom of Prussia, thereby pre-dating the so-called German Empire (1871–1918), the precursor to the current nation-state of Germany. Though the historical figure Kant spoke and wrote German, he is in hindsight thought to share a national identity that came long after him.

The complexities entailed in even casual uses of "society," let alone "identity," mean that the term should always be used as a handy but limited shorthand, one that requires a fair bit of elaboration and background theory for the uninitiated. As Jonathan Z. Smith (1938–2017) once observed, much like the commonsense, but equally complicated, claims about recovering an author's intention, "[s]tudents in introductory social sciences know that there is such a thing as a society that functions, and they effortlessly observe it doing so" (see the "Afterword" to the second edition of *Studying Religion: An Introduction* [2019], 126). Rather than imagine the disparate things that many designate *as* society—from languages and preferred foods to styles of dress, flags, and anthems—as continually reproduced by a series of prior assumptions and practices, thereby continually making and remaking the impression of society among its members, we need to see the concept within inherited structures that are not of the individual's making (something examined in detail in Mitsutoshi Horii's essay "Historicising 'Society' in the Discourse of 'Religion'," published in a special issue of the journal *Implicit Religion* devoted to the discourse of religion in contemporary social formations [2021]).

In this volume see: classification, comparison, culture, definition, description, explanation, function, gender, identity, ideology, politics, power, race, redescription, religion, sacred/profane, status

In *Religion in 50 More Words* see: church, civil religion, dialogue, piety, reformation, ritual, tradition

46 Status

Status is one of those terms that has numerous and often overlapping sets of meaning, all of which revolve around issues of what are often believed to be intrinsic notions of worth and value. The term can be used, for example, to signal the inferior position of the so-called non-believer, especially when juxtaposed against the superior status of the believer. All groups—including those known as religions—have an often-complex set of discourses on the status of outsiders. Within our field, consider that Muslims, to use one concrete example, have had (and continue to have) a different status—both social and legal—under Islam (both historically and in the present) than do non-Muslims. Historically, this has given Muslims certain values and privileges not available to those who are not Muslims. The same, of course, can be said about the non-Jew in Judaism, the non-Christian in Christianity, the non-Hindu and Hinduism, and so on and so forth. This difference in legal and social status reveals, once again, to just what an extent one's (or a group's) worth is contingent upon political, economic, and social factors despite the fact that such differences are often coded as religious in nature. It is, thus, important for the critical student of religion to be aware of how one's structured (and often ranked) relations to others—in all of their complex and overlapping ways—creates a set of privileges (or restrictions) that often have nothing to do with religion, but are nonetheless justified by it. As with the term identity or even power, we should not regard status as something intrinsic to those who hold it (whether so-called high status, low status, or that which is located somewhere in between), but as a value assigned from without, often to justify, to legitimate, and otherwise maintain forms of social prestige and political capital. This is done, moreover, only by those—priest, legists, interpreters, and those who are imagined to possess status—invested by tradition to make such moves. Status, again, shows us to just what extent those groups popularly known as religions are no less invested in the maintenance of the social and political order.

The English term status derives from the Latin *state*, also used in English, which refers to a person's or object's physical conditions, circumstances, situation, arrangement. From this, it could quite easily be extended to refer to one's station in life, rank, standing, prestige, or legal position—always judged in relation to those of others. Originally in English "status" referred to the physical height of a person or thing, presumably with the assumption that the taller or bigger something or someone was, the more status it or they possessed (akin to "you carry a lot of weight around here" indicating that someone exercises influence). In 1577, for example, we read in Raphael Holinshed's *The firste (laste) volume of the Chronicles of England, Scotlande, and Irelande*: "The height of a man is *Status*, & supposed to be all one with the lesser fadam, or extention of his armes." Also reflecting this earlier usage, status came to define the legal position of belonging to a group which, in turn, makes one subject to certain legal rights and/or limitations. This is often associated with the bestowal of the freedom of movement or action and/or citizenship in the nation-state. Thus, we read in *Considerations on the Origins of the American War* (1865), by H. W. Fisher: "Therefore his *status* as free or slave depended on the laws of Missouri" (84). In the nineteenth century the term takes on its more familiar connotation of social or professional rank, position, or standing, something that now refers to a person's relative importance or lack thereof in society. We now witness the definition and creation of categories to differentiate "high status" from, for example, "low status."

Status in the present primarily refers to someone's or something's worth—again, always relative to others and standards of judgment. Elites, for example, have a higher status on account of the social and financial benefits that their birth affords them, and which society sanctions. When it comes to the study of religion, status is usually constructed in terms of one's privileged access to the so-called sacred. If, however, the sacred is ultimately a social construct, as a critical scholar would likely maintain, then we have to admit that those who derive special status from proximity to it—for example, priests, rabbis, monks, among others—necessarily possess considerable political, economic, and social power. Here we would do well to remember that religions—which, as Émile Durkheim (1858–1917) reminds us, both reflect and maintain the social order—play a huge role in bestowing and legitimating such status and are thus heavily invested in replicating the status quo.

Status now can be understood as a principle that organizes and categorizes people and objects based on what is imagined to be their intrinsic worth or value in comparison to others. Moreover, the rhetoric and authority of religion functions as a convenient overlay to sublimate such practices, elevating the mundane to the level of metaphysics. Religious texts, for example, receive canonical status (or not) based on the fiat—often grounded in highly political and ideological decision-making processes—of those with power. These include those known as prophets, religious founders, priest, and subsequent commentators and jurists that interpret such texts. Those with such high status are then justified by their position to determine the often subservient (legal, social, political) status of, for example, women or the marginalized (legal, social, political) status of those who belong to other religions or, increasingly in the modern world, to no religions. Though such status is, to reiterate, believed—even by those who lack such high status—to be part of the cosmic order and thus somehow intimately connected to the presumed inherent worth of the object or person in question. In this regard, the assignment of status is how elites maintain their power and how they seek to exert it over others.

Religion is, as Bruce Lincoln notes in his book, *Holy Terrors: Thinking about Religion After September 11* (2003), "a discourse whose concerns transcend the human, temporal, and contingent, and that claims for itself a similarly transcendent status" (5). Naming something as a religion in this fashion, then, means that a scholar pays particular attention to the ability to recode any mundane human claim and make it seem to be part of the so-called divine, and thus superior, order. This recoding becomes a convenient way to protect (by naturalizing and thereby legitimizing) one's own status (along with the *status quo*, or current state of affairs) and, in the process, to minimize those who are either different (in terms of religion, gender, race) or with whom one disagrees. Status, then cannot be understood apart from its self-interested investment in political power.

In this volume see: authority, canon, classification, comparison, experience, gender, identity, ideology, interpretation, politics, power, race, religion, sacred/profane, text

In *Religion in 50 More Words* see: civil religion, commentary, cult, dialogue, idol, initiative, piety, pilgrimage, priest/prophet, renunciation, sacrifice, symbol, tradition, value

47 Text

Despite the important place of both archeology and anthropology in the history of the field, written documents, in various formats, have historically been the major focus within the study of religion. Indeed, philology—the academic field of studying the structure and historical derivation of, including the relationships between, language—was among the founding specialties in the history of the field. Perhaps this is not surprising given at least part of the field's investment in the onetime scholarly tradition known as Orientalism, which, among other things, sought to comprehend others through the translation of, and commentaries on, their normative writings. Despite the fact that recent years have witnessed the rise of those subfields known as lived and material religion, that have each attempted to decenter the larger field by focusing on data other than texts produced by elite classes, texts—broadly conceived—still play a large role. While there is considerable disagreement on how to understand or interpret texts signified as "religious," the role of texts remains significant, often assumed to be transcripts of the experiences and intentions that supposedly animate them. There is therefore a tendency to read such texts in ways that often simply reproduce the same methods used by practitioners when they comment on their own texts, often through the act of description and interpretation. The result is that scholars tend to accept them at face value by focusing only on their content as opposed to examining them as cultural productions and material artifacts. To analyze them in this manner then means that we ought to inquire into an assortment of issues behind their composition, (re)production, distribution, and use, including by whom and for what effect—all the while being mindful of issues of power and politics.

Like so many other modern English words, the noun "text" comes from the French, specifically the word *texte*, which in turn derives from the Old Northern French *tixte* or *tiste*. The term was originally used to refer to the Bible, making it synonymous with scripture. In fact, as recently as the mid-nineteenth century even the modern "textbook" signified not only

DOI: 10.4324/9781003140184-48

a manual in any subject area but also a book that collects scriptures, such as *The Scripture Treasury*, which was the second part of *The Scripture Textbook Arranged for the Use of Ministers, S.S. Teachers, and Families* (1847). The word is found in English as early as the fourteenth century—and consistently used over the past centuries—with William Langland's (ca. 1325–ca. 1390) *Piers Plowman* (1393) serving as an example: "Ich theologie þe tixt knowe." Or again, consider *The Parliament of Chryste Avovching and Declaring the Enacted and Receaued Trueth of the Prefence of His Bodie and Bloode in the Bleffed Sacrament, and of Other Articles Concerning the Same Impugned in a Wicked Sermon* (1566): "Therefor being moued with an other holie fpirit of his own thus he turned the text: *Take, eat, this fignifieth my bodie . . .*" (Second Book, 155). This meaning was still alive and well in William Shakespeare's day (1564–1616), where we read in his *Henry IV* (1600), just as Prince John enters the stage and utters the following:

When that your flock, assembled by the bell,
Encircled you to hear with reverence
Your exposition on the holy text,
Than now to see you here an iron man,
Cheering a rout of rebels with your drum,
Turning the word to sword, and life to death.
(Act 4, Sc. 1, 233)

In time, though, the term would be used to refer to the wording of anything written or, later, printed, including the overall structure formed by the words in their structured order. For example, there's the following commentary on Plato's followers who were, at least according to the English clergyman, Ralph Cudworth (1617–1688), writing in his *The True Intellectual Syftem of the Universe* (1679), "ufing all manner of Arts, and offering all kinds of violence to his Text" (Book 1, 240). The term is then used so widely, especially with the rise of print culture in Europe (from the late fifteenth century onward), that today it has even come to name succinct electronic messages let alone the action of writing and transmitting one (i.e., text messages and texting).

The academic study of religion, however, tends to implicitly retain the older meaning of the term, since the great majority of the documents studied in the field are primarily those that can loosely be called scriptural, but now expanded to include other genres of texts. As early as 1825 we witness Sir Graves Chamney Haugton (1788–1849), a military cadet for the East India Company (established in 1600 and becoming central wing of the British colonial project) and subsequent Professor of Hindu Literature in the East-India College, which was founded in 1806 to train "writers," i.e., administrators, for the East India Company, showing again how, as per Edward Said's (1935–2003) Orientalism thesis, textual study and knowledge of the other was intimately caught up with notions of empire and empire maintenance. In his *Mánava-dherman-sástra; or, The Institutes of Manu* (1825), a critical edition of said text, Chamney Haugton informs his readers as follows: "Though the Calcutta edition has been made the foundation for the present text, I have, after a careful comparison with several mss assumed to myself, the right of an editor, to substitute whatever conceived a better reading" (vol. 1, 313). Indeed, this era's desire to create such translations and critical editions of religious texts, especially those of other cultures, has played a large role in the field, and especially during the time of classical Orientalism, which seems safe to include as a precursor to the field. Witness, for example, one of the widely acknowledged founders of the field, F. Max Müller (1823–1900), the Boden Professor of Sanskrit at the University of Oxford, and his once celebrated 50-volume *Sacred Books of the East* library. Despite the fact that those engaged in such textual study not infrequently claim that they have interest in neither theory nor any sort of interpretation ("we study only the texts—and the texts do not lie!!" is a common refrain among these descriptivists), we see from Chamney Haugton's account above that the production of critical editions of religious texts, like any other act of translation and interpretation, is based on choice and decision-making on the part of the scholar. After all, in many cases, there are no such things as definitive, complete, or authoritative originals and so the work of such editions—not unlike the processes of producing a canon itself—is to sift through competing variants and disjointed fragments, often from dramatically different historical periods, to create the impression of a coherent text that can then be thought to mean this and not that. In like manner, a 1893 catalogue from the British Museum describes ancient Babylonian and Assyrian tablets as "fragments of religious texts." Such texts, broadly conceived, are thought of as religious or sacred on account of not just some features of their content (e.g., accounts of the world's origins or end) but also their presumed use in social acts designated by the scholar as religious, such as rituals or ceremonies. Though it is, of course, unclear whether such texts are deemed sacred by virtue of their use in the ceremony or liturgy or vice versa. According to *Religious Reading: The Place of Reading in the Practice of Religion* (1999), by the theologian, Paul J. Griffiths, a religious text is one that is open to a "religious reading," namely a reading in which religious believers allow their minds to be furnished and their hearts to be instructed by a sacred text, which is itself read and understood in the light of what they see to be an authoritative tradition. Again, though, the (over) use of terms such as sacred, religious, and authoritative in such an approach should alert the critical reader to the imprecision of terms and methods—terms and methods that often either implicitly or sometimes explicitly favor the reproduction of the participant's viewpoint.

There has therefore been a tendency in the academic study of religion to take texts signified *as* religious at face value, and without inquiring into their modes of production. The Quran, for example (though we could certainly use almost any other example from texts commonly designated as scriptures), is assumed to have been revealed by Allah—or, at the very least edited into its final form under the rule of the 4th caliph (successor to Muhammad) Uthman (d. 656 ce)—because this is what something called the tradition tells us to be the case. However, when we simply accept such postulates as the starting point for our scholarly work, we lose sight of the political tensions that went into the creation of texts, e.g., by whom and why was something written down, edited, and later reproduced, especially at times and in settings where writing was not a widely practiced skill? And so, against what now lost position(s) might the text have been written and only later, by yet other readers, some generations apart, codified as worth remembering and citing? As the literary critic Barbara Johnson (1947–2009) succinctly put it, "[w]hat is at stake in writing is the very structure of authority itself" ("Writing" in *Critical Terms for Literary Study* [1995], 48). We also often lose sight of what is entailed in working with a text, or what is commonly called reading, including the many hindsight projections onto the markings on clay, parchment, or paper that comprise the text in question (as opposed to what many once assumed simply to be *finding* things in a text or getting meaning *from* a text), all done to suit the always contemporary purposes of its users. In fact, this latter point was a central argument to the so-called "death of the author" movement of the mid- to later twentieth century, in which the idea of an intentional author imbuing a text with meaning was argued to be a continual creation of readers working with documents, resulting in the very idea of meaning itself being the reader's creation as well. So, rather than look into the production, redaction, and use of such texts, such as how they recycle earlier themes and texts, a method that can certainly be offensive to some current religious participants, there is instead the more general approach that shows the ways in which religious texts are understood by later communities. To stay with the Quran as an example for just a little longer, rather than finding studies devoted to the prehistory of this text and how it draws on and reproduces late antique ideas and yet other texts (a topic that would be seen as more germane to late antique studies or perhaps Islamic studies), there is a tendency to take the text for granted, as a settled and canonical fact. We see this in many studies of scriptures throughout the field, though with more attention to the compositional history of some than others—and this, by the way, is the power of textualization, or what Vincent L. Wimbush and Richard Newton alike would both refer to as the process of scripturalization: to manage meaning and identity through the appearance of being static, permanent, and therefore authoritative. Case in point, in an article titled "Islamic Origins and Incidental Normativity" (*JAAR* 84/1 [2016]), Jonathan Brockopp admits that, despite the fact that we know *very little* about the early Islamic period, including how the Quran as a text came to be, we are nevertheless able to use the later sources to *imagine* how later Muslims themselves *imagined* the earlier period and thus themselves as Muslims. This is a common approach in the study of religion, one where the emphasis is put on trying to understand or interpret, often in an outrightly speculative manner, how religious texts were or are understood by religious people. In terms of studying the Quran, we thus see in the field works with titles such as Anna Gade's *Perfection Makes Practice: Learning, Emotion, and the Recited Qur'an in Indonesia* (2004) or Bruce B. Lawrence's *The Qur'an: A Biography* (2007; an audiobook appearing in the "Books That Changed the World" series). While both of these works are important and informative, they are not interested in textuality, understood here as the study of writing and reading as an always situated human and thus social technology—and this, we would argue, is an unfortunate pattern common throughout the field. This, of course, should come as no surprise, if we are correct in our assessment of the field's longstanding and still implicit phenomenological bias. Within this context, religious texts are studied by many as a site where something non-empirical and timeless is made manifest—in this case, not necessarily an experience of the sacred but, more than likely, an experience of meaning.

Also problematic is when scholars assume—as many still do—that religions can somehow be boiled down to or summed up via the contents of their normative religious texts (or, we should add, texts that influential members within the group see and use as normative) and their own orthodox commentaries on them. In the aftermath of 9/11, for example, many scholars of Islam were, predictably perhaps, asked by the media about what the Quran actually said about "non-Muslims" or committing violence against them—this also exemplifies how scholars of religion are sometimes put into the position of being spokespeople for those whom they study—something far more apparent in some subfields. For it was assumed that the religious text somehow justified—and could thus explain—the murderous acts. Such a question, animated by certain assumptions on the role played by scriptures within communities, betrays a understanding closely associated with the largely Protestant Christian origins of the field, and thus overlooks the fact that many of the texts studied in the field only make sense to their followers—and often a specialized subgroup among them—when interpreted through an often lengthy and nuanced commentary tradition (yet other texts). Moving in the opposite direction, we also see how some try to show that because a particular religious text does not promote, say, violence, then those that do so in the name of religion cannot be truly or authentically religious or, if they claim to be, then they do not understand their own tradition properly. This is, for example, the tenor of Jonathan Sack's *Not In God's Name: Confronting Religious Violence* (2015). Curiously, despite frequent calls to "take religion seriously" and to empower and thereby describe and not theorize a religious participant's own self-understanding and self-reports, those scholars adhering to such a method have little difficulty suspending such approaches when the people under study fail to live up to the scholar's sometimes rather specific understandings of how the religion ought to be practiced.

In all of this, however, we would do well to heed Bruce Lincoln's words in the fourth of his "Theses on Method" (*MTSR* 8/3 [1996]): "The same destabilizing and irreverent questions one might ask of any speech act ought to be posed of religious discourse. The first of these is 'Who speaks here?,' i.e., what person, group, or institution is responsible for a text, whatever its putative or apparent author" (advice which is also part of his 2006 essay "How to Read a Religious Text" in *History of Religions* 46/2: 127–139). This, we would argue, is the basic and necessary requirement of treating any text as a human production, i.e., resisting the urge to assume that they have fallen from the sky fully formed. He goes on:

> Beyond that, "To what audience? In what immediate and broader context? Through what system of mediations? With what interests?" And further, "Of what would the speaker(s) persuade the audience? What are the consequences if this project of persuasion should happen to succeed? Who wins what, and how much? Who, conversely, loses?".

Religious texts, then, are not simply about sublime ideas that inspire people to be better, they are instead—like *any* text or speech act—invested in often very mundane issues of situation, propaganda, ideology, and, ultimately, power.

As mentioned at the outset, members of the recently established subfields of lived religion and material religion have consistently tried to move the field away from textual study to other, seemingly more mundane, artifacts. They also emphasize the study of the bodies of those texts' various users, often comprising marginalized or under-studied people, with the understanding that the traditional study of religion has largely overlooked the members of such groups. Since the body is now regarded as a medium of expression, it becomes like a text—a significant expansion of the word from its earlier and more traditional applications to just written documents.

This is a move indebted to decades of postmodern critiques, such as the work of the French philosopher Jacques Derrida (1930–2004), in which the situation that surrounds a document, or what was once distinguished as the text's context is now seen as part of the text as well, from the grammar that allows its symbols to be read as meaningful to the economy that produces and circulates it and the people able to use it. In Derrida's famous formulation: "*il n'y a pas de hors-texte*" ("There is no out-of-text"). This "somatic turn," as it is sometimes called, is therefore the result of larger forces in the academy that include various philosophical, sociopolitical, and cultural trends (also including feminist and disability studies). In her *The Body in Religion: Cross-Cultural Perspectives* (2017), for example, Yudit Kornberg Greenberg seeks to "highlight religion's role in constructing and shaping our body" while simultaneously investigating the ways "that our embodiments themselves contribute to our religious beliefs" (xxv).

While a critical scholar surely welcomes the movement away from the assumption that what scholars have usually termed texts (i.e., written documents) are the sole repository of religion, it would not seem enough to say that the body is like a text. For then the body, just like the documents once studied by our predecessors, would need not simply to be read as yet another inherently meaningful site awaiting the scholarly decoding but, rather, to be theorized and historicized. This would involve all of the nuance implied by the critical study of the categories included in this present volume— after all, "body" is no less self-evident than "text" let alone "indigeneity" or "identity." But the temptation simply to naturalize the rules and implications of reading, by simply describing content, are great, as is the tendency to conceptualize the item in question as a neutral medium conveying information from distant people to modern readers. Shifting to the body does not necessarily address this shortcoming and neither does critiquing earlier scholars for exclusively studying written documents as if they were somehow merely disembodied ideas anchored in a text. All texts are ultimately items of material culture—suggesting that the turn to material religion is not such a great turn after all, especially if the new medium in question is not itself theorized as a site of structured, human activity, something that also includes the scholarly observer. In like manner, it does not seem to be enough to say that the body as text is now another site to examine religion without actually looking at the intellectual work that the term "religion" or "religious" are performing. Yet in these newer subfields, not unlike the field at large, we often see the same lack of attention to such basic issues of definition and classification.

The perhaps misleadingly simple term "text" therefore invites the critical scholar also to examine such related terms as authors, readers, and editors/redactors. This, of course, is also to say nothing about intentionality, context, and meaning, along with the necessarily involved processes of representation, interpretation, reproduction, codification, and, in some cases, canonization. Such a scholar will do so while heeding Lincoln's advice by ensuring that no stage in the meaning-making process is seen as autonomous or self-sufficient. Rather, it will all be approached as an historical, and thus contestable, site of human production, which means both agency and structure, i.e., creativity and limit, are taken seriously.

In this volume see: description, experience, interpretation, lived religion, material religion, method, orthodoxy, phenomenology, politics, power, sacred/profane

In *Religion in 50 More Words* see: commentary, hagiography, theology, tradition, understanding

48 Theory

Everyone engages in theory, whether they admit it or not. The translation of a gerund as an adjective in a religious text, for example, is governed by a theory of translation. In like manner, when we decide to work on one text as opposed to another, or if we opt to do our fieldwork in one village and not the one next to it, we engage in theory—whether or not self-consciously and carefully, and thus in a manner that could withstand some scrutiny from our peers. Theory, then, could name the lens between an interpreter (be it a translator, a historian, an anthropologist, or the like) and that item on which they focus, their data, and thus what they deem to be significant and thus worth their attention. Far from being a natural act or set of acts, as many suppose, the way that scholars bring any item into focus and then analyze it is something to which theory should ideally attune us. Theory, in other words, forces the critical scholar to ask questions (often uncomfortable ones, thus why theory has long been a controversial term and activity in our field) not just about our data but also about ourselves as scholars. Unfortunately, the word "theory" signifies too many things to too many people and, for this reason, it becomes rather difficult to define with any precision. While it may be helpful to say, as we have here, that theory forces us to contemplate on where, when, why, and how we derive data, it can signal more than just that. For perhaps there are better and worse theories, with the adjudication between the two not simply being based on whether or not something is in accord with what one does, thinks, or hopes. After all, phenomenology provides a theory of religion—whether its proponents would phrase it in that manner—that is based on the presumed essence of the sacred. Yet while such an approach is still in use, as a general theory to account for religion it no longer seems particularly helpful, let alone all that useful.

Our English word "theory" (along with the verb "to theorize" and the noun "theorist") derives in the late sixteenth century from the Middle

DOI: 10.4324/9781003140184-49

French *theorie* and, prior to that, the Latin *theoria*, and even the ancient Greek *theoría*, meaning vision and thus the act of contemplation, in distinction from involvement in practical activities. It is therefore often used to name a branch of study that deals with speculation and thereby forming the conceptual basis of a subject or area of study, including the methodical intellectual constructs used to explain facts or phenomena (we see this use as early as the early seventeenth century). The term can also be used to describe purely abstract knowledge of a subject, as opposed to practical, empirical knowledge (as early as the middle seventeenth century), with the late-eighteenth-century term "theorism" once naming a stance, as in the onetime Colonial Treasurer of Hong Kong, Robert Montgomery Martin (1801–1868): "I cannot bring myself to believe that the theorism of Lord Grenville will, in the face of facts and common sense, be acted on" (140), as found in his 1832 treatise called *The Political, Commercial and Financial Condition of the Anglo-Eastern Empire in 1832: An Analysis of Its Home and Foreign Governments, and a Practical Examination of the Doctrines of Free Trade and Colonization, with Reference to the Renewal Or Modification of the Hon. East-India Company's Charter*. In its most basic sense, then, theory refers to a conception of something that is to be done, or of reflection afterward on the method of doing something, thus a way of devising and scrutinizing the procedures to be followed. Thus we read in the 1588 work, *A discoursiue probleme concerning prophesies how far they are to be valued, or credited, according to the surest rules, and directions in diuinitie, philosophie, astrologie, and other learning* by the English astronomer, John Harvey (1564–1592), under the pseudonym I. H. Physition: "Full silly and sorrie artists in any kinde, especially in the sound Theorie, and effectuall practise of the woorthiest, and noblest sciences, mathematical, philosōphicall, and other of like auailable effect" (5). We also see in the early use of the term the beginnings of a distinction between theory, on the one hand, and practice, on the other. This distinction between theory and practice (or what yet others will refine as praxis, i.e., theory put into practice) became increasingly prominent in the course of the seventeenth century, as seen in the following quote by Francis Bacon (1561–1626): "The means, hithero propounded, to effect it, are in the practice, full of error and imposture, and in the theory, full of unsound imaginations" (*Sylva Sylvarum* [1626], sec. 327). Likewise, in Sir William Hope's *The Compleat Fencing-Master in which is full described the whole guards, parades & lessons belonging to the small-sword: As also the best rules for playing against either artists or ignorants with blunts or sharps: Together with directions how to behave in a single combat on horse-back: Illustrated with figures representing the most necessary postures* (1687), and often referred to by its short title: *The Scots Fencing-Master*. According to him,

> for I have given you the Directions, which is all lyeth in my Power to make you a *Sword-Man*, and if you put them not in practice the fault is your own; for you must not expect that the simple reading of what I have here given you, will ever make you a *Sword-Man*; No no, it is practice that must do that; its true your reading of this little Piece may make you talk, and discourse learnedly enough of *Fencing*; But what will that avail a Man, when he is either to make use of *Blunts* or *Sharps?* Certainly, in such a case *Theorie* without *Practice* will serve but for little: It is therefore *Practice* joyned with it which in such a case must do the business; Reading therefore will as I said give you the *Theorie*, which is also absolutely necessary for a *Sword-Man*, but it is *Practice* which must make you act . . .
>
> (164–165)

Closer to our own field, the term could also be used to refer to a "divine theory," with the notion of creation, revelation, and ultimate redemption (as supplied, not surprisingly, by the Christian figure of Jesus). Thus we read in Joshua Spalding's (described as a "Minister of the Gospel of Jefus Christ") *The Divine Theory: A System of Divinity, Founded Wholly Upon Christ; which By One Principle, Offers and Explanation of All the Works of God* (1808):

> Diftinct, therefore, and oppofite in its nature, as this tree was from the tree of life, ftill, as it fprang up neceffarily in the garden of God, from the divine and moft beneficent operation, which caufed there to grow a tree of life, its exiftence, the exiftence of evil is neceffarily compromised un the argument of the divine theory.
>
> (240)

The term, of course, can also be used in the more scientific sense of giving an account of something, as we encounter, for example, in *The Glacier Theory* (1840) by James David Forbes (1809–1868), a Scottish physicist and glaciologist. "According to this theory," he writes, "the glacier melts, not only at its upper surface, but at its lower one, owing to the contact with the ground beneath, which has a temperature above 32 degrees" (21). In this sense, the term comes to refer to a set of interrelated propositions about something in the world, aimed to address a curiosity or anomaly, that has predictive and thus testable/replicable capacity, such as the title of a work by John Williams Lubbock (1803–1865), the English mathematician and astronomer, *On the Theory of the Moon, and on the Perturbations of the Planets* (1834). Whether the way to test such a theory is to confirm its truth empirically (as claimed by those in a school of thought known as Logical Positivism, who aimed to empirically verify theoretical claims as the way to distinguish them from what they termed metaphysics) or, as argued by the philosopher of science, Karl Popper (1902–1994), to attempt to prove it wrong (i.e., falsify it), then becomes a debate across the twentieth century. Those scholars of religion who advocate generating explanatory and thus reductive accounts of the cause or function of religion certainly employ the term in the manner of this intellectual tradition.

But in mid-twentieth-century scholarship the word "theory" increasingly came to be associated with a more rigorous approach to the study of literature, the arts, and culture that incorporated terms and concepts from disciplines such as philosophy, psychoanalysis, and the social sciences. We now see the emergence of such terms as "literary theory" or "literary criticism." Proponents of this type of theory positioned themselves in a manner that sought to challenge or, at the very least, provide an alternative to long-established or traditional methods and interpretations. The British Marxist literary critic, Terry Eagleton, phrases it as follows in his influential *Literary Theory: An Introduction* (1983): "the history of modern literary theory is part of the political and ideological history of our epic" (169; quoting from the 2008 Anniversary Edition), including critiques of capitalism and other neoliberal systems. Eagleton further sees the job of the theorist to "preserve this discourse, extend and elaborate it as necessary, defend it from other forms of discourse, initiate newcomers into it and determine whether or not they have successfully mastered it" (175). This discourse called theory, though vaguer than its use in the natural sciences, is instead a network of signifiers that casts its web over meanings, objects, and practices. Theory, on this reading, becomes the interrogation of authority and the status quo. Indeed, this would also seem to be behind the volume that has many ways inspired the present one: Raymond Williams's (1921–1988) *Keywords: A Vocabulary of Culture and Society* (1976). Therein, he describes his work as "the record of an inquiry into a *vocabulary*: a shared body of words and meanings in our most general discussions, in English, of the practices and institutions which we group as *culture* and *society*" (13).

If theory is often distinguished from practice, this does not mean that the latter term cannot be theorized. Perhaps nowhere is this on clearer display than in the work of the French sociologist, Pierre Bourdieu (1930–2002), whose widely read *Outline of a Theory of Practice* (1977) developed precisely such a theory of practice, around the concept of *habitus*, i.e., those unconscious acts whereby social actors develop strategies that are adapted to the structures of the social worlds that they inhabit. Bourdieu also stressed the importance of what he called "reflexive sociology," in which sociologists ought to be self-conscious of their own positionality, including their own set of internalized structures, which have the potential to distort or otherwise prejudice their appeals to objectivity, and thus be aware of their own *habitus*.

The term theory has a lengthy history of its own in the field of religious studies, going all the way back to those commonly considered to be its founders. Up until fairly recently, religious studies has had a fairly stable set of theorists that form the core of any department's annual undergraduate or graduate seminar devoted to some variation on the theme of "theories," "theory or method," or alternatively "approaches to the study of religion." This usually involves the trademarked journey from Rudolf Otto's (1869–1937) numinous creaturely feeling of the so-called *mysterium tremendum* (*The Idea of the Holy* [1917]), to Émile Durkheim's (1858–1917) understanding of what was then called primitive classification and the role of collective effervescence in social formation (*The Elementary Forms of the Religious Life* [1912]), to Sigmund Freud's (1856–1939) focus on patricide and totemism (*Totem and Taboo* [1913]). Not uncommonly we also find James George Frazer's (1854–1941) search for the illusive and ever-expanding Golden Bough in order to understand an ancient ritual (*The Golden Bough: A Study in Comparative Religion* [1890]), etc., something that usually culminates with Mircea Eliade's (1907–1986) notion of kratophanies, hierophanies, and irreducibility of the sacred (*The Sacred and the Profane: The Nature of Religion* [1957]). All of these theories—if that is what they should be termed, thus continuing to use this term rather loosely in the field—are different, radically so, from one another. Presumably, however, this is the point. Theory is a shared discourse that allows us to talk to one another and we have to, to invoke Eagleton again, teach it to others, but, of course, not in such a manner that it is either static or unproblematic.

After Eliade, and with some notable exceptions (to be discussed shortly), we could certainly make the case that theory or theorizing about religion is no longer about finding some grand account to explain the existence and persistence of this thing that many of us problematically call "religion." In more recent years, especially under the influence of those like J. Z. Smith (1938–2017), theory has become less about universalizing concepts and more about ongoing self-reflection on scholarly choice and situation, including the various motivations and implications that attend to the inevitable selections we make. In other words, it designates for some an awareness of our *habitus*, to invoke Bourdieu. Because of the deconstructive nature of some of this work and the fact that it can be uncomfortably pointed at other colleagues in the field, let alone the practical conditions of our work and the institutions in which it takes place, the more irenic-minded can deem it as being too "deconstructive" thereby writing it off as too problematic inasmuch as they portray it as a self-involved form of navel-gazing. This is, for example, how the scholar of visual religion, David Morgan, once characterized it in a December 12, 2013, interview with the Religion in American History blog: as pointless theory-wonking. In fact, it is even often deemed angry, perhaps because it is contemporary and seeks to historicize the category "religion" and all that travels in its wake. As perhaps evidenced in such attempts to write it off as impractical because "too theoretical," such theory is indeed politically charged, in that it seeks to identify the regnant discourses that the status quo produces.

Despite the fact that theory and theorizing can be open-ended, this does not mean that theory is a relativistic activity in which anything goes. It is therefore not equivalent to opinion or belief. For if the term "theory" is to have analytic utility in scholarship one cannot just say, "I have my theory about [insert topic here], and you have yours." Scholarship is a collaborative and thus social endeavor in which one must—as Bruce Lincoln once famously phrased it in the close to his *Theorizing Myth: Narrative, Ideology, Scholarship* (1999)—show one's work and thus be able to demonstrate to colleagues how one got from there to here. Lincoln then went on to elaborate that this is the role of footnotes and citations, though we must not forget that they also function to authorize work by linking it to possibly canonical predecessors. There are ways of talking about religion in general and religions in particular, that are more empirical than others, i.e., open to refutation. If a theory is predicated on inner experience or based on one's assumptions as a religious practitioner, and it is therefore untestable or analyzable, it cannot be a theory. Critical scholarship, in other words, cannot be based on an array of feelings, moods, perceptions, dispositions, and states of consciousness that can be neither empirically nor scientifically verified. Indeed, as Brent Nongbri cogently puts it: "If a concept is defined as 'beyond language,' it is, then, by definition not something that can be discussed" (*Before Religion: A History of a Modern Concept* [2013], 23).

Theorizing, of the old variety—that is, creating grand accounts meant to be of universal applicability—are not a historical relic, however. There have been recent attempts, such as Thomas A. Tweed, whose *Crossing and Dwelling: A Theory of Religion* (2006), seeks to demonstrate how religion situates people in time and space, positioning them in the body, the home, the homeland, and the cosmos—and allows them to cross various boundaries. Tweed's work uses, at least to some extent, the work of the cognitive science of religion (CSR), a recent subfield that, compared to other parts of the current field at least, is very interested in theorizing about religion, if by that we mean trying to identify the psychological, biological, and evolutionary causal mechanisms that make people religious.

In his *Religion Explained: The Evolutionary Origins of Religious Thought* (2001), for example, Pascal Boyer seeks to explain how ideas imagined *as* religious (such as those involving agents with counterintuitive features or capabilities) are acquired, stored, and, possibly, transmitted better than other (non-religious) ideas.

In the final analysis, however, we must not lose sight of the fact that theory, not unlike its frequent partner, method, is what ultimately permits scholars to conjure data into existence from the limitless background of things taking place in the world, and thus to frame what we think of as curious, puzzling, anomalous, or significant (or not), and, of course, to critique the frames and accounts offered by those with whom we disagree. Too many say that they have no time for theory and that they would rather "get their hands dirty" by looking at what they consider to be "real" data (though they would probably not use the last term, inasmuch as it is sometimes critiqued as dehumanizing when applied to social actors). However, as we hope should be clear by now, even such a claim is one that is grounded in theory—an implicit, an unreflective theory of religion and the human, to be sure, but a theory nonetheless. It is for this reason that we favor the term "data," we should add before closing, given that it can prevent confusion between, on the one hand, that which the scholar *chooses* to examine and, on the other, some imagined world in-and-of-itself that supposedly contains self-evidently interesting things. Thus, the word "data" preserves for the critical scholar a trace of the very topic of this entry, making plain to critical scholars' readers, students, and colleagues, that they work to take into account their own role in producing knowledge about the world.

In this volume see: belief, definition, description, essence, explanation, function, interpretation, method, phenomenology, practice, sacred/profane, text

In *Religion in 50 More Words* see: commentary, dialogue, emic/etic, theology, understanding

49 World religions

A map of the world's religions will likely bear a specific color of some sort for each world religion. South America, for example, would almost uniformly be one color (for Roman Catholicism) and pretty much all of north Africa another (for Islam). That a designator, "world religions," which is only a couple of hundred years old is now so common should strike us as curious and worthy of investigation. And large segments of the globe, moreover, might have once been presumed not to have any religion whatsoever (e.g., the Soviet Union or Communist China), but which now comprise what some scholars of religion now refer to as, and thereby study as, the religion of no religion. Here we have in mind here the so-called Nones, i.e., those answering "none of the above" on surveys about their religious affiliation, let alone those who refer to themselves as atheists and agnostics. All of this indicates just how successful this idea of religion has been in being extended and applied in novel situations in pretty much every corner of the world.

We certainly recognize that the term "world religions" is by now commonplace in a variety of languages. For example, the French *les religions du monde* or sometimes even *les grandes religions* (akin to the onetime "the great religions" in English), or the German *Weltreligionen*, and so on. To consider that the term may have a history, and perhaps a modern function, might be considered counterintuitive by many. But coming after our attempt to historicize and thereby complicate 48 other key terms in the modern study of religion, many of which might themselves be no less familiar to readers, it seems to be the right time to ask about "world religions." This is especially the case given the central role that it plays in the history of the field, not to mention its current shape (e.g., in classrooms, at conferences, or in the scholarly literature), including, of course, its popular usage. What may become apparent is that recent critiques of the category, though widely acknowledged and often cited approving by scholars, seem to have had little effect on slowing down what Suzanne Owen seems to have coined as the world religions paradigm.

DOI: 10.4324/9781003140184-50

This makes not just its history but also its resilience something that also ought to attract our attention. Indeed, the category may play such a fundamental role in modernity that doing without it, no matter how persuasive the criticisms may seem to be, might turn out to be an impossibility.

As already noted in other entries, the common practice of adding a qualifier to the noun religion can be a dubious move, inasmuch as the added specificity is attached to a noun that is usually left undesignated and thus utterly vague. Such is the case with "world religions." Although a member of a larger linguistic family (including such terms as "world affairs," "world class," "world cinema," "world peace," "world première," "world record," "world traveler," and "world war," not to mention "worldwide"), it is not so simple as to assume that the term is used in the same fashion. The term "world" is not a geographic designator, merely signifying religions *around* the world, let alone meaning religion *in* the world (thinking of a phenomenological approach concerning some ethereal religious essence manifested in worldly objects). In fact, it has meant different things at different times over the past two centuries, ranging from its early use to imply that certain religions are (or are not), for lack of a better term, world class to designating an exclusive subset of so-called great religions. This is not far off what the Canadian scholar of Islam, Wilfred Cantwell Smith (1916–2000) once wrote near the opening to his *The Meaning and End of Religion* (1962): "It is customary nowadays to hold that there is in human life and society something distinctive called 'religion'," Smith observed, adding, "and that this phenomenon is found on earth at present in a variety of minor forms, chiefly among outlying or eccentric peoples, and in a half-dozen or so major forms. Each of these major forms is also called 'a religion,' and each one has a name: Christianity, Buddhism, Hinduism, and so on" (15, citing the 1991 edition). He concludes by recommending that "we might investigate our custom here, scrutinizing our practice of giving religious names and indeed of calling them religions." This latter is a recommendation with which we agree, but we must add, for rather different reasons than Smith's, inasmuch as he claimed that by finetuning our nomenclature, with the addition of the term faith, we could better identify the essence of religion.

Given its changing uses, it might be clear that by opting for this term today few probably mean by it what Rev. John Henry Barrows (1847–1902) did. He was an American Presbyterian minister who was the president of the once celebrated World's Parliament of Religions, a religious pluralism event held at the 1893 World Columbian Exposition in Chicago. His set of Barrows Lectures of 1896–1897, entitled *Christianity The World-Religion*, was funded by Caroline E. Haskell (1822–1900), whose will also established the once noted Haskell Lecture in Comparative Religion at the University of Chicago, which brought "the religions of the East to the Christian

West" as phrased in the foreword to the published version of Hu Shih's (1891–1962) own 1933 Haskell Lectures (*The Chinese Renaissance* [1934], vii). Delivered in India and Japan by Barrows himself in its inaugural year (after whom the Barrows Lectures were named), the series was intended to convey (as Haskell's October 12, 1894 letter to the then President of the University of Chicago, William R. Harper, phrased it) "the truths of Christianity, its harmonies with the truths of other religions, its rightful claims, the best method of setting them forth to the people of India" (as quoted in the opening to the 1897 edition of Barrows's previously delivered lectures). Thus, the then hyphenated term "world-religion" took a rather different inflection from today's common usage, inasmuch as Barrows touted the "world-wide aspects," "world-wide effects," and "world-wide authority" of Christianity alone, not to mention his third lecture being entitled "Christian Theism as the Basis for a Universal Religion." The surprising distance between, on the one hand, this early example and, on the other, widespread contemporary understandings in which a more generous and relative status is apparently extended to all members of the family—but just how large *is* that family and *who* gains and governs admission?—should confirm the curiosity that might have been inspired by considering those world religions maps.

To get from Barrows to today, consider what we find in a February 1799 letter written by the noted poet, Samuel Taylor Coleridge (1772–1834) to the English abolitionist, Josiah Wedgwood (1730–1795). He discusses the conditions that eventually led to the adoption of Christianity in the Roman empire:

> It gradually therefore suffered the National Religion to sink into contempt, & took up a World-Religion—such as had always existed in Asia, from the largeness of the Asiatic Empires. To this cause I am inclined to attribute the easy Propagation of Christianity—which was in truth the World-Religion common to the great Empires in Asia, divested of Asiatic forms & ceremonies.
>
> (*Collected Letters*, vol. 1, 465, quoting from Earl Leslie Griggs's 1966 edition)

Here we see not only an early example of comparative religion being practiced, but also some of the categories that were once important in those early comparative enterprises, such as the then common distinction between a so-called national religion (understood as the religion of a kin group, large or small, that has not spread far from its original home) and a so-called world-religion (one that has spread and is therefore capable of spanning far larger groups by converting people). Although offering what seems to be a contemporary definition, Ron Geave's *Key Words in Religious Studies* (2006) nicely, though perhaps unintentionally, sums up this earlier sense of the term when it offers the following: "World religions are those whose numbers or influence interact with and transform human history" (111). Judging by the ever expanding contents to the world religions textbook over the past several decades—a genre that shows no signs of slowing, judging by the new additions let alone new editions that continue to be published, such as the 14th edition of David S. Noss and Blake R. Grangaard's *A History of the World's Religions* (2020) and the 10th edition of Mary Pat Fisher's *Living Religions* (2017), to meet the needs of university classrooms whose faculty rely on the enrollments that such courses bring to their departments. Now, virtually any religious group can be seen to somehow fit into the taxonomy that goes by the name of world religions, with the sequence of their chapters usually implying historical causality (with Judaism coming before Christianity and Islam, and Hinduism prior to Buddhism). In addition to this, we also see chapters with such designations as New Religious Movements (NRM) replacing what was once termed cults (with their members thereby gaining admission to the world religions club) and chapters on indigenous religions today replacing the onetime designation of primitive, primordial, or nature religions—let alone chapters organized around geography or national frameworks, e.g., Chinese religions. Though mid-twentieth-century books produced in Europe and North America, obviously, included a relatively small number of chapters, and while the earliest use of the term was often limited to just Christianity and Buddhism (the only two once presumed to have significantly moved beyond their original settings), they often included subdivisions within the larger designation. Christianity, for example, often had whole chapter devoted to Roman Catholicism, and another on Protestantism. We see this, for example, in the British historian of religions, Robert C. Zaehner's (1913–1974) once widely adopted *The Concise Encyclopedia of Living Faiths* (1959) which, to its credit perhaps, included more than just the above-named five but, while devoting a lone chapter to each of Judaism, Islam, and Hinduism had four separate chapters for Christianity alone (along with three on Buddhism).

This onetime focus on a more complex representation of that with which the reader feels familiar betrays the work that the world religions category has done over the years. No matter its level of detail, the discourse still offers an essentialized and condensed image of its topic, as if it moves through time, developing, certainly, but in an almost Hegelian sense, and thus more so revealing or even manifesting itself. For example, despite many scholars now agreeing that the designation of "Hinduism" (once spelled "Hindoo") is a fairly recent, mid- to later nineteenth-century development and one that groups together a specific set of claims, practices, texts, and institutions originally local to India—as understood by British colonial administrators and Indian intellectuals alike—we still use the term as if it names something. In this regard, see Richard King's still important book *Orientalism and Religion* (1999), in addition to Brian Pennington's *Was Hinduism Invented?: Britons, Indians, and the Colonial Construction of Religion* (2005). While contemporary so-called Hindu nationalists would surely disagree with such a construction, of course, given how it undermines their efforts to use a timeless Hindu identity to authorize their politics, the traditional textbook's common narrative nonetheless begins with "its" ancient origins and chronologically follows "it" through time and region, as "it" takes shape in different times and places. Thus, the phenomenological basis to the genre, evident in its descriptive and comparative approach, along with the methodologically agnostic stance required of its readers, indicates that the category, along with its classes and its resources, not to mention the way the intellectual work of the field is strictly divided among the religions (e.g., scholars professionally identifying themselves by the religion they study, along with its region or time period), are, or so the critical scholar may conclude, a curious artifact from an earlier time in the field's history, one that has somehow survived to our time so as to structure our work and identities as scholars. But, unlike what earlier anthropologists might have meant by designating something that has outlasted its original context and purpose as a "survival," we suggest that the category may continue to perform a crucial role in modern life, thereby explaining its continued use.

There is perhaps no one more associated today with rigorously historicizing the world religions category, and thereby examining its role, than the University of Michigan's Tomoko Masuzawa. Her book, *The Invention of World Religions Or, How European Universalism Was Preserved in the Language of Pluralism* (2005), has already influenced a generation of scholars (who, we should also note, still largely carry out their studies and teach their courses from *within* the paradigm . . .) by tracing the history of the term in European scholarship. Most notable here is that which was carried out in the nineteenth century in Dutch (using the term *Wereldgodsdiensten*) and German (using the term *Weltreligionen*), both of which were often translated into English first as Universal Religion, such as Masuzawa's example of Cornelius P. Tiele's (1830–1902) Dutch work, titled in English as *Outlines of the History of Religion to the Spread of the Universal Religions* (1884, 3rd ed.), or Abraham Kuenen's (1828–1891) 1882 Dutch lectures which were later published as *National Religions and Universal Religions* (1901). But even by the time of the British popular writer, George Thomas Bettany's (1850–1891) book, *The World's Religions: A Popular Account of Religions Ancient and Modern* in 1890 (a volume that predictably opens with a chapter on "Religions of Uncivilized Peoples") we see our own familiar term used, as in his use of Tiele's own above work, to detail what was once the common view on the development (even evolution) of religion across time. We witness this movement from what Tiele named as animism and so-called nature religions or tribal religions to polytheistic national religions and then monotheistic religions based on scripture or law (what was once called nomistic religions). "These last," Bettany then quotes Tiele as writing, "contain the roots of universal or world-religions" (22). The movement from earlier usage (i.e., religions that are universalistic are considered world-religions) and Bettany's (whose chapters, despite bearing the assumptions of his era, would strike a modern reader as rather familiar, with treatments of religions in Australia, India, Africa, the Americas, China, Japan, the Middle East, Europe, etc.) is worth noting. But despite the increasing openness that characterizes this genre over time, with it continually expanding over the coming century, and in spite of the common assumption that—as Masuzawa phrases it—what we see across this period is "a turn away from the Eurocentric and the Eurohegemonic conception of the world, toward a more egalitarian and lateral delineation" (13). The movement toward what she then characterizes as a "decentralized order of representation," as she immediately goes on to note, created pluralist ethos that now seems to define the field, of which the world religions paradigm is emblematic, and is something we need to question by inquiring about the "interests and concerns [that] animate this doctrine and keep it viable?" These, it seems to us, are the *very* questions that a critical study of religion ought to be posing—of the self-reports offered to us by the people we may study no less of the way our very field is organized and practiced.

And so, we return to that map of South America and north Africa, each represented in one uniform color. Critical scholars see something going on in such simplistic representations. For it distills a wide array of historical and cultural, not to mention regional, racial, gendered, economic, generational, etc., differences in both places to a seemingly essential and homogenous core of religious beliefs that are presumed to be expressed publicly by members in their practices. These are then seen as "principal areas of the respective faith," as phrased on the preface to *The New Lion Handbook of the World's Religions* (2005)—all of which are said to group masses of people together into some sort of shared, timeless identity that can then either be arranged along an evolutionary continuum, or assumed to name a relatively uniform group of more or less peers, the world religions paradigm can be redescribed as a modern governance tool that efficiently manages global populations. As such, it is not merely a descriptive term giving names to obvious self-evidences in which we can see "the unique genius of each 'tradition'" (as phrased by Masuzawa [320]). Instead, this designator and the larger system of which it is representative—a system that arose just as modern nation-state was also arising, and which is now linked to how governments identify and organize their populations—can be seen to play a role in helping to craft a certain sort, and thus sense, of the modern, governable subject, given the close association between ideas of the individual and religion as being a site where a presumably essential human nature is experienced and expressed.

This redescription is rather different from the usual critique of the world religions paradigm, which amounts to identifying the Protestant Christian prototype that implicitly drives the discourse, thereby refashioning different religions in its own image, and efficiently extending its hegemony in the guise of openness to difference. And so we arrive at the commonplace presumption that all religions have founders, sacred texts, a view on the afterlife, rituals that express the people's faith, etc. This is what Naomi Goldenberg exemplifies in how Judaism is now described not just as a religion but as a faith, with "Jews representing themselves more and more in Christian terms." (See her "What's God Got to Do with It? A Call for Problematizing Basic Terms in the Feminist Analysis of Religion" in *Feminist Theology* 15/3 [2007]: 283; in this regard, see also Suzanne Owen's helpful essay, "The World Religions Paradigm: Time for a Change," *Arts & Humanities in Higher Education* 10/3 [2011]: 253–268 and Rosalind Shaw's "The Invention of African Traditional Religion," *Religion* 20 [1990]: 339–353.) Instead of seeing the problem as being with how religions do or do not play well together, we suggest here a more critical tradition, one to which Goldenberg, Owen, etc., contribute, and that theorizes the very designation of religion itself (of which "world religions" should be considered as but a subtype). Such a tradition argues that, as phrased by Tim Fitzgerald, "'world religions' [was] invented by orientalists, missionaries, colonial administrators, and some sections of the indigenous (male) elites" as part of a modern system of othering, useful "in the normalization of Liberal fictions as though they are 'natural'" ("Negative Liberty: Liberal Faith Postulates and World Order," in *Religion as a Category of Governance and Sovereignty* [2015], 248). By such fictions he means the integrity of the lone individual, the freedom of belief, the tolerance of the state, the division between the religious from the secular, etc.

If this critique is read as persuasive, then identifying people not just in terms of their religious beliefs but then also grouping them together into one or another thing called a world religion can be seen as being closely intertwined with how modernity has come to be organized and regulated. Indonesia, for example, today understands religious freedom as eligible only to those who follow a recognized, and thus protected, world religion, thereby distinguishing "religion" from a variety of indigenous or local practices. It should not surprise us that, despite this critique, the category

World religions 309

of world religions has "persistently remained a part of teaching and the disciplinary organization of Religious Studies departments" let alone still playing a role in the laws of liberal democratic governments around the world. (We quote here from Teemu Taira's "Doing Things with 'Religion': A Discursive Approach in Rethinking the World Religions Paradigm" in the important edited collection in *After World Religions: Reconstructing Religious Studies* [2016].) If so, then scholars should probably learn to live with it, not by continuing to carry out work from within the discourse but, rather, by learning to study this discourse itself, its past, its contemporary effects, and its linkages to far wider systems of governance. This can be done, for example, by teaching the world religions paradigm *as* data (as Steven Ramey phrased it in the subtitle of his chapter in *After World Religions*). Thus, making a shift that we have recently seen elsewhere in the field, such as in Christopher Cotter's novel approach to studying the so-called Nones (*The Critical Study of Non-Religion: Discourse, Identification, and Locality* [2020]), the very designation can be understood as an identifier of practical effect, a performative and consequential act that should attract the attention of the critical scholar. For, as so nicely modeled by the French scholar of African politics, Jean-François Bayart in his *L'Illusion identitaire* (1996; published in English as *The Illusion of Cultural Identity* [2005]), the issue now becomes how the discourse on culture—or, in our case here, on world religions—is being used, by whom and toward what ends.

In this volume see: belief, cognition, comparison, culture, description, essence, experience, history, indigeneity, interpretation, lived religion, material religion, methodological agnosticism, primitive, redescription, religion, sacred/profane, secular

In *Religion in 50 More Words* see: animism, civil religion, east/west, founder, god, magic, nones, paganism, piety, pilgrimage, shamanism, spirituality, theology, tradition, understanding

50 Worldview

If some regard religion as a species of the larger genus ideology, there are those who instead propose to subsume religion within the broader category "worldview." The latter place those things known as religions alongside other worldviews that—or so the argument goes—exhibit a sufficient number of similarities so as to warrant all being treated as examples of the same thing, context, or process. This approach persists today, with the use of the category "worldview" along with "religious worldview" (as but one among other possible worldviews) increasing dramatically in English over the last third of the twentieth century. In fact, judging by some recent publications, it shows no sign of disappearing from many scholars of religion's vocabulary. Whether a more critical approach should follow this trend is the question, however.

Originally a hyphenated term (world-view), and attested in mid-nineteenth-century works, the word is generally seen as an attempt to provide an English equivalent to the German *Weltanshauung* or one's viewpoint on, or perception of, the world (*Welt*). The still common English use of the German original is often traced to a May 24, 1868, letter from the early American psychologist, William James (1842–1910) to Thomas W. Ward (a friend from his youth; see Ralph Barton Perry's *The Thought and Character of William James* [1935], vol. I, 160). Thus by worldview many today mean an overarching, total, or comprehensive viewpoint on the world, and thus the stance or set of assumptions that allow a mere setting to be signified as meaningful or coherent. This is akin to how the French scholar, Michel de Certeau (1925–1986) was interested in the way in which hectic space could be made into a specific sort of place by its dominant inhabitants (see his *The Practice of Everyday Life* [1984]).

The prominent use of "worldview" in scholarship on religion today is prompted by many scholars' effort to make sense of the so-called decline in religion. Though once predicted by the onetime influential secularization thesis (i.e., the more secular a society becomes the more likely its members are to become non-religious), recent scholarship has concluded that what has in fact declined is participation in what is now often qualified as *institutional* religion. The result is a variety of terms (e.g., spirituality) now used to name what some see as the continuing function of religion but being carried out well outside one's regular attendance at a worship service, for example. Should one imagine religion as playing a function that also happens beyond the walls of traditional religious institutions, then the appeal of a term such as worldview may make sense. Following a long-standing practice in the study of religion, scholars now even differentiate organized from personal worldviews. (See, for example, the essay "'Worldview': The Meaning of the Concept and the Impact on Religious Education," *Religious Education* 108/2 [2013]: 210–228, along with the same authors' essay, published in the same journal, "The Merits of Using "Worldview" in Religious Education," 112/2: 172–184.)

The term's use is linked to a specific theory of religion and the now widely accepted revision to the secularization thesis, concerning a decline of religious membership that is now seen as linked to a rise in so-called personal religion. The latter builds upon a long-used category that dates to earlier (theologically inspired) scholarship on Hellenistic religion, where assumptions were made concerning the region irresistibly moving in the direction of what scholars once portrayed as the truly personal religion of Christianity. A classic example of such an approach is found in the French Catholic theologian, Andre-Jean Festugiere's (1898–1982) *Personal Religion Among the Greeks* (1954). There may be no better example of this move in the study of religion that the work of the Scot, Ninian Smart (1927–2001), noted for his role in the study of religion at both Lancaster University, in the UK, and the University of California at Santa Barbara in the United States. Smart, a phenomenologist noted for his early and strong advocacy of the non-theological, publicly funded study of religion, is remembered today for, among other things, his efforts to develop educational materials. These included a variety of textbooks, like his last, *Worldviews: Crosscultural Explorations of Human Beliefs* (1983). This shift to the larger category was a logical extension of his prior emphasis on what he described as the seven dimensions of religion: the ritual, mythic, experiential, social, ethical, doctrinal, and material dimensions that more or less characterize all religions. (On these dimensions, see Bryan S. Rennie's "The View of the Invisible World: Ninian Smart's Analysis of the Dimensions of Religion and of Religious Experience" *Bulletin of the Council of Societies for the Study of Religion* 28/3 [1999]: 63–69). First using the term in his earlier world religions textbook, *The Religious Experience of Mankind* ([1969], 31), Smart's dimensions approach has been influential. He was able to capture the mid- to late-twentieth-century desire of scholars of religion to apply their tools well beyond the once strict definitions of religion (notably those of scholars who maintained that religion was unique and utterly distinct from the so-called profane). Dependent upon which of Smart's dimensions we emphasize when studying a group, such socio-political movements as Marxism (as exemplified in the history of Russia or China, for example) might easily be seen to function for their members akin to how religions might. Whether we then follow Edward Baily (1935–2015) and name and then study these other religion-like things as "implicit religion" or, instead, proceed with Smart and demote religion to one instance of how people organize their environments into habitable (i.e., knowable, actionable, organization, and thus meaningful) worlds is a question each scholar will have to answer for themselves. Both approaches, however, exemplify a widespread suspicion among current scholars concerning the onetime sharp distinction between the so-called sacred and the profane.

Today, Ann Taves, also at the University of California at Santa Barbara and onetime president of the American Academy of Religion, is likely the best representative of a scholar who has adopted Smart's notion of a worldview. She sees what we might traditionally classify as religion as but one among other instances of such world-making "ways of life," as she sometimes phrases it. (See, e.g., "From Religious Studies to Worldview Studies *Religion* 50/1 [2020]: 137–147; and on religion as a form of world-making see William Paden's essay "World" in the edited *Guide to the Study of Religion* [2000].) Such renaming is focused on a better way of characterizing and thus studying religion and other religion-like systems (which, for Taves, goes in the direction of a cognitive science of religion), as opposed to examining the very effort to group certain human activities together as deserving a common designation and scholarly approach will not be lost on the critical scholar, though its emphasis on the fluid nature of categorial boundaries will surely be of interest as well.

In this volume see also: classification, comparison, environment, ideology, religion, sacred/profane, secular, world religions

In *Religion in 50 More Words* see: civil religion, dialogue, piety, tradition, understanding

Appendix
A word on etymologies[1]

Words define words, in an endless cycle. As such, words derive from yet other words, which change over time, sometimes subtly or even dramatically. For the scholar, there might be something gained by knowing about these changes and trying to understand them in the light of other shifts in the wider social world of those who use them. Words, after all, do not float free of their usage, nor are they used apart from those who exist within the social acts of speaking and writing them—activities that are hardly idle or disinterested. There are reasons for talking or creating a text, after all, as well as effects to both, whether intended or not—among the reasons might be dissatisfaction with some of the work being done by a scholarly field's key terms.

We are here reminded of Jonathan Z. Smith's (1938–2017) point that the King James Bible, like Shakespeare's plays, is an Elizabethan text. Despite this, only the English of the former is presumed to be transparently meaningful to modern readers since the latter usually comes with a hefty scholarly apparatus in the footnotes, to help readers make sense of what sometimes reads like a foreign language. (In fact, in the Fall of 2015 it was reported that the Oregon Shakespeare Festival had decided that Shakespeare's English was just too difficult for contemporary audience to decipher, so it commissioned playwrights to translate the English-language plays into an English that moderns might understand.) As Smith goes on, "the word 'let' often means to stop somebody from doing something, and the word 'prevent' at times means to let them go ahead and do it." His point? "One gets odd moral conclusions by reading the King James Bible without such footnotes, and yet our mutual lie is that it is infinitely accessible while Shakespeare is accessible with difficulty" (from his Afterword to *Studying Religion: An Introduction* [2019], 125). The lie of which Smith writes is the hard work that scholars often hide from their students and their readers, making something that took years to acquire or figure out seem almost effortless and self-evident. This, or so he argues, does not benefit a field that tackles the study of something (i.e., religion) that so many people think is equally self-evident and effortless to understand. In part, this volume has been our attempt to address this shortcoming. Doing so requires us to make the roots and the changes more apparent, and it is within this context that each of the previous entries opens by offering an etymology, providing at least a glimpse into the historical derivation and uses of the terms included.

While neither of us are etymologists (and knowing our readers likely are not as well), we have relied on the work of those who have enabled us to provide insight into some of the twists and turns of the words so important in our work today. But, with the entry on origins in mind, we resist seeing any of these as definitive. Instead, these entries are suggestive and representative of the archival materials that happen to remain and that have come to the attention of the curious etymologist. Indeed, the very word "etymology" comes into English around the fourteenth century, by way of the Middle French *ethymologie* (and as is so common, from the Latin *etymologia* and prior to that the ancient Greek *étumología*). According to the *Oxford English Dictionary*, early on the term came to be used in the sense of providing an account of a word's origin by explaining its composition. Among the OED's early examples is Richard Sherry's 1550 *A Treatise of Schemes & Tropes*: "Etymologie or shewyng the reason of the name. . . ." So, contrary to discourses on origins that posit a linear development from some pristine source, we advise seeing these as exemplary and representative of a far sloppier history, comprised of the many other words that inhabit the sometimes overlapping and shifting orbits of the words in question.

For more details on what we have offered in the preceding entries we of course advise interested readers to stop by the OED for themselves, to explore the proposed derivations and examples of what John Locke once (ungenerously, mind you) called "a web of perplexed words" (*An Essay Concerning Human Understanding*, vol. II, Book III, 32, quoting the 1813 edition).

Note

1 This appendix, like the introduction, appears in both this volume and in *Religion in 50 More Words*.

Index

We leave it to readers to see the main entries in this volume for topics of interest and then to follow the suggestions at the close of each entry for supplemental readings elsewhere in the book. The items indexed here are therefore the mostly contemporary scholars mentioned throughout the present volume as well as the critical concepts that are each discussed in detail in the follow-up volume, *Religion in 50 More Words: A Redescriptive Vocabulary*, and which are also relevant to the entries in this book. Following this model, this volume's main entries will likewise be indexed in *Religion in 50 More Words*, allowing the two volumes to work more smoothly together.

Adorno, Theodore 53
afterlife, 108, 308
Alderton, Zoe 141
Alokan, Olusegu 80
Alston, William P. 92
Althusser, Louis 128, 132
Altman, Michael 237
Ammerman, Nancy 154
Anderson, Benedict 282
Anderson, Victor 238
animism 4, 183, 307
Armstrong, Karen 207
Arweck, Elizabeth 177
Asad, Talal 207, 216–7, 275, 276
atheism 29, 126, 175–7, 200
Avalos, Natalie 233

Bailey, Edward 155, 312
Bainbridge, William Sims 108
Baldwin, Matthew 98
Barrett, Justin 45
Barrett, Tim 251
Barrows, John Henry 303–4
Bayart, Jean-François 125, 237, 309
Beaman, Lori 204

Bellah, Robert 253
Beliso-DeJesus, Aisha 233
Benjamin, Walter 53
Berger, Peter L. 107, 134, 174–6, 177, 179, 274
Berlant, Lauren 11
Berry, Damon T. 233
Bird, Elizabeth 83
Bleeker, C. Juoco 21
Blum, Jason N. 93, 180
Bond, Sarah 237
Bourdieu, Pierre 14, 192, 223, 224, 298, 299
Boyer, Pascal 45, 301
Brauer, Jerald C. 169
Braun, Willi x, 183, 186, 221
Brewitt-Taylor, Sam 271
Brockopp, Jonathan 291
Brown, Anne S. 154
Brubaker, Rogers 125
Butler, Judith 55, 113–14, 128

Cantrell, Michael A. 179
Carloye, Jack 73
Certeau, Michel de 157, 221, 310

Chidester, David 163, 228, 233
Chin, Catherine Michael 98
church 5, 24, 32, 33, 174, 187–8, 199, 201, 216, 226, 252, 267, 271, 272, 276
civil religion 253
Clayton, Richard R. 191
Clifford, James 119
Collier-Thomas, Bettye 234
commentary 5, 52, 54, 146, 194, 280, 288, 291
conversion, 21, 126, 127, 228, 304
Corrigan, John 16
Cotter, Christopher 309
creation 2, 80, 145, 181, 185, 215, 297
Crenshaw, Kimberlé Williams 123
cult 58
Curtis, Edward E. 234
Cusack, Carole 139

Darwin, Charles 37, 173, 182, 227
Davis, Charles 176, 179
Deleuze, Gilles 11
Delgado, Richard 237
Derrida, Jacques 293
dialogue (interreligious) 3, 30, 54, 90, 103, 120, 191, 199, 203, 255, 256, 262
Dinham, Adam 258
Doniger, Wendy 169
Douglas, Mary 60, 268, 269
Driscoll, Christopher M. 233
Dubuisson, Daniel 250
Dudley, Carl S. 154
Dumpty, Humpty 66–7
Durkheim, Émile 39, 60, 99, 106, 107, 229, 258, 266, 268, 281, 282, 285, 299

Eagleton, Terry 130, 208, 298, 299
Earhart, Byron H. 249
east/west 3, 55, 80, 91, 95, 189, 196, 228, 231, 255, 270, 303
Eikelboom, Lexi 93
Eliade, Mircea 72, 81, 82, 86, 91, 98, 117, 118, 146, 156, 160, 169, 170, 171, 197, 217, 263–4, 266, 268, 299
emic/etic (insider/outsider) 35, 75, 123, 174, 192, 284
endtimes 2

Engelke, Matthew 155, 165
Engels, Friedrich 132, 280
Engler, Steven 167
Ernst, Carl 217
Esack, Farid 83
Esposito, John 62
Everton, Sean 127
evil 2, 12, 65, 263, 297

Fatubarin, Ayo 80
Feil, Ernst 249
Finley, Stephen C. 235
Fisher, Mary Pat 305
Fitzgerald, Timothy 134, 178, 179, 276–7, 308
Forbes, Cheryl 154
Foucault, Michel 52, 55, 216–17, 238
founder 16, 39 203, 258, 274
Frazer, James G. 138, 170, 299
Freud, Sigmund 106, 108, 170, 299
Führding, Steffen 119
fundamentalism 124

Gade, Anna 291
Gates, Henry Louis 223
Geaves, Ron 9, 305
Geertz, Clifford 148, 223, 276
Gennep, Arnold van 269
Giddens, Anthony 223, 224
god 2, 4, 5, 27, 29, 30, 36, 43, 45, 50, 80, 84, 92, 98, 99, 101, 102, 108, 109, 117, 143, 150, 175, 177, 178, 201, 213, 214, 248, 258, 270, 297
Goffman, Erving 224
Goldenberg, Naomi 134–5, 252–3, 308
Gould, Rebecca Kneale 154
Gramsci, Antonio 132
Gray, Biko Mandela 235
Greenberg, Yudit Kornberg 293
Gregory, Peter N. 148
Griffith, R. Marie 77, 154
Griffiths, Paul J. 289
Grim, John 81
Guattari, Pierre-Félix 11
Gushee, David 202
Guthrie, Stewart 45

Hall, David D. 154
Hall, Stuart 123

Harris, Angela 237
Harvey, Paul 237
Hastings, James 183
Hedges, Paul 23–4
Heidegger, Martin 85–6
Heiler, Friedrich, 169
Hermann, Adrian 119
Hermkens, Anna-Karina 163
Hervieu-Léger, Danièle 154
Hewitt, Marsha Eileen 133
Hick, John 43, 201
Hill, Peter C. 16
Hirsch, E. D. 259
Hood, Ralph W. 16
Horii, Mitsutoshi 250, 252, 283
Horkheimer, Max 53
Hoyt, Sarah F. 249
Husserl, Edmund 85–6, 195
Huxley, Aldous 92
Huxley, Thomas 173
Hyman, Gavin 178

icon 163
idol (idolatry) 102, 175
initiation 4, 9, 298
Irigaray, Luce 113
Isomae, Jun'ichi 250

Jackson, Jean E. 138
James, William 13, 62, 92
Jantzen, Grace 92
Johnson, Barbara 290
Johnson, Greg 136, 141
Johnson, Paul C. 77
Johnson, Sylvester 237
Johnston, Jay 8
Jones, Timothy W. 163
Jones-Matthews, Lucinda 163
Jun, Alexander 235

Katranji, Abdalmajid 82
Katz, Steven 92
Keller, Mary 178
Khan, Jonathon S. 235
King, E. Frances 163
King, Rebekka 238
King, Richard 233, 306
Kitagawa, Joseph 169, 171, 251
Krämer, Hans Martin 251
Kristensen, W. Brede 85

Kristeva, Julia 223, 224
Kugle, Scott 145

Lang, Andrew, 230
Lauterbach, Karen 179
Lawrence, Bruce B. 291
Lawson, E. Thomas, 43, 46, 109
Lease, Gary 134
Le Bras, Gabriel 154
Leeuw, Gerardus van der 85, 195, 196, 214
Lehrich, Christopher 247–8
Lévi-Straus, Claude 39, 223
Lincoln, Bruce 15, 24–5, 99, 117, 118, 172, 180, 185, 208, 217–18, 233, 261, 268, 286, 292, 294, 300
Linnaeus, Carl 36
Lloyd, Vincent W. 235
Lofton, Kathryn 247
Long, Charles H. 169, 238
Lopes, Ana Cristina 77
Lopez, Donald S. 31, 93
Ludwig, Theodore, 196
Luhmann, Niklas 134
Luhrmann, Tanya 180
Lum, Katheryn Gin 237
Lynch, Gordon 269

Mack, Burton L. 244–5
MacQueen, Graeme 144
magic 138, 164
Mahmood, Saba 206, 217
Mahomed, Nadeem 83
Malinowski, Bronislaw 104
Marchand, Suzanne L. 234
Marcus, George E. 119
Marcuse, Herbert 53
Marett, R. R. 183
Martin, Craig 180
Martin, Lori Latrice 235
Martin, Richard C. 217
Marx, Karl 3, 85, 108, 132, 170, 213, 223, 280, 281
Masuzawa, Tomoko 183, 306–7
Mauss, Marcel 39
Maxey, Trent E. 250
McAvoy, Thomas T. 154
McCalla, Arthur 116, 117, 122
McCance, Dawn 223
McCauley, Robert N. 43, 46, 109

318 *Index*

McDannell, Colleen 164
McDonald, Frances 11
McGill, Jenny 129
McNamara, Patrick 93
McNally, Michael 154
McQuire, Meredith 153
Mead, Margaret 112
meditation 91, 164
Mellor, Philip 266
Merleau-Ponty, Maurice 85
Miller, Monica R. 233
Mogahed, Dalia 62
monotheism 30, 36, 80, 95, 203, 225, 230, 231, 307
Moore, Diane L. 259
Morales, Harold D. 235
Moran, Dermot, 195
Morgan, David 163, 300
Moyser, George 210
Mueller, Max Perry 235
Müller, Friedrich Max 33, 39, 50, 85, 289
Murphy, Joseph M. 7
myth 4, 9, 50, 67, 73, 99, 117, 118, 169, 170, 172, 181, 207, 243, 244, 245
mysticism 65, 92, 148

Needham, Rodney 39
Newton, Richard W. 170–1 237
Ninh, Thien-Huong T. 235
Nongbri, Brent 144, 250, 300
nones 191, 302, 309
Noss, David S. 305
Nye, Malory 233

Olupona, Jacob K. 140
Orsi, Robert 98, 152, 154, 158, 197, 267
Ortner, Sherry 223
Orzech, Charles 163
Otto, Rudolf 88, 91, 98, 196, 214, 265, 299
Owen, Suzanne 136, 302, 308

Paden, William E. 266, 312
Paderson, Joshua 235
paganism 9, 38, 191, 225, 273
Painter, Nell Irvin 237
Parker, Stephen 258

Patton, Kimberly 198
Patton, Laurie L. 253
Pease, Paul 18
Peña, Elaine A. 15, 26, 260
Penner, Hans H. 109, 196, 197
Pennington, Brian 306
Pettazzoni, Raffaelle 169, 230, 231
piety 13, 59, 203, 206, 248
pilgrimage, 50 164, 170
Pintchman, Tracy 163
Plate, S. Brent 161, 162, 163, 197
polytheism 36, 95, 230, 231, 307
Popper, Karl 74
prayer 50, 62, 162, 174, 215
priest 2, 4, 120, 267, 272, 273, 284, 285, 286
prophet 2, 4, 65, 174, 226, 286
Prothero, Stephen 80, 154, 196, 259, 260
Proudfoot, Wayne 90

Ramadan, Tariq 75
Rambelli, Fabio 163
Ramey, Steven 187, 188, 309
Ramsey, Frank 197
Rana, Junaid 234
Reformation 21, 155, 182, 188, 274, 276
Rennie, Bryan S. 311
renunciation 148, 210
Ribi, Alfred 138
Ricoeur, Paul 106
ritual 4, 9, 27, 30, 44, 46, 50, 61, 67, 73, 74, 75, 92, 99, 102, 112, 117, 143–4, 155, 162, 164, 170, 172, 177, 188, 196, 207, 220, 245, 246, 248, 265, 269, 276, 299, 311
Rosenwein, Barbara H. 17
Rudolph, Kurt, 135
Russell, Bertrand 174
Ryle, Gilbert 165

Sacks, Jonathan 292
sacrifice 145, 218, 264
Safi, Omid 75
Sahlins, Marshall, 224
Said, Edward W. 36, 185, 289
salvation 2, 65, 89, 121, 122
Sanderson, Susan 18

Sandy, Peggy Reeves 113
Sanford, A. Whitney 93
Sartre, Jean-Paul 155
Savage, Barbara Dianne, 77
Schaefer, Donovan 13, 14
Scheer, Monique 14, 17
Schleiermacher, Friedrich 14, 27, 90, 91, 147
Schmeiser, Peggy 152
Schmidt, Leigh Eric 154
Schmidt, Wilhelm 230
Schonthal, Benjamin 151
Scott, Joan Wallach 157
Searle, John 223
sect 152
Sedgwick, Eve Kosofsky 16
sexuality 83, 111–14, 123, 145
shamanism 2
Sharf, Robert 90, 94
Sharpe, Eric J. 2–6, 256
Sheedy, Matt 204–5
Shilling, Chris 266
Siewert, Hubert 207
Simmons, K. Merinda 113, 237, 238
Slingerland, Edward 68
Smart, Ninian 133, 147, 148, 174, 177, 179, 311
Smidt, Corwin 222
Smith, Huston 259
Smith, Jonathan Z. x, 34, 39, 49, 51, 74, 75, 99, 168–9, 171, 184, 207, 243, 244–5, 247, 248, 250, 253, 265, 266, 283, 299, 313
Smith, Leslie Dorrough 98, 119, 170–1
Smith, Wilfred Cantwell 107, 169, 171, 249, 303
soul 14, 28, 42, 70, 102, 108, 206, 212, 214
Spencer, Herbert 173
Spickard, James 60
spirituality 62, 81, 90, 192, 249, 275, 311
Spooner, Brian 20, 22
Stace, W. T. 92
Stang, Charles 162
Stark, Rodney 108, 177, 244
Stausberg, Michael 167
Storm, Joseph Ananda Josephson 250
Stuckrad, Kucko von 8

Suit, Natalia K. 163
Sullivan, Brenton 68
Sullivan, Winnifred Fallers 152, 207
Supp-Montgomerie, Jenna 16
Suzuki, D. T. 91
Swidler, Leonard 203
Syahbudin, Atus 82
symbol 30, 77, 79, 86, 90, 97, 98, 99, 142, 170, 181, 194, 196, 197, 221, 223, 224, 235, 238, 248, 261, 293
syncretism 190

Taira, Teemu 309
Tarocco, Francesca 251
Taves, Ann 268, 312
Taylor, Bron 81
Taylor, Charles 270
Taylor, Mark C. 9, 31
ter Borg, Meerten 215
theism 29, 177, 304
theology 2, 27, 74, 82, 84, 91, 103, 121, 122, 143, 154, 168, 174, 175, 176–9, 214, 231, 276
Thomas, Jolyon Baraka 251
Thurman, Robert 147
Tiele, Cornelis P. 85, 306–7
Tillich, Paul 23, 247
Tomkins, Silvan 16
totem 4
Tsonis, Jack 141
tradition 6, 8, 9, 23, 63, 67, 75, 80, 83, 86, 102, 103, 118, 131, 145, 190, 191, 201, 249, 258, 284, 289, 290, 292, 307
transcendence 39, 86, 150, 148, 163, 177, 178, 249, 286
Trost, Theodore 77
Trouillot, Michel-Rolph 119
Tuckett, Jonathan 195
Tucker, Mary 81
Turk, Mladen 222
Turner, Victor 269
Tweed, Thomas A. 300
Tylor, Edward Burnett 46, 61, 66, 109, 170, 183, 228

understanding 3, 43, 53, 54, 67, 73, 82, 91, 106, 120, 147, 170, 171, 197, 199, 205, 210, 228, 243, 255, 259

Vähäkangas, Mika 179
value 6, 18, 22, 43, 54, 60, 74, 80, 81, 85, 99, 115, 176, 187, 201, 211, 252, 258, 261, 279, 280, 284, 285
Vandenburg, Brian 18
Vertovec, Steven 77
Vial, Theodore 90, 232
Visweswaran, Kamla 63

Waardenburg, Jacques 21
Wach, Joachim 169
Weber, Max 64–6, 81–2, 282
Webster, Joseph 163
Wedemeyer, Christian 169
Weisenfeld, Judith 235
Welch, Christina 23–4
Wettstein, Howard 215
Wexler, Jay 65
White, Hayden 119
Whitehouse, Harvey 44
Wiebe, Donald 176–7, 179
Wilkinson, Greg 34
Williams, Raymond x, 1, 7–8, 58, 60, 89, 235, 298
Wilson, Ann 163
Wittgenstein, Ludwig 65, 197
Wu, Jiang 34

Zaehner, Robert C. 305
Zemmin, Florian 274
Zoloth, Laurie 82